Erratum
Please note that the co-ordinates
for Djibouti below the plan on
page 180 should read
11°36'·9N 43°08'E and
not as printed.

Indian Ocean Cruising Guide

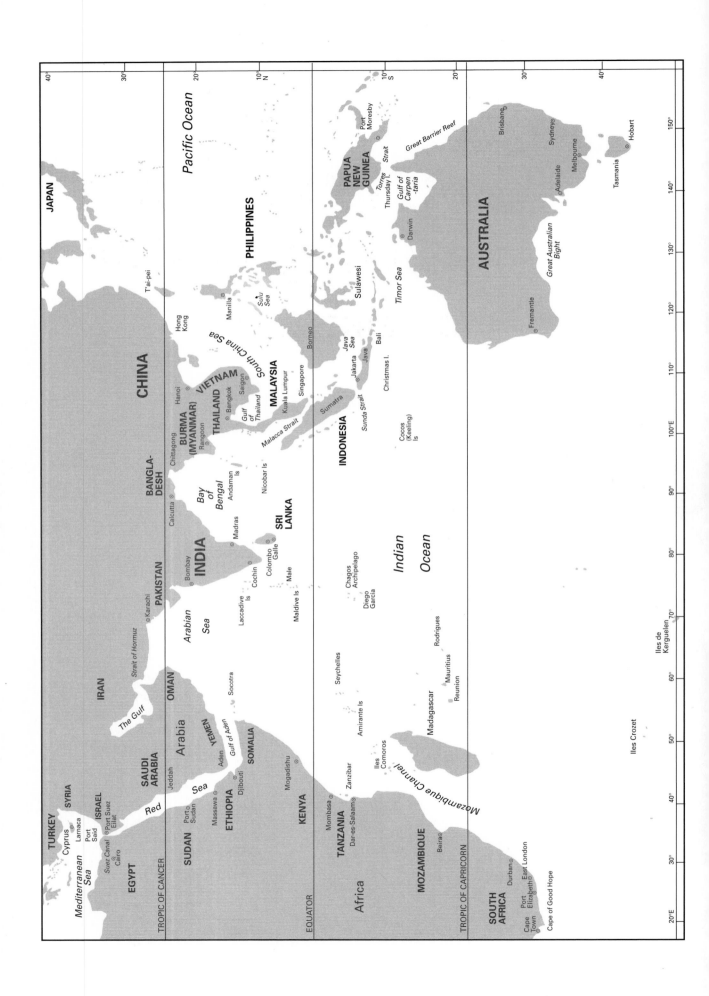

Indian Ocean Cruising Guide

ROD HEIKELL

Imray Laurie Norie & Wilson Ltd
St Ives Cambridgeshire England

Published by
Imray, Laurie, Norie & Wilson Ltd
Wych House, St Ives, Huntingdon,
Cambridgeshire PE17 4BT, England
☎ +44 (0)1480 462114 *Fax* +44 (0)1480 496109
E-mail ilnw@imray.com
1999

ISBN 0 85288 295 5

British Library Cataloguing in Publication Data.
A catalogue record for this book is available from the
British Library.

PLANS
The plans in this guide are not to be used for
navigation. They are designed to support the text
and should at all times be used with navigational
charts.

CAUTION
Every effort has been made to ensure the accuracy of
this book. It contains selected information and thus
is not definitive and does not include all known
information on the subject in hand; this is
particularly relevant to the plans, which should not
be used for navigation. The author believes that its
selection is a useful aid to prudent navigation, but
the safety of a vessel depends ultimately on the
judgement of the navigator, who should assess all
information, published or unpublished.

CORRECTIONS
The editors would be glad to receive any
corrections, information or suggestions which
readers may consider would improve the book, as
new impressions will be required from time to time.
Letters should be addressed to the Editor, *Indian
Ocean Cruising Guide*, care of the publishers. The
more precise the information the better, but even
partial or doubtful information is helpful if it is
made clear what the doubts are.

CORRECTIONAL SUPPLEMENTS
Imray pilot books are amended at intervals by the
issue of correctional supplements. Supplements, if
available, are supplied free of charge with the books
when they are purchased. Further supplements are
available from the publishers. The following should
be quoted:

1. Name of book
2. Date of edition (above)
3. Date of last supplement (if applicable)
4. Name and address to which supplement should
   be sent, on a stamped addressed A4 envelope.

The last input of technical information was April
1999.

Printed in Great Britain by Bath Press Colourbooks,
Blantyre, Scotland

Contents

ALSO BY ROD HEIKELL
Imray Mediterranean Almanac (Editor)
Mediterranean Cruising Handbook
Mediterranean France and Corsica Pilot
Greek Waters Pilot
Italian Waters Pilot
Ionian
Saronic
Turkish Waters & Cyprus Pilot
The Danube – A river guide
Yacht Charter Handbook
The Turquoise Coast of Turkey NET
Mediterranean Sailing A & C Black Ltd

For Miles

KEY TO SYMBOLS USED ON PLANS

3 : depths in METRES

: shallow water with a depth of 1 metre or less

: drying (mud or sand)

: rocks with less than 2 metres' depth over them

: rock just below or on the surface

② : a shoal or reef with the least depth shown

: wreck partially above water

: eddies

: overfalls

: wreck

④ Wk : dangerous wreck

: rock ballasting on a mole or breakwater

: above-water rocks

: cliffs

: coral

⚓ : anchorage

: prohibited anchorage

: church

: mosque

: windmill

: chimney

: castle or fort

✈ : airport

: ruins

: houses

: harbour master or port police

: fish farm

: customs

: travel-hoist

c : yacht club

: water

: fuel

✉ : post office

: Telecommunications

𝒊 : Tourist information

: mangroves

: palms

: electricity

⊕ : waypoint

: yacht berth

: Local boats (usually shallow or reserved)

: bn

: port hand buoy

: starboard hand buoy

: mooring buoy

Characteristics

: Light

: Lighthouse

F : fixed

Fl. : flash

Fl(2) : group flash

Oc. : occulting

R : red

G : green

w : white

m : metres

M : miles

s : sand

m : mud

w : weed

w : rock

co : coral

How the information is organised

The pilotage is divided into two sections: Part I Northern Indian Ocean and Part II Southern Indian Ocean. The equator is the dividing line. The countries are dealt with from the east to the west which is the most common direction for yachts to be travelling in.

The different countries have an initial section devoted to general information. The pilotage information follows. Not all countries have the full complement of general information and the level of detail depends on the country's size, the extent of its cruising area and the popularity of the country on cruising routes.

Charges

Where charges are made in harbours or marinas, because the exchange rates change and pricing policies change, I use a charge band system so you have some idea of what a place will cost if it is known. This is as follows. The charge is for a 12m yacht in high season (if applicable) for 24 hours and prices are in £GBP.

Charge band 1 Free
Charge band 2 under £15 (approx US$24)
Charge band 3 £16–£25 (approx US$26–40)
Charge band 4 £26–£35 (approx US$42–56)
Charge band 5 £36+ (approx US$58)

Preface

This book began with a request to write a successor to Alan Lucas' *Red Sea and Indian Ocean Cruising Guide,* the first proper cruising guide for the Indian Ocean which for a long time served its purpose well.

What to do? I decided to sail down there and do the research for new guide. Twenty years ago I had planned to go down the Red Sea and on to Southeast Asia from the Mediterranean. In between then and now events had conspired to keep me out of the Indian Ocean. It probably took me all of ten minutes to pull out a chart of the Indian Ocean and plot a track across it. Now all I had to was get *Tetra* ready, say goodbye, and cast off.

However, it wasn't really that simple. *Tetra* was in a dire state and basically needed to be rebuilt. In Turkey I contacted Yusuf at Yat Lift and together we worked out what had to be done. Everything was removed from the interior, the mast and keel came off, and *Tetra* was rebuilt and finished off with cloth and epoxy on the hull and decks. In between there came new chainplates, skin fittings, ports, deck hardware, pulpit and bow roller, the list went on and on and the costs escalated. Down below modifications were made and everything was beefed up for the trip to Southeast Asia and back.

In September 1995 I set off for Cyprus and there picked up my cousin Frank whom I hadn't seen for nearly twenty years and an old friend, Colin Mitchell. Going to Southeast Asia against the prevailing winds and currents was a bit of an epic, some 7500 miles to windward in the end, but strangely enough we were quite used to life on an angle by the time we arrived. In late 1996 I went out to bring *Tetra* back to the Mediterranean and going with the prevailing winds and current was infinitely preferable to the trip out. On the way out it took three weeks to beat to windward from Mukalla to Cochin. On the return trip it took thirteen days of easy sailing off the wind to cover the same distance. And while beating up the Red Sea is not a picnic for anyone, at least I knew what to expect.

One of the problems with a book that covers this sort of area is getting first hand information on places and conditions along the way. In the northern Indian Ocean I managed to cover most places with a few exceptions. For the southern Indian Ocean I got in touch with a number of people coming across and detailed what sort of information I needed. Others I met along the way who had cruised extensively in the Indian Ocean (north and south) were quizzed exhaustively and I thank everyone for their patience. In the end you who sail in the Indian Ocean must judge how this book succeeds and I welcome any material that adds to it.

One thing I do take exception to is the photocopying of books. A lot of work goes into putting a guide like this together and I would hope that its usefulness would more than repay the purchase price. Yet there seems to be a culture of poverty (mostly of spirit) amongst some cruising yachtsman whereby it is perceived as a fair cop to photocopy books and charts. It is opportunistic theft in both the legal and moral sense and I am weary of hearing the tired excuses of this benighted group of cruisers. I don't have a villa in the south of France and nor do I drive a Swan 50. The publishers are not awash with long expensive lunches and their profits are modest. In fact were it not for the enthusiasm and drive of Willie Wilson at Imrays, then these sorts of books would probably not be published at all. You are under no obligation to buy this book, but please do not steal it by photocopying it. Just to be on the safe side I got a shaman in India to shake up a curse for those who photocopy. The curse involves contrary winds and unpopular receptions wherever they go, amongst other things. Hey, don't say you weren't warned.

I have to confess to going a bit 'tropo' in the Indian Ocean. There were places when I turned to my companions and suggested that we should just stay here, not tell anyone where we were, and just go with the flow in 'tropo' land. It meant that the laptop wasn't fired up too many times, hence the time between the initial research and the publication of this book. In the end I hope you find it useful and that all your cruising in the Indian Ocean is enjoyable. Fair winds and if you have to beat to windward may there be cold beer waiting for you at the end of the voyage.

Acknowledgements

Many people helped with the information in this book, with practical advice and help on the trip, and with simple good cheer in bars or cockpits. To all of you my thanks and while I would like to mention everyone, it is just not possible. To the following my special thanks:

To Alan Lucas for his *Red Sea and Indian Ocean Cruising Guide* although the work here is my own. To all those who wrote and edited the British Admiralty pilots which although not the easiest reading, assisted along the way with a mass of detailed descriptions.

To Frank Whelan, alias Captain François, able crew from Cyprus to Malaysia, good company, courageous, and makes the best pikelets in the Indian Ocean. To Colin Mitchell for crewing from

Cyprus to Aden and for brandy sours under arduous conditions. To Yat Lift and all the crew for putting *Tetra* back together. To Jody for occasional smiles. To Yusuf Civilekoglu and crew for the passage from Thailand to Cochin. To Yener, for sails and canvaswork, I hope you take your own boat to the Red Sea some day. To Graham Sewell for crewing at the Kings Cup (and winning), glad you survived. To Arthur Hind and Jill Murray for looking after *Tetra* and information on Malaysia. To all those who rescued *Tetra* when the mooring broke in Kamphong Bahru. To Andy at Yacht Services Phuket. To Wen and Ti. To Horst at Big 'A' in Ao Chalong. To Eric and Robin Lambert for good cheer and information on the southern routes and for proof reading this manuscript. To Hans van Rijn for information and proof reading. To Harry and Dorothy (more Parker than Wizard of Oz) of S.Y *Whimbrel* for information and good liquor. To the late Nigel Morley and Julie Smart for information on Kenya. To Omar, Mr Fix-It, in Aden. To Mike in Massawa. To David Macmillan for cold white wine in parched Port Sudan. To Alison for cake. To Barry Sheffield for information on the Red and Arabian Seas. To AB and Adrienne, may you sort out those moral dilemmas. To Stephen Davies and Elaine Morgan for information. To Captain Mick for fortuitous encounters. To Mike and Christine of S.Y *Sea Topaz* for information. To Peter, hope you got to India. To Roy Stacy, mission control, for keeping everyone in touch and looking after things while I was away.

To the Seychelles Tourist Board in London my thanks for information and photos. To Willie Wilson for all his help and care and to everyone at Imrays who checks, draws and double-checks, my thanks.

Rod Heikell
London 1999

Introduction

The Indian Ocean and the limits and purpose of this book

The Indian Ocean is the third largest ocean after the Pacific and Atlantic. It is divided into two by the equator with a collection of seas in the northern Indian Ocean and the large mass of the southern Indian Ocean stretching down to the Southern Ocean. In this book I take this easy division of the northern and southern Indian Ocean as the dividing line for the various chapters. Starting in the east the first section covers the northern Indian Ocean and the countries westabout from Singapore to the Red Sea. The second section covers the southern Indian Ocean and the countries westabout from Australia to East Africa. This is a just a convenient division to organise the text and for routes which criss-cross from the northern to the southern Indian Ocean you will need to flick between the sections. You've got to do something with the large amount of information to organise.

For certain areas I touch only briefly upon the information and pilotage for an area if there are other useful books which provide relevant information. The following list gives those areas which are already well served by other pilots.

Indonesia
Cruising Guide to Southeast Asia Volume II. Papua New Guinea, Indonesia, Malacca Strait, West Thailand by Stephen Davies and Elaine Morgan.
Riau Islands Cruising Guide by Mathew Hardy. Available locally.
Thailand
Sail Thailand collated by Thai Marine & Leisure. Available locally.
Red Sea
Red Sea Pilot by Elaine Morgan and Stephen Davies.
Australia
Australian Cruising Guide by Alan Lucas.
Seychelles
Les Îles Seychelles by Alain Rondeau. (In French and English)
East Africa, Madagascar and the Comoros
East Africa Pilot by Delwyn McPhun.
South Africa
South Africa Nautical Almanac by Tom Morgan.

Vital statistics and odd facts

Total area 73 million km²/28 million miles². About 20% of the world's total ocean area.

Maximum depth 7,725m/25,344ft in the Java Trench between Java and Christmas Island.
Average depth 3890m/12,762ft.
Subsidiary seas Northern Indian Ocean: Gulf of Aden/Red Sea, Persian Gulf, Arabian Sea, Bay of Bengal, Andaman Sea.
Salinity 34–36 parts per 1000 except for W side of Arabian Sea which is 36–37 parts per 1000.
Wave height Wave heights of 20m plus recorded over the Agulhas Current.
Precipitation The W coast of India can receive up to 4000mm during the SW monsoon. Parts of the Shillong Plateau in the far NE of India have received up to 26m in a year.
Cyclone seasons Bay of Bengal April to December, Arabian Sea May to November, southern Indian Ocean November to April.
Worst cyclone damage 300,000 dead in Bangladesh from storm surge after 12 November 1970 cyclone.
Endangered marine species Dugong, Leathery turtle, Hawksbill turtle, Olive turtle, Loggerhead turtle, Blue whale.

Characteristics and history

The Indian Ocean is a divided sea. The northern Indian Ocean is for the most part a calm sea except for the occasional tropical storm that ploughs its surface. It is also blessed with two distinct seasons where the change in wind direction makes it comparatively easy to sail back and forth across it. By contrast the southern Indian Ocean is rougher, especially down towards the Southern Ocean. Hemming in the southern Indian Ocean on the W and E are the tip of Africa and the bottom of Australia, both difficult turning points separating the oceans on either side.

The relatively benign northern Indian Ocean and the reversal of wind directions between the NE monsoon and the SW monsoon provided early traders with convenient wind patterns to complete a trading voyage within a year. Hecateus of Miletus (520 BC) mentions India as does Megasthenes (300 BC). The Greeks called the Indian Ocean the Erythrean Sea, but there is little evidence they explored it, although it is likely some voyages were made. Not until the first century AD are there concrete references by Pliny and the unknown Greek author of the *Periplus (Circuit) of the Erythrean Sea*. Pliny refers to the SW monsoon as the Hippalus, named after a pilot called Hippalus who discovered that the SW monsoon could take you clear across to India. This discovery by Hippalus opened up the route to Roman vessels and there was soon a regular trade across the ocean and back to the Red Sea and the Gulf. Pliny also mentions the land of Chryse the Golden beyond India and it is reasonable to surmise that he was talking about Southeast Asia and China.

Less than a century later Marinus of Tyre acquired information on passages in the Indian Ocean from a sailor called Alexander who had sailed to the Malay Peninsula and on to China. This information was used by Ptolemy to draw his world map with a workable representation of the northern Indian Ocean.

For western voyagers the exploration of the Indian Ocean pretty much ceases with the demise of the Roman Empire. All the spices, silks and precious stones coveted in Europe were transported by Arab traders to the Levant where European traders purchased them. It was Arab traders who were to dominate trade in the Indian Ocean until the arrival of the Portuguese under Vasco de Gama at the end of the 15th century.

Voyages by Indian and Arab traders were in dhows, the hull shape much like the dhows still seen around the Arabian Sea and down the east coast of Africa. These craft were constructed using coir to bind the planks together, a method that used readily available materials and that could be easily repaired anywhere in the Tropics that coconut palms grew. Small craft are still made like this in some parts of India. Iron was in short supply in the region so nails could not be fashioned for alternative construction – any iron ore was used to make swords and spears. Craft of this type were certainly making voyages across the northern Indian Ocean in early times. The Greek author of the *Periplus* mentions these craft and the fact they voyaged across to Indonesia. In what was the Middle Ages in Europe, this part of the world was alive with trade and there were a number of rich Arab trading cities around the Middle East and Arab trading outposts around Africa, India and Indonesia. From the Gulf to the Hadramaut in Yemen and Hijaz in the Red Sea, traders journeyed all across the northern Indian Ocean spreading Islam to India and Indonesia and the Malay Peninsula. Even into the period of European domination this influence continued as recorded in Conrad's *Lord Jim* where European and Arab traders competed for trade in the Indies.

There were other voyagers as well. The Waqwaqs from Indonesia voyaged in large outrigger canoes similar to those used on Polynesian voyages in the Pacific across to Africa and colonised Madagascar around 300–400 AD. These voyages were direct over 3500 miles from Indonesia to east Africa and Madagascar using the SE trades. Some nine tenths of the Malagasy vocabulary is derived from the Waqwaq language and in fact Waqwaq is probably a term that referred to the sound of this foreign tongue.

The other great voyagers in this period were the Chinese and although references to them are scarce, they certainly must have made numerous trading forays over the years. In the 13th century Marco Polo voyaged on Chinese junks backwards and forwards across the Indian Ocean. In the 14th century the Three Jewel Eunuch, the Grand Admiral Zheng He, effectively brought much of the northern Indian Ocean under Chinese control. Chinese junks were formidable and capable sea-going ships compared to the coir bound Arab dhows and they possessed not only the knowledge to navigate by the stars and reckon latitude, but also the magnetic compass, which had only been introduced into Europe from China in the 12th century. Richard Hall provides the following description of a Chinese expedition under Zheng:

'The number of big junks sailing in each of the expeditions varied from about forty to more than a hundred, and each had several support vessels. These armadas of the Xia Xiyang ('Going down to the Western Ocean') were the wonders of the age. The ships carried doctors, accountants, interpreters, scholars, holy men, astrologers, traders and artisans of every sort: on most of his seven expeditions Zheng had as many as 30,000 men under his command, in up to 300 ships of varying types. Flags, drums and lanterns were used to send messages within the fleet. To work out positions and routes the heavens were studied with the use of calibrated 'star plates', carved in ebony.'

Empires of the Monsoon Hall

Zheng effectively brought the countries around the Arabian Sea under Chinese authority although no land garrisons were ever left to maintain control. The sight of one of these huge armadas sailing into a port would have been more than enough to quell any uprising.

In 1498 Vasco da Gama arrived in India with his small fleet and so began the period of Portuguese colonisation of India and adjacent countries. The influence of the Portuguese can be seen everywhere from the architecture to the Catholic faith to Indians and Malays called Diaz or Fernandez. The Portuguese were followed by the Turks who gained possessions in the Red Sea, but ultimately failed to displace the Portuguese from India, by the Dutch who were established in the East Indies and established colonies in Ceylon and South Africa, and finally the English who by the 19th century had colonised just about every country around the Indian Ocean including much territory that was formerly Portuguese and Dutch.

Most of the charting of the Indian Ocean was carried out in the 19th century by English ships and in fact most of the present day charts are based on 19th-century surveys. The French were here as well and established colonies in and around the SW Indian Ocean and charted some of the difficult coral strewn waters here. But the overwhelming influence was English, so much so that the Indian Ocean was dubbed the 'English Lake'.

In the 20th century the Indian Ocean countries have largely been returned to the indigenous peoples or whoever was the longest standing coloniser. Some small island territories remain British or

French, but for the most part the countries around the Indian Ocean are independent states.

The arrival of that largest of 20th-century industries, tourism, has come late to many of the countries around the Indian Ocean. There are huge areas which see little in the way of tourists and in other countries the tourism is concentrated in relatively small areas. In some countries civil wars or general civil unrest have turned tourists away. Eritrea, Yemen, Somalia, Mozambique, Madagascar, and Myanmar (Burma) have all had long civil wars and in a way, at the end of the 20th century, if you really want to get away from it all, then choose a country that has just had a civil war and you will find it uncluttered except for the locals and UN relief workers. Other countries like Pakistan and Sri Lanka have ongoing civil war affecting part of the country and have suffered a dramatic decline in tourist numbers. Some countries like Saudi Arabia and Oman are not keen on visitors and others such as much of the Laccadives and the Andamans and the Nicobars, are off limits to tourists.

Some islands like the Maldives, Seychelles, Mauritius and Réunion have turned themselves into tourist meccas and are now largely dependent on tourist receipts for as much as 50% of GDP. Other countries like Thailand, Kenya and, until recently, Sri Lanka, are also heavily dependent on tourism. Inevitably other areas will follow and parts of the west coast of India are now being developed as resort areas while other countries are also making plans to cash in on the tourist bonanza.

Cruising in the Tropics

Coral

Corals are related to sea anenomes and can be thought of as a polyp living in a limestone case. Each coral secretes its own design of limestone case and over time old limestone cases build up to become a reef. Over thousands of years coral reefs build up as polyps die and new polyps overlay the old. Corals need a sea water temperature of 20°C plus and relatively clean water to grow in. Anywhere there is a lot of silt or mud restricts the growth of coral which is why you find little coral around river estuaries and a lot of coral around the Red Sea where there are no major rivers. Coral grows at just below the surface down to 70m. From just below the surface down to 20m you get the widest variety of species and the best conditions for growth. Contrary to popular belief, coral grows very slowly at around 0·3–0·6m (1–2ft) every hundred years on the ocean side and 0·5–1·5m (1·6–5ft) every hundred years in sheltered reef areas. These are maximum rates and are frequently slowed by storm damage or conditions that are less than ideal. Charts made from old surveys 50 or even a 100 years ago will pretty much reflect what is down there now assuming the survey was correct in the first place. In some areas the charts are known not to be reliable

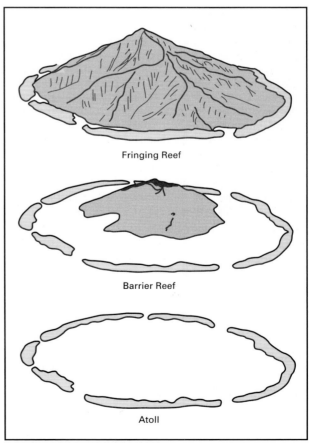

Fringing Reef

Barrier Reef

Atoll

CORAL REEF CLASSIFICATION

whereas in others the surveys are meticulous and wonderful pieces of work. In some areas the reef may have less water than shown, but then again it may have more water than is shown. What has usually been missed in a survey are isolated coral heads or 'bombies'.

A coral reef is a complex and varied ecosystem that also supports a wide range of other marine species either in a commensal fashion, as food, or most importantly, as a habitat sheltered from the power of the sea and waves. Coral reefs are classified pretty much along the lines suggested by Darwin in 1842 as follows and represent the evolutionary process of reefs from fringing to barrier to atoll.

Fringing reef Formed by the growth of coral close inshore on rocky coastlines. On the seaward side the drop-off may be gradual or abrupt. Inshore from the ocean there is usually just low coral reef with rock pools which have formed from storm damage or subsidence. There are not usually any natural passes through a fringing reef except where rivers exit, there is a very deep natural indentation, or a sub-strata like crumbly basalt exists which is unsuitable for coral to grow on. Artificial passes may have been blasted through the fringing reef. Fringing reefs are found all around the Red Sea, the Yemen and Oman, parts of India, the Andamans and Nicobars, parts of Thailand and Malaysia, Christmas Island, Seychelles, Mauritius, Réunion, parts of Madagascar, the Comoros and along some of East Africa.

Barrier reef These reefs are separated from the land by a lagoon, usually due to coastal subsidence during which the seaward reef builds upwards. The barrier reef is typified by the Great Barrier Reef on the east coast of Australia. There are usually natural passes through the reef where coral cannot grow or where storm damage has broken through and the tidal streams are too violent for coral to grow well. There may also be artificial passes which have been blasted through the reef. Barrier reefs are found in some places in the Red Sea, the Andamans and Nicobars, the Seychelles, Mayotte and parts of East Africa.

Atolls An atoll is a barrier reef where the original island it built around has subsided underwater and the barrier reef builds upwards and in the end is all that is left. Sand accumulates on the barrier reef to form low-lying islands or *cays*. Within the central lagoon there can often be considerable depths and in places there will also be very variable depths and bombies. On the seaward side an atoll typically drops off abruptly to considerable depths. There will nearly always be one or more natural passes through the reef into the lagoon, although in some cases the pass will be shallow and also possibly dangerous if it is on the side where the prevailing winds cause large seas which break across the entrance to the pass. Atolls are found in the Laccadives, the Maldives (from

where the word 'atoll' comes), Cocos Keeling, Chagos archipelago and around the outer islands of the Seychelles.

Navigating in coral

There are a few things to know about coral which are useful if you are new to it.

Coral reefs are not normally exposed except for a few hours at MLWS. Coral cannot survive being exposed to the hot sun for more than a few hours, so in most places the coral will be just under the water or at the surface for most of low water. At high water it may well be a couple of metres under the surface. Where coral is above water it has generally been raised by the land underneath being pushed up by the tectonic plates and this is dead coral. In places coral boulders may be thrown up by storms onto the reef and these are a useful visual indication of a part of the reef.

In less than 20m great care is needed when navigating in coral as it is in these depths that coral grows most prolifically and irregularly. Bombies grow anywhere that they can, on old coral accretions, on the higher parts of submerged land, on wrecks, and can vary in size from a pillar to a fair sized clump or small isolated reef. If you are under 20m and see the depthsounder fluctuating wildly then slow down and send someone aloft.

When approaching a reef anchorage always time the approach for between 0900 to 1400 or 1500 at the very latest. For reef approaches towards the east the approach should probably be made no later than 1300–1400 although we are nearly all guilty of later approaches. After 1400 the sun is starting to dip lower in the sky so that it is in your eyes and identifying reefs becomes a lot more difficult. For reef approaches towards the W 1500 is OK, although time it earlier if possible. It constantly surprises me how many boats make an approach through coral late in the afternoon and for many it is sheer luck that they do not hit anything. Even with someone conning you in over the radio and utilising GPS positions it is dangerous to approach through coral late in the afternoon. You may misunderstand an instruction or there may be bombies that the person conning you in did not see. Some do not make it through safely when making an approach late in the afternoon and the Red Sea, in particular, has its fair share of wrecks.

A pair of *Polaroid* sunglasses is essential to navigating through coral or in relatively shallow water anywhere for that matter. Other sunglasses will not do. Only *Polaroids* cut out the light from one plane and so remove much of the reflected light from the surface making it much easier to see the relative depths in shallow water. As a general rule the following colour coding applies for the depth of water: brown to yellow-brown means 2m or less, green 2–5m, blue-green 5–25m and dark green-blue 25m plus. This is in relatively calm water with the sun overhead. On days when there is scattered cloud identification is more difficult as you will get dark shadows moving over the water which make it difficult to see what is going on. Caution is needed interpreting these colours as under 10–15m the nature of the bottom confuses the scheme with sandy bottoms giving the clearest indication while rock and weed make things look darker and shallower. Weed clumps on the bottom can give you a heart attack as they look closer to the surface than a sandy bottom or light coral and it can be difficult to judge whether a patch of weed is a coral outcrop or what it actually is – weed. In disturbed water where the sand has been whipped up or blown off the shore the water is murkier and it is more difficult to work out the depths. Around the outflow of rivers there can be a lot of silt in the water which severely reduces visibility so that it is all but impossible to see anything. How coral grows under these conditions it is difficult to know, but around Thailand and Malaysia you will commonly encounter visibility of less than 2m and this makes it impossible to con your way around reefs.

Currents around the reefs are generally strong and variable in direction and it can be alarming to watch your boat being sluiced sideways through the reefs when in fact your heading is elsewhere. Through channels one side of a reef will generally be fairly steep-to compared to the other side, although this is not a hard and fast rule and you may encounter areas of 'bombies' that appear to obstruct a channel, but can in fact be navigated through with good nerves. Currents outside of reefs of any type will often have a set towards the reef, a benign phrase that could be replaced with reef-sucking currents (however you say it). Constant attention must be paid to currents when near to reefs as they can be as much as 2–3kts in places and inattention to your navigation can lead to catastrophic results.

Equipping for cruising in the Tropics

Water

In many places getting good drinking water ashore can be difficult and sometimes impossible. It may be that there is no water (usually the case on atolls) or that the water available ashore is suspect for some reason. Carrying adequate amounts of water on board backed up by jerrycans is just common sense although the quantity you carry will self-evidently be determined by the strictness of the water regime on board. If you use salt water for some purposes such as washing dishes, washing yourself, and for cooking (around a quarter for rice and pasta, around a third for vegetables), then you can get by on very little. And you can always rinse yourself and the dishes off with fresh to keep that saltwater stickiness away.

To augment water supplies the answer for many lies in the rain that regularly falls in most parts of the tropics. Most yachts cruising in the tropics are equipped with some sort of rain-catching device. Many adapt the bimini for this purpose by either putting gutters on either side with a run-off to the

water tank or a jerrycan, or by simply having a fitting in the middle which can take a hose and some way of depressing the middle of the bimini to form a hollow to collect the rainwater. Another method which I used was to collect the run-off from the furled main and sail cover. By simply dropping the boom a bit substantial amounts gush out of the end of the main and cover and by the simple method of shoving a bucket under the end it was possible to catch a fair amount of water. The only drawback with any rain catching device is that if a squall accompanies the rain, most of the water is blown away and in bumpy conditions at sea the motion of the boat tends to slosh the water off the bimini. Whether using the bimini or the sail cover it is necessary to let it run for a bit to wash off salt and dust. For the first amounts collect a few bucketfuls which can be used for washing clothes or yourself. One of the advantages of catching rainwater is that you know it is potable.

Increasing numbers of yachts, even some quite small ones, are installing watermakers. These have become a lot more reliable with filter elements which need less attention and last longer than many earlier models. I know of one 28ft cruising yacht which relies on its 12 volt watermaker and although I don't recommend you carry a radically reduced amount of water with a watermaker, in practice some yachts do. In the area covered by this book places to get spares are few and far between so carry adequate filters and any other bits you might need.

Water from a suspect source ashore can be treated by adding a little bleach (sodium hypochlorite at around 3%), potassium permanganate crystals, or proprietary tablets like *Puri-tab* at the recommended dosage. If you are really worried then boiling for around 10 minutes is the only sure-fire solution as the chemical regime above will not remove all nasties.

Anchoring

Anchoring over coral means you need to have chain and lots of it. Coral cuts through rope in a shorter time than you can believe possible and there is no way out of using chain. However in practice some yachts use a chain-rope combination where the water is very deep and with care this is a perfectly adequate solution. The reason is really that in places the water is so deep around coral that you could be anchoring in 30m plus and anchor winches and human-power have difficulty with the straight up and down pull of 30m of chain and the anchor on the end. Any anchor winch needs to be man enough for the job and at the very least small yachts need a snubber for the chain and enough muscle on board to get the anchor and chain up in deep water.

When anchoring in coral you do need to take care of where you anchor. Coral is a delicate slow-growing organism and careless anchoring can destroy coral that can take decades to re-grow. Multiply that by numerous yachts anchoring on coral and you have significant damage to coral caused by careless anchoring. Many governments now realise the damage being caused and have put down moorings in popular anchorages. These should always be used when available. If there are no moorings then search out a patch of sand. This often means anchoring in deeper water, but avoids not only damage to the coral but also the possibility of your chain getting snagged on lumps of coral on the bottom. For some reason chain has a magnetic attraction for the most undercut coral ledge and can be extremely difficult to free – often the only solution is to dive on it or get someone with tanks to dive on it for you and free the chain from the coral. Chain caught under coral on a low tide may endanger your boat if at high tide the scope of chain left is less than the total depth of the water and consequently the chain is trying to pull the bows of the boat underwater.

Tenders

The best sort of arrangement for getting ashore is not always the most practical to carry on board and so many of us end up with a compromise. You need to be properly equipped before you leave as getting a replacement tender can be a difficult job and practically only in Australia, Singapore, Malaysia, Thailand and South Africa, will you be able to replace a tender lost or damaged in the Indian Ocean region. You could of course get something flown out to other places, but the cost of doing this is exorbitant and you will still need to get it out of the grip of customs. Some yachties have been inventive enough to build small ply dinghies in out of the way places although the results have been mixed depending on the abilities and materials available.

A rigid dinghy is certainly the best option and aluminium has the advantage over GRP when it comes to coral. For lots of yachts stowing a rigid dinghy is not practical and an inflatable is then the choice. What you get really depends on what is available, but Avons are in mine and others experience the best choice in terms of durability. Many cover the top of the tubes with a canvas cover to stop UV deterioration and when stowed on board the inflatable should be covered as well.

I like to row, even in an inflatable, which has to be the worst kind of rowing machine invented, but

In many places there is a lot of gooey mud at low tide so allow time for getting ashore and back for either side of high tide.

most people end up getting an outboard – as did I. It is a matter of the distances. Sometimes you will have to anchor ¼ or ½ a mile off the shore, and rowing back and forth with others in the inflatable and to carry supplies, against a chop or against the current, becomes just too much even for dedicated rowers. Outboard spares are fairly common in most places because many local boats now utilise outboards and UN programmes seem to hand outboards out in the belief that this is a good way to encourage modern fishing methods.

One very cheap accessory for a tender is an umbrella. Most of the countries in the Indian Ocean have cheap umbrellas for sale and it is worth getting a couple. If the person sitting forward in the tender puts the umbrella up in front of them most of the spray coming over the front when there is a bit of chop will be deflected from coming on board. Believe me, it is more effective than a dodger on the front. If you are alone then wedge the umbrella in the front as a makeshift dodger. It can be angled for spray coming over one or other side and if there is a downpour, you can use it to keep dry. When it gets rusty just throw it away and get another.

And do carry a good pair of oars even when you have an outboard. I twice had to rescue tenders drifting away into the distance when outboards failed.

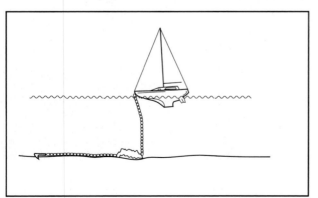

If anchor chain gets caught under a large coral head it can pull the boat under or cause other damage on a rising tide.

One other thing, and this is a true story, don't be tempted to tow your dinghy on long passages as one would-be sailor I met en route was going to – and no, it wasn't a wind-up.

Shade and ventilation

Under the tropical sun a permanent bimini is a must. The construction of a bimini depends on the cockpit layout, but if you are constructing one from new or getting new canvas work made up, it is a simple enough matter to have side-screens made. On my bimini the side-screens simply rolled up or down and were secured by *Velcro* tabs. A side-screen cuts out the sun when it is low in the sky and also importantly cuts out some reflection off the water. Although you may be worried about using a side-screen when sailing, in practice it doesn't seem to make much difference except when conditions are really boisterous. And there is something nice about rolling them up at the end of the day, a sort of nautical equivalent to closing the curtains at night in a house.

Ventilation is an important consideration in the tropics and if you are doing a major refit it is worthwhile thinking about extra deck hatches and opening ports. All hatches and ports need screens to keep mosquitoes out although it is useful if the screens can be removed for anchorages where mosquitoes are few because any screen impedes the flow of air below. Wind-scoops for deck hatches are important and I favour the type with a four-way entry (see diagram) as it doesn't need adjustment to work properly when the wind is fluky, the tide keeps the boat at a contrary angle to the wind, or when you are moored fore and aft or berthed in a harbour.

One design element I missed and had to rectify later was to put zips either side of the middle window of the spray hood so it can be rolled up at anchor or in calm conditions at sea. Spray-hoods tend to be fairly permanent affairs on a cruising boat and being able to roll up the middle panel allows a flow of air into the cockpit area and also allows cooking smells and moisture to get out. Boats with permanent cuddies likewise need an opening window in the front to allow a flow of air into the cockpit.

Tetra looking aft showing the solar panels permanently installed on the bimini. Although not the optimum site for solar panels, it meant they were always there producing a squirt of power for the autopilot and lights.

If you leave the boat somewhere for a while get a cover made up to protect the decks from sun, rain and bird deposits from those little critters who treat your rigging as home. You don't want to come back to a floating island of guano.

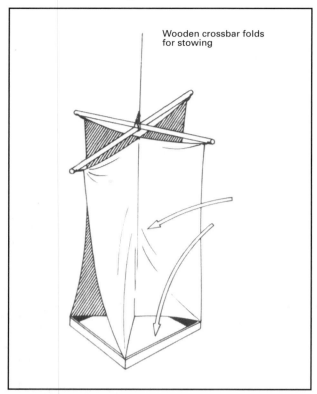

Windscoop - this design works whatever
the wind direction relative to the boat

Wooden crossbar folds
for stowing

Mast-steps

For cruising in coral mast-steps are a must. Being able to get up the mast gives you a much better idea of what is going on on the sea bottom and also gives you a wider perspective on channels through coral. Mast-steps need only go up to the first set of cross-trees as this will give you a good enough view and going higher means more motion aloft if there is any sea running. Ratlines between the shrouds are a possible alternative, but are not as easy to use when a sea is running. Mast-steps will allow you to hold onto the mast for security. Some yachts have a form of crow's nest on the mast, but in most situations it is comfortable enough sitting on the cross-trees with a leg either side of the mast.

GPS

This little miracle box of tricks considerably simplifies navigation through the reefs and islands and in the approaches to harbours and anchorages. Apart from the obvious uses of plotting latitudes and longitudes and plumbing in waypoints, it is extremely useful in giving the true course taking into account current, as opposed to the compass course. Currents can vary greatly around the islands and reefs with variable strength and direction and often at variance with indicated currents from the collected hydrographic data. The reef-sucking phenomenon is often noted in logs with lots of exclamation marks directed at currents that seemed only to suck towards a reef, often at rates of 1–1½ kn.

It should always be remembered (and I am continually surprised by how often cruising folk neglect to do it) that the chart datum must be selected for the GPS readout or significant errors can result. For the plans in this book waypoints are given to WGS 84 datum (usually the default setting for most GPS receivers) wherever possible although some are related to GIS (Geographical Information Systems) which utilises information on all relevant errors using satellite photographs and data to give a position which should be close to WGS 84. This is not always the case and care is needed using GIS positions although where I have been able to check them they appear to correspond well to WGS 84 positions.

The matter of chart datum is at best hazy for unmetricated charts and obscure for some of the new metricated charts. Most modern charts refer to

A permanent bimini is a must. If possible get side-curtains made for when the sun is low in the sky. Most of the time they can be used when sailing and on *Tetra* we only ever rolled them up over Force 5–6.

WGS 84 or WGS 72, but in some cases there are references to simply WGS datum or to a country datum source that is not commonly used or does not exist in the chart datum sources logged into the memory of the GPS. In some cases a correction is given which must be applied to lat and longs. For unmetricated charts there is generally no datum source given and I have been unable to track any down for most of the fathoms charts. Where a WGS 84 GPS position is known a correction can be worked out for the general area the chart covers and while not perfect, will be better than nothing.

In practice it is best to operate with a guard zone, a circle of error (COE), of at least 1M from dangers to navigation until positive visual identification of landforms or conspics are made. In some cases the COE should be up to 3M. Depths are a good guide although in some areas there are significant discrepancies and in others there are unsurveyed areas of water. Extra vigilance is needed where charts are known to show serious errors concerning the lat and long or over depths. There are also discrepancies between overlaps on the charts where an islet can have a fringing reef on one chart and none on the other. A certain amount of prudence is needed when determining just how far to stay away from a danger and if in doubt keep at least 3M away.

Astro

There are a few hardy souls out there who think GPS is a misbegotten beast of the late 20th century and who rely solely on the sextant and tables to get around. There are also those who like to keep a check on the black box by taking occasional sights in case the batteries go flat or the GPS gives up (and they do sometimes). For all of this area taking sights is straightforward and indeed visibility is usually good by day and night with one exception. The Red Sea usually has so much haze above the horizon that it is difficult to pull objects down to it and I would recommend GPS, even for ephemeris die-hards, when navigating in the Red Sea. This warning also applies to the Malacca Straits if smoke from the forest fires on Sumatra reduce visibility dramatically as has happened in recent years.

Stores along the way

Stocking up with food and fuels along the way varies dramatically around the Indian Ocean and forward planning is essential. In the introduction to each country covered in this book I give some idea of what is available and so here I will just make some general comments.

Diesel

Is not always readily available although in most places it can be found. It pays to fill up your tank and any reserve tank or jerrycans wherever possible. Most of the harbours which get a significant number of cruising yachts will have either a fuel quay to go alongside or a fuel barge. In a lot of cases you need to make an appointment to take on diesel and

Around most of the Indian Ocean spares and repairs are hard to come by. Equipment on board should be serviced regularly, especially before any hard passages such as the Red Sea or around the bottom of Africa. Here at Changs in Malaysia you need to fight off the snakes when cleaning the bottom.

sometimes there is paperwork to carry out. In some places you must pre-pay for fuel. In a number of places the only way to get diesel is to jerrycan it from the shore which means you need to do a lot of trips to replenish the tank(s).

In places the quality of the fuel can be appalling. Water in the diesel is the most common complaint and in Massawa and Port Sudan, for example, I estimate that the fuel contained around 7–8% water. This means you are going to be cleaning your water separator and filter at frequent intervals and after taking on new fuel it should be checked regularly for water. It also pays to carry a good stock of fuel filters. In some places diesel-bug is also a problem and if you get it there is no solution except to clean out the tank and fuel lines and filters.

If you are topping up the main tank from jerrycans I recommend the 'Eric' siphon method to avoid splashing diesel over the decks or having to suck on the pipe and get a mouthful of the awful stuff. Simply lead the siphon pipe from the bottom of the jerrycan into the fuel filler and then take a short piece of pipe which you seal into the air space in the top of the jerrycan with a piece of rag and your hand. By blowing into the short tube and the air space in the top, or using your inflatable pump, diesel is forced up the siphon tube and in a second away it goes starting the siphon. So elegant and simple, I wish I had thought of it myself.

What you pay for fuel varies either because it is taxed heavily or because the one and only supplier is taxing you with higher prices. In general it is fairly cheap throughout the region with the exception of Australia, India, and the Seychelles. In the Red Sea you may pay a bit more for the agent to supply it although if you can find a source ashore it is not expensive.

Petrol
Usually only available from a petrol station in town although as most people only require small amounts for outboards, this is not too much of a problem.

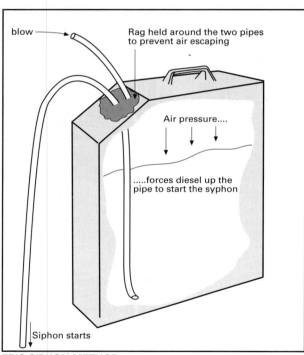

blow

Rag held around the two pipes to prevent air escaping

Air pressure....

.....forces diesel up the pipe to start the syphon

Siphon starts

ERIC SIPHON METHOD

Lubricating oils
Most of the well-known brands of lubricating oil can be found or at least a viable alternative. Specialist hydraulic fluids are harder to find and a good stock should be carried in case you can't locate the type you need.

Gas
In most main centres gas bottles can be refilled IF the depot has the right connector. For this reason it is a good idea to carry a collection of connectors which can simply be plumbing adapters whereby you can alternate between male and female thread sizes. The only alternative to this is to drain gas from local bottles into your own, a procedure which should only be carried out in a well ventilated area which cigarette smokers are banned from. Draining seems to have varying degrees of success. I have not had much success with the method and it can take a long time to even get a bottle half-full.

You also need to be careful of the depot over-filling a bottle. I had one bottle over-filled in Galle in Sri Lanka which started to fizz violently around the rubber seal when I got it back to the boat. Not wanting to live with a bomb on board I heaved it into the water just before the seal went. The bottle acted a bit like a torpedo out of control, alternately diving to the bottom and then erupting out of the water into the air – all accompanied by a wonderful hissing sound. The marines stationed in the harbour zoomed over in their runabout and it was all I could do to persuade them that it was not a Tamil Tiger attack and that they should not shoot it. The consequence of them shooting at the bottle doesn't even bare thinking about. Ever since I have kept a beady eye on anyone filling my gas bottles.

Paraffin
Is easily found in most of the countries around the Indian Ocean. In some countries such as India a special permit is needed for large quantities unless you get it through one of the boat-boys. Methylated spirits is not always as easy to get and in some places such as the Red Sea it is relatively expensive.

Basic provisions
Most basics including rice, pasta and pulses are readily available in most countries. Depending on the local diet in a country, some items will be of exemplary quality while others will often be of poor quality and expensive to boot. So rice is cheap and of good quality in India while pasta produced there makes a glutinous mess when cooked. The colonial past of a country needs to be taken into consideration with the result that you can buy excellent pasta in Eritrea courtesy of the old colonial rulers, Italy. In general the Indian Ocean is the place for rice and pulses and if you like pasta then stock up in places where there is good imported pasta or the local stuff is known to be good.

Wheat flour is available everywhere and rolled oats, essential for muesli, are also widely available in vacuum packed tins. Dried milk is commonly available although the ability of the powder to mix properly with water varies dramatically from brand to brand – try some before you buy a lot of it or stick to a brand you know. Biscuits vary a lot although in general countries which have been British colonies in the past tend to have the best biscuits. This applies to cakes as well and both India and Sri

Lanka have very good dark fruit cakes of one sort or another.

Tinned goods vary greatly and if possible it is best to stock up in either Australia, Singapore, Malaysia and Thailand, or South Africa. Cooking oil is available everywhere although olive oil is scarce and expensive.

Fruit and vegetables

In most countries except the atolls and in the Red Sea, fresh fruit and vegetables are excellent and cheap. India and some of East Africa probably have the best fruit and vegetables going with all sorts of recognisable varieties and some unusual species which should be tried. In a few odd places like the Yemen, fresh fruit and vegetables are better than you might think. Some places like India have excellent dried fruit and nuts and others like Madagascar have spices such as vanilla and nutmeg at bargain basement prices.

Meat and fish

For most of the region meat is not butchered or kept in the sort of conditions most people are familiar with. The sight of freshly butchered meat hanging in local butchers shops, sometimes with a lot of flies around, may put some people off. For the most part it is quite OK and will have been freshly killed that morning. Because it has not been hung it is not as tender as most meat westerners are used to, but the taste is often better, even if a good serrated knife is needed to cut it. In some places including Australia, Singapore, Malaysia, Thailand, Sri Lanka, India and South Africa, good frozen meat can be found at reasonable prices.

Fish is everywhere fresh and good value. The Indian Ocean offers better and more reliable fishing than any other ocean I know of and around coasts with a shallow continental shelf there are prawns and shrimps aplenty. In India and Sri Lanka and

Frank's tomato storage. Soft fruit like tomatoes mostly go off when touching each other. Using an egg carton to separate them like this meant tomatoes for nearly two weeks on passage, even 10° off the equator.

sometimes in Thailand and Malaysia, excellent tiger prawns can be found. In Thailand there are farmed prawns everywhere, but these are not a patch on the free range variety.

Alcohol

In most of the countries around the Indian Ocean beer and local spirits will be found. The exception is in Muslim countries around the Red Sea. In Oman, Yemen and Sudan alcohol is banned and you cannot buy it except on the black market or in a few luxury hotels where it is very expensive (between $US5–7 for a small can of beer in Yemen). In some countries with a more benign Muslim aspect such as Malaysia and Egypt, alcohol will be available although not everywhere. In some duty-free areas along the way, notably Langkawi in Malaysia, alcohol is very cheap and yachts tend to stock up in quantity. In other places like India where the locally made rum is good and cheap, additional stocks can be taken on.

It is one of those little ironies that in countries where alcohol is banned, like Yemen, that you will be constantly asked for it and a cheap bottle of any description can buy you just about anything you want and ease the way in all sorts of transactions.

Good wine is difficult to find and when you do it can cost an arm and a leg. The exceptions are Australia and South Africa which produce excellent wines at reasonable prices. In Langkawi you can find quaffable wines at reasonable duty-free prices and in Réunion, Mayotte and Djibouti French wine is imported, though at a price.

Boat bits

Basic items like shackles, polypropylene ropes, basic paints and varnishes, oil filters, and the like can be found in most of the large coastal towns or cities. Yacht chandlery can be found in Australia, Singapore, the west coast of Malaysia, Phuket and South Africa. Specialist gear and spares will only be found in Australia, Singapore, Phuket and South Africa. Specialist antifoulings can be found in Australia, Singapore, and South Africa. Soft antifouling can be found in Malaysia, Thailand, Sri Lanka, India, Yemen, Seychelles, Mauritius, Réunion and Kenya. You may also be able to track down soft antifouling in a few other places as well. Resins, both polyester and epoxy, can be found in most of the places where there is antifouling of any sort although the shelf-life should be checked as the storage can be suspect.

If you need to have spares sent out then get them sent to Australia, Singapore, Malaysia, or South Africa. Failing that get them sent via a courier such as DHL or Federal Express. Do not have anything sent to India, Madagascar, the Comoros or Egypt if you can at all help it, either because the bureaucratic process is cumbersome or in some cases corrupt. Langkawi in Malaysia is a popular place to have gear and spares sent to because it is a duty-free area with good communications and you simply receive the goods and put them on board without any fuss.

War Zones and civil unrest in the Indian Ocean.
1. Indonesia: Riots and the possibility of civil unrest as the economy collapses.
2. Sri Lanka: Bloody civil war in the north of the country.
3. The Gulf: Possibility of conflict involving Iraq.
4. Yemen: Short civil wars in the recent past.
5. Somalia: State of anarchy prevails with warlords controlling different parts of the country.
6. Hanish Islands: Armed dispute over ownership between Yemen and Eretria.
7. Sudan: Ongoing civil war mostly in the south of the country.
8. Egypt: Terrorism by Muslim fundamentalists.
9. Mozambique: Recent civil war now ended.
10. Kenya: Civil unrest.

Piracy areas in the Indian Ocean.
A. Indonesia: Low risk for yachts. Some risk for merchant shipping.
B. Singapore: None to low risk for yachts. High risk for merchant shipping.
C. Malacca Strait: Low risk for merchant shipping. No risk for yachts on Malaysia side.
D. Southern India: Incidents reported. Low risk for yachts.
E. Strait of Hormuz: Moderate to high risk for merchant shipping.
F. Yemen: Incidents reported. Low risk for yachts.
G. Somalia and Socotra: High risk for yachts and merchant fishing.

WAR ZONES AND CIVIL UNREST AND PIRACY AREAS IN THE INDIAN OCEAN

Beer is the staple drink in most of the Indian Ocean and is nearly always palatable, especially in frosty cold bottles in the heat of the day.

Piracy

The question of piracy is one question often asked and too little backed up by reliable reports. In general piracy world-wide is on the increase again after a period where there was a marked decrease in the numbers of pirate attacks reported. There are areas in the Indian Ocean detailed below where care is needed and few areas to be actively avoided, but much of what passes between cruising boats is often fourth or fifth hand, much embellished, and in the worst cases totally unsubstantiated. Some cruising folk seem to make a bit of an industry out of dissembling rumour and paranoia as reliable reports. Some of this comes from local craft approaching yachts, not to attack them, but out of mere curiosity, or in some cases to get something to eat or medical attention. Many of the countries around the Indian Ocean are amongst the poorest in the world and life on the water is a hard business. Many of the fishermen look like something out of a pirate movie and your first impulse is to take evasive action and tell them to go away. I have encountered local fishermen in Egypt, Sudan, Eritrea, Yemen, India, Sri Lanka, Thailand and Malaysia without ever really feeling threatened. Often these piratical looking types have tied alongside and come on board. At times it has been necessary to control the situation by just having them alongside or tied off astern without an invitation aboard and I always leave the VHF on Ch 16 and turned up so that they know I am in touch with the outside world. I have yet to feel threatened although at times some caution has been necessary. In return for hospitality I have had more fish than you can poke a stick at and enjoyed an hour or so of the locals company. I don't recommend you do as I do at all, I can almost see the letter arriving telling me about a fisherman in Gondwanaland who went berserk or stole everything off your boat, but I do counsel some caution over received opinion about pirates or theft in some areas.

Indonesia

There have been odd reports of yachts being chased by local craft in Indonesian waters, but as many boats pass through here in company on the series of races starting in Darwin and finishing in Singapore, it is difficult to know what the situation is. For yachts not travelling in company there are few reports of piracy I can track down. For cargo ships the area is considered a piracy blackspot with numerous well documented incidents. The sea area between Indonesia and the Philippines, notably the South China Sea and Sulu Sea, is considered the worst piracy area in the world for commercial shipping. Recent incidents on cargo ships have occurred off Sandakan, Borneo, and Sumatra. In one case it is believed that the customs officers used the customs boat to supplement their income with a little piracy on the side and in another incident the 'pirates' were wearing Indonesian marines uniforms. The incident of the M.Y. *Baltimar Zephyr*, a commercial ship which was attacked by pirates in the Sunda Strait and in which two officers on board were killed in December 1992, still rankles with the shipping community as the Indonesian government refuses to accept that it was an act of piracy.

Singapore

Phillips Channel has long been a notorious area for pirate attacks on merchant shipping with 82 cases reported by The Singapore National Shipping Association (consists of 180 shipping companies) between 1990 and 1995. Attacks on yachts appear to be few and far between and it seems likely that these pirates are interested mainly in the valuables carried on large ships. Yachts regularly use this area and I know of no recent reported cases of piracy.

The area is covered by the Regional Piracy Centre in Kuala Lumpur ☎ (03) 292 1333 *Fax* (03) 298 7972.

Malacca Strait

Incidents of piracy in the Malacca Strait have declined dramatically in recent years with no recent cases of yacht piracy reported. If you are travelling along the west coast of Malaysia the chances of piracy are very low to negligible.

The area is covered by the Regional Piracy Centre in Kuala Lumpur ☎ (03) 292 1333 *Fax* (03) 298 7972.

Malaysian Royal Navy Piracy Headquarters ☎ (03) 235 7671 *Fax* (03) 232 0910.

Southern India

There have been reports of fishing boats approaching yachts and stealing items off the deck. Most yachts including myself have not experienced any problems with fishermen in the area who do approach yachts to ask for cigarettes, alcohol or to attempt to sell fish, but are not pirates or even threatening, although their boathandling can be a bit erratic at times.

Oman

There have been reports of attacks on merchant shipping in the Straits of Hormuz just north of Ras Musandam and also a report indicating an increase in attacks in Omani territorial waters, but I have no reports of attacks on yachts in Omani territorial waters. Mina Raysut is a naval base and it is unlikely there would be pirate attacks in the vicinity.

Yemen

There have been reports of yachts attacked off the Yemen coast including a Japanese yacht boarded by three men. The captain was reported to be kidnapped while the wife locked herself in the cabin and radioed for help. I cruised the Yemen coast stopping in numerous places in 1996 and visited again in 1997 and cannot confirm this report. As far as I know the coast is relatively safe and no yachts I know of have encountered problems.

Somalia and Socotra

Socotra Island at the SE corner of the Gulf of Aden has always been well known as an area to keep clear of because of the possibility of pirate attacks. Now the threat of piracy around the island has spread all along the shores of Somalia right up to the approaches to Djibouti. After the abortive attempt of the UN and the USA to bring peace to Somalia, the country has disintegrated into areas dominated by local war-lords who have no compunctions about extending their territory offshore. There is no legitimate government for the whole country and no-one to bring order to the situation. There are no

established links with the war-lords controlling the separate areas and no medical or hospital facilities. For this reason the area should be steered well clear of and the zones shown as danger areas on the map from the French Navy should be given a wide berth.

In 1995 the area off Somalia was declared a no-go area for all shipping by the IMO (International Maritime Organisation) with the recommendation that vessels travel in convoy or keep close to the Yemeni coast. In April 1995 the maxi yacht *Longobarda* was fired upon and chased for over an hour in the area south of Socotra until the arrival of a Canadian frigate scared the attackers off. Another report from 1995 cited an attack on a ship by speedboats in the vicinity of Bossaso on the S side of the Gulf of Aden in which 5 were killed and the ship looted.

Chris Bonnet who sailed up the coast between Socotra and Somalia on incorrect information that the UN was policing the area collected the following disturbing data.

- There have been 15 attacks on ships, fishing boats and yachts between 1994 and May 1995 in the areas shown on the map. 5 attacks were on yachts.
- Three pirate vessels have been identified as (i) 20m long wooden hull, no bridge deck. (ii) 15m long steel hull, bridge at the stern. Reg. no. Djibouti 304. (iii) Speed boat, no other details.
- The speed of the first two vessels is estimated to be about 10kn.
- Weaponry involved includes handguns, AK47s, rockets, and nets for fouling propellers.

The French Navy in Djibouti will respond to MAYDAY calls on VHF or SSB. Their emergency Imarsat no. is 8731111351. They have a patrol aircraft in Djibouti available for emergency response and reconnaissance.

For most yachts crossing the Indian Ocean it is fairly easy to avoid this area by sailing to either Salalah in Oman or Mukalla or Aden in Yemen keeping close to the Yemen coast. I sailed along this coast in 1995–1996 and again in 1997 and experienced no problems. For yachts coming from Mauritius, South Africa and Kenya to the Red Sea the problem is a little more complicated and the best bet is probably to head out to sea giving Socotra a wide berth and then angle into the Yemen coast (or vice versa when leaving the Red Sea towards the southern Indian Ocean).

Useful contacts

International Maritime Organisation Piracy
   department ☎ (0171) 735 7611 Ext 3155.
Hydrographic Office Warnings to Mariners
   ☎ (01823) 337 900
Hydrographic Office France (SHOM) ☎ (33) (98)
   220460
Foreign Office Travel Desk ☎ (0171) 270 4129
Maritime safety Agency ☎ (01703) 329 100

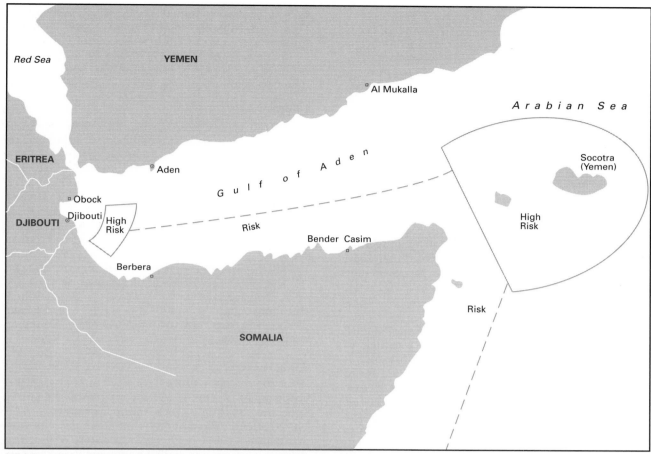

PIRACY AREAS AROUND SOMALIA AND SOCOTRA (BASED ON FRENCH NAVAL INFORMATION)

War zones and civil unrest

Indonesia

In May 1998 the corrupt regime of Suharto and his cronies and family finally fell after popular demonstrations against him. Riots broke out in most major cities and eventually he was forced to resign and his first minister B J Habibe was appointed president. It is uncertain whether Habibe can calm the situation in Indonesia, but for the time being things are settled and Habibe has made some gestures such as freeing political prisoners, reforming the electoral rules and promising parliamentary elections in May 1999 and presidential elections in December 1999.

Around the coast and islands cruising yachts are pretty much away from political goings-on in Jakarta, but it would pay to monitor events prior to visiting and get any feedback from other yachts which have recently cruised here.

Sri Lanka

The bloody civil war between the mainly Singalese Sri Lankan military and the Tamil Tigers resistance fighting for an independent Tamil state in the north of Sri Lanka has been going on since the mid-1980s. All the actual fighting is concentrated in the N and NE of the island, but the Tigers use suicide bombers and frogmen to mount attacks elsewhere, notably in Colombo.

The on-going violence means there is considerable internal security and this applies to any yachts visiting the island. In effect there is only one harbour, that at Galle, used by yachts, and here your yacht will be searched (a fairly cursory procedure) by the navy and at night small depth charges are randomly dropped into the harbour to deter Tamil frogmen from entering and placing explosives on craft. Despite the state of unrest many travel inland and up to the highlands and like many areas of civil unrest, there is an unnerving feeling of normality nearly everywhere you go. I spent a week motorcycling around Sri Lanka and did not feel worried at all. Obviously you should stay away from the northern half of the island where Tamil activity takes place.

Persian Gulf

At the time of writing the most recent confrontation over Iraq has died down. If heading up this way it would be wise to monitor the situation although paradoxically any stand-off means a large presence of naval forces making the area relatively safe.

Yemen

Yemen has been through numerous civil wars between the north and the south culminating in the last civil war in 1994 in which the north won. The country is now united although much resentment smoulders between the north and south. Away from the cities and large towns the odd group of tourists are kidnapped by local sheikhs who hold them to ransom, usually for something the government has promised like a school or a hospital. Those kidnapped are usually well treated. Along the coast you are unlikely to run into any problems of this nature.

Somalia

A state of anarchy exists in the country with different parts of the country ruled by war-lords. Yachts should keep well away from the coast because of the risk of piracy. See the preceding section on piracy.

Eritrea and the Hanish Islands

In December 1995 Eritrea invaded the Hanish Islands which had traditionally been regarded as Yemeni territory. I was in fact in the Hanish Islands just a couple of days before the invasion and heard of it on the BBC World Service between the Hanish and Bab El Mandeb. The occupation of the islands has effectively put them out of bounds to yachts and there have been reports of a yacht being fired on in the vicinity of the islands since the invasion. Since the Eritreans use small craft it could be either side firing on yachts around the islands. At the present time there is a stand-off and mediation between the two claimants to the islands. Given the volatile situation the islands should be given a good offing although in 1997 I saw no activity in the area when I passed by.

In May and June 1998 and again in March 1999 there were serious armed clashes over disputed territory between Eritrea and Ethiopia. Asmara has been bombed and military forces in both countries have been mobilised. Most of the disputed area is in the southwest corner of Eritrea. At the present time it would be wise to avoid the port of Assab and monitor the situation for Massawa. On no account should a yacht go anywhere near an area used by the military.

Sudan

Sudan is a country riven by civil war and famine, governed by an Islamic party that has introduced *shariya* law, a country which has disputes with every country it borders and that includes Eritrea, Ethiopia, Kenya, Uganda and Egypt. It has surprised many that the government is still in power and given recent rebel advances in the south, it is imperative that the situation is monitored closely. What is surprising given the situation in most of the country is that Port Sudan exudes such an air of normality. In 1997 and 1998 the port was open to visiting yachts and most services were easily accessed. Despite the apparent air of normality in Port Sudan yachtsmen should take special care in Sudanese waters and follow the situation in the countryside carefully. It would be wise at present to avoid all border areas although there have been no major problems in recent years.

Egypt

While the coastal areas are stable, inland there is some terrorism from fundamentalist groups who want Egypt to become an Islamic country along the lines of Iran or Sudan. These two countries are accused of aiding the terrorist groups. There have been several attacks on tourists, mostly on coaches visiting areas around the Nile, and the massacre in late 1997 at Luxor which left over 40 dead and many injured. This has severely dented the tourist industry and internal security by the army is now much in evidence everywhere. It is unlikely a yacht cruising along the coast will be targeted by terrorists and no incidents have occurred to date. When travelling inland it is probably wise to go by taxi although in real terms the risk on other modes of transport is low.

Mozambique

After the madness of the civil war here between the government (Frelimo) and the resistance (Renamo) sponsored by South Africa, things are reported to be on the mend. The country cannot be described as stable just yet, but neither is it in a state of flux any more since an accommodation was reached between Frelimo and Renamo in 1992. Although things have improved greatly there is still much poverty and isolated incidents from bandits. For the most part cruising yachts will know nothing of this as the coastal regions are rarely affected.

Kenya

The re-election of Daniel arap Moi in late 1997 was contentious and it is likely incidents of unrest will increase in Kenya between the various opposition parties and Moi's KANU party. At the moment outbreaks of tribal violence mirrored by the various political parties and violent crime in the urban centres has severely dented the tourism business in Kenya. For the most part the coastal regions have been little affected but it would pay to monitor the situation in Kenya in case full scale tribal violence breaks out.

Diving

Much of the Indian Ocean lies within the tropics and the diving in this region is some of the best in the world. Here all I will do is briefly detail well known dive sites. For most of these areas I am talking about snorkelling as well as subaqua diving and one of the delights of the Indian Ocean is that there are numerous areas where the marine life is so prolific that there is more than enough to see just snorkelling around the reefs and shallow diving without tanks. For additional information contact dive holiday operators or dive centres in the countries concerned.

Indonesia Has numerous good dive sites around the smaller islands. Around many of the large islands the silt brought down by rivers reduces visibility. With over one quarter of the world's coral reefs there just has to be a lot of little known good diving around the islands.

Malaysia Has some areas of coral reef but in general the silty water reduces visibility too much for it to be a good diving area. Some offshore islands like the Pulau Payer Marine Park between Langkawi and Penang are far enough away from the coast for clearer water.

Thailand Like Malaysia suffers from generally bad visibility making it necessary to visit the offshore islands. Around the Similan and Surin Islands there is good diving. Good dive facilities in Phuket.

Andamans Reported to have excellent diving around the offshore reefs with prolific marine life everywhere. Schools of manta rays and sharks aplenty are reported.

Sri Lanka The only good area for diving is in the north where the civil war is going on so you can strike it off your list.

India In general the water is too silty making visibility so bad it is not worth diving in most places. Around the Laccadives the diving is reported to be excellent, but it is a restricted area.

Maldives This atoll chain has long been renowned for its diving and little else needs to be said. The diving is excellent everywhere with lots of pelagic fish including mantas and sharks. Good healthy reefs although care is needed in places of strong currents. Good dive facilities and some of the islands have small hotels devoted to dive holidays.

Yemen Good diving around the reefs and islands although the present stand-off between Yemen and Eritrea makes it a bit tricky to dive here.

Eritrea Superb diving around reefs that have seen little fishing during the long civil war. At the time of writing the new conflict between Eritrea and Ethiopia means it would be prudent to avoid dallying overlong around the coral reefs. Monitor the situation to see if things calm down. A marine soup where you can really just watch everything go by. Lots of sharks including hammerheads.

Sudan Superb diving around the reefs which are little touched by commercial fishing.

Egypt Already well known on the dive scene. Away from popular dive sites like Hurgadha the diving is excellent. Good dive facilities.

Cocos Keeling Superb diving over the reef and near the anchorage at Direction Island there is a drop-off where fishing is banned.

Chagos Outstanding diving over the reefs. It should be remembered this is a marine reserve and fishing, catching turtles, living ashore, etc. is prohibited.

Seychelles Good diving over the reefs. Around the outer atoll groups the diving is reported to be excellent, but you need a permit to go there. Many of the hotels have dive facilities.

Mauritius and Réunion Don't have a lot in the way of reefs and several artificial reefs have been created by sinking small hulks.

Madagascar Has several superb diving areas around the offshore islands. There is a lot of coral and marine life and the visibility is OK away from the main island coast.

Mayotte First class diving reported around the barrier reef.

Comoros First class diving reported around Moheli.

South Africa Sodwana Bay (Sordies) close to the border with Mozambique is reported to have first class diving with lots of sharks. Aliwal Shoal close to Durban is also reported to be a good place to see lots of sharks.

Mozambique Reported to be superb diving, especially in the north between Ibo and Ilha Mozambique with St Lazarus Bank offshore recommended. Around some areas the water is silty from rivers flowing into the sea and visibility much reduced.

Tanzania Good diving around offshore reefs with the Pemba Channel a well known world class diving area. Lots of manta rays, sharks and good coral.

Kenya Popular dive area although close to Mombasa it tends to be overpopulated. Bad visibility in places from silt brought down by rivers.

Diver's code
- Do not collect living shells and coral.
- Do not buy shells, coral, souvenirs made from turtle shell or other marine knick-knacks. Turtle shell is protected under CITES and can be confiscated by customs.
- Respect marine reserves and the regulations governing them. If it is prohibited to fish in an area leave your speargun and lines behind and just look. Yachtsmen can get to out-of-the-way places like Chagos where regulations are sometimes flouted so self regulation is necessary or the numbers of places yachts can go to will be curtailed – something which has happened in parts of the world already.
- Do not litter or feed fish with unsuitable food. Plastic bags can suffocate life on the bottom and cause death to animals like turtles or dugongs which get caught in them.

- Do not anchor yachts on coral and always use moorings if they are provided.
- Do not pollute the water with diesel or oil.
- Do not walk on reefs if you can help it. In some areas repeated numbers of people walking on reefs has caused a visible effect on coral growth.

Fishing

Fishing around the Indian Ocean is some of the best fishing anywhere and that includes the Pacific and Atlantic. There were days when we had to declare a 'no-fish' day, and I love fish, but in the end you can get sick of it day after day. I'm not a dedicated fisherman but I don't mind trolling a line out the back and in some parts of the Indian Ocean you can dangle just about anything off the back and catch fish.

Most of the fish you are going to get will be tuna of some sort, including yellowfin, dogtooth and occasionally albacore, mackerel and wahoo, and dolphinfish (mahe-mahe). You will also get barracuda and sharks. Personally I don't mind barracuda and small shark for eating, but if there is other fish around I usually throw them back. The mackerel in the Red Sea and Indian Ocean are beautiful fish with an almost white flesh and less oily than other mackerel I have caught.

Theories on lures vary, but a good lure like those made by Rapallo are worth carrying. When you have lost them all then you can get down to making your own. Tuna will go for just about anything including white cloth wrapped around a hook. What you will need is a good stainless trace, preferably 3 or more metres long, and good strong swivels. Sometimes you will find the trace has just been cut in half with hardly a tug on the line and in this case you really don't need to know what was on the end of it. Nor do you need fancy kit, just some good strong nylon line and a bit of elastic cord ('stretchy') to take the sting out of the initial strike. We used to use either a clothes peg to hold the slack line after the elastic or to loop it around the winch so it turned the winch when there was a strike. It's a good idea to carry a good stock of line, stainless traces, swivels and hooks, not only to replace those that you lose, but also as gifts for fishermen in out of the way places.

Catching the fish is comparatively easy in the Indian Ocean, but getting it on board can be more difficult. For hard-lipped fish like tuna you can just haul them up or gaff them through the mouth. For soft-lipped fish like dolphinfish, you need to gaff them through the gills or through the body. For shark and barracuda the trick is to get them off any way you can without getting bitten or cut from the shark's skin. It's a delicate process, especially on a smaller yacht, and care is needed – those teeth are very sharp and even a small shark or barracuda can do a fair bit of damage.

Once on board the head should be severed to cut the spinal cord and kill it as quickly as possible. It

Cuttle fish catch in the harbour in Mukalla. To my taste cuttle fish is better than squid.

also lets the flesh bleed and stops toxins accumulating from a struggling fish. I used to stun the fish with a baseball bat and then hold it down and sever the head. The fish can then be gutted and filleted or cut into steaks. For small bony fish that are going to be pan-fried the easiest thing to do is to cut the head off and then cut along the bottom (ventral) of the fish so it can be flattened out to fit in the pan.

Cooking fish

Arguably the best way to eat fish which has just been caught is to pan-fry it. Following are a few tips.

- With tuna or any other fish than can be cut crosswise into steaks, get a plastic bag, put some flour and a bit of pepper and salt into the bag, and then just throw the steaks in and shake them around inside the bag. This cuts out a lot of mess and you can keep the bag to be re-used with the flour until it begins to smell a bit fishy.

- The oil in the pan should be hot and to stop the fish sticking sprinkle a bit of salt into the oil.
- For a bit of variation on pan-frying put some garlic cloves into the oil (you can leave the skin on), some sun-dried tomato, a few chillies, or anything similar or whatever combination of all these that suits your palate. It just gives a suggestion of taste to the fish. And remember fish is not salty so it needs a bit of salt for flavour.
- Never keep fish for more than a few hours without refrigeration or more than 6–10 hours with refrigeration. Tuna is a good fish to freeze, but do make sure it is frozen. If fish tastes prickly to the tongue, smells ammoniacal or very fishy, then throw it out. Food poisoning from bad fish is not something you need in mid-ocean.

Rod's fish stew
For four
- 1kg of fish
  If you can get them, mussels (canned mussels are not too bad) or any other shellfish or things like shrimps.
- 2 large onions and several cloves of garlic.
- 1 can tomatoes (plus a handful of chopped sun dried tomatoes if you have them or some tomato paste).
- Any other suitable vegetables like green peppers, courgettes, or even a few potatoes chopped into small pieces. You don't need to use any of these but be inventive.
- Oil, salt and pepper, and basil and bay leaves if you have them.
- Aniseed spirits like ouzo, raki, *Pernod* or similar. Or brandy if you don't have any aniseed flavoured spirits.

Chop the onions and saute. Chop the fish into bite sized chunks and add to onion with crushed garlic, seal the fish on either side. Add all the other ingredients and simmer gently for 10 minutes with a lid on. Add a glug of aniseed spirit or brandy to taste. Simmer for another 2 minutes with the lid on. Serve with rice or noodles.

BBQ fish
Wrap fillets or steaks of the fish in tinfoil with a slice of tomato and green pepper on top and if you have it, a piece of mozzarella or similar – even camembert or brie work OK.

You can also mix up some curry powder and other condiments you fancy with butter or margarine (or oil at a pinch) and smear the mixture onto fillets or steaks. Don't wrap with tinfoil but just BBQ directly.

Other good uses of fish are for fish cakes or if you have plenty of gas, oven-baked in tinfoil.

Cultures and poverty
The Indian Ocean has a mixture of cultures ranging from Muslim to Hindu to Buddhist to Christian to Taoist with a bit of Animism and a lot of variation thrown in. Some are well-developed and economically prosperous cultures and others are very poor. These diverse cultures often co-exist and all are overlaid with different colonial experiences and some home grown influences that have formed them into the particular culture they are. For the yachtsman encountering these very diverse cultures for the first time there can be an element of fear and concern about how safe, honest, friendly and approachable these cultures are.

Let me put it this way. I sometimes think that if I had to live a poor and menial existence in one of these cultures then I would seize upon the opportunity to steal from these plump westerners in their fancy yachts and rip them off whenever I could. Yet you are unlikely to have anything stolen by the poor in this part of the world and the honesty of people with very little leaves me gasping at the concept. You are far more likely to have something stolen in your own highly developed country than in most of these underdeveloped countries where the word 'underdeveloped' applies only to the economic situation and not to their morals and ethics.

In a few places it pays to take precautions against theft from items left on deck and from tenders on the shore and there are details on these places in the relevant sections in the main body of the text. But in many places I did not bother to lock up the boat and during my whole time in the region nothing was stolen from the boat, even when left unattended, not even anything inconsequential, except on one occasion, and the likely culprits were some of the crew from a coaster berthed nearby.

Certainly I have a rekindled respect for the dignity and honesty of the poor. I left *Tetra* for 3 weeks in Cochin and nothing was stolen. I left her again in Malaysia for 6 months up the Dinding River and nothing was stolen. I left her for a day or two in all sorts of anchorages and harbours and not a thing was touched. I have fumbled with bundles of *riyal* in Yemen and had some returned because I counted out too much. I have had a Thai fisherman help me to move from an anchorage that was becoming untenable. I have had an Indian farmer hand me a forgotten package as the train pulled out. I have been so often humbled by acts of generosity and friendliness from the poor that I have lost count.

You will of course come across sharp practices, but these will generally be perpetrated by those hanging around tourist areas or a well-known yacht harbour or anchorage. Anyone who calls themselves an agent should always be treated with suspicion if they are not already well known to the cruising community. There are places like Sri Lanka or the Suez Canal where you need to use an agent and there is no point in arguing the point. In some places touts and taxi drivers can be a pain and will overcharge you while in others a good taxi driver will prove to be a Mr Fix-It who will be able to locate services and take you to the best places to buy provisions. In some countries confidence tricksters will regale you with a hard luck story involving the loss of money, family, goods, whatever, all through absolutely no fault of their own and only because they happened to be standing in the wrong place when the sky fell on their head. You need to be wary over such stories which you will likely find have been repeated to most of those in the anchorage or harbour.

Drugs are a no-no in all of the countries around the Indian Ocean and should you be caught there are harsh penalties which may involve the loss of your yacht. In Malaysia and Singapore the death penalty applies for smuggling hard drugs. In other apparently tolerant countries like India there are hundreds in primitive prisons awaiting trial for drug related offences. Ashore you may be offered various substances, although often you may not get what you think. Some dealers will report you to the police and many pass off packets which contain not a milligram of an illicit substance but do come with a lot of assurances.

Begging is a contentious issue and I for one adopt a random approach based on a gut feeling. You cannot pass all those deformed limbs and gazelle eyes without succumbing and you cannot satisfy them all. When I feel it is time to give a few coins I generally make sure I have an escape route like a shop or office which the beggars will not enter. In countries like India a single coin dispensed will attract other beggars in an instant. Cochin in fact bans beggars from the streets, but if you travel to other urban centres prepare for constant attention from gangs of beggars.

In most of the areas you visit a small gift or some hospitality on board is only human. For fishermen hooks and line are treasures and it is worthwhile carrying a stock of shiny hooks and line for gifts. Containers, especially plastic containers, are also valuable currency. In Arab countries a small packet of tea is a symbolic gift of friendship and in cultures where sweets and sugar are in short supply a packet of fairly ordinary biscuits is a treat for isolated fishermen. In places like India your rubbish can be a treasure trove for the dispossessed and at the Bolgatty Hotel it was sorted through and recycled in next to no time when left near the landing stage. For other communities a T-shirt or a hat with the name of the yacht on is a nice link between you and them and for others a pen with the yacht's name on it will also go down well.

In most of the region a 'business' card with your address and other details on it is *de rigeur* and people you meet will expect you to have one and will give you their card in return. Alcohol of any sort is a useful gift in countries where it is banned or in short supply and in some places can significantly ease your passage through bureaucratic procedures. Cigarettes are important currency in Sudan and Egypt although you will find that some haggling is in order and at times a downright refusal must be made to extortionate demands by minor officials.

For any situation some interpretation of what is going on will be required and amongst cruising yachts the word on what the going rate is, what gifts are useful or appreciated, and where and when to say 'no' will be frequently discussed. Using common sense in a situation is one thing, but there are some cruising folk around for whom the milk of human kindness has dried up and who are downright mean in their dealings with the locals. Perhaps it is worthwhile reflecting on what your own attitudes are to yachts cruising your own home waters and how you react to those arriving in your country. How would you like to be treated as a second class citizen in your own country?

The matter of dress and appearance is important in many countries and can be taken as a reflection of your worth and standing. If you go ashore in cut-off shorts and a dirty T-shirt you are not likely to be treated with the same respect as someone who takes a bit of time to don long trousers and a shirt. This is a difficult one because you know that what you wear on board at sea means nothing in terms of how you cope with the sea and its dangers and many of us would like to think that somehow our intrinsic worth shines through. It does not. Things will be a lot smoother ashore if you make an effort to look neat and tidy and don't offend the norms and mores of the local population. For many Muslim societies it is offensive for men and especially women to show flesh around the mid-riff and a lot of leg. In some Muslim societies women should wear a head scarf. When visiting any religious temple or shrine modest and neat attire is expected and appropriate. You wouldn't walk into a church or go to see your bank manager in your own country dressed in swimming trunks or a pair of tatty shorts, so why expect to do it in another country.

Body language in different countries is also something that can be a bit confusing. Seemingly innocent gestures or postures used in our own country can be offensive in others. For many cultures it is offensive to point with a finger or to beckon someone with a crooked finger. Use the hand palm down to make a gesture to 'come here'. Using the left hand to eat or touch things with is often offensive because in many countries this is the hand used to carry out necessary toilet activities in the absence of loo paper. To touch the head in Buddhist countries is to touch the most sacred part of the body and to touch anything with your foot, the least sacred part of the body, is to contaminate it or express disgust. Affectionate embraces and kissing in public is also inappropriate in Buddhist cultures. Raising your voice often means a loss of face and you will have less credence if you do so.

It's a complicated old world out there – but interesting.

Health matters

Visitors to the Indian Ocean will be encountering a good number of countries in which there will be health risks not normally associated with their own country. Partly this is to do with the tropical environment and partly to do with standards of hygiene, poor living conditions and low standards of health care in some of the countries. In each of the general sections on a country in the main body of the text I have briefly detailed what to expect in the way of health care in a particular country. Before you go there is much in the way of preparation to reduce the likelihood of contracting disease and here I will briefly give an overview and advice on minimising the risks.

Stock up on any special medication you are on (for high blood pressure, angina, diabetes, etc.) for the duration of the trip. Asthma sufferers should ensure they take adequate refills for inhalers and any other necessary medication. Asthma sufferers usually find the sea air helps their breathing but in some cases the humidity can aggravate their condition. Hayfever sufferers should take whatever medication they require with them and not assume that because they are going to areas where the pollen count should be low, that they will have no reaction. It may be that different types of pollen will cause a severe reaction when actual counts are low. And don't forget a spare pair of glasses and your lenses prescription.

Insurance

Medical insurance including repatriation in the event of serious illness should be seriously considered. I make it mandatory for any crew coming with me on the boat although thankfully it has never been necessary to claim on it. A good policy need not be overly expensive and it is worthwhile looking around and getting a few quotes on premiums. Many companies do not make an additional charge if you are on a yacht although do check because some do. Most insurers do have exemptions for sports like sub-aqua diving, water-skiing and the like so you may need an additional premium to cover you for accidents involving these activities.

Medical insurance for the Indian Ocean should be for one million pounds (or 1½ million dollars) and should include air ambulance costs of around ½ a million pounds (¾ million dollars). Often the medical insurance component can be obtained as part of a general travel insurance policy although it can be cheaper to get it separately or you may decide that the general travel insurance part is too expensive and not worthwhile.

Vaccinations

Yellow fever Should be kept up to date. It lasts ten years and evidence of immunisation is required in some countries.

Tetanus and polio Ensure your jabs are in date. Tetanus and polio jabs last ten years.

Hepatitis A is only a moderate risk but Hepatitis B is on the increase. Hepatitis B is only transmitted by sexual contact or contaminated blood. For Hepatitis A gammaglobulin is not now widely used and the only effective vaccination is the new Hepatitis A (*Havrix*) vaccine. *Havrix* can be given in conjunction with other vaccinations.

Japanese encephalitis Is on the increase in a few tropical areas. Effective vaccines are available.

Typhoid Is a risk only in a few areas. Injectable or oral vaccines last only three years so check with your doctor.

Cholera Is low risk in most areas. As the vaccine is only 60% effective and lasts for only 3–6 months it is not normally recommended. If there has been a recent cholera outbreak in an area you are going to a doctor will be able to advise you if vaccination is useful. A cholera exemption certificate may be useful although I have never heard of anyone being asked for one.

Rabies Not normally recommended as the incidence is extremely low.

TB Children should be immunised at any age.

Meningitis Is a risk in certain areas. Check with a doctor on vaccination.

Smallpox Not required for most countries but check with your doctor.

Children should be protected against diphtheria, whooping cough, mumps and measles if they have not already had them. Consult your doctor.

Advice on vaccinations can be obtained from your doctor, the Department of Tropical Diseases in a main hospital or in the UK from MASTA (Medical Advisory Services For Travellers Abroad). In the UK MASTA is the most likely to have the latest information and can be telephoned on 0891 224100. Calls are charged and you must give answers to a recorded answer-phone system with a fairly tedious system of pressing numerals in response to questions. You will be sent a print-out detailing health risks and recommended vaccinations as well as the latest health warnings from the countries you have specified.

Malaria

There is a risk of contracting malaria in many of the countries around the Indian Ocean. In some countries the incidence of malaria is increasing and there are also some new strains of malaria which are resistant to the normal prophylactic regime. Whether or not to take prophylactics in a malaria risk area is a much debated point on cruising yachts. In some countries the coastal areas are little affected by malaria whereas inland there is a high risk. This does not mean you will not contract the disease in a coastal region and in some areas the local population has some resistance to the disease which new visitors will not have. Many believe that by taking sensible precautions and avoiding being bitten that there is therefore no reason to take prophylactics which in any case may not be effective.

It is important to know that while malaria is transmitted by mosquito bites, it is only transmitted by the *anopheles* mosquito. Mosquitoes are common in most parts of the world, but the majority of species do not transmit malaria. Because there are mosquitoes around does not mean you are at risk and in fact *anopheles* normally come out in the evening and at dawn only.

The choice of treatment is between the old fashioned prophylactic regime of two proguanil (commonly *Paludrine*) a day and two chloroquine a week (commonly *Nivaquine* or *Avloclor*) or one mefloquine (commonly *Lariam*) a week. While the weekly regime may seem more attractive it does produce side effects in a certain percentage of people thought to be as high as 10% although only 0·7% experience serious side effects. These side effects are dizziness and for a small group rapid mood changes or depression. The latter can be long term for the 0·7% so affected. If you have any history of dramatic mood changes or depression it is suggested that you do not use mefloquine. The possibility of depression on a small yacht invites some scary scenarios.

The best protection against malaria is to prevent mosquito bites. Some boats have mosquito screens fitted, but unless you are going to stay below on balmy evenings this is not much of a help. In the following section on dealing with unwanted visitors there are suggestions for keeping mosquitoes (and other aerial visitors) at bay.

Unwanted visitors

By day there can be unwanted visitors like flies, wasps, bees, flying ants and an assortment of other creatures depending on where you are. Wasps and bees are the only ones which are dangerous and really only because you will have few clothes on and be more likely to be stung. Wasps and bees are attracted by the odour of food and drinks and if these are removed, they will soon disappear. They particularly like sweet drinks like colas and other fizzy pops, mixers in your evening tipple, jams and chutneys, and meats like ham and salamis. It is best not to try and swat them or they may get angry and sting someone.

One tip is never to drink out of a can whatever the beverage inside. I know of two incidences where a wasp crawled unseen into the can and stung the recipient in the throat while travelling down the oesophagus. The subsequent swelling in the throat obstructed the windpipe and nearly caused death in one case. Always tip canned drinks into a glass.

For stings take an antihistamine cream or something like *Waspeze* in an aerosol can which contains a mild local anaesthetic as well as an antihistamine.

In the evening and early morning mosquitoes and midges are a problem in many areas. Midges are not disease carriers but can inflict an irritating bite out of all proportion to their size. Mosquitoes in most areas are not malaria carriers, but the bite is irritating and some poor souls have an allergic reaction to the anticoagulant the mosquito injects which causes the irritation. If you know that mosquitoes or midge bites cause an allergic reaction take whatever medication is necessary. Putting screens over ports and hatches will keep mosquitoes out (although there always seem to be one or two which somehow get through) and once you set off to sea a good spray down below with fly spray or similar will kill any mosquitoes hitching a ride.

In the evenings cover yourself up with a long-sleeved shirt and long baggy trousers. Use a reliable mosquito repellent. Those that contain DEET are the most effective but in some people they cause an irritable reaction on the skin and they will also dissolve some plastics including watch straps and the like. Try some out on your skin before applying to clothing. There are various other repellents of varying effectiveness. Use vapour coils if these do not suffocate you and if the boat has a cigarette lighter adapter it is possible to purchase 12 volt tablet 'cookers' which plug into lighter adapters similar to the ones which plug into 220V mains sockets.

AIDS

The incidence of AIDS in the world still increases dramatically and rates in Southeast Asia and East Africa in particular are very high. The TravelSafe code from the Department of Health reproduced below should be followed at all times.

Avoid unnecessary medical or dental treatment and situations which may make this necessary.

Avoid having casual relationships but if you have sex with someone new, always use a condom.

Don't inject drugs or share needles and syringes.

Remember alcohol and drugs affect your judgement.

Avoid having a tattoo, acupuncture, or your ears pierced unless sterile equipment is used.

Within your medical chest it is worthwhile carrying your own sterile hypodermic syringes in case you need injections ashore.

Marine perils

Jellyfish Jellyfish stings are the most common injury encountered in the marine world. All jellyfish sting as that is the way they immobilise their prey and it is also their defence against predators. They will only sting if you bump into them or inadvertently become entangled in their trailing tentacles. Some jellyfish like the Portuguese man-o-war and some sea wasps are vicious stingers and the sea wasp causes a number of fatalities in Australia every year. Other jellyfish like the more common *Aurelia aurita* and *Pelagia noctiluca* are stingers but never fatal. Different people have different reactions to jellyfish stings. For some there is a violent allergic reaction with loss of breath and increased heart rate while for others the symptoms are just a mild irritating reaction on the skin. There are various treatments although none are 100% effective. Those likely to have a violent reaction should use anti-histamine creams and something like *Waspeze*. Other treatments are dilute ammonium hydroxide, neat alcohol, vinegar, lemon rubbed on the sting, and even meat tenderiser which is said to break down the protein base of the venom. One tip is to wear gloves when hauling up an anchor as jellyfish tentacles can become wrapped around it and will still sting you even if detached from the body of the jellyfish.

Sea urchins Can be a problem when wandering around rocky areas if you tread on one and get the spines embedded in your foot. Always wear shoes or sandals when walking in shallow water around rocky areas and watch where you put your feet. The spines themselves are not venomous but are difficult to remove and may cause an infection.

Coral Coral cuts are common when you go swimming or walking around reefs and for some reason take an age to heal. Coral does sting mildly, but this is not the cause of cuts taking a long time to heal. Any cuts should be washed with an antiseptic solution and then the cut kept dry. If necessary put a plastic bag on the foot with a rubber band around the ankle when going ashore in a dinghy or anywhere else the foot is likely to get wet.

Ciguatera Is not a well known disease but does claim a number of victims every year. Though it is seldom fatal its effects can be long term. It is caused by eating certain types of fish, usually reef fish, although others have been implicated, which for some reason become infected and pass the infection on to humans when eaten. The problem is that the disease affects fish which are normally edible and there is no way of knowing whether a fish is infected or not. It only affects tropical fish and has been associated with fish living around coral that has been damaged in some way. Fish caught on a line trolled behind a boat are seldom affected. Local fishermen normally know if *ciguatera* is around and consequently will not deliver certain types of fish to the market at certain times of the year. If you have been fishing around a reef ask the locals if the fish is OK to eat.

Seasickness

Most people suffer at some time or other from seasickness, some more chronically than others. If you know that you are susceptible take your preferred remedy with you.

Tablets A number of antihistamines are on the market, commonly *Avomine*, *Dramamine*, *Marzine RF*, and *Sturgeron*. Of these *Sturgeron* is widely accepted as the most effective. They all cause drowsiness to some extent, though *Sturgeron* is reported to do so to a lesser extent than the others. The tablets should be started prior to going sailing, sometimes as much as four hours beforehand. Other tablets such as *Phenergan*, *Kwells* and *Sereen* contain hyoscine hydrobromide which has a sedative effect and leaves the sufferer drowsy.

Patches A small elastoplast patch is stuck on the body, usually behind the ear, and releases the sedative slowly into the bloodstream. This has the advantage of a small continuous dosage as opposed to the instant dosage in tablet form and thus is less likely to cause drowsiness. Commonly contain hyoscine hydrobromide. Young children cannot use this system and it does have side effects on some people, usually drowsiness although a few souls have experienced mild hallucinations.

Homeopathic cures A number of homeopathic treatments are available: *Nux Vomica*, *Cocculus Indicus*, and *Ipecac*. Other natural remedies are ginger, glucose and Vitamin B12. Ginger appears to come out favourite.

Sea bands Elasticised bands with a small knob sewn into them. When slipped over the wrist the knob is supposed to press on the *nei-kuan* pressure point that reduces nausea. The problem is hitting exactly the right point – something an acupuncturist spends years learning to do.

In general someone who is seasick should be kept warm, but should stay in the cockpit if possible. Watching the horizon seems to have a curative effect and giving them something to do like steering, if they are able, seems to take the mind off the nausea. Any odours from diesel, gas, cooking smells and the like will aggravate the nausea. When seasick try to eat something like crackers or dry bread and drink plenty of water as vomiting causes dehydration.

Water

Water is a tricky issue and staying clear of waterborne diseases or complications cannot be solved by drinking bottled water. In any of the destinations you go to you will come into contact with it by virtue of eating ashore. Salad vegetables and fruit will be washed in it, local ice and ice-cream will be made from it, cooking and other utensils will be washed and rinsed in it, and you will wash and clean your teeth in it. Even the most fastidious amongst you will not be able to avoid contact with it in one way or another.

In most places the water is safe to drink although it may contain local micro-organisms which in themselves are not dangerous, but may cause a minor case of upset tummy and the runs until your digestive system adapts to them. If there are problems with water supplies in an area other boats will know about it. Otherwise my advice is to drink the local water as you will inevitably come across it in one way or another.

One last plea. Dispose of used water bottles in garbage containers. There are too many plastic water bottles littering the seas and beaches of the world and none of us should add to this very visual form of pollution.

Bureaucracy

An inevitable part of travelling by yacht is that you will often encounter long and tedious procedures for clearing in and out of a country or to prolong your stay in it. In most cases these regulations are not the making of the officials you encounter and I have been appalled at times to witness skippers shouting and lecturing to harried officials who are trying their best to clear them in or out. You will encounter little Hitlers in some places and almost invariably will come across corruption and requests for backhanders or gifts, but mostly you will encounter officials who are just doing their job and carrying out the procedure set down from on high. There is often no point hectoring some hapless official when he already knows that he is involved in a tedious paperchase, but must follow it through because that is the law.

When you do go to clear in make sure you are dressed neatly and soberly with long trousers and a shirt. Many officials will treat you with greater respect and process your paperwork a lot quicker if you are neatly attired. Wear a pair of swimming trunks and a grubby T-shirt and you will not be considered worthy of respect and your requests will not be taken seriously.

The following list will give you some idea of what to expect with officialdom in any given country, although obviously experiences can differ.

Singapore and Malaysia Paperwork carried out quickly with civility and honesty.

Thailand Paperwork carried out quickly with a smile and a small 'gift'. To leave a boat in the country you must lodge a bond for which a larger bribe is needed. Use an agent if possible for extensions and leaving a yacht in the country or go to Malaysia where it is straightforward to leave a yacht in the country.

Sri Lanka The Windsors are the official agents here for clearing in and out with a set fee.

India Clearing in and out is a prolonged affair although all officials are helpful and there are no 'additional' charges. Can be difficult to get visa extensions.

Maldives Use an agent at Male.

Oman Straightforward with no 'gifts' necessary.

Yemen Straightforward and efficient with just a few small 'gifts' to ease the way.

Djibouti Straightforward.

Eritrea Straightforward with no 'gifts' necessary.

Sudan Use an agent. A few small 'gifts' may be required.

Egypt Baksheesh rules. Use an agent at Suez. Elsewhere agents will approach you and can be used although they tend to be very expensive. For everything, even saying 'hello', you will be asked for baksheesh. Use your own judgement, but start out by refusing any until you get down to the absolute bottom base rate.

Seychelles Straightforward if tedious. You may be asked for some gifts along the way. All formalities are handled at Victoria.

Mauritius and Réunion Straightforward.

Madagascar and Comoros Confused and difficult process. Demands for 'extra' charges and 'gifts'. Check with others just what the going rates are.

Mayotte Straightforward.

South Africa Straightforward and friendly.

Mozambique Confused and you may be asked for 'extra' charges and gifts. Difficult to get visa extensions.

Tanzania Officious with occasional requests for small 'gifts'. Difficult to get visa extensions.

Kenya Straightforward and generally friendly.

For a voyage around the Indian Ocean it is useful to carry a wad of passport size photographs of yourself and crew and to have numerous crew lists made up. A ship's stamp is also useful to add authority to all documents and it can give some respite from the tedium by wielding it vigorously for all documents.

Obey the signs. It makes it pretty clear what will happen if you don't in Malaysia.

Technical information

Cruising highways

Most cruising yachts will be making a passage westabout across the Indian Ocean, usually as part of a circumnavigation. This passage uses the trades and the NE monsoon to get across from Australia and Southeast Asia to Africa and the Red Sea. It is a well known passage with reliable winds and generally easy seas except towards the southern half of the Indian Ocean.

Although the majority of yachts are cruising westabout along known routes, an increasing number of yachts are cruising eastabout or staying around the Indian Ocean area for longer periods and basing themselves in one or more places to enjoy the cruising to be had here. In the sections on passage making that follow I will flesh out some of the general comments here which give an overview on planning a cruise around the Indian Ocean and some pointers on where you might like to dally.

Once across the Pacific yachts arriving in Australia or eastern parts of Southeast Asia have a decision to make about crossing the Indian Ocean. From Darwin you can decide to strike out south of the equator for the Christmas Island, Cocos, Chagos, Seychelles route to Africa and the Red Sea with a split at Cocos where some yachts will head up to Sri Lanka and then across to the Red Sea. Alternatively yachts will head up through Indonesia to Malaysia and Thailand before crossing to Sri Lanka and on to the Red Sea north of the equator. Choosing between these routes is often a matter of time with the route south of the equator covering the distance to Africa or the Red Sea in large chunks with the reliable SE trades pushing you along at a good clip. The route up through Southeast Asia and then on across north of the equator generally has less reliable winds and a lot of coastal cruising along the way and will take longer because of distances and diversions to the straight sailing. It also has a whole series of regattas which link up to one another and which are detailed below.

From the middle of the Indian Ocean there is a decision to make on whether you are going up the Red Sea to the Mediterranean or down around Africa. The route up the Red Sea can be quite a bash to windward with awkward seas and strong winds on the nose. It comes as a bit of a shock to those who have been drifting with the wind around the world on the trades, but with a little preparation and attention to your gear it is not unduly arduous if you do not hurry over it. The passage around the bottom of Africa needs to be planned carefully with attention to weather forecasts, but in the southern hemisphere summer should be relatively straightforward.

Increasing numbers of yachts are basing themselves in Southeast Asia around areas like Singapore, Langkawi and Phuket and doing a circuit from these bases around the neighbouring countries and even back and forth to Australia. Others do longer circuits as far as Sri Lanka and Chagos and then back to Southeast Asia.

Around the eastern side there are yachts based in South Africa and Kenya which cruise to Chagos and neighbouring areas before returning to Africa.

Some yachts are now doing a regular run down from the Mediterranean to the Indian Ocean and then back to the Mediterranean over an 18 month to 2 year period with large charter yachts doing an annual circuit. The bash up and down the Red Sea can be a bit of pain but with adequate planning there is nothing too daunting to it.

Cruising bases

Australia/Darwin Easy access to Indonesia and Southeast Asia. Yachts can return to the east coast for the cyclone (willy-willy) season. Good facilities.

Indonesia/Riau Islands Easy access to Southeast Asia and to Singapore for facilities.

Singapore Restricted space in marinas. Easy access to Indonesia, Malaysia and Thailand. Good facilities.

Malaysia Convivial anchorages and some marinas opening up including Sebana Cove near Singapore. Admiral Marina near Port Dickson, Penang YC, Langkawi YC, and Rebak Marina. Facilities expanding. Duty-free import straightforward.

Thailand Convivial anchorages and two marinas. Facilities expanding. Restrictions on time that can be spent here.

Sri Lanka A few yachts have used Galle.

India Cochin and Bombay have been used by a few yachts. Maldives not too far away.

Seychelles A few yachts have spent extended time here. Convoluted bureaucratic procedures.

Mauritius and Réunion A few yachts (mostly French) have based themselves here for a season or two. Risk of cyclones.

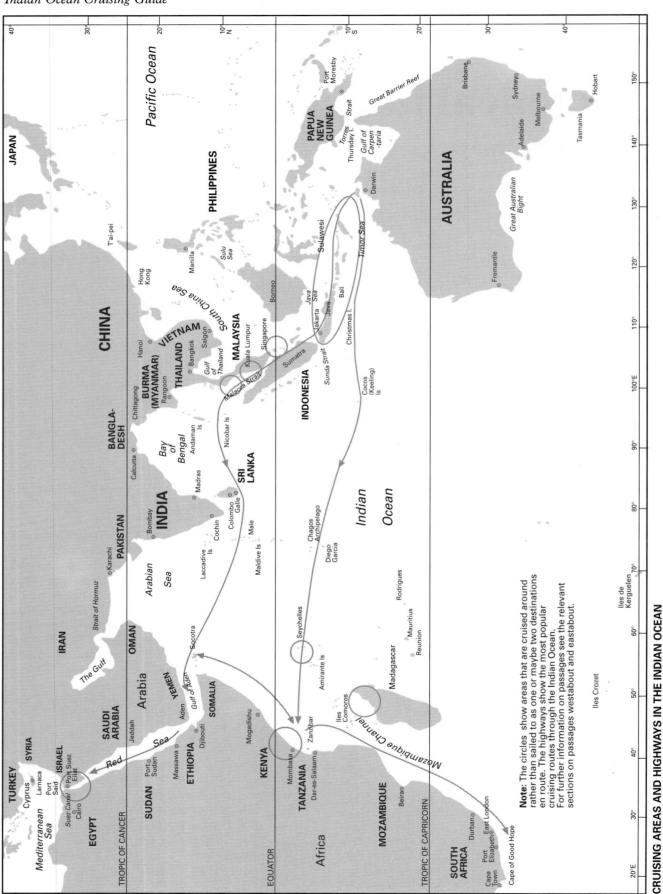

CRUISING AREAS AND HIGHWAYS IN THE INDIAN OCEAN

Note: The circles show areas that are cruised around rather than sailed to as one or maybe two destinations en route. The highways show the most popular cruising routes through the Indian Ocean.
For further information on passages see the relevant sections on passages westabout and eastabout.

South Africa Well developed facilities in Durban and Richards Bay. Easy access to Madagascar and East Africa.

Kenya Used by some yachts for a season or more. Restricted facilities but a lot of goodwill.

Off the beaten track

Indonesia A number of yachts now cruise the W coast of Sumatra en route to Australia or Indonesia. A look at the charts would indicate a lot of useful looking anchorages, but I have little hard information on Sumatra.

Malaysia While there are a number of well known places that yachts hole up in Malaysia, there are also a lot of rivers offering good protection and interesting places to explore. A few yachts I know of spend a fair bit of time pottering around the rivers and some leave the well known places like Lumut and Langkawi to spend part of the wet season up a river.

Thailand There are a number of sheltered areas behind islands and in estuaries where there are few yachts and tourists. Most of them are south of the main areas around Phuket Island along the mainland coast.

Andamans Not many yachts visit here and all that do report that it has wonderful diving and good anchorages not that far from Port Blair.

India Most yachts just touch at Cochin en route to the Red Sea, but a number spend a season here although the cruising is limited by the SW monsoon and cumbersome bureaucratic procedures.

Yemen I spent a fair bit of time cruising the Yemen coast and it has some interesting and remote anchorages.

Red Sea Eritrea and Sudan have a lot of anchorages and out of the way places to cruise although care is needed of the political situation in both countries.

Madagascar Sees an increasing number of yachts. There are numerous places to cruise and a lot of useful looking anchorages.

Mozambique and Tanzania By all accounts a whole new area with a lot of cruising to be had away from it all.

Kenya Has long been a base for yachts, but there are still remote areas to cruise.

Southeast Asia regattas

There is now an extensive series of regattas in Southeast Asia, many of which are aimed at cruising yachts heading up to Thailand from Darwin. Many of these regattas are well established events and are a lot of fun. The social side is often hectic and if you can survive the parties ashore and the racing on the water, you will survive just about anything. While it is unlikely that the regatta series will be postponed, partially or wholly, after the recent troubles, still it would pay to enquire in advance.

Darwin to Ambon Race late July to early August.
Began in 1976. Currently around 130–140 yachts take part. Useful race for cruising yachts as all paperwork and permits for Indonesia are arranged by the race committee. Race ends in Amahusu 8km from Ambon town centre.

Makassar Regatta mid-August.
Yachts sail at their own pace from Ambon to Ujung Pandang in South Sulawesi (a little over 600M) for two day race series.

Bali to Jakarta Yacht Race end of August to early September.
From Benoa on Bali to Surabaia and on to Pulau Pelangi in the Thousand Islands off Jakarta (around 650M).

Thousand Islands Regatta mid-September.
Two days of racing around the islands.

Jakarta to Nongsa Race mid- to late September.
From the Thousand Islands to Nongsa in the Riau Islands (around 440M).

Kasal Cup Regatta late September.
Olympic triangle race at Nongsa.

Note For Indonesian Regattas the following applies.
- Races are sailed under the *International Regulations for Prevention of Collision at Sea* rules and the *Yacht Racing Rules and Sailing Instructions* of the IYRU.
- Races are open to the following classes:
  Div. 1 Monohull Racing
  Div. 2 Monohull Cruising
  Div. 3 Monohull Rally
  Div. 4 Multihull
- Yachts must have a waterline length of not less than 7·3m and comply with IYRU Safety Regulations. Multihulls must have a waterline length of not less than 8m.
- An entrance fee for the series or for individual races applies. ($US200 in 1997).
- The Race Committee can arrange sailing permits for 3 months for Indonesia over the period of the races.
- For some races a valid CHS or IMS certificate is needed, although for cruising classes a rating will be allocated by the Race Committee if necessary.

For further information and entry forms contact: Secretariat, The Indonesian Sail Training Association, Cilangkap, Jakarta. ☎ (6221) 872 3162 *Fax* (6221) 871 1858.

Changi Sailing Club Regatta early November.
Three days of racing off Singapore. Contact Changi Sailing Club, 32 Netheravon Road, Changi, Singapore 1750. ☎ (65) 545 2876 *Fax* (65) 542 4235.

Raja Muda late November.
A week of races up the west coast of peninsular Malaysia from Port Klang to Langkawi including several Olympic triangles. Several of the early legs are sailed at night to take advantage of the land

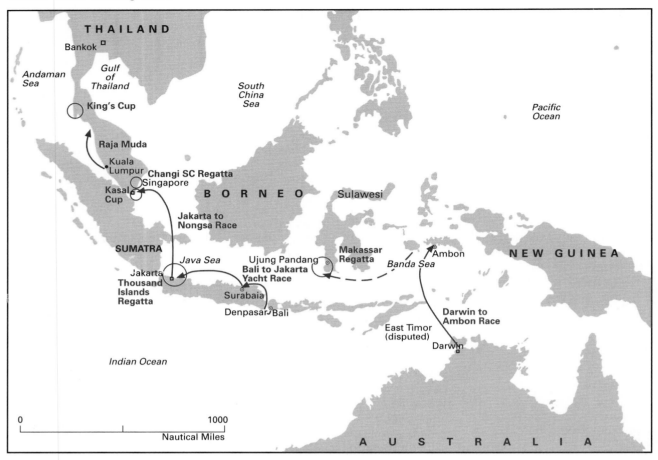

SOUTHEAST ASIA REGATTAS

breeze augmented by the NE monsoon.

Races are open to the following classes:

- *Racing Class A* CHS TCF of above 1·050.
- *Racing Class B* CHS TCF of 1·050 or below.
- *Cruising Class* No high tech sails or gear or you may be re-classified into one of the racing divisions.
- *Classic Class* Usually 25 years plus old. Handicap issued by the Race Committee.
- *Ocean Multihull Class* Minimum size eligible to MOCRA rule. Handicap by Portsmouth Yardstick or estimated by Race Committee.

Entrance fee in 1997 around $US150 depending on the number of crew. Valid CHS certificate required except for classic and multihull classes. For further information and entry form contact The Secretary, Royal Selangor Yacht Club, Jalan Limbongan, 42000 Port Klang, Selangor Darul Ehsan, Malaysia. ☎ (603) 368 6964 *Fax* (603) 368 8650.

Kings Cup early December.

A week of races out of the Phuket Yacht Club in Nai Harn. Several Olympic triangles and several longer races. Attracts a large number of international entries and is firmly established on the international yacht racing scene. Races are open to the following classes:

- *Racing Class* CHS hull factor of 7·6 and above.

Yachts with a CHS hull factor of 8·5 or less and CHS DLR greater than 195 may be permitted to race in the cruising classes.

- *Ocean Cruising Class* CHS hull factor of 7·5 or lower and a TCF of 1·050 or above.
- *Cruising Class* CHS hull factor of 7·5 or lower and a TCF of 1·049 or less.
- *Classic Class* 20 years plus old and assessed CHS hull factor of less than 6·5. Handicap by the Race Committee.
- *Ocean Multihull Class* Anything from 25 foot up approved by the Race Committee.

Entrance fee in 1997 around $US600 depending on crew. Valid CHS certificate required except for classic and multihull classes. For further information contact The Regatta Secretary, Phuket Kings Cup Regatta, 9th Floor Pacific Place, 140 Sukumvit Road, Bangkok 10110 Thailand. ☎ (662) 254 9900 *Fax* (662) 254 5311.

Envoi

A lot of cruising yachts decline to enter these races for reasons which range from an inverse snobbery to mutterings about the expense. In truth they are not expensive and the amount of fun to be had is vast. In 1996 I entered the venerable old *Tetra* in the classic class of the King's Cup and to my own and a few locals' surprise won the classic division. The racing on the water is adrenaline buzzing stuff, even in the classic class, and the entertainment ashore makes you wish for a quiet night on board – except you might miss some of the fun, not to mention the booze and food, so you don't. At the end of the whole affair there is a wonderful calm as you realise that today you don't have to get up and party or race. I'm going back for more.

Prevailing winds

This section covers winds over the open seas away from thermal effects generated by land masses and strong winds generated by depressions or tropical storms. For details on coastal winds there is a section included in the general information on the specific country. For information on tropical storms and cyclones and the ITCZ refer to the relevant sections which follow.

The prevailing winds in the Indian Ocean can be conveniently sliced into those in the northern and southern Indian Ocean although there is some interaction between the northern and southern systems. The accompanying wind charts give the general pattern for direction over the Indian Ocean. For more detailed information on direction and frequency when closer to land refer to the tables in the introduction to each country.

Northern Indian Ocean

The northern Indian Ocean is dominated by the NE and SW monsoons. Although there are other areas which have monsoon seasons, the northern Indian Ocean is the archetype of the monsoon and indeed the name comes from the Arabic *mawsim* meaning a fixed season. The word monsoon applies equally to the prevailing winds and to the characteristics of the season in terms of rainfall, cloud cover and temperature.

The NE monsoon is known as the cool season and is generally dry with clear skies and moderate temperatures making it the best time to be in the area. The SW monsoon is known as the rainy season and brings rain, often torrential, and moist humid conditions which can be oppressive at times. It also brings impressive thunderstorms with awesome lightning displays. The transitional period from April to May is known as the hot season until the relief of the rain in the SW monsoon arrives.

The monsoon winds are dictated by pressure differences caused by the warming and cooling of the Asian landmass between the northern summer and winter in relation to the adjacent sea mass which remains at a fairly constant temperature. In the summer the landmass heats up and draws air off the sea mass towards Asia and the Indian subcontinent setting up the SW monsoon. In the winter the landmass cools and the warm sea mass draws air off the land setting up the NE monsoon.

Southwest monsoon The SW monsoon blows during the northern summer from around May to October, although allowance must be made for the onset of the season with the SW monsoon occurring earlier in the S than in the N. During this period it blows with great constancy and can be relied upon for 90% or more of the time. Its influence stretches right across the northern Indian Ocean from the Andaman Sea to the Gulf of Aden. In strength it is typically stronger in the Arabian Sea than it is in the Bay of Bengal. In July it often blows at Force 7 or more for long periods in the Arabian Sea.

In the Bay of Bengal wind speeds over the open sea in July are generally Force 4–6 (10–25kn) although there will be occasional days of Force 7 and possibly 8 (30–40kn). In June and August wind speeds are a little less.

In the Arabian Sea wind speeds over the open sea in July are generally Force 5–7 (18–32kn) although there will often be days of Force 7–8 (30–40kn). In June and August wind speeds are a little less but still substantial and there is more than enough wind to shift you along.

In the Andaman Sea and along the coasts of Thailand and Malaysia the SW monsoon lifts over the land and the constancy and direction of the wind is less marked, although a heavy swell will still set onto any exposed coast.

In the Gulf of Aden the wind is channelled to blow from the W to WSW by the shape of the gulf until it joins the main SW flow of air in the Arabian Sea.

The constant winds from the SW have a long fetch which creates moderate to heavy seas over much of the area. The SW monsoon also spawns a good number of thunderstorms which can cause a localised area of confused and violent sea. On any exposed coast heavy seas will be encountered and not surprisingly many ports on the W coast of India are closed for the duration of the SW monsoon.

Northeast monsoon The NE monsoon blows during the northern winter from around November to March. In general it occurs earlier in the N and lasts longer in the S so that it is dominant in the northern areas from November to February and in southern areas from December to March. During this period it blows with reasonable constancy and can be relied upon for 75% or more of the time. Its influence stretches right across the northern Indian Ocean from the Andaman Sea to the Gulf of Aden. In strength it is typically less than the SW monsoon and rarely reaches Force 6–7 (25–30kn). Mostly it blows at Force 4–5 (10–20kn) over most of the northern Indian Ocean making for very pleasant passage making.

While the SW monsoon is fairly constant in direction, the NE monsoon tends to slightly different directions over the sea area. In the Andaman Sea and Bay of Bengal it can at times have an easterly or northerly component although mostly it is from the NE. In the Arabian Sea it blows from the N near the W coast of India to NE over most of the Arabian Sea until the Gulf of Aden where it is funnelled to blow from the E and at Bab El Mandeb is funnelled to blow from the SE and increases in

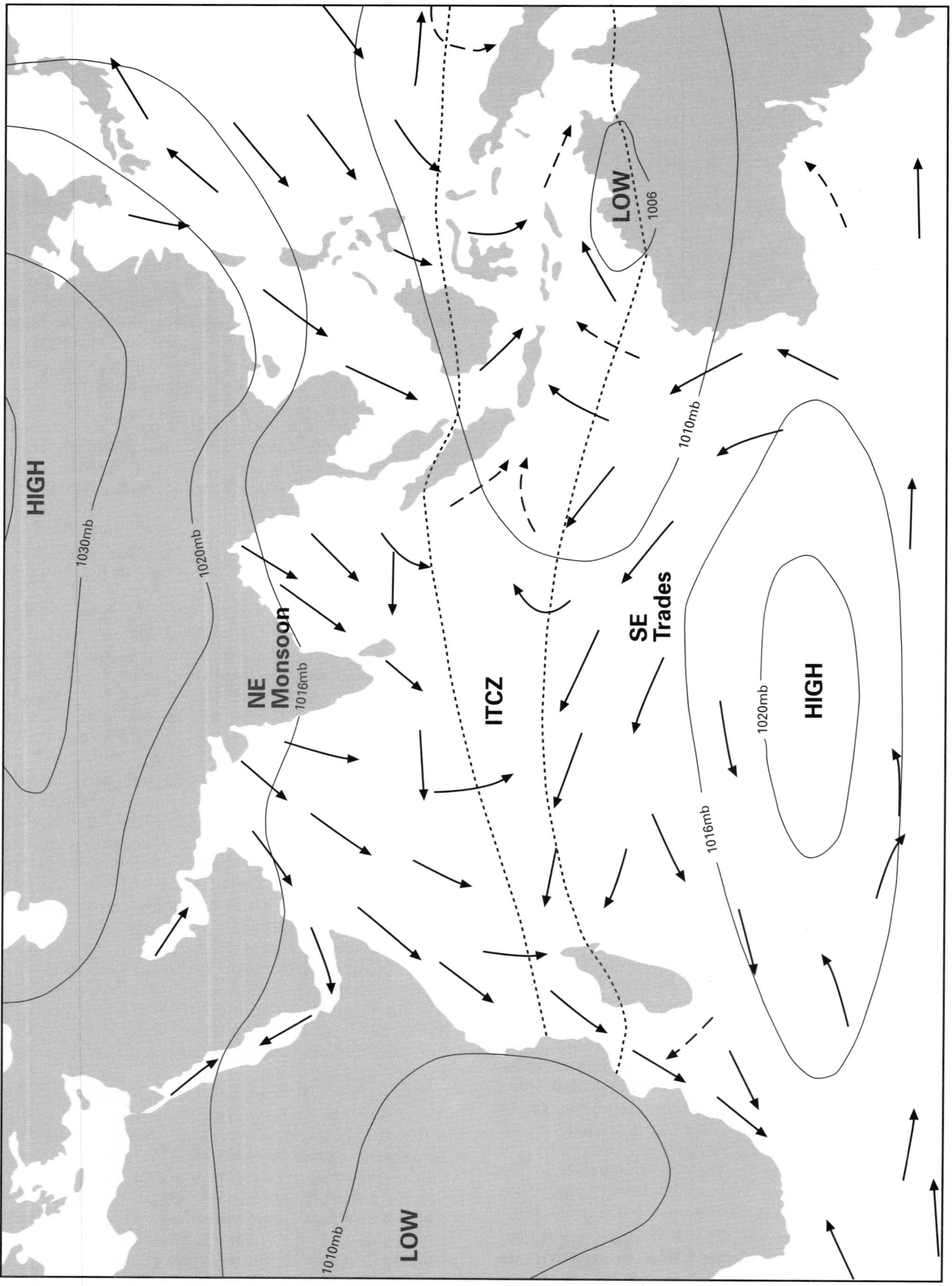

HIGH

1030mb

1020mb

NE
Monsoon

1016mb

ITCZ

LOW

1010mb

LOW

1006

1010mb

SE
Trades

1016mb

HIGH

1020mb

1016mb

PREVAILING WINDS IN THE INDIAN OCEAN: JANUARY

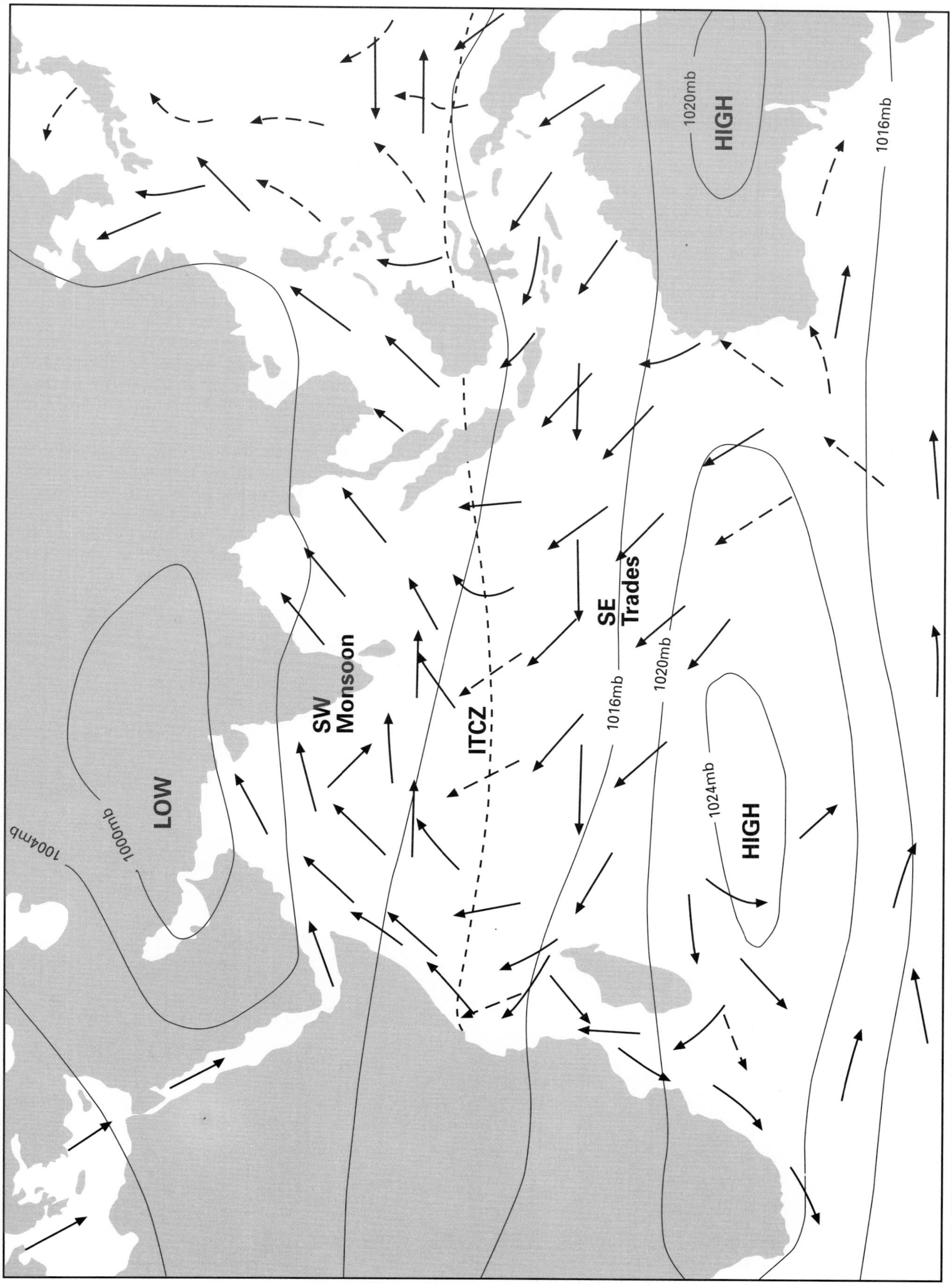
LOW
1000mb
1004mb
SW
Monsoon
ITCZ
SE
Trades
1016mb
1020mb
1024mb
HIGH
HIGH
1020mb
1016mb

PREVAILING WINDS IN THE INDIAN OCEAN: JULY

strength up to Force 7 (30kn) in the bottom of the Red Sea.

The moderate winds blowing off the land cause only a moderate and at times slight sea which is generally regular and easy for passage making. Generally conditions are clear with little cloud and rain.

Transition periods Between the two monsoons there are transitional periods in April to May and September to November. During these periods the wind direction becomes variable and there may be some days when the wind changes between monsoon directions or goes light and variable. There are also more days of calm. Before the arrival of the SW monsoon there can be violent thunderstorms accompanied by strong squalls and heavy rain. At the end of the SW monsoon there will be similar conditions.

Gale force winds (For tropical storms see the relevant section that follows.)

Red Sea

The Red Sea is a special case with northerlies prevailing for most of the year. The accompanying maps show the prevailing winds over the Red Sea and for more detailed information you should consult *Red Sea Pilot* by Elaine Morgan and Stephen Davies.

Southern Indian Ocean

The southern Indian Ocean is dominated by the SE trades. These blow across most of the southern Indian Ocean all year round between approximately 5° to 25°S, although the extent of the SE trades extends and recedes over the top half of this area between the equator and 12°–15°S during the NW monsoon. In the far S after 30°S, the prevailing winds are the westerlies of the Southern Ocean which become progressively stronger the further S you go to the roaring forties, furious fifties and screaming sixties.

SE Trades The SE trades blow consistently and often at some strength over most of the Indian Ocean outside the wind shadow of the surrounding continents. Clear of the wind shadow of Australia and Sumatra the SE trades kick in. On the western side the African continent stops the wind or the influence of the NE monsoon makes itself felt, more

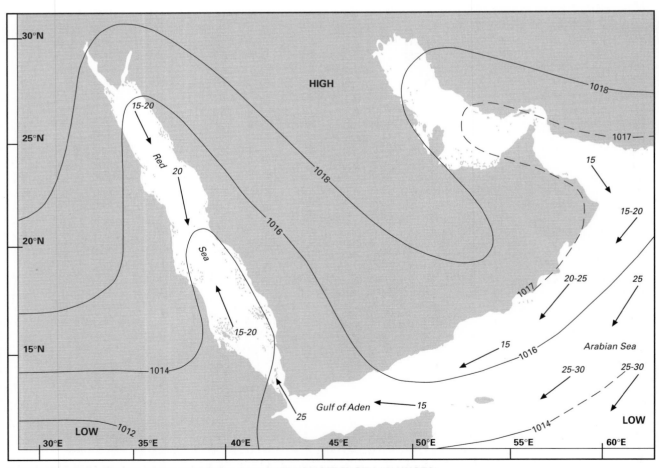

BAROMETRIC PRESSURE , WIND DIRECTON AND AVERAGE STRENGTH (IN KNOTS) FOR THE RED SEA AND GULF OF ADEN: JANUARY

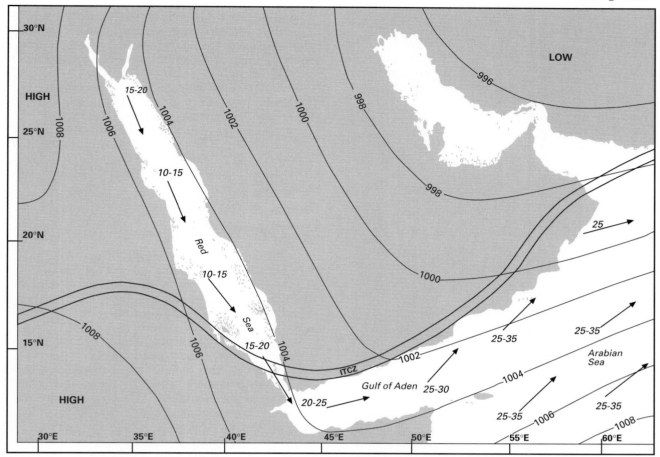

BAROMETRIC PRESSURE , WIND DIRECTON AND AVERAGE STRENGTH (IN KNOTS)
FOR THE RED SEA AND GULF OF ADEN: JULY

of which later. Where land masses funnel the wind such as in the Torres Strait and the Mozambique Channel, the wind direction can be altered and winds forced into the channel are usually stronger than over the open sea.

From April to November the trades blow consistently over the whole of the southern Indian Ocean at around Force 4–6 (12–25kn) becoming lighter towards the equator depending on the position and extent of the ITCZ and somewhat stronger towards Madagascar as the wind is deflected by the African continent. At times the wind will get up to Force 7 (30kn) for a few days and will then generally die down to its norm of around Force 4–6. At other times it will die down to a benign Force 4 (12–15kn) before rising again. It will sometimes become more easterly then SE, but never goes into the north except for the area under the northwest monsoon caused by the northeast monsoon in the northern Indian Ocean.

The SE trades season between April and November corresponding to the southern winter is a warm settled time to travel with typical trade wind clouds and regular if quite large seas over the long fetch across the southern Indian Ocean. This is the dry season and temperatures and humidity make it the most pleasant time to be in these latitudes.

Northwest monsoon Between December and March the SE trades are pushed to the S and over the area from the equator to approximately 12°–15°S when the northwest monsoon prevails. The northwest monsoon is something of a misnomer because although the prevailing wind is NW, it is not a consistent wind like the NE monsoon in the northern Indian Ocean and you can expect to have variable winds on many days and unsettled weather with fluky winds and thunderstorms. The NW monsoon is an extension of the NE monsoon in the north which is deflected to the NW by the African continent and the retreat of the winter high pressure over the southern Indian Ocean. The influence of the NW monsoon is along the west coast of Africa and from the equator down to 12°–15°S to about 80°–90°E. In the same band under the equator winds from around 90°E to Sumatra and Australia are predominantly from the S, usually S–SW, although some W–NW winds will blow as well.

If all this sounds a little messy it is because this band of wind down to 15°S is not as consistent and true as the SE trades. Often the wind is modified by thermal effects from land masses and by the position and extent of the ITCZ which has a much broader spread at this time of the year. In the introduction to each country I have described the weather patterns

Beating up the Red Sea seems to go on and on forever. Nothing for it but to buckle down and keep at it.

Waterspouts are fairly common in tropical water, but fortunately rarely seem to cause damage to yachts. This one is a fairly small affair in the Langkawi archipelago in Malaysia.

during this time and reference can also be made to the tables for wind and weather given for an area. Between the maps and the data for each country, more specific information can be identified than a textual description is able to give.

The northwest monsoon is known as the wet season corresponding to the southern summer and there are often thunderstorms which may be accompanied by squalls. It is also the cyclone season. Cyclones breed at the junction of the NW monsoon and SE trades between 5°–10°S although they do not usually become destructive until they have tracked south for a while.

ITCZ

The Intertropical Convergence Zone, the ITCZ, can be simply defined as the convergence zones of northern and southern weather systems around the equator. It is now usually called the ITCZ, but may also be referred to as the Equatorial Trough or the Doldrums belt. More properly the ITCZ is a complex interaction of weather and oceanic factors demarcating a meteorological equator.

The ITCZ lies around the equatorial trough where the prevailing winds in the northern and southern hemisphere meet to form a low pressure feature. These prevailing (trade) winds, laden with

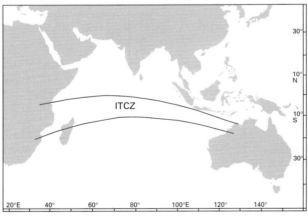

ITCZ: January

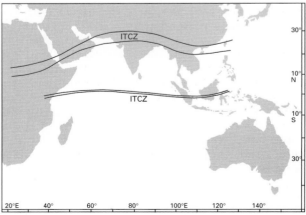

ITCZ: July

heat and moisture after their passage across the sea, converge to form a zone of increased convection, rain and cloudiness. Although the prevailing winds provide the engine for the ITCZ, oceanic factors like the prevailing surface currents, deep ocean bottom currents causing an upwelling of colder water and the warm surface water carried by the prevailing swell, also influence the formation of the ITCZ. The ITCZ plays a critical role in the global weather picture restoring equilibrium by the release of latent energy generated by the prevailing winds in their passage over the sea.

So much for the meteorological description. In sailing terms the ITCZ is neither simple to pin down nor well understood. Let us get a few misconceptions out of the way and make some general comments on the ITCZ.

- The ITCZ is not always a well defined area. It can be a zone perhaps 50 miles wide with well established limits or it can extend over 300 miles with ill-defined boundaries.
- The ITCZ does not stay in the same place at any given period. Although the maps show the average position of the ITCZ for the time of year, this is only an average as the ITCZ is continually shifting in response to weather systems and can be a long way N or S of its given position before moving back again.
- Although the ITCZ is also called the 'doldrums', (specifically in the Atlantic), it is not always a windless zone with calm seas. In the Indian Ocean it frequently has violent thunderstorms and has been known to have few days of calm. In my experience there was wind for 75% of the time and others report struggling with strong winds and awkward seas for long periods. The wind will often be variable although towards the boundaries of the zone the winds become more consistent and more or less from the direction of the prevailing wind outside the ITCZ zone.
- In the Indian Ocean there is nearly always rain, often torrential, and sometimes continuous for days on end. I have experienced two days of solid torrential rain and along with the almost continuous cloud cover the effects on morale of sailing in the ITCZ zone should not be underestimated.
- The lightning displays can be dramatic and scary. I am sure I have seen ball lightning in the ITCZ and even called the crew out to witness it. Then again I am not 100% sure of what ball lightning looks like as I have never seen it elsewhere. This is also the region where St Elmo's fire was reported in the days of yore and I for one am not keen on seeing this weird display of atmospheric ionisation.

In truth getting through the ITCZ, whether you are stuck in it on an outer edge or cutting across it, is a matter of luck. Because the ITCZ zone changes not just seasonally, but daily as well, you may have just a day or so of variable winds and calms or you can get a week of variable winds, thunderstorms, rain and awkward seas. It pays to keep in touch with other yachts on HF to get an exact picture of what is going on although even a few days later ITCZ boundaries can change dramatically.

Seasonal changes
The ITCZ is difficult to work out for the Indian Ocean and various sources give one of two explanations. One has the ITCZ around and just below the equator for all of the year although it moves S during the northern winter/southern summer. The second has the ITCZ around the equator or just S of it for the northern winter/southern summer, but when the SW monsoon kicks in for the northern summer/southern winter it has the ITCZ situated across the top of India curving around to the southern Red Sea. In fact it is likely that the Indian Ocean has two convergence zones (as the Pacific does) for the northern summer/southern winter with a weaker convergence zone around the equator and a higher one over the Asian landmass. This is shown on the map below.

In general the ITCZ hovers around the equator or just below it during the southern winter/northern summer and then moves S and expands over a wider area across the top of Madagascar, extending in an arc to the top of Sumatra and down to 20°S over Australia for the southern summer/northern winter.

The northern convergence zone also separates winds in the Red Sea and over the Persian Gulf area. The Red Sea convergence zone is usually located around 12°–18°N in July and over the top of Somalia in January. However I have encountered it as a clearly defined zone at around 15°N in January and others report similar experiences, so it is likely to sit around here even in January when it is supposed to be much further S.

It must be stressed again that these are average positions and the ITCZ moves about all over the place either side of the equator and no doubt in the split affecting higher latitudes as well. The ITCZ also extends across land masses so it affects coastal regions as well, although thermal winds may dissipate its effects at times. One thing is sure, you will recognise it when you enter the zone.

Tropical storms and cyclones

Tropical storms originate between 7°–15° north or south of the equator and then spin off to the north in the northern hemisphere and to the south in the southern hemisphere. In the Indian Ocean the term cyclone is used to describe what are called hurricanes in the Atlantic and eastern Pacific and typhoons in the western Pacific. They are also called 'willy-willies' in Australia.

Tropical storms require certain conditions to develop. The ocean temperature needs to be in the region of 26°C or above. If atmospheric conditions

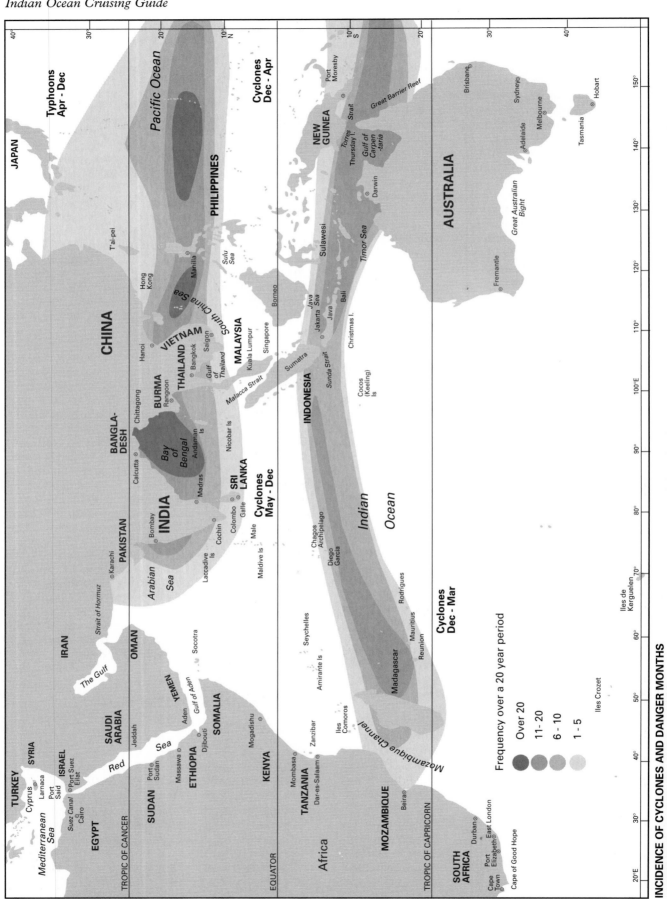

INCIDENCE OF CYCLONES AND DANGER MONTHS

are favourable, which usually means that there are calms and increased convection in the ITCZ, then humid air rises, cools and condenses to form thunderclouds. Air is sucked in to replace the rising air and if the process goes on the winds strengthen and begin to swirl around a low pressure centre. In the northern hemisphere rotation is anticlockwise and in the southern hemisphere rotation is clockwise. Although the pressure at the centre is around that of a mid-latitude depression, because the depression is over a smaller radius, (typically 500 miles for a cyclone as opposed to 1500 miles for a mid-latitude depression), the pressure gradients are tighter and therefore the wind speeds greater. Tropical depressions are graded on the following scale.

- *Tropical depression* Winds of Force 7 (30kn)
- *Tropical storm* Winds of Force 8–9 (35–45kn)
- *Severe tropical storm* Winds of Force 10–11 (45–63kn)
- *Cyclone/hurricane/typhoon* Winds of Force 12 and over (64kn plus)

In any cyclone the winds are of a destructive nature and yachts cannot sail in these conditions. Even large ships have difficulty manoeuvring and may founder. A cyclone is accompanied by torrential rain and with the wind speeds mountainous waves are set up. In the eye of the storm there will be a period of calm or variable winds and the seas, without any wind to drive them and coming from different directions, will be steep and treacherous. It hardly needs to be said that avoiding action must be taken at the earliest possible moment and in both the northern and southern Indian Ocean the action is the same: head for the equator. I will elaborate on avoiding action later.

Northern Indian Ocean

Bay of Bengal In the northern Indian Ocean the Bay of Bengal is the danger area. The British Admiralty gives an average of 5–6 tropical storms and 2 cyclones a year for the Bay of Bengal measured over a 50 year period. Dr Landsea of Colorado University gives an incidence of tropical storms for the whole of the northern Indian Ocean at 5·4 and for cyclones 2·5 per year measured over a 20 year period to 1990. The two sets of data would suggest that the average for the Bay of Bengal is around 5–6 tropical storms a year and 2 cyclones a year. It must be remembered these are averages and there may be just 1 in a year followed by 4 in another year. For all of the northern Indian Ocean Dr Landsea gives the most tropical storms occurring in any year as 10 and the least 1, while the most cyclones in any year are 6 and 0 over the 20 year period from 1968 to 1989.

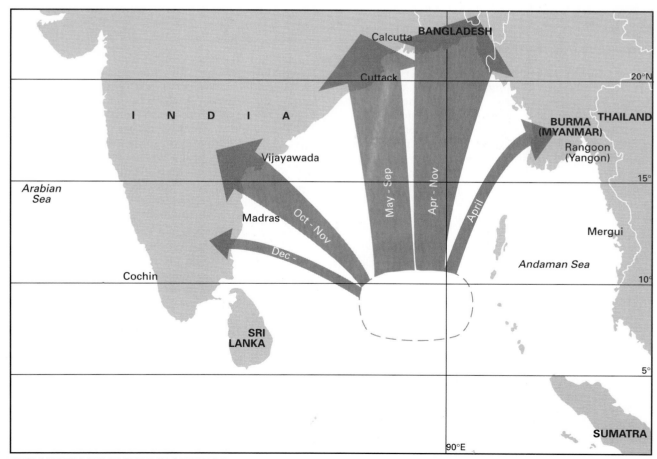

CYCLONE TRACKS IN THE BAY OF BENGAL

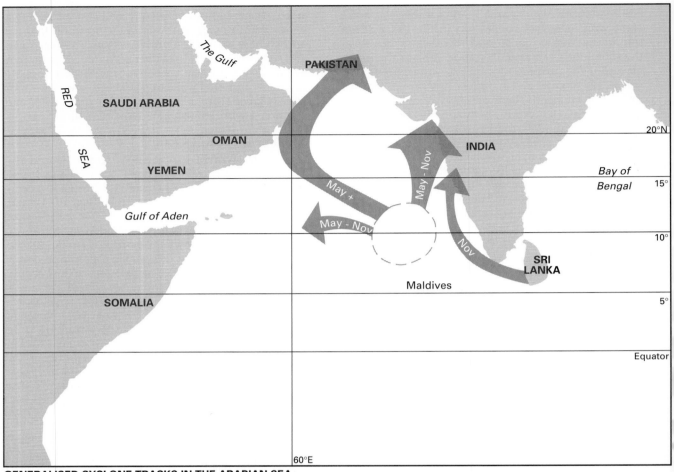

GENERALISED CYCLONE TRACKS IN THE ARABIAN SEA

In the Bay of Bengal the cyclone season runs from late April to early December although the most dangerous months are May, October and November. The table below gives an idea of the incidence of tropical storms and cyclones on a monthly basis for the Bay of Bengal. Figures are from British Admiralty records and are the totals over a 50 year period.

Month	Tropical Storms	Cyclones
Jan	4	1
Feb	1	0
Mar	6	3
Apr	14	8
May	21	13
Jun	24	3
Jul	23	5
Aug	16	2
Sep	22	7
Oct	32	14
Nov	39	16
Dec	20	5
Total	222	77

Cyclones in the Bay of Bengal typically originate in the sea area between 88°E to 94°E and around 10°N of the equator, except for the later season cyclones in October-November which can originate around 5°N of the equator. The cyclones typically move off in a northerly direction towards Bangladesh except for late season (Oct-Nov) cyclones which may curve NW to the Indian coast around the region of Andurapesh in the crook of the E coast or curve NE across to Burma. In November 1996 a cyclone tracked across to Andurapesh causing much damage and some loss of life. Typical tracks for cyclones in the Bay of Bengal are given in the accompanying map, but it should be remembered that these are the typical tracks and cyclones can take atypical tracks from as far S as Sri Lanka to across the Andamans.

Arabian Sea The Arabian Sea has a much smaller incidence of tropical storms at just 1–2 tropical storms a year. Some of these will develop into cyclones, but the incidence is much less than the Bay of Bengal. There are two distinct periods for tropical storms in the Arabian Sea. The first is from May to June. In this period tropical storms originate in the general area around the Laccadives and move off to the N or NW. Occasionally these storms will curve back to the NE. The second period is from October to November and these tropical storms originate in the Bay of Bengal and move W or NW across India into the Arabian Sea. Tropical storms have been recorded in other months, but the overall incidence is low as the table below shows. Figures are from British Admiralty data and are totals over a 74 year period to 1975.

Month	Tropical Storms	Cyclones
Jan	5	5
Feb	0	0
Mar	3	1
Apr	9	8
May	32	25
Jun	24	12
Jul	7	0
Aug	11	3
Sep	10	5
Oct	54	30
Nov	70	36
Dec	29	13
Total	254	134

Note To roughly compare the frequency with the table for the Bay of Bengal reduce these figures by one third.

Southern Indian Ocean

SW Indian Ocean The SW Indian Ocean has the highest incidence of tropical storms and cyclones for the whole ocean. The average from the British Admiralty is around 11 tropical storms per year and 4 cyclones per year. Dr Landsea gives the incidence at 10·4 tropical storms per year and 4·4 cyclones per year. Like other areas these are averages and there may be 1 cyclone in one year followed by 8 in the next year. For the SW Indian Ocean Dr Landsea gives the most tropical storms occurring in any year as 15 and the least 6, while the most cyclones in any year are 10 and 0 over the 20 year period from 1968 to 1989.

In the SW Indian Ocean no month can be regarded as totally free of tropical storms, but the period of highest incidence is from November to April with December to March considered the worst months. The table below from British Admiralty data gives the average annual occurrence of tropical storms and cyclones for the different months.

Month	Tropical Storms	Cyclones
Jan	3–4	1–2
Feb	3–4	1
Mar	2–3	1
Apr	1	0·4
May	0·2	rare
Jun	rare	rare
Jul	rare	rare
Aug	rare	rare
Sep	rare	rare
Oct	0·33	rare
Nov	0·4	rare
Dec	1–2	0·5
Total	11	4

Note Figures are averages per year.

Cyclones in the SW Indian Ocean breed between 5°S and 13°S of the equator in the ITCZ zone and between 50° to 95°E, although the majority breed between 60° to 80°E. They then track to the SW before recurving to the S and SE. Some will travel as far as the E coast of Africa and the Mozambique Channel and may recurve across Madagascar. Others will recurve before Madagascar and threaten

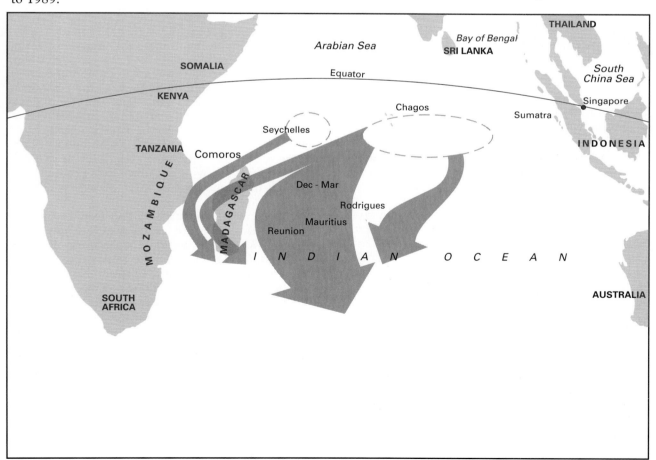

GENERALISED CYCLONE TRACKS IN THE SW INDIAN OCEAN

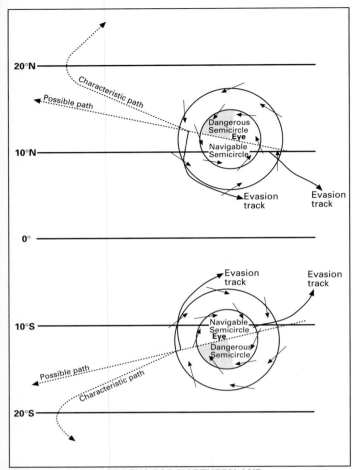

**TROPICAL STORM TRACKS FOR NORTHERN AND
SOUTHERN HEMISPHERES**

Réunion, Mauritius and Rodrigues. The Seychelles
are outside the cyclone zone and Chagos is rarely hit
by destructive winds.

SE Indian Ocean and Australia In the area
covered by this pilot tropical storms and cyclones
(willy-willies) are rare. Cyclone Tracy which hit
Darwin in 1976 was an anomaly in the overall
picture and the area from Darwin to Christmas
Island is rarely affected. In March 1999 cyclone
Vance hit close to Exmouth 780 miles NW of Perth
causing extensive damage. *Vance* was classified as a
category 5 cyclone with winds up to 140mph and is
one of the strongest cyclones on record to have hit
the NW coast of Australia.

Warning signs

If you are not on the receiving end of HF
communications or a weatherfax warning of a
developing cyclone, there are a number of warning
signs of a developing cyclone which can give some
indication of what is going on. In practice, though,
it can all be a bit nebulous.

- If you have a barometer corrected for height,
  latitude, and temperature and you are equipped
  with tables for the diurnal variation, then a
  sudden drop of 3 millibars below the mean

pressure for the time of year should put you on
your guard. If there is a drop of 5 millibars or
more then it is definitely time to take avoiding
action and the likelihood is that you are already
experiencing an increase in wind strength.

- If there is an abrupt change in wind direction and
  strength this is a good indication assuming you
  are not in the ITCZ or there is thunderstorm in
  the vicinity. Buys Ballot's law states that if you
  face into the wind the centre of the storm will be
  around 100°–125° on the right hand side in the
  northern hemisphere and on the left hand side in
  the southern hemisphere. This will be when the
  eye of the storm is around 200 miles away. As the
  centre gets closer the angle becomes nearer to
  90°.
- A long low swell, usually with a long period,
  contrary to the prevailing swell, will sometimes
  emanate from the eye of the storm. Most yachties
  are pretty tuned in to the pattern of swell when
  on passage and contrary swell with a long period
  can be a useful indicator.
- Solid amounts of cirrus followed by altostratus
  and then broken cumulus advertises the approach
  of a tropical storm.

Avoiding action

If a tropical storm is known to be forming or the
signs are that one may, it is necessary for all sailing
yachts to take avoiding action in the early stages.
Basically the action is to head for the equator if you
are on a typical east or westabout passage along the
principal sailing routes.

In the northern hemisphere the storm revolves in
an anticlockwise direction and travels somewhere
between NW and N. If you are to the E of the storm
then it is necessary to head towards the equator in
whatever fashion you can. This will be difficult
because the winds will be predominantly SW–S, but
you will just have to do the best you can. Even
making little progress is better than 'following' the
storm which will only bring you closer to stronger
winds. If you are W of the storm then proceeding S
towards the equator will be easier because winds will
be mostly N–NW.

In the southern hemisphere the storm revolves in
a clockwise direction and travels somewhere
between W–SW. If you are E of the storm then it is
a matter of struggling N for the equator again. If you
are W of the storm then it is an easier matter to head
for the equator as winds will be S–SW.

The two diagrams show the scenario although not
the conditions at sea. Even towards the equator with
the storm travelling away from you it is likely that
you may have to heave-to for a day or two
depending on the distance from the storm. The
waves generated can be very high and the swell can
travel long distances. I have not been in the sort of
destructive winds generated by a cyclone, but I have
been around the perimeter and even at a distance of
700 miles the seas generated are considerable.

For weather information on cyclones and forecasts
see the next section.

Weather information

For most cruising yachts weather information comes from HF communication or weatherfax. There are also a number of other options which I list here as well.

Radio weather services

Indonesia (Sumatera)
Dumai (PKP)
Navigational warnings
8457kHz at 0100, 1300. 12682·5kHz at 0230, 0630. 17184·8kHz at 0500. In English
Belawan (PKB)
Navigational warnings
8686kHz at 0200, 0600, 1100, 1300. 12970·5kHz at 0230, 0630. 16861·7kHz at 0600, 1400. In English
Palembang (PKC)
Navigational warnings
8705·5kHz at 0100, 0500, 0900, 1130 in English

Indonesia (Jawa)
Jakarta (PKX) (E)
Weather messages
8542, 12970·5, 2690kHz at 1100. Storm warnings, 24h Fcst, synopsis and analysis in English for Indonesian waters and China Sea.
Navigational warnings
8542, 12970·5kHz at 0200, 1000, 1800. In English
Jakarta-Kemayoran (8BB)
Weather messages
11500, 16200kHz at 0830. Storm warnings, synopsis, 24h Fcst in Indonesian and English for Indonesia.
Surabaya (PKD)
Navigational warnings
8461kHz at 0200, 0730. 12704·5kHz at 0000, 1100. 8794, 13110kHz at 0100, 0900. In English

Singapore
Singapore (9VG) (C)
Weather messages
4369kHz at 0005, 1205
6412, 4322kHz at 0118, 1318
6323·5, 8420·5, 12579·5, 16807, 22381kHz at 0130, 1330
Storm warnings, situation in English for South China Sea, Malacca Straits, Andaman Sea. 12h Fcst in English for Phuket, Malacca, Tioman, Bunguran, Condore, Reef
Navigational warnings
8728kHz at 0005, 0405, 0805, 1205
VHF Ch 24 at every odd H+05 (0105-1105) 4322kHz at 0118, 0518, 0918, 1318, 1718, 2118
6412kHz at 0118, 0518 0918, 1318
For South China Sea, Malacca Strait, Bay of Bengal

Malaysia
Kuching (9WW20)
Weather messages
4249, 6632·5kHz at 0120, 0520, 0920, 1320, 1720, 2120
Storm warnings, synopsis and 12h fcst for Phuket, Malacca, Tioman, Bunguran, Condore, Reef, Samui, Palawan, Sulu, Labuan, Terumbu Layang Layang
4249, 6632·5kHz at 0120.
Navigational warnings
8522kHz at 0200, 0600, 1000, 1400, 1800, 2200
2130kHz at 0300, 0700, 1100, 1500, 1900, 2300
4371·1 or 8767·2kHz at 0100, 0500, 0900,1300, 1700, 2100

Pinang (9MG)
Weather messages
6353·9, 8698kHz at 0148, 0548, 0948, 1348, 1748, 2148
17172·4kHz at 2148
2790, 8719kHz at 0205, 0605, 1005, 2205
Storm warnings, synopsis, 12h Fcst in English for Phuket, Malacca, Tioman, Bunguran, Condore, Reef, Samui, Palawan, Sulu
Navigational warnings
6353·9, 8698kHz at 0148, 0548, 0948, 1348, 1748, 2148
17172·4kHz at 2148
2790, 8719kHz at 0205, 0605, 1005, 2205
In English for China Sea, Malacca Strait, Bay of Bengal

Thailand
Krung-Thep (Bangkok) (HAS) (HSJ) (F)
Weather messages
7955, 8573·5, 8686kHz at 0150, 0750, 1150
Storm warnings, in English for area 4°N–20°N, 98°E–115°E. Synopsis, in English, for area 0°N–30°N, 90°E–120°E. 24h Fcst, in English

Sri Lanka
Colombo (4PB)
Weather messages
8473kHz at 0530, 1330. Gale warnings, synopsis, Fcst in English.
0600, 1300. Fcst in English for Sri Lanka and vicinity
Navigational warnings
8473kHz on receipt. At the end of the next silence period. 0600, 0900, 1330. On request. In English for area within 200 n miles of Colombo.

India
Bombay (Mumbai) (VWB) (G)
Storm warnings
8630, 12710kHz at 0448[1], 0848, 1248[1], 1648, 2048[1], 2348[2]. In English for Arabian Sea.
Weather messages
8630, 12710kHz at 0848, 1648. Synopsis and Fcst in English for Arabian Sea.
8630, 12710kHz at 0420[1], 0820, 1220[1], 1620, 2020[1], 2320[2]
Situation, Fcsts of wind, weather visibility and sea state in English.
Navigational warnings 8630, 12710kHz On receipt. At the end of the next silence period. 0648, 1548. On request. In English for the area within 200 n miles of Bombay between 21°N and 17°N including Gulf of Khambat (Cambay)
1. Bcst in the event of a tropical storm having developed
2. Bcst in the event of disturbed weather
Bombay (Mumbai) Naval (VTG)
Weather messages
4268, 8634, 12808·5, 16938, 22628·5kHz at 0900
2072, 4268, 6467, 8634, 12808·5kHz at 1500
Navigational warnings
2072, 4268, 6467, 8634, 12808·5, 16938, 22628·5kHz at 0500, 1500 on day of receipt or 1500 on day of receipt and 0500 following day. Repeated at 0900 on days 2, 5, 8, 12, 16, 20 and 24 (day of second main Bcst taken as day 1). On request
NAVAREA VIII warnings in English
2072, 4268, 6467, 8634, 12808·5, 16938, 22628·5kHz Sat 0500, 1500
Numbers of all NAVAREA VIII warnings in force. Repeated at 0900 Sun, Wed
2072, 4268, 6467, 8634, 12808·5, 16938, 22628·5kHz

Sun 1215. Summary of important NAVAREA VIII warnings between 24 and 42 days old
2072, 4268, 6467, 8634, 12808·5, 16938, 22628·5kHz at 1400. List of vessels W of 80°E holding overdue INSPIRES reports

Goa (VWG)
Weather messages
417·5kHz at any H+00[1]
0420[2], 0820[2], 1220[2], 1620, 2020[2], 2320[3]. Situation, Fcsts of wind weather, visibility and sea state in English
Navigational warnings
417·5kHz On receipt. At the end of the next silence period. 0648, 1548. On request. In English for the area within 200 n miles of Goa between 13°30'N and 16°30'N

Mangalore (VWL)
Weather messages
438kHz at any H+00[1]
0420[2], 0820, 1220[2], 1620, 2020[2], 2320[3]. Situation, Fcsts of wind weather, visibility and sea state in English.
Navigational warnings
438kHz On receipt. At the end of the next silence period. 0648, 1548. On request. In English for the area within 250 n miles of Mangalore between 10°30'N and 14°N including the Lakshadweep Islands.

Cochin (VWN)
Weather messages
460kHz at any H+00[1]
0420[2], 0820, 1220[2], 1620, 2020[2], 2320[3]. Situation, Fcsts of wind weather, visibility and sea state in English
Navigational warnings
460kHz On receipt. At the end of the next silence period. 0648, 1548. On request. In English for the area within 300 n miles of Cochin between 5°N and 12°N including the Lakshadweep Islands.

Madras (Chennai) (VWM) (P)
Note Bcsts reported unreliable (Nov 1994)
Storm warnings
8674·4kHz at any H+00[1]. At the end of the next silence period. At the end of the next silence period for single-operator ships. 0030[2], 0430[3], 0930, 1330[3], 1830, 2130[3]
Weather messages
8674·4, 12718·5kHz at 0030, 0930, 1830. Synopsis and Fcst in English for Bay of Bengal
1. Bcst in the event of the unexpected development of a tropical storm
2. Bcst in the event of a tropical storm having developed
3. Bcst in the event of disturbed weather

Djibouti
Djibouti (J2A)
Weather messages
8628kHz at 0430, 1700[1].
12728kHz at 0900[1]. 12h Fcst in French and English
8628, 12728kHz. On request. Fcst in French or English
1. Bsct includes updated information
Navigational warnings
8682kHz at 0430, 1700. 12728kHz at 0900. In French and English for coastal waters of Dijibouti, Red Sea, NW Indian Ocean.

Australia
Darwin (VID)
Storm warnings
4272·5, 8487kHz at every odd H+48 for up to 6 hours. Gale warnings for coastal waters Torres Strait (10°41'S 142°00'E) to Exmouth Gulf (21°47'S 114°10'E).
2201, 4426, 6507, 8176, 12365kHz and VHF Ch 67 every even H+33 (on frequencies in use at the time). Gale and strong wind warnings for coastal waters Torres Strait to Exmouth Gulf.

Weather messages
8487kHz at 0018. 4272·5kHz at 1018. 2201, 4426, 6507, 8176, 12365kHz and VHF Ch 67 at 0233, 1233 (on frequencies in use at the time). Gale and strong wind warnings, synopsis, 24h Fcst for coastal waters Torres Strait (10°41'S 142°00'E) to Exmouth Gulf (21°47'S 114°10'E)
Navigational warnings
4272·5, 8487kHz at 0018, 1018 (on frequencies in use at the time). For coastal waters Torres Straits to Kuri Bay.
NAVAREA X warnings repeated on days 2–6. Numbers of NAVAREA warnings in force (more than 6 days old). 2201, 4426, 6507, 8176, 12365kHz and VHF Ch 67 at 0233, 1233 (on frequencies in use at the time).
NAVAREA X warnings repeated on days 2–6. Numbers of NAVAREA warnings in force (more than 6 days old) 2201, 4426, 6507, 8176, 12365kHz and VHF Ch 67 at 0833, 2233 (on frequencies in use at the time). For coastal waters Torres Straits to Exmouth Gulf.

Seychelles
Seychelles (S7Q)
Navigational warnings
8770kHz at 0518, 1548. In English for area within 200 n miles of Seychelles

Mauritius
Mauritius (3BM)
Weather messages
8554, 12831kHz at 0830, 1630.
16978·4kHz at 1630
22587kHz at 0830. Storm warnings, synopsis 24h Fcst in English
4282kHz at 0130, 2030.
8554, 12831kHz at 0130, 0430, 1330, 2030
22587kHz at 0430, 1330. Cylcone warnings (only bcst when cyclones affect Fcst Areas), in English
Navigational warnings
4282, 8554, 12831, 16978·4, 22587kHz at 0130, 0430, 0900, 1630. Coastal warnings in English

Mauritius (3BT)
Weather messages
3188, 7693, 15955kHz at 0930. Surface Anal for area of La Réunion, southwest Indian Ocean including the Seychelles.

Réunion
Radio Réunion (Radio-France Outre-mer (RFO))
Weather messages
666, 729kHz at 0235, 0828, 1355. Fcst for the coastal waters of the Mascarene Islands and approaches, in French
666, 729kHz at 0355, 1440. Synopsis, 24h Fcst for La Réunion, in French

South Africa
Cape Town (ZCS)
8719kHz and VHF Chs

Alexander Bay	04	Port Nolloth	01
Hondeklip Bay	25	Doringbaai	87
Cape St Martin	23	Saldanha Bay	27
Milnerton	25	Constantiaberg	26
Franskraal	85	Struisbaai	84
Albertinia	26		

Storm warnings
As above. On receipt. On request. At the end of the next silence period.
Weather messages
As above at 0948, 1748.

Navigational warnings
As above. On receipt. On request. At the end of the next silence period. Urgent NAVAREA VII; urgent local and coastal warnings for the area from Cape Cross to Cape Recife.
0918, 1718. NAVAREA VII warnings, repeated on days 1, 2, 3; thereafter every 4th day for 6 weeks. Local and coastal warnings are bcst on all frequencies and channels at the scheduled bcst times for the area from Cape Cross to Cape Recife.

Port Elizabeth (ZSQ) (I)
VHF Chs

Knysna	23	Kareedouw	24
Port Elizabeth	27	Governorskop	83
East London	26		

Storm warnings
As above. On receipt. At the end of the next silence period.
Weather messages
As above at 0933, 1733.
1340. Reports from selected meteorological observation stations, gale warnings.
Navigational warnings
As above. On receipt. At the end of the next silence period. Urgent NAVAREA VII; urgent local and coastal warnings for the area from Cape Hangklip to Cooper Lt (Natal)
0933, 1733. NAVAREA VII warnings, repeated on days 1 and 2 and thereafter every 4th day for 6 weeks or until cancelled. Local and coastal warnings for the area from Cape Hangklip to Cooper Lt (Natal), repeated daily until cancelled.

Durban (ZSD) (O)
VHF Chs

Port Shepstone	26	Port Edward	27
Bluff (Durban)	26	Empangeni	26
Cape St Lucia	25	Sodwana	16
Kosi Bay	16		

Storm warnings
As above. On receipt. At the end of the next silence period.
Weather messages
As above at 0903, 1703. On request.
1303. Gale warnings, reports from selected observation stations.
Navigational warnings
As above. On receipt. At the end of the next silence period. After the first silence period in each subsequent single-operator watch period until they are included in the next scheduled bcst. Urgent NAVAREA VII; urgent local and coastal warnings for the area from Cape Recife to Ponta do Ouro.
0903, 1703. NAVAREA VII, local and coastal warnings for the area from Cape Recife to Ponta do Ouro, repeated until cancelled for a maximum of 6 weeks.

Walvis Bay (V5W)
Storm warnings
VHF Ch 26, 27. On receipt and at the end of silence periods until incorporated in the general weather bulletin.
Gale warnings and weather forecasts
VHF Ch 26, 27 at 0935, 1235, 1635. For coastal waters and Trades area.
Navigational warnings
VHF Ch 26, 27 at 0905, 1605. NAVAREA VII and coast of Namibia.
Lüderitz (V5L)

Storm warnings
1764kHz. On receipt and at the end of silence periods until incorporated in the general weather bulletin.
Gale warnings and weather forecasts
1764kHz at 0935, 1235, 1635. Coastal and Trades area.
Navigational warnings
1764kHz at 0905, 1605. NAVAREA VII and coast of Namibia.

Kenya
Nairobi (5YE)
Weather messages
9043, 17441·6kHz at 1200. Storm warnings, general situation including sea state and visibility and 24h Fcst, in English.
9086kHz at 1245. Storm warnings, general situation, fcst in English

HF nets and Ham

The majority of yachts on passage communicate on informal nets and someone ahead of you can give accurate information on the weather you can expect. Below are a number of established amateur nets.
All times UT unless stated.

Thailand
Rowdy's Net 14316kHz USB (OOZULU)
Phil Hollywood 14320kHz USB (irregular)

South Africa
Durban Maritime Mobile Net
14316kHz USB at 0630 (ZS5GC).
14316kHz USB at 1130 (ZS5MU)
Run by the Campbells in Durban. Synoptic and coastal weather.

Kenya
East African Marine Radio Net (call sign *Kiore*)
4483kHz USB at 0430
8101kHz USB at 0445Z
14316kHz USB at 0500 (call sign *5Z4FZ*)
Run by Tony Britchford in Kilifi. Synoptic and coastal weather.

Eastern Med Net
7080kHz LSB at 0530.
East Med weather.

Weatherfax

If there is one thing that is certain in the world, it is that weatherfax transmissions are often not on time. The following frequencies and times should be checked whenever possible against the data from anyone else trying to receive weatherfaxes.

Darwin (AXI) (Facsimile)

5755	10	0900–2300
7535	10	0900–2300
10555	10	H24
15615	10	2300–0900
18060	10	2300–0900

Map Area

A				(a)	B				(a)
30°N	120°E	30°N	180°		30°N	70°E	30°N	130°E	
35°S	120°E	35°S	180°		35°S	70°E	35°S	130°E	
C				(a)	D				(a)
30°N	70°E	30°N	180°		29°N	96°E	34°N	142°E	
35°S	70°E	35°S	180°		43°S	110°E	34°S	155°E	

E (a)
23°N 100°E 23°N 170°E
23°S 100°E 23°S 170°E
AUST (b)
10°S 90°E 10°S 170°E
50°S 90°E 50°S 170°E
IO (c)
    10°S – 90°S
    0° East to 180°
SH (c)
    10°S – 90°S
    All longitudes
SWAUST (a)
25°S 110°E 25°S 120°E
37°S 110°E 37°S 120°E

H
25°N 80°E 25°N 180°
25°S 80°E 25°S 180°
RSW (a)
0°.100°E 0.180°
50°S 100°E 50°S 180°
SWP (c)
    20°S – 90°S
    150° East to 70°W
SEAUST (c)
31°S 148°E 31°S 156°E
40°S 148°E 40°S 156°E

Schedule

	AI/AXM Schedule (2 parts)	0015 1215	120/576
	Information notice	0045	
	IPS recommended fx for AXM	0100	
	IPS recommended fx for AXI	0130	
AUST	24h Surface Prog.	0200(00) 1515(12)	
RSW	Regional significant Wx Prog.	0215(18) 0715(00) 1300(06) 1900(12)	120/576
H	Current warnings summary (on WT(HF) plain language)	0230 0815 1445 2045	
AUST	Surface Anal.	0245(00) 0845(06) 1430(12) 2015(18)	
	500 hPa Anal.	0300(00)	
D	Darwin tropics significant WX Prog.	0330(18) 1000(00) 1530(06) 2200(12)	120/576
AUST	24h 500 hPa Prog.	0400(00) 1600(12)	
SEAUST	Sea surface isotherm (SE Australia) (Updated Wed)	0430	
	250m isotherm (SE Australia) (Updated Wed)	0445	
SWAUST	Sea surface isotherm (SE Australia) (Updated Wed)	0500	
A	Gradient level wind Anal. Part A	0600(00) 1800(12)	
B	Gradient level wind Anal. Part B	0623(00) 1823(12)	
C	Surface pressure Anal.	0645(00)	
IO	Indian Ocean surface Anal.	0730(00) 1915(12)	
AUST24	wind/wave ht(m) Prog.	0745(00) 1930(12)	120/576
	24h swell/wave ht(m) Prog.	0800(00) 1945(12)	120/576
SWP	South Pacific Ocean surface Anal.	0830(00) 2000(12)	120/576
C	250 hPa streamline	0900(00)	

	Anal.	2100(120	
	500 hPa streamline	0920(00)	
	Anal.	2120(12)	
	700 hPa streamline	0940(00)	
	Anal.	2140(12)	
SH	48h Southern Hemisphere 500 hPa Prog.	1030(00) 2230(12)	
	48h Southern Hemisphere Surface Prog.	1045(00) 2245(02)	
	Southern Hemisphere 500 hPa Anal.	1115(00) 2303(12)	
E	Sea surface Anal. temperature (Updated Tues)	1130	
AUST	36h Surface Prog.	1200(12) 1515(12) 2330(00)	
IO	36h Indian Ocean Surface Prog.	1245(12)	120/576
SWP	48h Pacific Ocean total waves	1315(00)	
IO	48h Indian Ocean total waves	1330(00)	
SWP	Pacific Ocean, Sea surface temperature (Updated Weekly)	1345	
IO	Indian Ocean, Sea surface temperature (Updated Weekly)	1400	
AUST	500 hPa Prog.	1500(12)	
IO	48h Indian Ocean Surface Prog.	2345(12)	

Note Weather charts are also available by fax through: INMARSAT +613 9273 8046. *Fax* 019 725 046

Krung-Thep (Bangkok) (HSW) (Facsimile)

(HSW64)	7396·8	3·0
(HSW61)	17520	3·0

Map Area

A		1:20 000 000 (a)	
50°N	45°E	50°N	160°E
30°S	45°E	30°S	160°E

Schedule

A	Test chart	0500	
	Fcst for shipping (English plain language)	0100(00) 0400(03) 0700(06) 1000(09) 1300(12) 1700(17) 2300(17)	
	Surface pressure fcst	0120(12)	
	Surface Anal.	0140(18) 0500(00) 1020(06) 1720(12) 2320(18)	
	24h surface pressure fcst	0300(12) 0720(12)	120/576
	48h surface pressure fcst	0320(12) 0740(12)	
	72h surface pressure fcst	0340(12) 0800(12)	
	24h 850 hPa wind/temp fcst	0420(12) 0820(12)	
	850 hPa Anal.	0520(00)	
	700 hPa Anal.	0540(00)	
	500 hPa Anal.	0600(00)	

New Delhi (ATA) (ATP) Facsimile)

ATA57	7403	B9W	10	1430–0230
	(White +400kHz)			
ATP65	14840	B9W		0230–1430
	(Black −400kHz)			

Note Bcsts are centred 1900Hz away from the carrier frequencies, listed above, in the USB

Map Areas

A	1:20 000 000 (a)		B	1:20 000 000 (a)	
45°N	30°E	45°N 125°E	40°N	30°E	40°N 125°E
25°S	30°E	25°S 125°E	0°	30°E	0° 125°E
E	1:20 000 000 (a)		F	1:20 000 000 (a)	
60°N	25°E	60°N 120°E	25°N	55°E	25°N 100°E
0°	25°E	0° 120°E	0°	55°E	0° 100°E
H	1:20 000 000 (a)				
67°·5N	0°	67°·5N 180°E			
15°S	0°	15°S 180°E			

A	Surface Anal.	0011(18)
		0634(00)
		1211(06)
		1820(12)
H	24h 250 hPa Wind/Temp Fcst	0030(12)
		1230(00)
	24h 500 hPa Wind/Temp Fcst	0050(12)
		1248(00)
	24h 850 hPa Wind/Temp Fcst	0110(12)
		1306(00)
B	Significant Wx Prog.	
	for period 0300–1500	0130(18)
	for period 0900–2100	0834(00)
	for period 1500–0300	1324(06)
	for period 2100–0900	2040(12)
A	ECMWF[1] 96h 500 hPa Fcst	0150(12)
H	24h 400 hPa Wind/Temp Fcst	0210(12)
		1400(00)
	24h 300 hPa Wind/Temp Fcst	0238(12)
		1342(00)
	24h 700 hPa Wind/Temp Fcst	0300(12)
		1506(00)
	24h 200 hPa Wind/Temp Fcst	0320(12)
		1430(00)
	24h 150 hPa Wind/Temp Fcst	0340(12)
		1448(00)
A	ECMWF[1] 48h 200 hPa Wind Fcst	0400(12)
	ECMWF[1] 72h 500 hPa Fcst	0420(12)
F	7 day mean sea surface Temp	0440 120/576
	Satellite Imagery (Infrared)	0600(12)
	Test chart	0622 1810
A	850 hPa upper air Anal.	0654(00)
		1910(12)
	700 hPa upper air Anal.	0714(00)
		1928(12)
	500 hPa upper air Anal.	0734(00)
		1946(12)
	300 hPa upper air Anal.	0753(00)
		2004(12)
	Surface Prog.	0812(00)
		2022(12)
	200 hPa upper air Anal.	0856(00)
		2100(12)
A	850–500 hPa thickness	0916(00)
		2118(12)
	500 hPa upper air Prog.	0936(00)
		2223(12)
	Digital Significant Wx (Tokyo)	1005(00)
		2205(12)
A	300 hPa upper air Prog.	1025(00)
		2241(12)
	250 hPa upper air Prog.	1055(00)
		2259(12)
	200 hPa upper air Prog.	1115(00)
		2317(12)
	Tropopause/Max wind Prog.	1135(00)
		2335(12)
	100 hPa upper air Prog.	1135(00)
		2353(12)
E	850 hPa relative vorticity	1840(12)
	500 hPa relative vorticity	2136(12)

1. ECMWF – European Centre for Medium-range Weather Forecasts

Diego Garcia

NKW relay from US Navy, Guam on USB

7580kHz	1400-0159
12804kHz	1100-2300
20300kHz	0200-1359

0000/1200	*Fax* schedule
0235/1435	36 hour surface analysis
0435/1635	Preliminary surface analysis
0505/1705	Sig wave height analysis
0525/1725	48 hour surface prognosis
0540/1740	N. Indian Ocean satellite image
0555/1755	S. Indian Ocean satellite image
0700	Tropical cyclone warning
1020/2220	Preliminary surface analysis
1150/2350	24 hour surface prognosis

Saint-Denis Météo (HXCP) (FZS63) (Facsimile)

(HXP)	8176	1·0
(FZS63)	16335	1·0

Map Areas

A			(c)	B		(a)
0°	15°E	0°	90°E	2°N 18°E	2°N	70°E
60°S	15°E	60°S	90°E	32°S 18°E	32°S	70°E
C			(a)			
2°N	31°E	2°N	100°			
44°S	31°E	44°S	100°E			

Schedule

	Test chart	0430 0730	
C	12h 850/700 hPa Winds Prog.	0433(12)	
	12h 500/200 hPa Winds Prog.	0445(12)	120/576
	12h Vertical shearing 850/200 hPa Prog.	0457(12)	
	12h Vorticity/divergence 850 hPa Prog.	0509(12)	
	12h Vorticity/divergence 200 hPa Prog.	0521(12)	
	12h Steering current Anal. and Prog.	0533(12)	
	24h & 48h Steering current Prog.	0545(00)	
A	Surface Anal.	0733(00)	
		1105(06)	
B	TEMSI–Significant Wx, air	0744(09)	
C	24 & 48h Surface pressure Prog.	0755(00)	
	24h 850/700 hPa Winds Prog.	0807(00)	
	24h 500/200 hPa Winds Prog.	0819(00)	
	24h 300/250 hPa Winds Prog.	0831(00)	
	24 & 48h Vertical shearing 200/850hPa Prog.	0843(00)	
	48h 850/700 hPa Winds Prog.	0855(00)	
	48h 500/250 hPa Winds Prog.	0907(00)	
	Test chart and schedule	1030	

C	24h Vorticity/divergence 850 hPa Prog.	1041(00)	
	24h Vorticity/divergence 200 hPa Prog.	1053(00)	
	48h Vorticity/divergence 850 hPa Prog.	1116(00)	
	48h Vorticity/divergence 200 hPa Prog.	1128(00)	
A	12h Surface wind Anal. & Prog.	1140(00)	
	24h & 48h Surface wind Prog.	1152(00)	

Pretoria (ZRO) (Facsimile)

Facsimile (USB):

(ZR05)	4014		6·0	1600–0800
(ZR02)	7508		6·0	H24
(ZR03)	13538		6·0	H24
(ZR04)	18238		6·0	H24

RTTY (USB):

(ZR05)	4016	F1B	6·0	1600–0800
(ZR02)	7510	F1B	6·0	H24
(ZR03)	13540	F1B	6·0	H24
(ZR04)	18240	F1B	6·0	H24

Map Areas

ASZA:1:20 000 000   (a)   FSZA   (a)
0°   20°W   0°   70°E   10°S 5°W 10°S   30°E
60°S 50°W 60°S 90°E   50°S 20°W 45°S   50°E
(Shipping Chart)   (forecast Area for Numerical Model)
AOZA: (a)
25°S 15°E 25°S 34°E   15°S 8°E   15°S   21°E
38°S 15°E 38°S 34°E   34°S 8°E   34°S   21°E
(Eastern Coastal Area)   (Western Coastal Area)
XXZA: (c)
20°W to 30°E
Antarctic Coast to edge
of Pack Ice

Schedule

FSZA	ECMWF[1] Surface Prog.	0405(12)
		0730(12)120/576
ASZA	Surface Anal.	0445(00)
		1000(06)120/576
		1500(12)
		2200(18)
	Schedule	0505 120/576
FUZA	ECMWF[1] Upper air Prog.	0630(12)120/576
AOZA[2]	10 day Mean sea Surface temp Anal.	0710 120/576
XXZA	Antarctic Ice limits	0800 120/576

1. ECMWF – European Centre for Medium Range Weather Fcsts
2. Monday, Wednesday and Friday – East Coast of Southern Africa. Tuesday, Thursday and Saturday – West Coast of Southern Africa

Nairobi (5YE) (Facsimile)

	7464·4		1800–0600
	9045	6·0	H24
	12315		
	16186·9		0600–1800
	17445·6	6·0	H24
	11867		

Note Transmission is centred 1900Hz above the registered frequencies. It is intended for the broadcasts to be received within a 3000 n miles radius of Nairobi

Map Areas

B	1:15 000 000 (a)	C 1:7 500 000 (a)
	55°N 20°W 55°N 90°E	22°N 25°E 22°N 60°E
	35°S 20°W 35°S 90°W	02°S 25°E 02°S 60°E

D	1:15 000 000 (a)	E	1:15 000 000 (a)
	30°N 15°E 30°N 70°E		20°N 30°E 20°N 70°E
	30°S 15°E 30°S 70°E		30°S 30°E 30°S 70°E

Schedule

	Test chart	0350 0830[1]
B	24h 500 hPa Prog.	0844(00) 2055(12)
	24h 300 hPa Prog.	0903(00) 2114(12)
	24h 250 hPa Prog.	0922(00) 2133(12)
	24h 200 hPa Prog.	0941(00) 2152(12)
D	Surface Anal.	1057(06) 1638(12) 120/576
	Upper air Anal.	1112(06)
	24h change of pressure/variation	1127(06) 1455(12)
	24h Surface Prog.	1142(06) 1802(12)
B	700 hPa Anal.	1210(06) 1820(12)
	500 hPa Anal.	1229(06) 1839(12)
	300 hPa Anal.	1248(06) 1858(12)
	250 hPa Anal	1307(06) 1917(12)
	200 hPa Anal.	1326(06) 1936(12)
E	Surface Anal. (Indian Ocean)	1345(06) 1708(12) 120/576
C	Low level convergence zone	1430(12)
D	850 hPa upper air Anal.	1653(12)

1. Changes to the schedule will be transmitted in place of the normal test chart

NAVTEX

See map.

Internet

The following web sites may be useful. All of them carry a warning along the lines of: *Not to be used as an accurate forecast or for navigation purposes.* Nonetheless many of them do have the best forecasts and the most recent weather maps and satellite images.

Tropical weather sites

Some of these have real time weather analyses and real time tropical storm warnings. They also have other links.

gopher://geografl.sbs.ohio-state.edu:70/1Tropical

www.taifun.org gives up to date warnings for the Indian Ocean.

Weather

http://cirrus.sprl.umich.edu/wxnet/servers.html useful links

http://lumahai.soest.hawaii.edu/Tropical_Weather/tropical.html

http://banzai.neosoft.com/citylink/blake/tropical.html

http://www.supertyphoon.com/indian.html has pressure, wind and satellite photos.

http://www.wmo.ch/web-en/metinfo.html useful links.

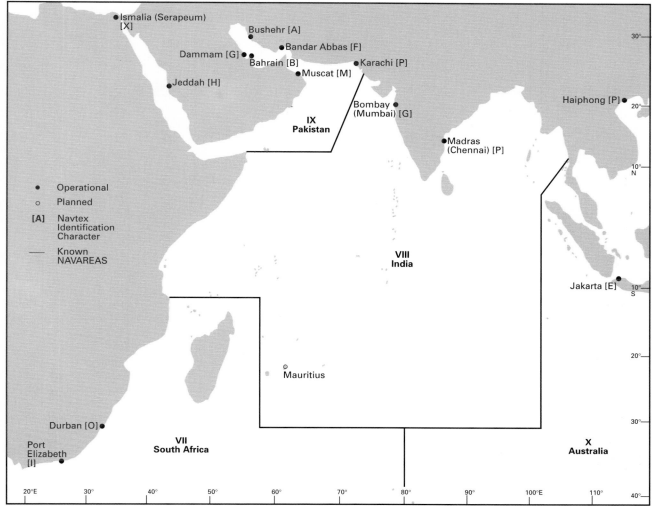

NAVTEX SERVICES

Currents

Like the prevailing winds for the Indian Ocean, it is useful to look at the predominant currents for the northern and southern Indian Ocean separately. Here I will look at the oceanic currents while currents around the coast are discussed in the introduction to each country. It must be emphasised that in coastal waters currents can be contrary to the main oceanic flow or can be in the same direction but greater. There can also be considerable onshore sets augmented by local tides (the 'reef-sucking' currents) and some care is needed plotting courses. Keep an eye on that ever-useful GPS reading for cross-track error.

Bay of Bengal The pattern of currents in the Bay of Bengal changes radically between the NE and SW monsoons. Basically the NE monsoon sets up a W−flowing current with a clockwise circulation in the northern half of the Bay of Bengal. The SW monsoon sets up an E-going current with an anticlockwise circulation in the northern half of the Bay of Bengal. In the southern half of the bay, which is the bit that concerns most cruising yachts, the currents are reasonably strong and consistent. Rates can be appreciably higher than the averages provided by hydrographic publications and it is not unusual to have rates of 1–1½kn on passage between Sri Lanka and Southeast Asia. Around the bottom of Sri Lanka rates of up to 2kn can be encountered where the current is pushed down around the island.

With the NE monsoon the current starts to die down in March-April and the clockwise circulation spreads further S. Rates are still considerable enough with a W-going current of around ½-¾kn in the south of the Bay of Bengal. In May the E-going current from the SW monsoon is established although it does not reach full strength until July. By July there can be rates of 1–1½kn of E-going current. In October the current dies to be replaced by a generally N–NW-going current which is deflected S by the E coast of India and accelerates down the coast at rates of 1–2kn until the full NE monsoon pattern is established later on.

If you are on passage against the prevailing currents it pays to get down towards the equator where there is less current and towards the end of

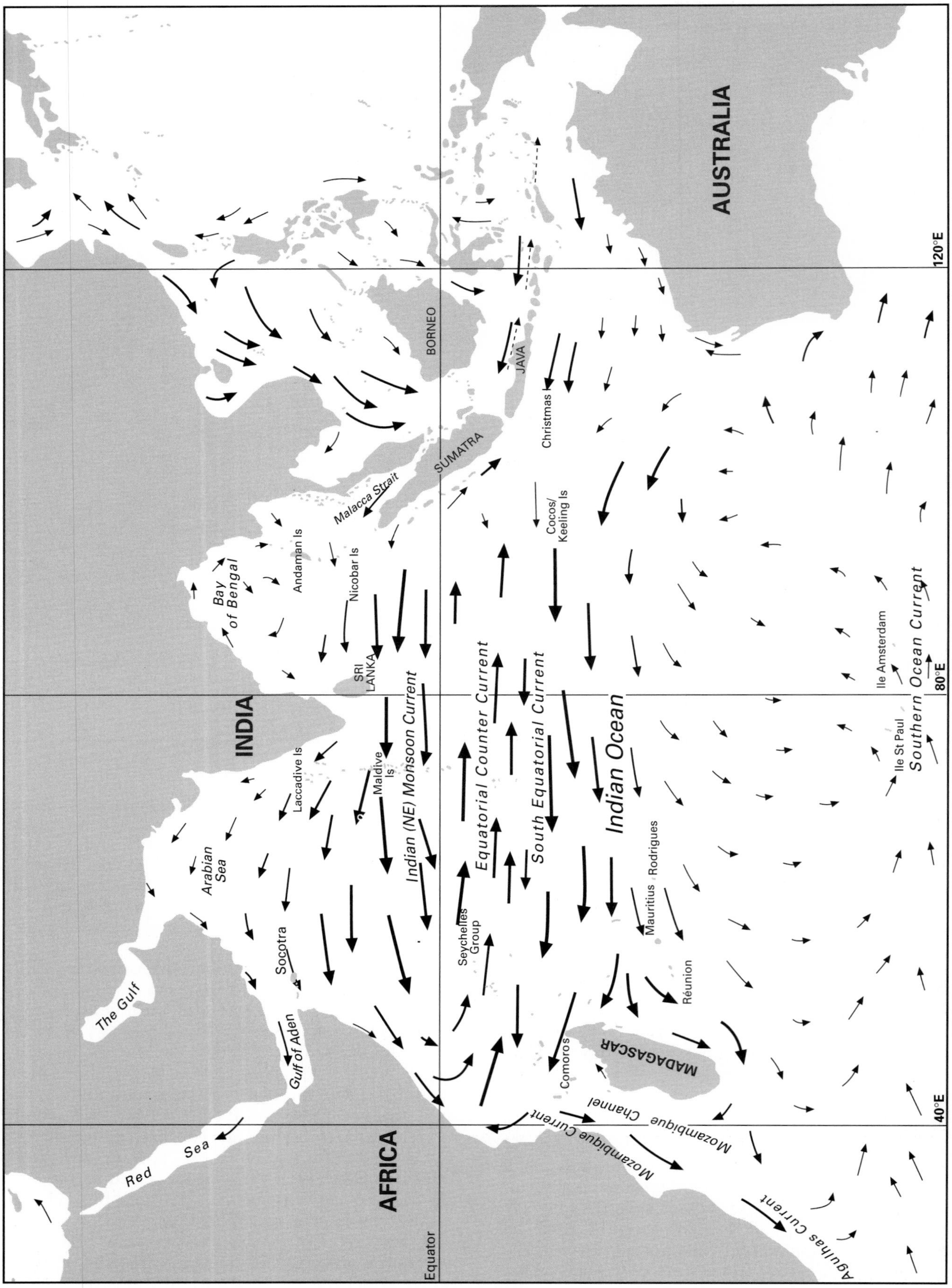

AUSTRALIA

120°E

BORNEO

JAVA

Christmas

SUMATRA

Malacca Strait

Cocos/
Keeling Is

Andaman Is

*Bay
of Bengal*

Nicobar Is

SRI
LANKA

Indian (NE) Monsoon Current

Equatorial Counter Current

South Equatorial Current

INDIA

Indian Ocean

Ile Amsterdam

80°E

Laccadive Is

Maldive
Is

Southern Ocean Current

Ile St Paul

Mauritius · Rodrigues

*Arabian
Sea*

Socotra

Seychelles
Group

Réunion

The Gulf

Comoros

MADAGASCAR

Gulf of Aden

Mozambique Current

Mozambique Channel

Red   Sea

AFRICA

40°E

Agulhas Current

Equator

CURRENTS IN THE INDIAN OCEAN: JANUARY

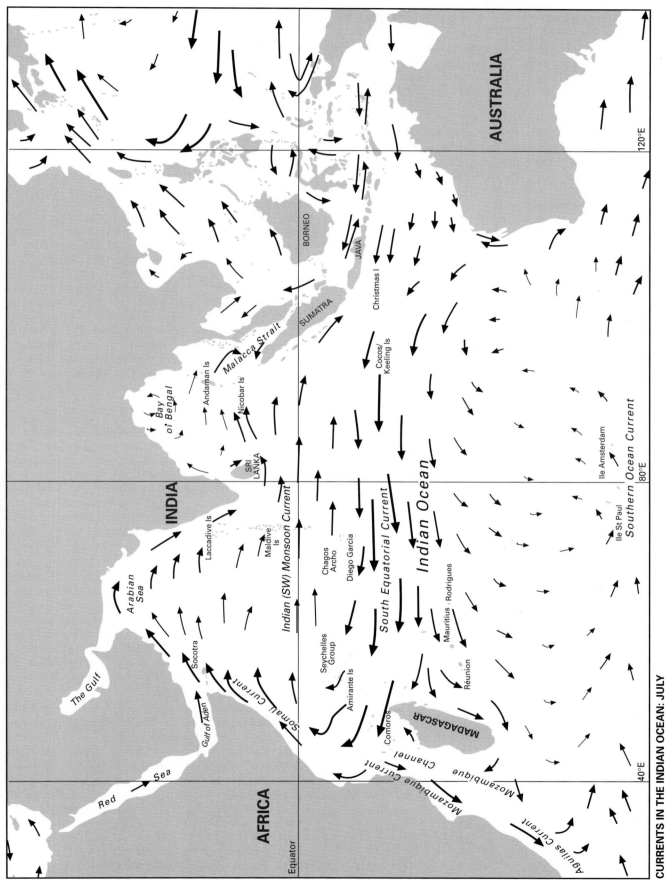

AUSTRALIA

BORNEO

JAVA

SUMATRA

Malacca Strait

Andaman Is

Nicobar Is

Bay of Bengal

SRI LANKA

INDIA

Laccadive Is

Maldive Is

Christmas I

Cocos/ Keeling Is

Indian (SW) Monsoon Current

South Equatorial Current

Indian Ocean

Chagos Archo

Diego Garcia

Seychelles Group

Amirante Is

Mauritius · Rodrigues

Réunion

Comoros

MADAGASCAR

Mozambique Channel

Mozambique Current

Ile Amsterdam

Ile St Paul

Southern Ocean Current

80°E

Agulhas Current

The Gulf

Arabian Sea

Socotra

Gulf of Aden

Somali Current

Red Sea

AFRICA

Equator

40°E

120°E

CURRENTS IN THE INDIAN OCEAN: JULY

49

the NE monsoon you can even pick up favourable counter currents.

Arabian Sea As for the Bay of Bengal, current patterns change radically between the NE and SW monsoons. The NE monsoon sets up a predominantly W-going current although in the early stages the current around the bottom of India and Sri Lanka tends to flow NW up the coast before being pushed W. The current is typically stronger in the southern half of the Arabian Sea at around ¾-1kn than it is in the northern half where rates are ¼-½kn and may be more variable in direction.

The SW monsoon sets up an E-going current which tends to curve around the top of the Arabian Sea and flow SE down the W coast of India. Rates are typically ½-¾kn except around the bottom of India and Sri Lanka where the current is compressed by the land and rates can be ¾-1kn or more. During the SW monsoon there is generally a weak southerly flow around the equator, although the current may reverse to a weak W-going flow in places.

In the intervening periods between the monsoons the currents die, become variable in places, and then pick up as the new monsoon wind takes over.

Gulf of Aden With the NE monsoon the W-going current is squeezed into the gulf and can be strong in places, up to 1½kn in the Gulf of Aden and 2–2½kn through Bab El Mandeb and the very S of the Red Sea. With the SW monsoon the current is predominantly E-going out of the Gulf of Aden and S–SSE out of the bottom of the Red Sea.

Southern Indian Ocean

Current patterns in the southern Indian Ocean are somewhat more complex than in the north. It is useful to talk about the separate currents, which are all well developed and known individually. Sometimes a textual description can be confusing, but a glance at the accompanying maps should clarify matters.

South Equatorial Current In general there is a W-going current between 10°S and 25°S throughout the year known as the South Equatorial Current. The N limit of this current butts onto the S limit of the SW Monsoon Current or the Equatorial Counter-Current according to the season (see below). Its S limit is the Southern Ocean Current. Out of the Timor Sea and across through Christmas Island, Cocos, to the top of Madagascar, this current flows strongly with rates up to ¾-1kn and more at times. Generally it is stronger and less variable in the N than in the S. During the southern hemisphere winter it flows around the bottom of Chagos and the Outer Islands of the Seychelles. In the southern winter it is pushed up around the top of Madagascar into the Somali Current and the Mozambique Current. In the southern summer it divides at Madagascar to flow S down the E coast of Madagascar and across to the African coast.

Equatorial Counter-current When the NE monsoon is blowing in the northern Indian Ocean a counter-current is set up between the equator and between 8°S to 10°S. Its S limit is the South Equatorial Current. This current flows to the E during the southern summer (northern winter) while the NE monsoon is blowing. At this time it affects the Seychelles, Chagos and right across to Sumatra where it is deflected SE by the coast of Sumatra. It is a solid current with rates around 1–2kn with the higher rate usually found at the beginning and end of the season. Rates of 4kn have been reported.

SW Monsoon Current When the SW monsoon is blowing in the northern Indian Ocean an E-going current is set up between the equator and 5°S to 8°S. This effectively replaces the Equatorial Counter-current during the southern winter (northern summer) and although the direction is basically the same, it has important implications around the region of the Seychelles. The Equatorial Counter-current is fed from the N in an anticlockwise direction while the SW monsoon is fed from the S in a clockwise direction. If you are on passage in this area the two contrary 'feeds' to the two currents can be important. The SW Monsoon Current is consistent and strong with rates around 1–2kn. Like the Equatorial Counter-current it is most consistent and strong at the beginning and end of the season.

Southern Ocean Current Also known as the Circumpolar Current. This current flows eastwards around the Southern Ocean propelled by the continuous westerlies that circulate here unhindered by any landmass. In the southern winter there is a SE to SW anticlockwise flow between 30°S to 40°S while in the southern summer there is predominantly a SW flow between 30°S to 40°S except where the current is deflected back around the SW tip of Australia. Below 40°S the flow is to the E.

Mozambique Current The Mozambique Current runs S along the E coast of Africa from around the top of Madagascar where the South Equatorial Current divides. It is a strong current with rates of up to 4kn recorded. Usually it runs at around 1½-2kn, less in the southern winter. Up the W coast of Madagascar a weaker N-going current runs at around ½-1½kn. It is useful for yachts headed N up the Mozambique Channel.

Agulhas Current Around the tip of Africa there is a continuation of the Mozambique Current augmented by the South Equatorial Current known as the Agulhas Current. It has a strong SW flow curving W and then NW following the coastline. The current is always strong and rates of 5kn have been regularly recorded at all times of the year. Rates of at least 2kn can be expected although in places rates are around 1½kn. The inside boundary of the current is said to be the 200m line, so yachts wishing to get out of the current should go inside 200m. Around East London the current divides and one arm circulates anticlockwise to join the

Southern Ocean Current. The Agulhas Current is known and feared by many as it can give rise to exceptionally steep seas with a short period when a SW blow comes through. Yachts should listen carefully to weather forecasts in the area when on passage around the tip of Africa.

Somali Current This current runs up or down the coast of Somalia and Kenya depending on the season. When the NE monsoon is blowing in the northern Indian Ocean it flows SW down the coast. It is a strong current running at 2kn with 3–4kn not unusual at certain times. When the SW monsoon is blowing it flows NE up the coast and often attains rates of 3kn with 4kn not unusual.

Passages westabout

Passages westabout take the normal trade winds route and this is the most common direction for yachts to go as part of a circumnavigation or starting off from Australasia for a cruise of the Indian Ocean region. There are a lot of variations, but for the most part yachts will travel through Southeast Asia and then across to Sri Lanka/India and then on across to the Red Sea and up to the Mediterranean. The alternative is to Christmas Island, Cocos/Chagos, Sri Lanka/India and on across to the Red Sea and the Mediterranean. Some yachts will go down around Africa, but the majority take the Red Sea option to the Mediterranean.

Note
Charts are small scale British Admiralty (BA) with a few exceptions where charts from another Hydrographic department are routinely used.

Sailing directions are British Admiralty. It is illegal to photocopy charts and pilots or to carry photocopies on board. It will invalidate an insurance policy covering your boat and makes you liable to maritime claims in a country including third party claims.

Season is the normal time yachts make the passage described.

Tropical storms gives the months when it is likely there will be a tropical storm although in some areas there is the possibility of a tropical storm all year round, but storms are rare in certain months.

The following brief descriptions identify the main routes going westabout.

W1 Darwin to Christmas Island/Cocos Keeling

Charts Aus *413*, BA *4071*
Pilots *NP17 Australia Pilot Vol V. NP34 Indonesia Pilot Vol II*

Darwin to Christmas Island 1490M
Christmas Island to Cocos Keeling 530M
Season May to October
Tropical storms December to April

This is the standard fast way out of Australia into the southern Indian Ocean. Once out of the wind shadow of Australia the SE trades blow consistently at 12–25kn although in May and again in November they are less consistent. Generally this is a fast passage with a relatively easy landfall at Christmas Island. Some yachts break the passage at Ashmore Reef. From Christmas Island yachts usually proceed on to Cocos Keeling. Some yachts will make the passage direct to Cocos Keeling because the anchorage at Christmas Island is uncomfortable with the swell pushed around into it with the SE trades. The anchorage at Cocos is safe and comfortable with the SE trades.

W2 Darwin to Langkawi or Phuket

Charts Aus *413*, BA *941B, 941A, 830.* You will of course need more detail than this bare minimum.
Pilots *NP34 Indonesia Pilot Vol II. NP36 Indonesia Pilot Vol I. NP44 Malacca Strait Pilot*

Darwin to Bali (Benoa) 970M
Bali (Benoa) to Singapore 985M
Singapore to Langkawi (Kuah) 420M
Langkawi (Kuah) to Phuket (Ao Chalong) 135M
Season May to December
Tropical storms December to April. (A small chance only in the Timor Sea.)

This is the more leisurely route when going west. Many yachts follow the regatta series beginning in Darwin with the Darwin to Ambon Race in late July and proceeding on to the Bali to Jakarta Yacht Race, Jakarta to Nongsa Race and the Raja Muda. There are numerous regattas and race series in between finishing up with the Kings Cup at Phuket in early December.

There will be periods of calms once you are amongst the Indonesian archipelago and in the Malacca Straits. The likelihood of tropical storms is very low and the only bad weather is likely to be squalls associated with thunderstorms including the notorious *Sumatra* in the Malacca Straits.

This route takes some people a year or two to do as there are a lot of places to explore along the way. Yachts going west will normally leave from Langkawi or Phuket.

W3 Fremantle to Cocos Keeling

Chart BA *4070*
Pilots *NP17 Australia Pilot Vol V. NP34 Indonesia Pilot Vol II*

Fremantle to Cocos Keeling 1585M
Season May to October
Tropical storms November to April

This is the quick route to the northern Indian Ocean during the SE trades. The passage will normally be a fast one and at times a wet and rolly passage. Some yachts sail up the W coast of Australia before setting out for Cocos.

W4 Phuket to Sri Lanka (Galle) and via the Andamans (Port Blair)

Charts BA *830, 827*
Pilots *NP21 Bay of Bengal Pilot, NP38 West Coast of India Pilot*

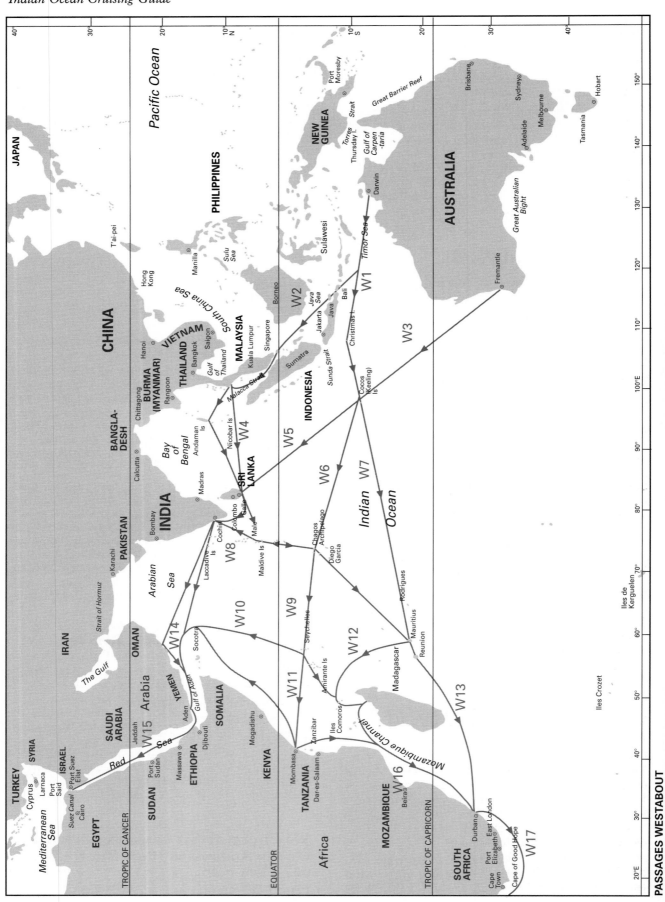

PASSAGES WESTABOUT

Phuket to Sri Lanka (Galle) 1100M
Phuket to Andamans (Port Blair) 410M
Andamans (Port Blair) to Sri Lanka (Galle) 850M
Season January to March although yachts sometimes leave in December.

Tropical storms May to December

Once clear of the wind shadow of Thailand the NE monsoon blowing at 12–20kn gives a fast passage to Sri Lanka. Yachts normally pass through the Great Channel between Great Nicobar Island and the N end of Sumatra, but can also pass through the Sombrero Channel between Katchall Island and Little Nicobar which is free of dangers. It is prohibited to approach or anchor off the Nicobars (see section on the Nicobars). In the approaches to Dondra Head, the southern end of Sri Lanka, traffic is squeezed into narrow separation lanes and there will be a significant increase in shipping. The best option is to go between the inside lane and the coast and although large numbers of fishing boats will be encountered, especially at night, this is a better option than mixing it with ships in the separation lanes further out.

The passage to Port Blair in the Andamans will usually be dogged by light winds until clear of the wind shadow off Thailand. Remember it is advisable to have an Indian visa with a stamp to visit restricted areas before leaving for Port Blair (see section on the Andamans). From the Andamans to Sri Lanka it is a downhill ride with the NE monsoon.

In the Andaman Sea there will often be upwelling currents producing a strange choppy sea in defined areas. This phenomenon occurs over most of the Andaman Sea between the Nicobars and Andamans and the Thai and Burmese coast. Around the Nicobars and Andamans there are variable currents, some producing overfalls, and there will often be an onshore set which needs to be monitored with the cross-track error on the GPS. Around the bottom of Sri Lanka there are also strong currents, some with an onshore set, which need to be monitored.

W5 Cocos Keeling to Sri Lanka (Galle)

Chart BA *4707*
Pilots NP44 *Malacca Strait Pilot.* NP38 *West Coast of India Pilot*
Cocos Keeling to Sri Lanka (Galle) 1480M
Season August to December
Tropical storms November to April in southern Indian Ocean/April to December in the Bay of Bengal.

This transequatorial route is pretty much clear of the tropical storm zones although even on the fringes the effects of a tropical storm can be felt with winds and especially big seas. The chances of a tropical storm once N of the equator are next to non-existent.

Because the route passes through the ITCZ, winds will be variable and the likelihood of thunderstorms and squalls is high. There are few who have much that is good to say about this route and it can involve lots of sail changes, dull rainy

weather and some motoring. Most yachts tend to make the passage in September to November. Closing on Sri Lanka a fair amount of commercial traffic will be encountered and a good lookout must be kept at this stage.

There are three different current flows to deal with here, but the overwhelming direction for the most popular time in September to November is towards the E and the Southwest Monsoon Current can flow at anything up to 2kn towards the E around the bottom of Sri Lanka. Allowance should be made for this overall push towards the E and while leaving the passage until December is an option, it doesn't seem to make a great deal of difference when compared to making an earlier passage.

W6 Cocos Keeling to Chagos (Salomon Islands)

Charts BA *4707, 4703*
Pilots NP44 *Malacca Strait Pilot*, NP39 *South Indian Ocean Pilot*
Cocos Keeling to Chagos (Salomon Islands) 1520M
Season May to October
Tropical storms November to April

Most boats make this passage around September to October when the SE trades have died down a bit, but are still consistent and strong enough to make for a speedy passage. The currents during this time are mostly W-going with the South Equatorial Current although the further N you get, the more likely the current will slow or even reverse towards the E as the Southwest Monsoon Current takes over. For most yachts this is a pleasant fast passage if occasionally a bit rolly when the trades go into the E.

W7 Cocos Keeling to Rodrigues, Mauritius and Réunion

Charts BA *4714, 4703*
Pilots NP44 *Malacca Strait Pilot.* NP39 *South Indian Ocean Pilot*
Cocos Keeling to Rodrigues (Port Mathurin) 1985M
Cocos Keeling to Mauritius (Port Louis) 2330M
Cocos Keeling to Réunion (Port des Galets) 2460M
Season May to October
Tropical storms November to April

For this passage it is important that the voyage is planned well clear of the cyclone season and with time in hand to leave the area for east Africa before the onset of the cyclone season. The three Mascarene Islands of Rodrigues, Mauritius and Réunion have a good chance of being hit by cyclones which develop in the area and there are not too many options available if a cyclone is predicted to pass by.

The passage will be a fast one although it is often reported as uncomfortable with big seas the further S you go and some days when the SE trades are somewhat more than boisterous. For this reason it is not a bad idea to make the passage around June before the SE trades get up to full strength and it allows some time to explore the Mascarene Islands before leaving.

The currents are all favourable for this passage and the landfall on the high volcanic islands is straightforward.

W8 Chagos (Salomon Islands), Sri Lanka (Galle), Maldives (Male) and India (Cochin)

Charts BA *4703, 4707*

Pilot NP38 *West Coast of India*

Sri Lanka (Galle) to Chagos (Salomon Islands) 835M
Sri Lanka (Galle) to India (Cochin) 355M
India (Cochin) to Maldives (Male) 390M
Maldives (Male) to Chagos (Salomon Islands) 595M

Season January to April

Tropical storms May to December

The rough triangle of routes here are mostly used during the NE monsoon period. Yachts en route to the Red Sea will often cross from Galle to the Maldives and a good number now go up to Cochin. Some yachts head down to Chagos and likewise some head from Cochin to the Maldives and then onto the Red Sea or down to Chagos. Winds can vary dramatically depending on the route.

From Galle to Chagos winds will initially be NE–E with the NE monsoon and then become variable in the ITCZ with a good chance of thunderstorms and squalls. You will also have to do a bit of motoring. Many yachts leave this passage until later in the season, around March or April.

From Galle to Cochin the passage will be boisterous where the NE monsoon is funnelled down through the gap between the bottom of India and Sri Lanka with winds of Force 7 (30kn) not uncommon for a day or so. Once up to the coast there will be land and sea breezes to Cochin.

From Cochin to Male there is a good breeze from the NE monsoon once you are clear of the wind shadow off India, although this tends to weaken as you get towards the Maldives.

From Male to Chagos the winds will be variable with thunderstorms and squalls in the ITCZ zone as for the Galle to Chagos passage.

W9 Chagos (Salomon Islands) to the Seychelles (Victoria), Comoros, Madagascar (Nosy Be)

Chart BA *4702*

Pilot NP39 *South Indian Ocean Pilot*

Chagos (Salomon Islands) to Seychelles (Victoria) 1010M
Seychelles (Victoria) to Comoros (Moroni) 860M
Comoros (Moroni) to Madagascar (Nosy Bé) 320M

Season May to October

Tropical storms November to April

The passage from Chagos to the Seychelles is usually a pleasant one with the SE trades providing a moderate breeze and hardly ever getting blustery.

The seas are not too big and the current is going in the right direction. The approach to the Seychelles needs to be made with caution and the final approach to Victoria should be by day.

The passage to the Comoros tends to get more windy as you go S and the seas start to get bigger and less pleasant.

The passage from Moroni to Nosy Bé tends to be sheltered from the worst of the swell by the bulk of Madagascar and the closer you get, the less sea there is.

For detailed information on passages around the Comoros and Madagascar see *East Africa Pilot* by Delwyn McPhun.

W10 Seychelles (Victoria) to the Red Sea

Charts BA *4703, 4704*

Pilots NP39 *South Indian Ocean Pilot*. NP3 *Africa Pilot Vol III*. NP64 *Red Sea and Gulf of Aden Pilot*

Seychelles (Victoria) to Red Sea (Bab el Mandeb) 1720M

Season June to October

Tropical storms May to June (small risk)

For this passage yachts need to hitch into the SW monsoon period which gives favourable winds and current. The problem is that when the SW monsoon is blowing at full strength there will often be gale force winds around the Horn of Africa and in the entrance to the Gulf of Aden. For this reason yachts normally make the passage in September to October when the SW monsoon has died down a bit, but there is still sufficient wind to shift you along and a favourable current.

Yachts should go well outside Socotra before heading into the Gulf of Aden because of the piracy risk around Somalia and Socotra. Yachts will probably head for Mukalla or Aden to break the voyage before tackling the Red Sea.

In the NE monsoon yachts will usually find light and variable winds from the NW–NE in October-November when heading towards the Gulf of Aden and when the NE monsoon is established there will be E winds in the Gulf of Aden itself.

W11 Seychelles (Victoria) to East Africa (Mombasa)

Charts BA *4703, 4701*

Pilots NP39 *South Indian Ocean Pilot*. NP3 *Africa Pilot Vol III*

Seychelles (Victoria) to East Africa (Mombasa) 950M

Season May to September

Tropical storms none

With the SE trades this is a fast and pleasant passage. The currents are favourable until you hit the Somali Current which flows strongly to the N up the coast of Kenya and Somalia. The width of the current is around 100 miles for the worst of the current and this has been recorded at 4–5kn at times. By all accounts getting through the current is a wet business and there seems little to be done except to expect a loss to the N. If this can be compensated by keeping as far S as possible in the approaches then so much the better. The current usually finishes around 30–50 miles off the coast.

W12 Mauritius (Port Louis) to the Comoros (Moroni) and Madagascar (Nosy Be)

Chart BA *4702*

Pilot NP39 *South Indian Ocean Pilot*

Mauritius (Port Louis) to Comoros (Moroni) 1065M
Mauritius (Port Louis) to Madagascar (Nosy Be) 825M

Season May to October

Tropical storms November to April

During the SE trades this is a downwind run that will be fast if a bit wet and furious at times. At the northern tip of Madagascar the wind tends to be particularly heavy although once around the top things get better. The seas up to Madagascar can be fairly big at times and it will not always be a comfortable trip. The currents are all favourable except for the counter current running up the W coast of Madagascar.

The voyage can be broken at a number of places around Madagascar or at Mayotte.

For detailed information on passages around the Comoros and Madagascar see *East Africa Pilot* by Delwyn McPhun.

W13 Mauritius (Port Louis) to South Africa (Durban)

Charts BA *4700*

Pilots NP39 *South Indian Ocean Pilot.* NP3 *Africa Pilot Vol III*

Mauritius (Port Louis) to Durban 1555M

Season May to October

Tropical storms November to April

This is the fast way out of the Indian Ocean around the southern end of Madagascar and to Durban or a yacht can continue on to the Cape of Good Hope and into the Atlantic. The SE trades die down towards the bottom of Africa and some SW winds and a SW blow will be likely. The SW blows against the strong Agulhas Current running down the coast of Africa can produce very steep and dangerous seas. It is worthwhile monitoring the weather in this area which has a bad reputation for small craft.

For detailed information on passages around Madagascar and South Africa see *East Africa Pilot* by Delwyn McPhun and the *South African Nautical Almanac* by Tom Morgan.

W14 India (Cochin) to Oman (Mina Raysut), Yemen (Aden) and the Red Sea

Chart BA *4705*

Pilots NP38 *West Coast of India.* NP64 *Red Sea and Gulf of Aden Pilot*

India (Cochin) to Oman (Mina Raysut) 1360M
India (Cochin) to Yemen (Aden) 1850M
India (Cochin) to the Red Sea (Bab el Mandeb) 1940M
Sri Lanka (Galle) to the Red Sea (Bab el Mandeb) 2240M

Season January to April

Tropical storms May to December

Yachts normally leave Galle, the Maldives and Cochin around January to February for the passage across to Mina Raysut (Salalah) or Aden when the NE monsoon is firmly established. Yachts can also leave in December when the risk of tropical storms is very low. Yachts heading for Aden or the Red Sea directly should not aim to make too much northing at first as the NE monsoon will be mostly N at first, gradually turning to NE and E at the entrance to the Gulf of Aden. This allows you to make the passage with the wind just aft of the beam all the way to the Gulf of Aden rather than going N and then rolling downwind to the Gulf of Aden. In addition the W–going current is strongest around 11°–12°N giving a useful boost to daily averages.

Likewise going to Mina Raysut, it pays to curve gradually up to the north rather than trying to make a lot of northing in the beginning.

This passage is considered to be one of the gentler ocean passages with only a moderate swell and winds hardly ever above Force 5 (20kn) and clear skies with few thunderstorms and squalls.

W15 Red Sea passages

Chart BA *4704*

Pilot NP64 *Red Sea and Gulf of Aden Pilot*

Bab el Mandeb to Port Suez 1210M

Season December to April

Tropical storms none

Getting up the Red Sea is complicated by the fact that the prevailing winds blow down the Red Sea from the N for most of the year. At the bottom of the Red Sea there will be southerlies from December to March/April blowing for anything up to 100–150 miles N of Bab el Mandeb. After that it is likely the convergence zone will be encountered and N of Massawa there will be northerlies. For the rest of the way up the Red Sea northerlies will blow, often quite strongly at Force 6–7 (25–35kn) with few days of calm. The short steep seas kicked up by the wind make going to windward a wet and bumpy business and the whole thing will come as a bit of shock to those who have been on passage downwind for some time. Unless you are in a hurry (in which case it will all just be wet and uncomfortable) it is best to take some time over the Red Sea passage.

For detailed information on passages in the Red Sea see *Red Sea Pilot* by Elaine Morgan and Stephen Davies.

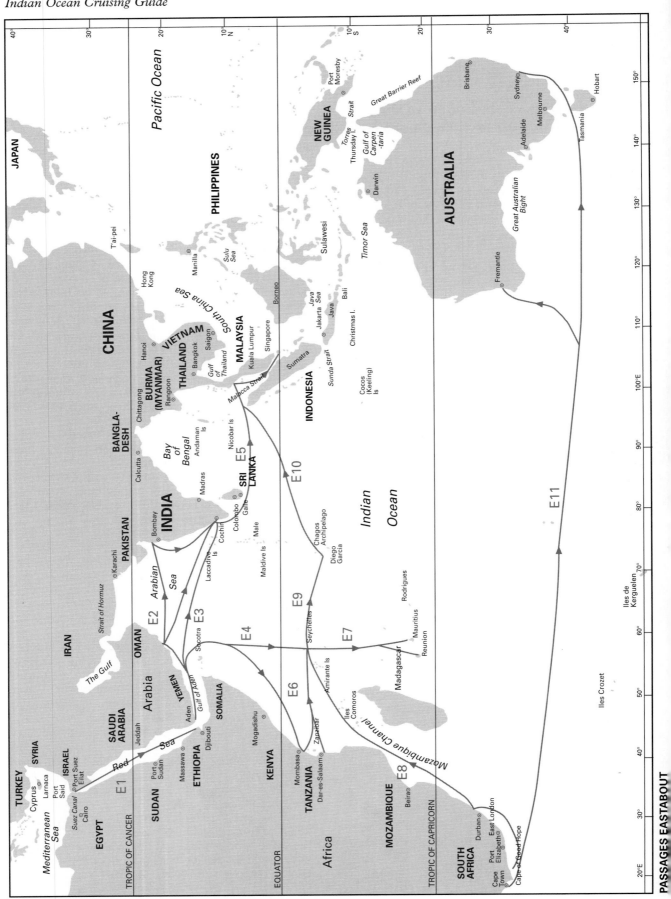

W16 East Africa passages

Charts BA 4701, 4700

Pilot *NP3 Africa Pilot Vol III.*

Kenya (Mombasa) to the Red Sea (Bab el Mandeb)
2150M (outside Socotra)

Kenya (Mombasa) to South Africa (Durban) 1750M

Tropical storms May to October

The passage from Mombasa to the Red Sea is best in October to December when the SW monsoon is dying out and the Somali current is still favourable. Late November to December are best as then the NE monsoon can be caught in the Gulf of Aden and southerlies are more likely in the bottom of the Red Sea. Yachts need to keep well clear of Somalia and Socotra because of the piracy risk there. Yachts will often break the passage at Mukalla or Aden.

The passage from Mombasa to Durban is rarely a direct one as there are lots of places to stop off en route. Yachts normally cruise down the coast of Tanzania to Mozambique and Madagascar in July to August aiming to be going down the Mozambique Channel in September to October.

The ramifications of current, winds, the cyclone season and the rainy season make cruise planning essential along the East African coast. For further information consult *East Africa Pilot* by Delwyn McPhun.

W17 Durban to Capetown and the Atlantic

Chart BA *4204*

Pilot *NP3 East Africa Pilot Vol III.*

Durban to Capetown 775M

Season January to March

The passage around the Cape of Good Hope can be a challenging one, but with attention to planning and constant monitoring of the weather forecasts there should be few problems in the southern summer. The main danger is of SW gales coming in and causing steep and potentially dangerous waves when it blows against the SW-going Agulhas Current. Wave heights of 20m have been recorded and the waves are very steep. Choosing your time and monitoring the weather forecasts, it is possible to coast around here without encountering bad weather.

For detailed information see the *South African Nautical Almanac* by Tom Morgan.

Passages eastabout

Passages eastabout are less common than the westabout trade winds route. Yachts will choose an eastabout passage if they want to get directly from the Mediterranean to the Indian Ocean, to get from east Africa to other cruising grounds, or to get quickly back to Australasia and the Pacific from the bottom of South Africa.

Note

Charts are small scale British Admiralty (BA) with a few exceptions where charts from another Hydrographic department are routinely used.

Sailing directions are British Admiralty. It is illegal to photocopy charts and pilots or to carry photocopies on board. It will invalidate an insurance policy covering your boat and makes you liable to maritime claims in a country including third party claims.

Season is the normal time yachts make the passage described.

Tropical storms gives the months when it is likely there will be a tropical storm though in some areas there is the possibility of a tropical storm all year round, but storms are rare in certain months.

The following brief descriptions identify the main routes going eastabout.

E1 Red Sea Passages

Chart BA *4704*

Pilot *NP64 Red Sea and Gulf of Aden Pilot*

Port Suez to Port Suez 1210M

Season All year

Tropical storms none

Getting down the Red Sea is easier than getting up. The prevailing winds are northerly for all of the year at least down as far as the bottom of Sudan. You can potter down the Red Sea or pick up a brisk northerly blow and fly down for as long as it lasts. For the southern end of the Red Sea the situation is somewhat different. With the NE monsoon blowing there will be strong southerlies, up to gale force, anywhere just S of Massawa to Bab el Mandeb. Add to these headwinds a current of anything from 1–3kn and it can be hard work getting out of the bottom of the Red Sea. When the SW monsoon is blowing northerlies extend further down the Red Sea and often there will be just a patch of variable wind or light southerlies at the bottom of the Red Sea.

The favoured time to make the passage is in July-August when you can pop out the bottom of the Red Sea and catch the last of the SW monsoon up to Mukalla or Mina Raysut before continuing on across to India or Sri Lanka. The only disadvantage to this is that it is very hot at this time in the bottom of the Red Sea and around the Arabian peninsula, often in the high 30s or 40°C.

For detailed information on passages in the Red Sea see *Red Sea Pilot* by Elaine Morgan and Stephen Davies.

E2 Red Sea (Bab el Mandeb) to Yemen (Aden), Oman (Mina Raysut), and India (Bombay)

Chart BA *4705*

Pilots *NP64 Red Sea and Gulf of Aden Pilot. NP38 West Coast of India*

Bab el Mandeb to Aden 100M
Bab el Mandeb to Mukalla 370M
Bab el Mandeb to Mina Raysut (Salalah) 690M
Mina Raysut to Bombay 1080M
Mina Raysut to Cochin 1360M

Season December to March and August to September

Tropical storms May to December (incidence in August to September is virtually nil)

Yachts normally try to exit out of the Red Sea into the Gulf of Aden around late July and through August and then proceed around the coast via Aden and Mukalla to Mina Raysut. The trick here is to avoid the SW monsoon when it is blowing strongest in July in the Arabian Sea and catch the tail end of the SW monsoon as it dies down in late August/September. Yachts normally cross to Bombay, Goa (Panaji) or Cochin in late August and through September. Although this is theoretically the cyclone season, the incidence of cyclones is very low.

It is possible to cross from the Gulf of Aden to India during the NE monsoon although a yacht must be able to efficiently go to windward. See E3 below.

Care must be taken to keep well clear of the coast of Somalia and Socotra because of the risk of piracy.

E3 Red Sea (Bab el Mandeb) to India (Cochin) and Sri Lanka (Galle)

Charts BA *4705, 4706*

Pilots *NP64 Red Sea and Gulf of Aden Pilot. NP38 West Coast of India*

Bab el Mandeb to Mukalla 370M
Bab el Mandeb to Ras Fartak 550M
Mukalla to Cochin 1615M
Ras Fartak to Cochin 1450M
Mukalla to Galle 1910M
Ras Fartak to Galle 1750M

Season December to March and August to September

Tropical storms May to December (incidence in August to September is virtually nil)

During the NE monsoon getting out of the Gulf of Aden against the prevailing easterlies and against the W-going current (1–2kn) can take some doing although it is possible to coast along Yemen until a good slant can be obtained from Ras Fartak. Around longitude 55°E the worst of the current should be over and it is then a matter of sailing hard on the wind to India or Sri Lanka. Initially it will not be possible to point in the right direction, but bit by bit the NE monsoon will turn to the NNE and then N and you will be able to pull around to Cochin or Galle. Although you are hard on the wind, the moderate breeze and moderate seas do not make this an unduly arduous passage.

With the SW monsoon it is a matter of catching the tail of the monsoon in August to September. It will be a rapid passage across to India or Sri Lanka and fairly wet at times. Although this is theoretically the cyclone season, the incidence of cyclones is very low.

E4 Red Sea (Bab el Mandeb) to Kenya (Mombasa) and the Seychelles (Victoria)

Charts BA *4705, 4703*

Pilots *NP64 Red Sea and Gulf of Aden Pilot. NP3 Africa Pilot Vol III*

Bab el Mandeb to Kenya (Mombasa) 2150M (outside Socotra)
Bab el Mandeb to Seychelles (Victoria) 1720M

Season November to March

Tropical storms May to December in Arabian Sea (incidence in August to September is virtually nil)

This passage should be made in the NE monsoon when there will be favourable winds and current once you get out of the Gulf of Aden. The latter can be a bit of a struggle and most yachts go up to Mukalla.

Yachts on passage to Kenya should not be tempted to squeeze through the passage between Socotra and Somalia because of the risk of piracy. Some yachts do take this shortcut, but there have been more than enough incidents to make this a very risky business. Once out from Socotra it is a downwind passage to Kenya with the Somali Current providing a useful increment to daily runs.

The passage from the Gulf of Aden to the Seychelles is straightforward once out of the Gulf of Aden although yachts usually run out wind for longish periods and a good supply of diesel will be necessary if you are not to take a long time over the passage.

E5 Sri Lanka (Galle) to Thailand (Phuket) and Singapore

Chart BA *4707*

Pilots *NP38 West Coast of India Pilot. NP21 Bay of Bengal Pilot. NP44 Malacca Strait Pilot*

Sri Lanka (Galle) to Phuket 1100M
Sri Lanka (Galle) to Malaysia (Kuah) 1180M
Kuah to Singapore 420M

Season January to March and June to August

Tropical storms April to December (June to August have a low incidence of cyclones)

This passage can be made during the NE monsoon although like the passage eastabout across the Arabian Sea, it means going to windward to get to Southeast Asia. It is not unduly arduous and in the approaches to Sumatra and Thailand there may well be long periods of calm or light winds where you will have to motor.

The passage can be made during the SW monsoon in June to August and although there is a risk of tropical storms, the risk is low and by keeping around 10°N or lower you should be able to take avoiding action if a tropical storm threatens.

Passage from Phuket or Langkawi down to Singapore is best made with the NE monsoon although the winds are much affected by the land and sea breeze pattern and there will be calms.

E6 East Africa to the Seychelles

Charts BA *4701, 4703*

Pilots *NP3 Africa Pilot Vol III. NP39 South Indian Ocean Pilot*

Mombasa to Seychelles (Victoria) 950M
Dar es Salaam to Seychelles (Victoria) 975M

Season All year

Tropical storms none

Although it is possible to make this passage all year round, the best time is during the NE monsoon when the wind is likely to be NNW–NW once across the Somali Current. You will also pick up the Equatorial Counter-current about halfway across. Winds are likely to be light and variable with some squalls as you get towards the Seychelles.

For detailed information on passages around East Africa see *East Africa Pilot* by Delwyn McPhun.

E7 Seychelles to Mauritius and Réunion

Chart BA *4702*

Pilot *NP39 South Indian Ocean Pilot*

Seychelles (Victoria) to Mauritius (Port Louis) 945M
Seychelles (Victoria) to Réunion (Port des Galettes) 985M

Season May to October

Tropical storms November to April

This is a windward route which cannot be made when the SE trades are partially displaced by the NW monsoon because of the risk of cyclones. Most yachts will tend to voyage down the coast of East Africa and then across to the Comoros and Mayotte before the final bash to Mauritius and Réunion.

E8 South Africa to Seychelles

Charts BA *4204, 4700, 4701, 4703*

Pilots *NP3 Africa Pilot Vol III. NP 39 South Indian Ocean Pilot*

Capetown to Durban 775M
Durban to Seychelles (Victoria) 2100M

Season May to October

Tropical storms November to April

Yachts proceeding around the bottom of Africa will have a hard job against the Agulhas Current. Passage up the Mozambique Channel should be in May or June as the chance of SW gales is highest in July and August. Once up towards Tanzania yachts can follow the passage as for E6.

For detailed information on passages around east Africa and South Africa see *East Africa Pilot* by Delwyn McPhun and the *South African Nautical Almanac* by Tom Morgan.

E9 Seychelles (Victoria) to Chagos (Salomon Islands)

Chart BA *4702*

Pilot *NP39 South Indian Ocean Pilot*

Seychelles (Victoria) to Chagos (Salomon Islands) 1010M

Season November to December and April

Tropical storms November to April

This passage is against the prevailing winds so a yacht should attempt to make it at the beginning or end of the NW monsoon which coincides with the cyclone season. In November and again in April the likelihood of a cyclone is rare and in any case a yacht will be pretty much out of the sea area affected by keeping N of 5°S. Just because you are not in the actual path of a cyclone does not mean that the weather and seas will not impede progress and any cyclone developing in the area will send a considerable swell up to 5°S and the weather can be squally with impressive thunderstorms.

To make the passage during the SE monsoon between May to October would mean you would have to beat to windward to get there, but there would be a negligible risk of tropical storms.

E10 Chagos (Salomon Islands) to Thailand (Phuket) and Malaysia (Langkawi)

Charts BA *4703, 4707*

Pilots *NP39 South Indian Ocean Pilot. NP 44 Malacca Strait Pilot*

Chagos (Salomon Islands) to Thailand (Phuket) 1760M
Chagos (Salomon Islands) to Langkawi (Kuah) 1815M

Season All year

Tropical storms none

On this transequatorial route the incidence of tropical storms is rare although like E9 the effects of a cyclone to the N or S can produce big seas and unsettled weather. The best time to make this passage is at the beginning of the SW monsoon period when with luck you will pick up good SW winds once across the ITCZ.

E11 South Africa to Australia

Charts BA *4072, 4070, 4060*

Pilots *NP3 Africa Pilot Vol III. NP39 South Indian Ocean Pilot. NP13 Australia Pilot Vol I. NP17 Australia Pilot Vol V. NP14 Australia Pilot Vol II*

Capetown to Fremantle 4710M
Capetown to Sydney 6320M

Season December to March

This fast route from South Africa to Australia should only be made in yachts built and equipped to withstand the rigours of the roaring forties. The winds around 40°S blow from the W around the globe and are frequently at gale force. The seas, driven by this wind and unchecked by any land can be mountainous. Most of us will have seen pictures of the Whitbread Race around the world (now the

Volvo Race) where the 60 to 70ft yachts look like dinghies in the mountainous seas and waves continually sweep over the decks. Cruising yachts should attempt to keep fairly well N so that they are on the edge of the roaring forties and do not get down to the furious fifties and the screaming sixties.

The passage in the southern winter should be avoided if possible as ice can drift a fair way N and the consequences of hitting even a small bergy bit in this desolate piece of ocean should persuade most people that summer is the season to do this trip. Even then it is for the hardy in a bullet-proof yacht that can withstand this ocean.

I. Northern Indian Ocean

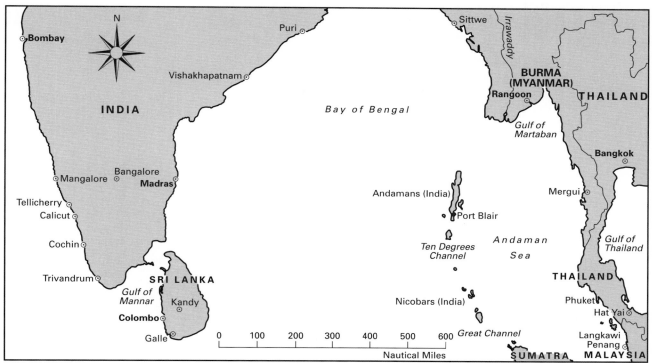

BAY OF BENGAL

Singapore

Current situation

Singapore is a stable democracy although it has been ruled with an iron fist by Lee Kuan Yew since secession from Malaysia in 1970. Lee himself resigned as prime minister in 1990 and was succeeded by Goh Chok Tong although Lee's tough policies are continued. In a sort of benign dictatorship, opposition to the government is strictly controlled and Singapore is one of the most orderly places in Southeast Asia. Littering, including dropping cigarette butts and chewing gum in public places, carries a fine. Vandalism and graffiti writing is punishable with a birching. These laws apply equally to visitors and the locals alike, so behave yourself.

The waters around Singapore are well patrolled and today the incidence of piracy inside the territorial waters is low for yachts.

Documentation and visas

Normal boats papers and a valid passport for all crew members must be carried. You may be asked for a radio licence and insurance documents although there will be few problems if you do not have them.

Most visitors to Singapore from Europe, the USA and Commonwealth countries will automatically get a visa on entry for two weeks. This is extendible for another two weeks and it is possible to get an extension up to 90 days. A yacht can be left here for long periods and visas apply to individuals only.

Entry formalities

On arrival in Singapore you must go to immigration and the port office after you have arrived. Immigration is at: Seaman's Section, #3-01B World Trade Centre, 1 Maritime Square, Telok Blangah Road, Singapore 0409. ☎ 273 0525/273 0053/4. Once stamped in here you must report the yachts arrival at the Port Clearance Office, Tanjong Pagar Complex.

Data

Area 620km² (239M²)
Coastline 193km (104M)
Maritime claims Territorial 3M. Exclusive fishing zone 12M.
Population 2,765,000
Time zone UT+8
Language Chinese, Malay, Tamil and English (all official). English widely spoken.
Ethnic divisions Chinese 76%, Malay 15%, Indian 6·5%, other including Europeans 2·5%.
Religion Chinese are mostly Buddhist, Malays are Muslim.

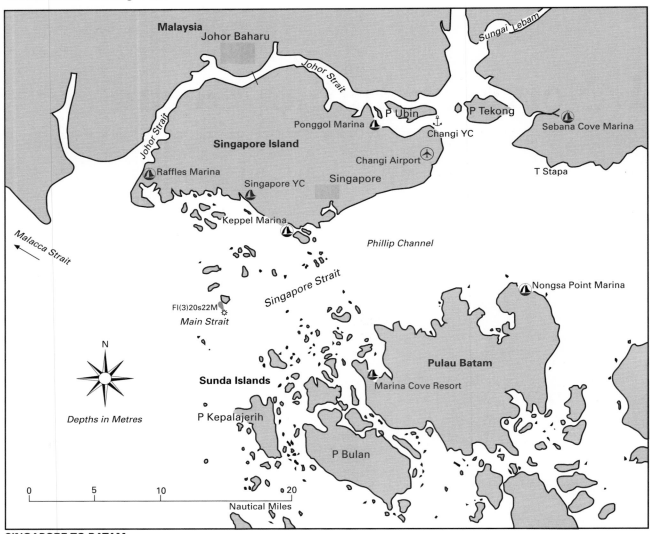

SINGAPORE TO BATAM

Public holidays
Jan 1 New Years Day
May 1 Labour Day
Aug 9 National Day
Dec 25 Christmas
Moveable
Jan/Feb Chinese New Year
Apr Good Friday, Hari Raya Punsa
Apr/May Vesak Day
Jun-Jul Hari Raya Haji
Nov Deepavali

Government Democratic Republic although one party has ruled continuously since 1970.

Disputes Two islands in dispute with Malaysia.

Crime Low level of crime with efficient police force. Drug smuggling in Singapore is harshly dealt with and can be punishable by death, so do not even think about it.

Travel
Internal
Good bus and underground system (MRT: Mass Rapid Transit) to all areas. Taxis and car hire. Ferries to many places.

International
Air Changi International Airport is an ultramodern affair that handles flights from all around the world. Singapore Airlines fly to many destinations including countries around the Pacific and to Europe. Most other major airlines also have services from Changi.

Ferries To nearby towns on the Malay peninsula and to the Riau Islands.

Train Singapore is the southern termination of the Malaysian railway network and is connected to the main line through Kuala Lumpur and Butterworth and so on to Thailand.

Bus Frequent bus services to Malaysian destinations.

Practicalities
Mail Reliable and efficient. Can be sent to Poste Restante but a private address is to be preferred.

Telecommunications IDD system. Country code 65. Phone cards and credit card dialling widespread. Digital phones with a GSM card work if your supplier has an agreement in Singapore. Fax service from agencies and hotels.

Currency The unit of currency is the Singapore dollar divided into 100 cents. Rates of exchange have been reasonably stable although it lost value with the Southeast Asian slump of 1997.

Banks and exchange Most of the major banks can be found in the Central Business District although there are others elsewhere. Most banks will change travellers cheques or cash and many can give a cash advance on major credit cards. Banks are open 1000–1500 weekdays and 1100–1630 Sat. Moneychangers (mostly located in Change Alley near the major banks) will exchange for cash and travellers cheques. They also deal in restricted currencies such as Indian rupees and it is useful to obtain some rupees here if headed for India (see the section on clearing into India). ATMs which will take major credit cards are common. Many shops and restaurants also accept major credit and charge cards.

Medical care Medical facilities are of a high standard and charges are medium. Most doctors and dentists will have been trained in Britain, Australia, NZ, or the USA. Chinese herbal centres are common and acupuncture centres will be found. The water is generally safe to drink.

Electricity 220V 50Hz AC.

For climate and weather see the section on Malaysia.

Harbours and anchorages

Changi

Charts BA *3831, 2569*

Cruising yachts will normally make for this anchorage off the Changi Sailing Club.

Approach

The anchorage lies on the NE corner of Singapore Island. Proceed around to Serangoon Harbour and anchor where indicated in Loyang Bay off the pier in 12–20m.

VHF Ch 16, 69 for Changi Sailing Club.

Dangers

1. In the approaches yachts with masts higher than 49m must keep outside the restricted area shown on BA *3831*.
2. Care is needed of the numerous craft using the eastern channels.

Mooring

Data 160 moorings. 300 dry berths ashore.

Anchor off the pier in Loyang Bay and then take the yacht tender around to Changi Sailing Club to sort out a mooring.

Shelter Adequate although there is continual wash from passing craft.

Authorities Commodore, club staff.

Anchorage It is often difficult to get a mooring at Changi, such is the demand, so yachts will often anchor out in Loyang Bay or under the lee of Ubin Island on the opposite side of the fairway. These spots are as good as any and you can still get temporary membership at the club and use the facilities.

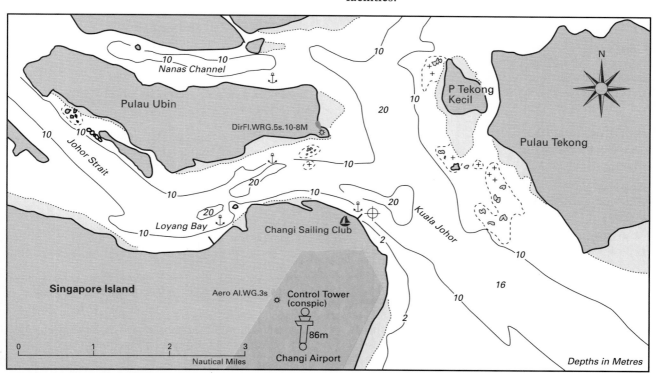

CHANGI AND NEARBY ANCHORAGES ⊕ 01°24′N 104°0′E

Facilities
Water At the club.
Repairs Slipway up to 10m and 6 tons. Repairs can be arranged.
Provisions Some shopping nearby.
Eating out Restaurants and local stalls. Good seafood at the beach restaurants.
Other 24 hour security. Library and chartroom. Swimming pool. Bus and taxi into town.
Changi Sailing Club, 32 Netheravon Road, Changi, Singapore 1750. (Can be used as a mailing address). ☎ (65) 545 2876 *Fax* (65) 542 4235.

General
Changi is a popular place for cruising yachts to stop and the club is a convivial and convenient place to be. To get into Singapore take the No. 29 bus from behind the club to Tampines where you can transfer to the MRT.

Ponggol Marina
Charts BA *2586*

Approach
Through the Johor Channel to the entrance at Ponggol. The first approach should only be made by day.

Mooring
Data 62 berths. 800 dry berths. Visitors berths.
Berth Where directed or anchor off.

Facilities
Services Water and electricity. Showers and toilet.
Repairs 70-ton travel-hoist. Most repairs can be carried out or arranged.
Other Clubhouse. Restaurant/bar.
Ponggol Marina, Lot 73, Ponggol, 17th Ave, Singapore 820000. ☎ (65) 385 3920 *Fax* (65) 385 3923.

General
Ponggol is more a place to haul out than a place to berth. It is a bit out of the way but there is public transport into downtown Singapore.

Keppel Marina
Charts BA *3833*
Marina 01°15'·9N 103°48'·66E WGS 84

Approach
The marina lies on Sentosa just S of West Keppel Fairway.

Mooring
Data 50 berths. 200 berths ashore under cover. Max LOA 25m.
Berth Where directed. Pontoons.

Facilities
Services Water and electricity. Showers and toilets.
Repairs 70-ton travel-hoist. 15,000lb marine forklift for dry berths. Most repairs including mechanical and engineering repairs, GRP repairs, wood repairs and painting and antifouling.
Keppel Marina, Bukit Chermin Road, Singapore 098832. ☎ (65) 270 6665 *Fax* (65) 273 7900.

General
Keppel Marina is more of a dryberth marina and yard than a fully fledged marina as such.

Singapore Yacht Club
Charts BA *3833*
The Singapore Yacht Club may have a berth available, but it is necessary to check and book a berth in advance.

Mooring
Data 30 berths. 120 dry berths.

Facilities
Services Water and electricity. Clubhouse.
The club plans to build new facilities on the W coast.
Singapore Yacht Club, 249 Lalan Buroh, Singapore 609832. ☎ (65) 265 0931 *Fax* (65) 265 3957.

Raffles Marina
Charts BA *3833*

Approach
The marina lies on the SW of Singapore Island a short distance up the Johor Strait. Merambong Islet is best left to port to avoid the Merambong Spit running out N of it.
VHF Ch 77 for marina office.

Mooring
Data 165 berths. Visitors berths. Max LOA 20m+8 megayacht berths.
Berth Where directed. Finger pontoons.
Shelter Good all-round shelter.
Authorities Harbourmaster and marina staff. Charge band 2.

Facilities
Services Water and electricity at all berths. Shower and toilet block.
Fuel Fuel quay.
Repairs 70-ton travel-hoist. Covered workshops. Mechanical and engineering repairs. GRP and wood repairs. Electrical work. Spray painting facilities. Chandlers.
Contact: Marina Yacht Services Pte Ltd ☎ (65) 862 4319/20 *Fax* (65) 862 4431.
Provisions Mini-market.
Eating out Restaurant and bar.
Other Telephone and fax services. Tennis, pool, and a gymnasium.
Raffles Marina, 10 Tuas West Drive, Singapore 638404. ☎ (65) 861 9000 *Fax* (65) 862 2280.

General
The marina is a bit out of the way from town, but downtown Singapore can be reached by taxi or bus.

Other services

Boatyards
Natsteel Marine, 72 Loyang Way ☎ 543 1651
Chandlers
Intermarine Supply Co. 12 Tuas 11 ☎ 863 3396
Marine International, 388 East Coast Road ☎ 447 3004
Electronics
Codar, 315 Outram Road ☎ 221 0310
Communication Systems, 67 Ayer Rajah Cres. ☎ 776 5191
VDO Southeast Asia, 51 Ayer Rajah Cres. ☎ 778 7772
Rico Pte Ltd, 80 Genting Lane. ☎ 745 8472
Charts
Motion Smith, 78 Shenton Way. ☎ 220 5098
Inflatables and liferafts
Supratechnic Pte Ltd, 16 A Joo Koon Circle. ☎ 862 2100
W H Brennan, 47 Loyang Way. ☎ 542 9722
Refrigeration
Marine Air-Con Systems, Hougang Ave 4. ☎ 288 0668
Rigging
Marintech Marketing, 101 Kitchener Road. ☎ 298 8171
Sails
Hip Jack & Co, Blk 642 Rowell Road. ☎ 291 5259
Sail Spirit Ltd, 1210 East Coast Road. ☎ 752 1088

Indonesia

For general information on Indonesia see *Cruising Guide to Southeast Asia Volume II* by Stephen Davies and Elaine Morgan. For information on the Riau Islands including Batam see *Riau Islands Cruising Guide* by Mathew Hardy available locally.

Batam

Charts BA *3831*, *3833*
There are two marinas on the N of Batam used by cruisers as an alternative to the marinas and anchorages around Singapore.

Nongsa Point Marina

Lies on the NE tip of Batam.

Mooring
Data 178 berths. Visitors berths.
Berth Where directed. Finger pontoons.
Shelter Good shelter.
Authorities Harbourmaster and marina staff. Charge band 2.
Nongsa Point Marina ☎ (62) (778) 761 333 *Fax* (62) (778) 761 330.

Facilities
Services Water and electricity at all berths. Showers and WC.

The marina is part of a hotel and condominium complex. Ashore there are restaurants and bars, mini-market, pool, and telephone and fax facilities. Mini-bus connection to other parts of the island.

Marina Cove

Lies S of Sekupang on the NW of Batam.
VHF Ch 14.
Dangers Care needed of shallow patches in the approaches.

Mooring
Data 60/150 berths. Visitors berths.
Berth Where directed. Finger pontoons.
Shelter Good shelter.
Authorities Harbourmaster and marina staff. Charge band 2.
Marina Cove Resort, Marina Clubhouse, Waterfront City, Batam. ☎ (65) 276 5179 *Fax* (65) 225 7526.

Facilities
Services Water and electricity at every berth. Showers and WC.

The marina is part of a resort as yet unfinished. There are restaurants and bars and a mini-bus shuttle operates to Batu Ampar and Nagoya where there is good shopping. The marina is next to Teluk Senimba ferry terminal which operates a service to Singapore.

Sumatra

Yachts crossing to Sri Lanka from Langkawi have reported putting into Sabang at the N end of Sumatra for a break en route. Details are a bit sketchy but it seems if you cite the usual engine problem or other minor breakdown then there are not too many problems.

Yachts with a sailing permit for Indonesia will sometimes take the outside route down the western Sumatran coast and report that it is an idyllic cruising area.

Malaysia

Current situation

Malaysia is a stable democracy although it has always been under the sway of the ruling party, the United Malay National Organisation (UMNO), since independence. The present Prime Minister, Datuk Seri Mahathir Mohamad, usually known as Dr Matathir, rules with an iron hand and is known for his Malay chauvinism and outspoken opposition to Western values, although none of this affects the visitor who will recognise many old British institutions and practices in the country. By and large the officials here are fair and there is less obvious corruption than in many other Southeast Asian countries.

Piracy in the Malacca Strait is now much diminished after the Singaporean, Malaysian and Indonesian authorities decided to co-operate on anti-piracy measures in 1992 and the few cases which occur here concern commercial shipping and not yachts. In 1993 there were no reported incidents involving pleasure craft although commercial shipping in the Malacca Strait is still a target for pirate attacks. Patrol boats are much in evidence up and down the coast keeping an eye on Indonesian boats smuggling workers into Malaysia and as a by-product the waters are well policed and piracy towards yachts virtually unknown in the last five years.

Documentation and visas

Normal boats papers and a valid passport for all crew members must be carried. You may be asked for a radio licence and insurance documents although there seem to be few problems if you do not have them.

Most visitors to Malaysia from Europe, the USA and Commonwealth countries will automatically get a visa on entry for 60 days. This is extendible up to 3 months and after that period you can go to Singapore or Thailand by road or air and on your return you will automatically be granted another 60 days extendible to 3 months.

Entry formalities

On entering territorial waters a yacht should proceed to the nearest port of entry. From S to N the ports of entry commonly used are at:

Port Dickson
Port Klang
Lumut
Penang
Kuah at Langkawi

You can also clear in at Malacca and Sebana Cove Marina. In most places, with the exception of Lumut, the relevant offices will be grouped together or within a short distance of each other. You must bring the following documents: ship's papers, all crew passports, last port clearance papers, crew and passenger list, and if you have them a radio licence, certificate of competence and insurance documents.

A Q flag and a Malaysian courtesy flag should be flown.

Note It is a serious crime to bring illegal drugs (of any sort, but especially heroin) and firearms into Malaysia. Firearms must be declared on entry. Smuggling illegal drugs into the country can carry the death penalty on conviction.

Go to the Marine Department to register your arrival, to immigration to be stamped into the country, to customs and the health office, and finally to the harbourmaster. You will be given various slips of paper to carry from one department to another and there is a modest charge for stamps on some of the documents such as the immigration registration.

On exit you must again visit all these departments and obtain a port clearance form. You will not need to clear immigration if you are going to another port in Malaysia. Officially you must clear in and out of each port you visit, but in practice many yachts will just clear in at the first port of entry and then clear out for the last port they visit before leaving Malaysia where they will again clear in and out, visiting immigration this time to be stamped out.

If you want to leave a yacht in Malaysia this is a fairly straightforward process and does not involve a bond. Simply visit immigration and customs and then the harbourmaster where the requisite paperwork will be handled. On entry it is a simple process to again visit these offices to collect the necessary paperwork for the yacht.

Data

Area 329,750km^2 (127,317M^2) (includes peninsular Malaysia and Sabah and Sarawak)
Frontiers 2669km (1441M). Brunei 381km (206M). Indonesia 1782km (963M). Thailand 506km (273M).
Coastline 4675km (2524M) total. Peninsular Malaysia 2068km (1117M).
Maritime claims Territorial 12M. Exclusive economic zone 200M.
Population 18,750,000
Capital Kuala Lumpur
Time zone UT+8
Language Bahasa Malay. Cantonese. English is widely spoken.
Ethnic divisions Malay and other indigenous 59%, Chinese 32%, Indian 9%.
Religion Malays mostly Muslim, Chinese Buddhist, Indians Hindu.
Public holidays
  Jan 1 New Year's Day
  Feb 1 City Day (Kuala Lumpur)
  May 1 Labour Day
  Jun 1 Yang di Pertuan Agong Birthday
  Aug 31 Malaysian Day
  Dec 25 Christmas
Moveable
  Jan/Feb Chinese New Year
  Apr/May Wesak Day
  Ramadan (Lunar calendar)
  Jul Hari Raya Haji
  Sep/Oct Mohammed's Birthday
  Oct/Nov Deepavali
There are many other national and local festivals and holidays as can only be expected from this intricate mix of Muslim, Buddhist, and Hindu cultures.

Government The Confederation of Malaysia was formed in 1963. It consists of 13 states in peninsular Malaysia and Sabah and Sarawak. The 13 states are ruled by Sultans, usually in direct succession from a royal family. Every 5 years an election is held for the Yang di-Pertuan Agong or 'King' of Malaysia. An elected government handles the real power and economic and law-making apparatus in the country. The UMNO party has been in power since 1963.

Disputes Dispute over the ownership of the Spratly Islands with China, Philippines, Taiwan and Vietnam. The state of Sabah is claimed by the Philippines. The old frictions between Singapore and Malaysia have largely been resolved. Some friction with Thailand over smuggling. Some irritation with Indonesia over the smuggling of workers into Malaysia.

Crime In general Malaysia is a safe country to travel in and there are few incidences of violence or robbery. Around Langkawi there was a problem in the past with smuggling between Thailand and Malaysia, but this has been pretty much eliminated and a large patrol boat stationed here keeps it that way. Piracy in the Malacca Straits is confined to the Indonesian side and to big ships. The crew on Malay fishing boats may look piratical, the boats look piratical as well, but they are a friendly lot and no danger. Theft from boats is infrequent, but take all precautions and lock the yacht securely before going ashore.

You should be aware that drug smuggling in Malaysia is punishable by death, so do not accept packages from strangers or acquaintances and pack your own bag.

Note Parts of Malaysia including Langkawi have predominantly Muslim populations and topless sun-bathing is offensive. It is also offensive for men to go into Muslim villages with bare torsos. Dress appropriately if you are going ashore.

Travel
Internal

Good air, rail and road links. Ferries link some of the islands or coastal towns. Car and motorcycle hire in some tourist areas.

Air Internal routes are nearly all operated by the national airline MAS. There are useful links between Langkawi, Alor Setar, Penang, Kuala Lumpur, and Johore Bahru or Singapore. There are also numerous links to Sabah and Sarawak.

Rail There are two main lines running close to the E and W coasts. The W coast line runs from Singapore to Kuala Lumpur and on to Penang and then to Thailand. The service is reliable, clean and cheap. It is much to be recommended and is worth taking a trip just for the trip itself.

Coach Most places in Malaysia are connected by coach and the service is efficient and cheap. Try to get an air conditioned bus if possible. At holidays and weekends it pays to book in advance.

Hire cars and motorcycles In the tourist areas (such as Langkawi and Penang) there are numerous hire car and motorcycle companies. Rates are cheap.

Taxis and rickshaws Taxis are common and will

either have a meter or you pre-pay for your destination. There are also numerous share-taxis which run along a more or less predetermined route. Long distance taxis operate on a full complement of four and are a cheap way of getting around. In places such as Penang there are rickshaws but these now charge an exorbitant price and are more of a tourist attraction than a means of transport.

Ferries There are numerous ferry services between Langkawi and Penang and Singapore and peninsular Malaysia. The ferries are often fast catamaran-type vessels. Ferry services also link other places along the coast.

International
Connections by air, land and sea.

Air Most international flights are from Kuala Lumpur. From here it is possible to fly almost anywhere in the world. The national airline MAS gives good deals on tickets and has an extensive international network using modern aircraft. There are some international flights from Penang and in the future there may be international flights from Langkawi. It is also possible to find flights out of Singapore.

Land There are good rail and road connections with Thailand and Singapore.

Practicalities
Mail Reliable and efficient. You can send letters to Poste Restante but it is better to use a private address if possible. If you are having duty-free items sent out get them sent to Langkawi which is a duty-free island. (See the notes on Langkawi.)

Telecommunications IDD system. Country code 60. Phone cards and credit card dialling to some countries including the UK, USA and Australia. Digital mobile phones with a GSM card work if your supplier has an agreement in Malaysia. Fax service from agencies and hotels in the larger centres. The telecommunications system is adequate and in general there are no problems dialling in and out.

Currency The unit of currency is the Malaysian dollar or *ringgit* divided into 100 *sen*. The *ringgit* used to be tied to the Singapore dollar but is now one of the currencies in the basket of ASEAN currencies. Rates of exchange have been reasonably stable over the last 5 years although it lost value with the Southeast Asian slump of 1997.

Banks and exchange In any city or tourist resort there are banks which will change travellers cheques or cash and give cash advances on major credit cards. Banks are open from 0830–1200 and 1300–1600 Monday to Friday. In some provinces including Langkawi, all offices and shops close at midday Friday and all day Saturday, but are open on Sunday as a normal day of business. There are also ATMs which will take major credit cards. Many shops and restaurants accept credit and charge cards.

Medical care Is generally very good in the cities and larger centres. There are well-staffed and equipped hospitals in the larger centres and tourist resorts and doctors are often trained in Britain or the USA. The cost of medical care is medium but it is advisable to have private medical insurance. The pharmacies are well stocked and there are few problems in obtaining any of the drugs you need. There are also numerous Chinese herbal centres and shops selling Chinese remedies.

In the major towns and big resorts the water is generally safe to drink. If you are unsure drink bottled water. For the most part any problems will be a reaction to local micro-organisms in the water to which you are not accustomed.

Electricity 220V 50Hz AC.

Curiosities and culture
Sons of the soil In 1969 violent riots broke out between the Malays and the resident Chinese population. The source of the dissent was the extent to which the Chinese controlled companies and business and the extent to which Malays were given privileges in land ownership, business licences and opportunities and positions in the government bureaucracy. Following the riots the government introduced the title *bumiputra* which means 'sons of the soil' and stipulated wide ranging reforms which gave the *bumiputras* more advantages. One of the main reforms was to define the amount of a company's shares which a *bumiputra* must hold in an attempt to wrest control of the nation's business away from the Chinese. Much of the talent and a lot of the wealth in Malaysia disappeared overnight as the Chinese left in disgust and it is fair to say that there is a good deal of resentment to this day.

While it was necessary to balance the wealth of the resident Chinese against the poverty of the native Malays, many feel that the concept of the *bumiputra* has done much to introduce laziness and minor corruption into Malay life when they are assured of job positions and opportunities over and above the other inhabitants of Malaysia. To a large extent the visitor doesn't see the effects of the system, but for anyone working here the sloppiness the system has introduced is all too evident.

Ancient rainforests Peninsular Malaysia has the most ancient rainforests in the world and the biodiversity of the region is astounding. In any anchorage away from centres of population the jungle teems with life and the extent of the flora and fauna is astounding. There are over 8000 species of flowering plants including 2000 trees. It has the world's highest tree, the *tualang*, which can reach 80m (260ft) and the world's largest flower, the *rafflesia*, which can reach one metre across and weigh up to 9kg, nearly 20lbs. There are 450 species of birds, 250 reptiles and 200 mammals. As for insects, there are an incredible 150,000 species.

Around Langkawi and any other places where you can get away from man you only need to sit in the cockpit with a pair of binoculars and marvel. There are huge flying sea eagles floating overhead, monkeys crashing through the canopy, bright flashes of colour from birds like hornbills, kingfishers, woodpeckers and sunbirds. It is not uncommon to see snakes swimming across a river or from an island to the shore as contrary to popular opinion, most of them swim very well. There are cobras including the spitting cobra, pythons including the reticulated python which is the world's longest snake at around 10m (32½ft) and not the anaconda as is commonly supposed, vipers and tree snakes. If you go ashore the sheer density of the jungle is off-putting and the best thing to do is to try and find an established path. Don't worry: most of the beasties there will retire when they hear you crashing through the undergrowth. Personally I try to make a lot of noise.

Eating out Eating in Malaysia is pure heaven with bounteous variety at unbelievable prices. You will find Chinese (Cantonese and northern and southern Chinese as well), Indian (again all regions), Malay and Indonesian dishes. Most of this food will be cooked fresh whether in an up-market hotel restaurant or at a market stall. Dishes often contain chicken, beef, pork or fish. Seafood is abundant with a wide range of fish and crustaceans at bargain basement prices. Add to this an abundance of fresh vegetables and tropical fruit and it is unlikely that anyone will not delight in the cuisine of Malaysia.

Strange fruits Apart from all the usual tropical fruits like pineapples, bananas, mangoes and pawpaws, Malaysia has a whole plateful of strange and assorted fruits. Some like the durian which smells like a sewer and tastes like sour ice cream are for aficionados only, and the durian for some reason has a lot of aficionados. Others should be tried and tried again. The rambutan is cousin to the lychee and tastes just as good. The mangosteen is the size of an orange but with a dark purple skin concealing white segments which taste like sweet and sour strawberries and grapes. The starfruit is a pale green and when cut has a star shape. It has a cool slightly sweet lime taste and is one of my favourite fruit juices. The custard apple or *zirzat* has a warty green exterior over a creamy white flesh that tastes of lemon. In the markets you can find stalls which do slices or segments of these fruits and so can taste all of them and then select what you want. You can also get a fresh fruit salad made up of those you fancy.

Useful books
Being an old English colony there are a number of local publishers in English and two English language daily newspapers.

Malaysia and Singapore Handbook Joshua Eliot. Footprint Handbooks.

Lonely Planet Malaysia, Singapore and Brunei Wheeler, Finlay, Turner & Crowther. Lonely Planet.

Remember a lot of Joseph Conrad's novels are set in Malaysia and Indonesia including *Lord Jim* and *The Shadow Line*.

Turtle Beach Blanche d'Alpuget. Penguin. On the arrival of the Vietnamese boat people and their detention ashore in horrific conditions.

Geography and climate
The coast Unlike Thailand, much of the W coast of peninsular Malaysia is made up of flat river deltas although there is often high land not too far away. Around Langkawi and in other places down the coast there are steep-to islands and coast jutting out of the sea, but not in the exaggerated way of the islands in Thailand. Like Thailand everything is covered in thick jungle and along the flatter parts of the coast there are extensive plantations of coconut and palm oil palms.

Coastal waters In the Malacca Strait the depths are everywhere below 100m and from Port Klang down to Singapore everywhere below 50m. Extensive shallows border the coast up to 10–15M off and in places like One Fathom Bank there are extensive shoals scattered across the width of the Malacca Strait. Off the coast there are also extensive drying mud flats bordered by large areas of mangroves. Around Langkawi you will often be sailing in waters just 3–4m deep for long periods and when you hit depths of more than 10m this is deep water around this archipelago.

Although the shallow depths are at first intimidating, you get used to following the contour lines and keeping an eye on the depth sounder. Because the water is fairly silty there is not a lot of fringing coral around the coast. For most of the coast you can sit on the 20m line which keeps you away from the shipping lanes further out and outside of the range of smaller inshore fishing boats. You will still meet lots of fishing boats although they tend to be in clusters off the main fishing ports.

The fishing boats are normally adequately lit although some will simply flash a light at you or will only turn their lights on when you are getting close. I won't pretend you will have any relaxed night sailing in the Malacca Strait, but you get used to it. One danger is unlit smuggling boats coming across from Sumatra, although they will usually keep well clear of you just in case you are a patrol boat. Closer inshore, there can be fishing platforms although these are now few and far between and most fishing seems to be by boat.

Most of the waters around the coast are murky and not at all clear. Visibility is often less than 2m. This is not because the waters are dirty but because of the river silt brought down and deposited by the numerous rivers in the Malacca Strait. Unfortunately manmade activities, mostly in developing tourist coastal projects, have severely exacerbated the situation by removing forest cover and allowing increased erosion. In the period 1989 to 1996 I have noted a discernible decrease in underwater visibility around the Langkawi archipelago and this can be directly related to the huge increase in coastal developments. Some estimates around the coast suggest there has been a 40% decrease in visibility over the last 20 years which can be directly attributed to an increase in the removal of jungle cover, coastal development and mining activities. It is ironic that tourist developments are killing off the main attraction by polluting the waters they are built close to.

Climate There are two distinct seasons corresponding to the two monsoon periods. The favoured season is during the northeast monsoon between November and April and the less favoured is the southwest monsoon between May and October.

The northeast monsoon is the dry season (although paradoxically it can be wet at Langkawi and Penang from September to December) and consequently the least humid season. Average temperatures range from around 31–32°C in November and December to 33–37°C in April. Temperatures are only a few degrees less at night. The average humidity at midday is around 66–71% over the season. The northeast monsoon will have settled down by mid-November and lasts through until mid-April with a consistent pattern. The best months are reckoned to be December, January, and February.

The southwest monsoon is from May to October. This is the hot season and later the wet season. Those unused to the tropics will find the humidity difficult to handle. Average temperatures are around 33–37°C from May through to October although temperatures will often reach 39–40°C. The average humidity is around 79–81% over the season. The humidity is uncomfortable at first throughout this season. The worst months are reckoned to be July, August and September.

At Penang	Av max °C	Av min °C	Relative humidity	Days 0·25 mm rain
Jan	32	23	68%	8
Feb	33	23	64%	7
Mar	33	23	64%	11
Apr	33	24	66%	14
May	32	23	66%	16
Jun	32	23	67%	12
Jul	32	23	67%	12
Aug	32	23	67%	15
Sep	31	23	69%	18
Oct	32	23	70%	21
Nov	31	23	71%	19
Dec	32	23	68%	11

Weather

Prevailing winds near the coast The prevailing winds in the area are basically determined by the monsoon season, but because the waters are much enclosed by large land masses, peninsular Malaysia on the E and Sumatra on the W, there is a lot of variation.

The wind blows from the northeast during the northeast monsoon and this is the favoured time to sail in this area when the wind is blowing off the land. However there is a distinct diurnal component promoted by sea and land breeze effects. The NE monsoon will often be held up in the afternoon by the sea breeze and augmented at night by the land breeze. By day you will often have to motor to get anywhere or there may be a NW or even W sea breeze when the NE monsoon is not fully developed

or in the transitional periods. At night you may well have to reef down as the land breeze/NE monsoon winds get up to 20–25kn, especially in the northern parts of the Malacca Strait. By mid-morning the wind will have died down and by afternoon it will often be calm or a light NW–W breeze again.

During the NE monsoon the diurnal effect of calm days and windy nights means it is worthwhile taking some care over where you anchor as although it may be calm or light NW–W in the late afternoon, the wind can get up in the night from the NE and there can be gusts off any high land.

During the SW monsoon there can be little wind in the Malacca Strait or strong southerlies blowing up the strait depending on the strength of the SW monsoon. When it is blowing strongly there are often squalls in the strait, especially around the N entrance. Throughout the strait this is the time when a *sumatra* is most likely. The diurnal effect is less pronounced during the SW monsoon because of the increased cloud cover over the land. Where a sea breeze does occur it will augment the SW monsoon and likewise any land breeze at night will diminish the effect of the SW monsoon.

At Penang	Prevailing winds	Calms
Jan	N–NE/45%	20%
Feb	N–NE/35%	20%
Mar	N–NE/35%+SW–W/35%	30%
Apr	S–SW–W/35%	30%
May	variable	35%
Jun	S–SW/25%	40%
Jul	S–SW/30%	35%
Aug	S–SW–W/35%	35%
Sep	variable	35%
Oct	variable	30%
Nov	N–NE/35%	30%
Dec	N–NE/50%	20%

Locally named winds
Bohorok Warm fall wind in Sumatra.
Sumatra Violent squall usually accompanied by rain and lightning in the Malacca Strait.

Gales
Gales are rare and winds of over 30kn account for around 1% of observations. These are mainly from squalls and particularly from *sumatras*. At the N end of the strait there is a marked increase to around 5% for winds over 30kn. Depressions do not normally travel over this area.

Tropical storms
Do not normally effect these low latitudes. Only two tropical storms have travelled close to the N entrance to the Malacca Strait in the last 50 years.

Thunderstorms and waterspouts
Thunderstorms are common in the area. They mostly occur during the SW monsoon and in the transition periods, but also occur during the NE monsoon. They can be spectacular affairs with a great deal of lightning, especially over high land. It is common to see thunderstorms most evenings in this area and lightning strikes do occur. In 1996 during the Raja Mudra regatta a small fishing boat

was hit by lightning and a fisherman's hand blown off. One of the competitors in the race noticed the fishing boat in distress and was able to provide assistance until the fisherman was rescued. These thunderstorms are often accompanied by squalls although mostly the wind will be in the range of 20–30kn and only last for an hour or two.

The exception to this is a *sumatra* which normally occur between April and November. They mostly occur in the evening and move from Sumatra itself in a roughly easterly direction to peninsular Malaysia. They can be spotted by a dark bank of cumulonimbus and are accompanied by an impressive lightning display and heavy rain. They can last anything from an hour to 4–5 hours and winds may reach gale force and above for brief periods. Winds up to 40–50kn have been regularly recorded. The squalls can hit in an instant with winds getting up to 30–40kn from a flat calm or a light breeze. You can expect 4–5kn *sumatras* a month from April to November with the area of highest frequency at the northern end down to the middle of the Malacca Strait.

Waterspouts are common in this area and I have had one close encounter at less than a mile away in the Langkawi archipelago.

Tides

In the Malacca Strait the tides are semi-diurnal with the time of the tide getting progressively later going down the Malacca Strait. Thus the tide at Iyu Kecil in the approaches to Singapore Strait is 10½ hours later than at Langkawi at the N end of the Malacca Strait. In general the tide sets SE down the Malacca Strait on the flood and NW out of the Malacca Strait on the ebb. With luck you can catch the tide on the flood for a good distance down the strait because it will be getting progressively later the further down you go. It is certainly possible to catch it from Langkawi just about down to Lumut in one go. On the ebb you will invariably encounter some tidal set against you although the prevailing NW current mitigates against the tidal stream (see below).

The tidal range varies from N to S in the Malacca Strait. At springs the range at Langkawi is 3·2m (10ft 5in), at Lumut 2·7m (8ft 9in), at One Fathom Bank 3·7m (12ft), after which it decreases to 1·8m (5ft 10in) off Melaka and then increases again to 2·6m (8ft 5½in) off Iyu Kecil. The range is considerable enough to mean that care is needed around the numerous shoal areas, especially off One Fathom Bank.

The tidal streams vary considerably and are affected by the constant NW-going current in the Malacca Strait. Tidal streams in the deeper water of the Strait are usually around 1–1½kn at springs except around One Fathom Bank where streams are variable but have been recorded at 3–4kn. Likewise in the shallow waters and channels close to the coast rates may be stronger, up to 2–3kn at springs. In general rates are less at the N end (around 1–1½kn off Kuah) and stronger at the S end, although at the

bottom of Singapore rates again decrease.

The tidal range at springs can expose considerable areas of mud when the tide is out and it pays to work out when to go ashore and when to come back if you do not want to be wading ashore through black sticky mud.

Currents

Currents in the Malacca Strait are generally from the SE in a NW direction throughout the year. The rate is on average ¾ of a knot although it can be less at times. At the N end of the strait there may be a weak SE set from May to September. Tidal streams as described above are the most important feature around the coast.

In this enclosed area the seas are seldom large and even wind against tide or current does not raise large seas.

Visibility

In 1997 smoke and haze from forest fires on Sumatra severely reduced visibility in the Malacca Strait and there were a number of collisions between ships and probably a fair number of small fishing boats that were run over and not reported. The sound of fog horns was commonplace in the strait and navigation was difficult and at times dangerous for yachts. Although the reduced visibility was put down to the dry conditions promoted by an El Niño year causing forest fires on Sumatra to burn out of control, reduced visibility has occurred from forest fires in other years, notably 1992, which was also a bad year for smoke and haze across the strait.

It is likely in the future that forest fires on Sumatra will get out of control or be purposely lit to clear land and that when the SW monsoon is late, or brings little rain to damp the fires down, that visibility will be bad in the strait. In 1997 it also made living in Sumatra, Singapore and the Malay peninsula hell and was reckoned to be the equivalent of smoking two packs of cigarettes a day.

Navigation

The coast has been surveyed in recent years around major harbours and in the main shipping channels. For some areas there have been no obvious surveys since the 19th century. The admiralty and other charts have corrections of around 0·1 minute eastwards to agree with WGS 84 datum. For metricated charts this allowance seems to be reasonable although there have been reports of errors up to 0·3–0·4 minute of longitude. I cannot confirm these errors and for the most part found the metricated charts to be accurate. In some areas, such as around Langkawi, the old fathoms charts are still in use, although it is likely that they will be either metricated or deleted from the catalogue. Where possible I have given GPS co-ordinates using WGS 84 datum. Other co-ordinates are schematic and should be treated with caution.

Despite there being no obvious discrepancies it is still necessary to exercise considerable care when close to dangers to navigation and when approaching anchorages. Because so much of the coastal waters are shallow it is necessary to watch the tide and use transits to get in and out of some anchorages. Likewise it is necessary to take care over the channels leading into river harbours or between sandbanks and mudbanks leading to a harbour or anchorage.

One danger in these waters is large trees and logs washed down the rivers and into the strait. There are not inconsiderable numbers of very large water-logged trees and logs floating just above the water or at water level which can do considerable damage to a yacht if you hit one. I have had several close encounters at night and it is an adrenaline pumping experience. In fact I believe that some accounts of yachts hitting uncharted reefs and rocks are more likely to be yachts running into nearly submerged trees or logs. There is little you can do except keep a good lookout by day and pray by night.

Harbours and anchorages

This section includes only those commonly used harbours and anchorages along the coast of peninsular Malaysia. There are a whole host of other anchorages and small harbours and a good number of rivers which can be explored for part of their length. The description is from S to N.

Sebana Cove Marina

Charts BA *2585*
Entrance 01°24'N 104°07'E
Marina 01°24'·7N 104°09'·8E

Approach

The marina lies just under 3 miles up the Sungai Santi River opposite the E tip of Singapore Island. Care is needed in the approach to the river mouth as a sand bar extends from the N entrance point to about half way across the entrance. Enter on a course which takes you midway between the S entrance point and the middle of the entrance. If in doubt of depths call up the marina on VHF Ch 71. Ideally the approach should be made on a rising tide. The river itself is buoyed with port and starboard buoys right up to the marina. Pilotage can be arranged by the marina if necessary.

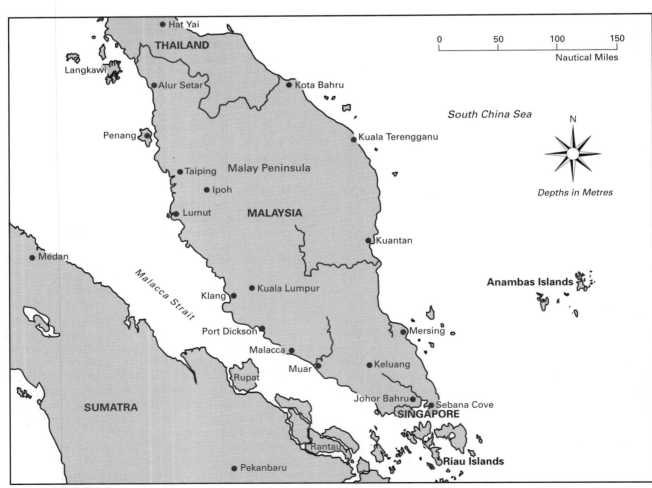

MALAY PENINSULA

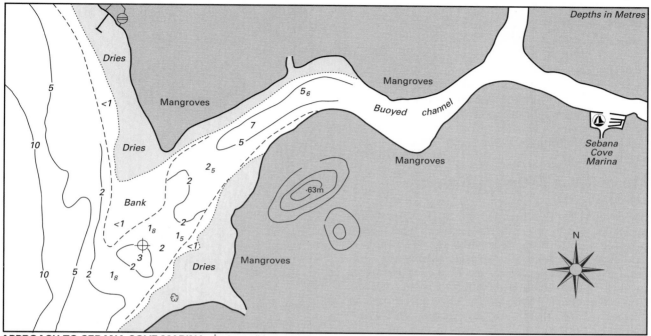

APPROACH TO SEBANA COVE MARINA ⊕ 01°24′N 104°07′E

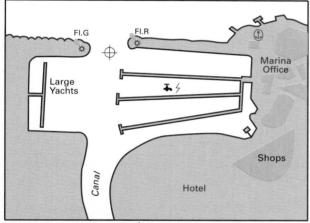

SEBANA COVE MARINA ⊕ 01°24′·7N 104°09′·8E

By night The channel buoys are lit Fl.G/Fl.R but a night approach is not recommended for the first entry into the river.

VHF Ch 71 for marina control. Call sign *SCM* (Sierra Charlie Mike).

Dangers Care is needed of the sand bank at the entrance as described above.

Note Speed limit in the river is 6kn and in the marina basin 3kn as long as you are not making excessive wake.

Mooring
Data 170 berths. Visitors berths. Max LOA 50m.

Berth Where directed. Finger pontoons.

Shelter Excellent all-round shelter.

Authorities Harbourmaster. Marina staff. Captain must report to the marina office after berthing. Authorities for clearing in and out are not stationed at the marina but the papers will be taken to the relevant authorities at 1100 and 1500 each day. If a yacht arrives after 1500 it can deliver the papers for clearing in for the next day to the office. Charge band 2.

Facilities
Services Water and electricity (110/220/420V) at every berth. Shower and toilet block.

Fuel Fuel quay in the marina.

Repairs Limited repair facilities. Most yachts will head for Singapore. There are plans to expand facilities in the future.

Provisions Mini-market. Duty-free zone. For better shopping go to Singapore.

Eating out Several restaurants and bars.

Other Exchange facilities. Telephone and fax communications from the office. Laundry service. Marina ferry service to Tg Belungkor where you can get a ferry to Singapore.

Sebana Cove Marina, PO Box 102, Bandar Penawar PO, 81900 Kota Tinggi, Johor Darul Takzim. Marina office ☎(07) 8252401 *Fax* (07) 8252054.

General
Sebana Cove Marina is part of a large shoreside development that includes a five star hotel, numerous condominiums and leisure facilities like a golf course, pools, a go-kart track, roller blade track and an archery range. It is a bit out of the way but affords all-round shelter and 24 hour security. To get to Singapore you can take the marina ferry to Belungkor or walk to the ferry station which connects with Changi on Singapore.

Johor Bahru

Charts BA *2586*

For many years the anchorage off the town to the E of the causeway has been technically prohibited and yachts have been informed they must move on. However recently (1997) there seem to have been a few foreign flag yachts anchoring off here and it may be worth trying. The anchorage is sheltered and handy to everything in Johor Bahru.

Muar River (Sungai Muar)

02°03'N 102°32'E

About 20M S of Malacca is the Muar River which has been used by a number of yachts. There is a bar over the mouth of the river with reported depths of just over one metre at low tide. Yachts normally cross from 3 hours plus on the flood and report no problems. The channel is reported to be marked. You can anchor off the town of Muar just inside the entrance. The officials are reported to be friendly and most things can be obtained in the town. It is about 45 minutes by bus to Malacca.

Malacca (Melaka)

Charts BA *3946*

Yachts sometimes anchor in the roadstead off the town. There is no harbour or river here. You need to anchor a fair way off, outside the buoys (around ½ mile out) and it is fairly exposed here. There is no protection from onshore winds and there is a fair amount of inshore traffic. The officials are on the waterfront and most facilities can be found in the town.

Port Dickson

Charts BA *1140*

An anchorage on the S side of the settlement. To the S of Port Dickson is the new development of Admiral Marina.

Approach

The approach is best made from the W between the Arang beacon (topmark ⦂) and the buoy marking the pipeline running out from the coast 0·6M to the N. There is also an inner passage between Bambek Shoal and the coast which has good depths. Care is needed of Bambek Shoal to the NW of Port Dickson which is extensive and has a significant part of it with less than 1m depths. In the immediate approach from the W there is no shoal water and a yacht can proceed into the roadstead between Port Dickson and Pulau Arang Arang just off the coast.

Conspicuous The settlement at Port Dickson will be seen and from the S the large development at Admiral Marina also stands out well. A number of chimneys and flares are conspicuous near the town. Arang beacon and Pulau Arang Arang can be identified in the closer approach.

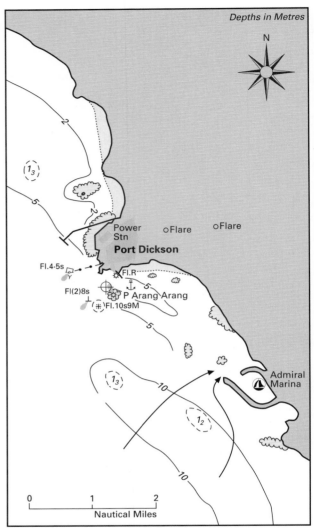

APPROACH TO PORT DICKSON AND ADMIRAL MARINA
⊕ 02°30'·9N 101°47'·7E

By night Although the approaches are well lit a night approach is not recommended. Use the light on Kuala Sepang Besar Fl.WRG.4s15-10M. The W red sector over 270°-311° covers Bambek Shoal. At the SE end of Bambek Shoal there is a light buoy Fl(2)R.10s. There is a fairway buoy LFl.10s2M S of Bambek Shoal SE buoy. The inner N has three light buoys from NW to SE: Q.G/Fl.G.2s/Fl.G.7s/Fl(3)G.10s. Arang beacon is lit Fl(2)8s. Pulau Arang Arang Fl.10s.9M. Buoy marking the end of the pipeline Fl.4·5s.

VHF Ch 16 for Port Dickson. Ch 69 for other yachts in the vicinity.

Dangers

1. From the N care is needed of Bambek Shoal as outlined above.
2. From the S care is needed of two patches of shoal water SE of Arang beacon
3. Off the SE side of Pulau Arang Arang there is a large area of shoal water although generally depths are 3m plus.
4. Yachts should not attempt to pass between the

buoy (Y) marking the end of the pipeline off Port Dickson as there may be floating hoses on the surface.

Mooring

Anchor off in the roadstead taking care not to obstruct the channel. There are convenient depths of 5–10m off the jetty. The bottom is mud and good holding. Shelter is good from northerlies but open to southerlies and to the *sumatra* from the W.

Authorities Immigration and customs are located in the town.

Facilities

Water and fuel ashore. Reasonable shopping for most provisions. Local restaurants. Banks and PO.

Admiral Marina

A large marina and apartment complex in an advanced stage of completion approximately 2½ miles SE of Port Dickson.

Approach

The approach should be made from the W and not directly from Port Dickson because of shoal water and several coral patches. Care is also needed of a shoal patch (least depth 1·2m) lying approximately 1M SW of the entrance.

Conspicuous The large high rise buildings of Marina Crescent at the SE end of the marina will be seen. The Marina Club building also stands out well.

By night Entrance lights are to be installed.
VHF Channel to be allocated but try on Ch 16.

Dangers
1. Care needed of the isolated shoal mentioned above.

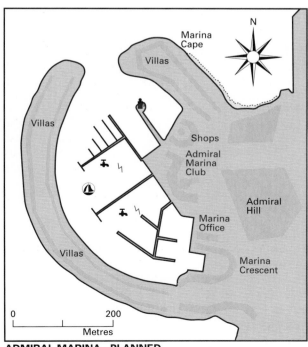

ADMIRAL MARINA - PLANNED

2. Care need of shoal water and coral patches to the N of the entrance.

Mooring

Data 180 berths. 94 stacking berths. Visitors' berths. Max LOA 60m. Depths 3·5–4m.
Berths Where directed. Finger pontoons.
Shelter All round.

Authorities Harbourmaster. Marina staff. Facilities for customs and immigration to be arranged so that yachts can clear in and out from the marina.

Facilities

Services Water and electricity to be installed at every berth.
Fuel Diesel and petrol dock at the entrance to the marina.
Repairs Basic repair facilities to be installed. Chandlers.
Provisions Supermarket.
Eating out Restaurants.
Other Laundrette, swimming pool and gymnasium to be built.
Admiral Marina BHD, Port Dickson, Selangor. ☎ (03) 248 1033 *Fax* (03) 241 7555.

General

The breakwaters for the marina are in place and basic infrastructure for yachts was expected to be ready by the end of 1998.

Port Klang (Kelang)

Charts BA *3453, 2152, 2153*

Approach

The approach is through the S Channel (Selang Klang Lumut) or through the N Channel (Selang Klang Utara). Both channels are deep (8–11m at MLWS) and marked by buoys or beacons into Port Klang.

Conspicuous The entrance to both channels is difficult to identify from the distance. The islands and coast are fringed with low-lying mangrove. Once up to the channel entrance the buoys (green conical and red can buoys) can be identified and lead to the North Port. The chimneys of the power station on the coast of the North Channel are conspicuous. Close to the North Port the cranes and gantries of the port will be seen. The channel leading into the South Port and the yacht club is marked by buoys and beacons.

By night Although the channel buoys and beacons are lit (Fl.G/Fl.R) a first time night approach is not recommended. Batu Penyu in the North Channel is lit Fl(2)5s10M.

Tides 5·7m at springs and around 1m at neaps. Tidal streams can be 3kn at springs and more if it has rained a lot and the river is running high. Assuming conditions are suitable there are numerous places in the shallow waters to anchor off and wait for the tide to turn.

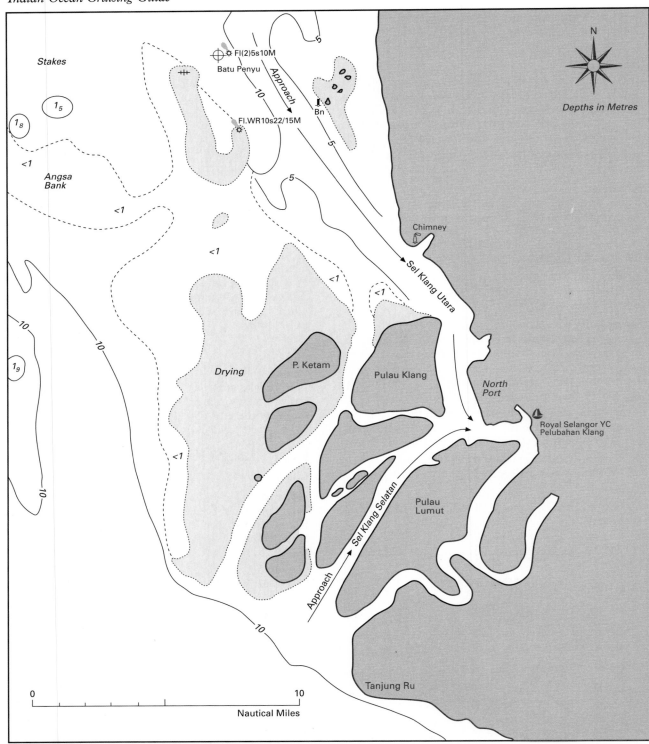

APPROACHES TO PORT KLANG ⊕ 03°13'·7N 101°12'·8E

VHF Ch 16 for Port Klang port control. Ch 72 for Royal Selangor Yacht Club (call sign RSYC1).

Dangers

1. Care is needed of fishing stakes off the coast and on some of the banks.
2. Commercial traffic has right of way in the deep water channels and must not be obstructed.

Mooring

Contact the yacht club to see if a mooring is available. Moorings are allotted on a temporary basis and the club does its best to accommodate visiting yachts.

Shelter Good all-round shelter.

Authorities The marine department, customs, health and immigration are situated in the South Port near

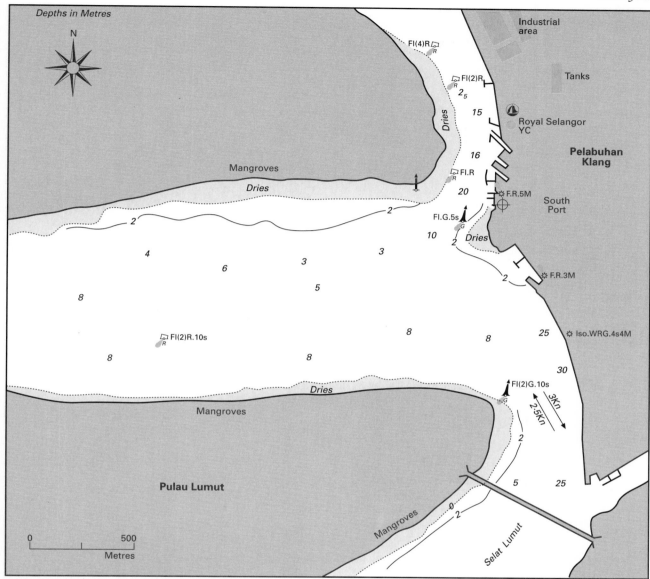

PORT KLANG ⊕ 3°00'·1N 101°23'·5E

the jetty. The yacht club makes a modest charge for mooring and use of the club facilities.

Facilities
Water On the yacht club pontoon.
Fuel At the yacht club.
Repairs The club has a slipway that can haul yachts up to 35 tons. It must be booked in advance and is often busy. Mechanical and electrical repairs. Chandlers and general hardware shops. Electricity on the club pontoon.
Provisions Good shopping in Klang.
Eating out Numerous restaurants and a restaurant/bar at the yacht club.
Other PO. Banks. Gas bottles can be filled. Telephone and fax at the yacht club. Laundry services. Taxis. Bus to Kuala Lumpur.
Royal Selangor Yacht Club, Jalan Limbongan, 42000 Port Klang, Selangor. ☎ (03) 368 6964 *Fax* (03) 368 8650 VHF Ch 72.

General
The yacht club opened in 1969 and in 1989 it obtained the title Royal Selangor Yacht Club. In 1990 the club organised the first Raja Mudra Regatta named in honour of the Life Commodore of the club, the son of the Sultan of Selangor. He is a keen sailor and well known on the local racing circuits. Recently he completed a circumnavigation in his Swan 68 *Jugra*. The club is a friendly place and makes visiting yachts welcome. There are club rooms, showers and toilets, a restaurant and bar and the club also provides a bum-boat to ferry you back and forth between the moorings and the club.

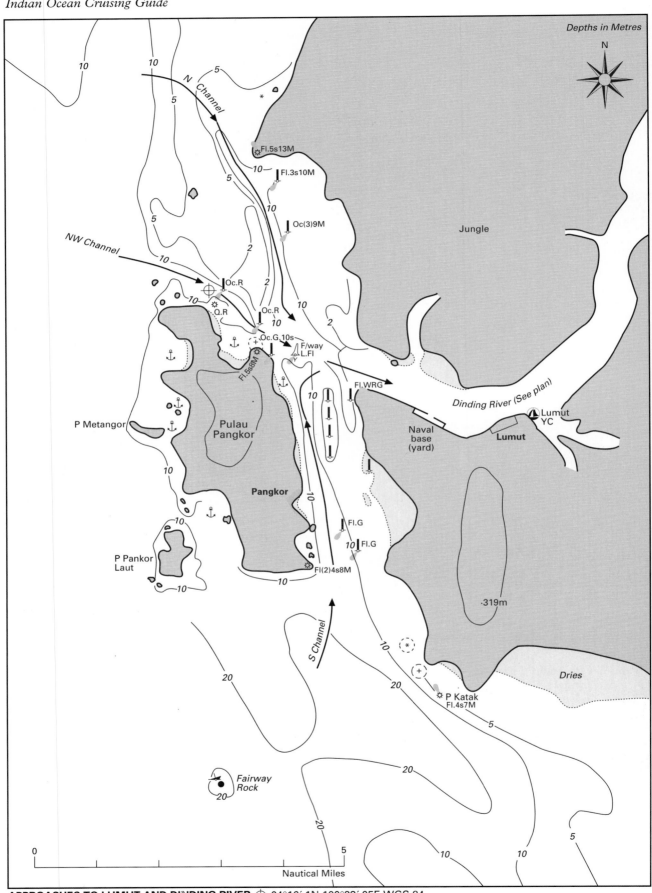

Depths in Metres

N

10 10 5 5

N Channel

*

Fl.5s13M

10 Fl.3s10M

10 Oc(3)9M

5

2

NW Channel

10

Oc.R

10 Oc.R

Q.R 10

2

10

2

Jungle

Oc.G.10s

F/way
L.Fl

Fl.5s8M

Fl.WRG

Dinding River (See plan)

Lumut
YC

P Metangor

Pulau
Pangkor

10

10

Lumut

Naval
base
(yard)

Pangkor

Fl.G

·319m

P Pankor
Laut

10

10

10 Fl.G

10

10

Fl(2)4s8M

S Channel

10

20

20

*

+

Dries

+

P Katak
Fl.4s7M

5

20

10

20

Fairway
Rock

20

20

5

10 10

0 5

Nautical Miles

APPROACHES TO LUMUT AND DINDING RIVER ⊕ 04°16′·1N 100°33′·05E WGS 84

Perak River

Charts BA *1353, 3944, 3945*
04°03'N 100°40'E (Fairway Buoy)

The Perak River can be navigated for at least 10M although passage is restricted at one point by overhead electricity cables. The entrance is buoyed and there are reported to be good depths for at least 10M. There is a yard up the river which some yachts have used.

Trawlers charging into Lumut on the tide are a good indication of the channel.

Platform type beacon in the W channel into Lumut.

Lumut (Dinding River and Kamphong Bahru)

Charts BA *792*

Lumut is the town inside the mouth of the river where there is a naval base and the Lumut Yacht Club with pontoon berths and some laid moorings. Further up the Dinding River there is Changs with laid moorings and posts to dry out on and further on up is Kamphong Bahru where there are laid moorings off the G7 chalet camp.

Approach
Three channels lead into the Dinding River as shown on the plan. The two easiest and deepest channels are the S Channel entered from the S end of Pangkor Island leading inside the island and Northwest Channel leading in from the W and across the N end of Pangkor Island. North Channel can also be used but it is not as easy to identify what is what in the approaches. Although it all looks a bit daunting in the approaches, the channels are in fact straightforward although it pays to keep an eye on the depth sounder. The channels are marked by buoys and beacons, the latter being a mixture of platform beacons and small towers.

Conspicuous Pangkor Island can be identified from some distance off. Closer in the islets off the N end of Pangkor Island and Pulau Pangkor Laut off the S end are easily identified. The outer beacons marking the channel are platform beacons which are conspicuous. Batu Mandi and T Awang Kecil light towers are both white girder towers and easily identified. In Teluk Dalam, the large bay on the N end of Pangkor Island, a hotel development is conspicuous. The village at Pangkor on the E side of Pangkor Island is easily identified. The mid-channel buoy (RW) where the three channels meet at the entrance to the Dinding River is easily identified. Once into the Dinding River the channel buoys are easily identified. The naval base on the S bank just inside the river mouth and Lumut town a little further on are conspicuous.

By night There are numerous lights in the approaches but without local knowledge I don't recommend a night approach.

Pangkor Island

Lights
T. Terengganu SE Pt Fl(2)4s8M
Hospital Rock Fl.R.6s5M
Batu Mandi Q.R.5M
T. Awang Kecil Fl.5s8M
Mainland coast
Pulau Katak Fl.4s7M
Putih Iso.4s7M
River Rock Fl.WRG.3s7-4M
Billik Ldg Lts 351°15' *Front* Oc(3)20s9M *Rear*
   Fl.3s10M
T. Hantu Fl.5s13M

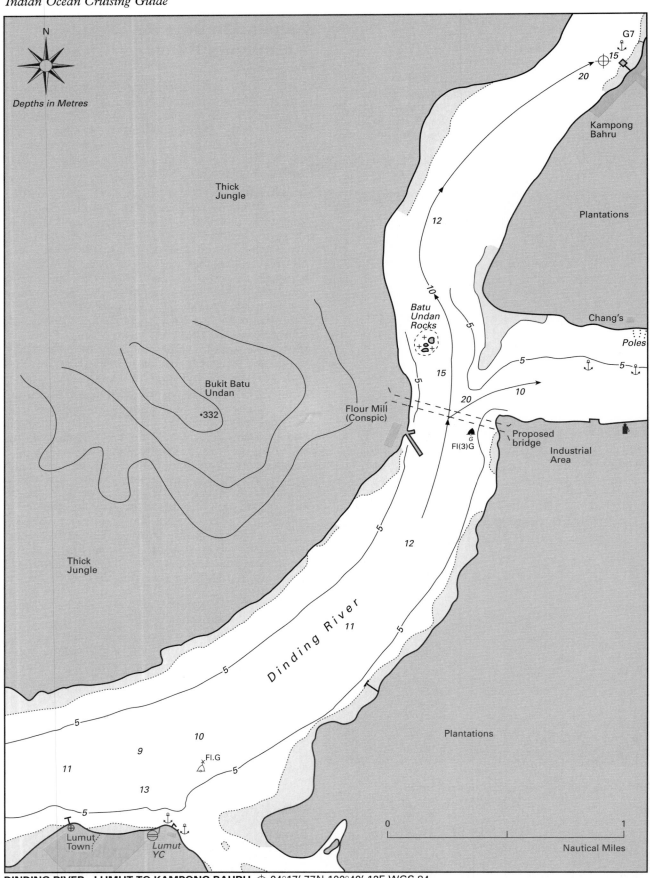

N

Depths in Metres

Thick
Jungle

G7

20

15

Kampong
Bahru

12

Plantations

10

Chang's

*Batu
Undan
Rocks*

5

Poles

Bukit Batu
Undan

•332

15

5

Flour Mill
(Conspic)

20

10

5

Dinding River

11

G
Fl(3)G

Proposed
bridge

Industrial
Area

Thick
Jungle

12

5

5

5

Plantations

5

10

9

.Fl.G

11

5

13

0   1

5

Lumut
Town

*Lumut
YC*

Nautical Miles

DINDING RIVER - LUMUT TO KAMPONG BAHRU ⊕ 04°17'·77N 100°40'·12E WGS 84

VHF Ch 69 for anyone listening on a yacht upriver. Ch 16 for harbourmaster at Lumut.

Dangers Large numbers of fishing boats including large trawlers are based here and numerous ferries criss-cross back and forth from Lumut to Pangkor. A good lookout needs to be kept in the immediate approaches and the channels. It is not always wise to follow the ferries and local boats which will take shortcuts across shoal water where there are insufficient depths for a keelboat.

Note The fishing fleet often anchors off Pangkor in one or other bays waiting for the flood to enter. When the tide turns they all charge in and so give a good indication of what the tide is doing. Tidal currents in the channels and in the Dinding River can be considerable at times and may run at 2–2½kn at springs.

Mooring

Yachts can make for one of three places not counting the anchorages around Pangkor Island or in the Dinding River.

Lumut International Yacht Club Lies at the E end of Lumut town just around the corner in Kuala Lumut. There are good depths in the channel which seldom are less than 7–8m and mostly 10m plus. Two floating pontoons with finger pontoons project out from the shore and clubhouse. Yachts up to around 100ft can be accommodated. Depths off the ends of the pontoons are around 5m at MLWS. There are also laid moorings which can be picked up to the NW of the club and a couple in shallower water to the SE of the pontoons. The latter afford the best shelter as there is less chop from the afternoon sea breeze that blows up the river. Likewise berths on the SE side are to be preferred. Shelter in general is good although there can be some wash from river traffic. Dinghies can be left on the pontoons.

Charge band Charge band 2 on the pontoons and a modest charge is made for the laid moorings.

Changs Lies around 2½M further up the Dinding River in a branch river on the right bank. From Lumut the large flour mill with a loading pier off it is conspicuous. The river is well buoyed up to the branch where Changs lies and up to the branch river there are mostly 10m plus depths. Once up to the branch keep near to the S bank to avoid the extensive sandbank on the NE corner (see plan). Part of the sandbank dries at low water. Dredging has been going on here so the navigable channel varies somewhat. A number of yachts on laid moorings will be seen and the best thing to do is pick up a free mooring and go across to Changs house and restaurant to see if moorings are available. Good shelter in this branch river but you are away from it all and it can be difficult to get into town. Dinghies can be hauled up on the beach.

Perak Yacht Club Right next to Changs on the W side is the Perak YC. No facilities are yet available to visiting yachts although it is planned to construct facilities.

Lumut International Yacht Club just past Lumut town.

The flour mill conspicuous on the port side on the way up to Changs and Kamphong Bahru.

The above-water rocks to be left just to port (shoal water on the starboard side) on the way up to Kamphong Bahru.

Kamphong Bahru Lies further up the Dinding River. From the flour mill it is necessary to keep close to the W side of the river to avoid the sandbank on the E side. Two large above water rocks will be seen on the W side and a yacht should pass just E of these rocks. There are a number of buoys but mostly depths are over 10m and often 15–20m. The village of Kamphong Bahru will be seen on the E side of the river and a number of yachts moored off the village will be also be seen. Pick up a mooring if one is free or anchor off. Depths are considerable at around 10–15m, but the bottom is mud and good holding. I left *Tetra* here for 6 months, mostly on anchor, and experienced no problems. Good shelter. Dinghies can be left on the pier off the village or at the G7 pier.

Note It is planned to build a bridge across the river from the bank opposite Changs to the other side. Surveys have been completed but work had not started in 1998. The last information was that it was to have an air height of over 20m under the highest span.

Authorities Immigration is a bus-ride away and customs and the harbourmaster are in Lumut. Customs is near the Lumut Yacht Club and the harbourmaster at the Pangkor ferry terminal.

Anchorage There are a few places up the river where you can anchor and around Pangkor Island a number of anchorages which can be used depending on the wind and sea. See the plan.

Facilities
Lumut International Yacht Club Water and electricity at every berth. Showers. Fuel in the town. A slipway with tractor and trailer where motor boats are hauled in and out. Dry storage ashore within a secure compound. Mechanical and minor engineering and electrical problems can be tackled. At the naval base there is a travel-hoist capable of lifting large pleasure yachts which is used by a contractor carrying out repairs and refits to pleasure craft. There are extensive workshops ashore. Reasonable shopping in Lumut town. Bar and restaurant at the yacht club. Other restaurants and bars nearby. Laundry in town. PO. Banks and ATM that accepts *Visa* and *Mastercard* for cash advances. Ferries to Pangkor and buses to Penang and Kuala Lumpur.
Lumut International Yacht Club, Lot 4182 Jalan Titi Panjang, 32200 Lumut, Perak. ☎ (05) 683 5191.

Changs Hose near the drying out posts although its potability is suspect. Fuel at the commercial docks opposite where the tugs berth. Concrete apron with posts to dry out alongside. Restaurant at Changs although it may not always be open. To get into town you will have to walk along a track through plantations for a good 30 minutes before you get to the road near Kamphong Bahru where you can get the local bus to Sitiawan. Alternatively if you have a RIB the easiest thing to do is head down the river to Lumut.

Kamphong Bahru Water and (cold) showers at G7. Small quantities of petrol by jerrycan at Kamphong Bahru. Limited shopping. A couple of basic Chinese restaurants and several Muslim restaurants (no alcohol). For shopping and other facilities it is a 20 minute bus ride into Sitiawan. Here there are several good hardware shops which stock some basic chandlery including sealants, paint and antifouling. Good shopping for provisions in several supermarkets and a good fresh fruit and vegetable market. Restaurants. Laundry. PO and bank. Buses to Lumut.

General
The river is a wonderful place flanked by thick jungle on the left bank and plantations on the right bank after the branch to Changs. There is

something appealing about chugging up a river and for the most part the Dinding River is well buoyed and the depths considerable.

Lumut is a bustling place serving the ferry terminal to Pangkor Island which is a popular destination for weekends and day trippers. The yacht club is a convivial enough place to stay and the bar and restaurant ashore has a shaded veranda overlooking the club swimming pool which catches just enough of the breeze to be a cool spot for a beer. On the road into Lumut town there are several good restaurants and bars that are used by yachties here as less formal watering holes.

Kamphong Bahru is a small village that I for one have a special affection for. There is a half reasonable restaurant ashore with good sweet and sour crab and cold beer. The locals are friendly and the yachting community convivial. A bus runs regularly into Sitiawan where most facilities can be found. Kamphong Bahru and Sitiawan have the charm of being almost entirely off the tourist map and I left the place with fond memories. It is a good place to leave a yacht if you need to get back home and *Tetra* survived the wet season virtually unscathed. Do get a cover made though, not for the rain but for the hordes of swallows that will use your

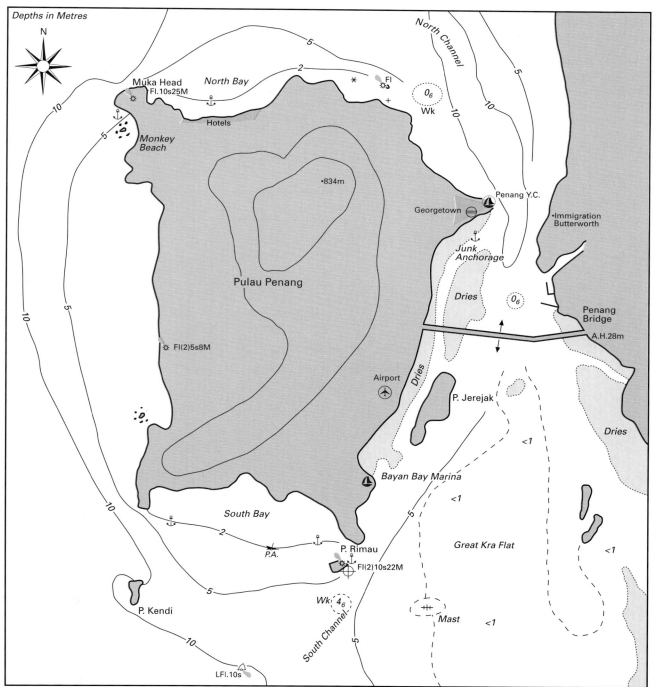

PENANG ISLAND ⊕ Pulau Rimau 05°14'.8N 100°16'.9E

rigging as a convenient perch and your deck as a public loo.

Pulau Penang (Pinang)

Charts BA *1366*

The large island lying just off the mainland between 05°15'N and 05°30'N. It has a navigable channel between the island and the coast although some care is needed to identify buoys and other navigation marks. The tide runs swiftly through the channel and often runs at 2–3kn for some time after the turn. This is not so important for the N approach where the tide runs less strongly if you are headed to the Penang Yacht Club or the old junk anchorage as they are fairly close to the NE end of the island, but is important when leaving to go S through the channel or when headed N up the channel to the Penang Yacht Club or the junk anchorage. A road bridge connects Penang to the mainland with an air height of 28m under the highest navigable arch. In theory you must get permission to pass under the bridge, but in practice no-one does.

Although the channel approaches from either end are lit, a night entrance into the channel between Penang and the mainland is not advised although the outer approach channels from the S and N are straightforward.

Yachts will normally make for the old junk anchorage or Penang Yacht Club. Some yachts go to Bayan Bay Marina close to the airport.

Bayan Bay Marina

Charts BA *1366*

A yard with laid moorings and shore berths at the S end of Penang Channel. The 'marina' is tucked around on the N side of Batu Maung Point to the E of the airport. The approach should be made from the SE to avoid the shoal water running out from Batu Maung Flat. Anchor off or go on the dock if there is room to inquire after a berth. Good shelter although there can be some chop across the bay and from craft using the S entrance to the channel.

Water and fuel available. Slipway at the yard. Most repair work including mechanical, engineering and electrical work can be arranged. Restaurants and bars nearby.

Bayan Bay Marina Club, 2 Sg Nibong, 11900 Bayan Lepas, Penang. ☎ (60) (4) 642 2339 *Fax* (60) (4) 642 2336.

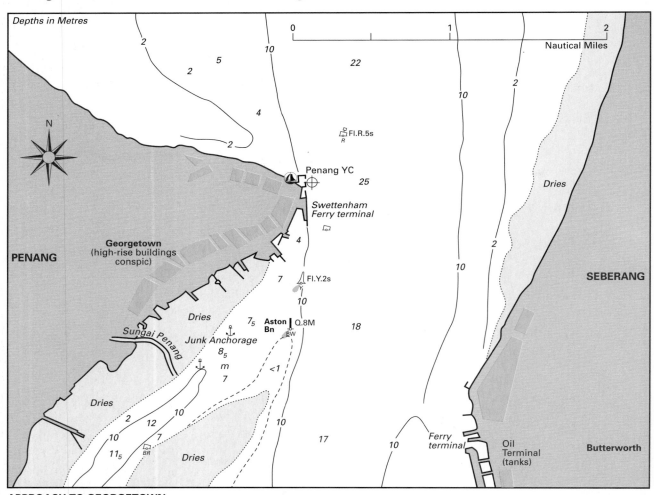

APPROACH TO GEORGETOWN
⊕ 05°25'·36N 100°20'·69E WGS 84

Junk Anchorage (Georgetown)

Charts BA *3732*

Anchor off the shanty town on stilts and rough piers along the shore where shown. You usually have to anchor in quite deep water, often 15–20m, despite what the chart shows. Care is needed not to get too close in as the bottom comes up quickly from considerable depths. The bottom is sticky black mud and good holding, but makes a mess of everything when you haul the anchor up. There is a considerable current here and it can be blowy at times, especially at night if there are thunderstorms around and a squall blows through.

Although it is dirty, rolly from the wake of passing craft, and the tide rips through the channel, you are close to all the facilities in Georgetown. Take the dinghy ashore to one of the rough piers where it will usually be safe although it may pay to padlock it on.

There has been some talk of reclaiming the land here and prohibiting yachts from anchoring. In 1998 the anchorage was still in use.

For facilities in Georgetown see under Penang Yacht Club.

Penang Yacht Club

Charts BA *3732*

Approach

The Penang Yacht Club marina lies on the NE end of the island.

Conspicuous From the NW approach the large skyscrapers of Georgetown are easily identified and

The road bridge across the Penang Strait (air height 28 metres).

the buoys marking the deep water channel into Penang Channel are easily located. There will often be ferries or commercial shipping entering or leaving by the deep water channel and this makes finding it relatively easy. Once into the channel follow it down until you can identify the pontoons of the Penang Yacht Club. The masts of any yachts and the superstructure of motor yachts make identification

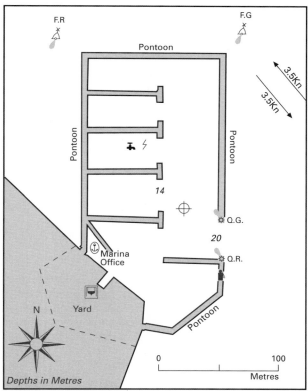

PENANG YACHT CLUB ⊕ 05°25′·36N 100°20′·69E WGS 84

Northern approaches to the Penang Yacht Club marina.

85

Pulau Rimau and lighthouse at the S end of Penang Strait.

straightforward. From the S follow the channel up until the Penang Yacht Club is identified.

By night A night approach from the N is feasible although the final approach is best left until daylight. A night approach from the S up the Penang Channel is not recommended.

Lights
From the S use
South Channel fairway buoy LFl.10s
Pulau Rimau Fl(2)10s22M
Bukit Teluk Tempoyak Besar Aero Fl.R.2·4s12M
Ldg Lts on 044° *Front* Fl.3s5M *Rear* Q.5M
Ldg Lts on 05° *Front* Fl.3s8M *Rear* Q.5M
Bridge navigable arch light Oc.WRG.10s10-8M
Aston Bn Q.8M
Buoy lights are correct for the entrance from seawards from the S.
From the N use
Muka Head Fl.10s25M
Fairway buoy Fl(2)7s
Deep water channel is lit (Fl.G/Fl.R) with direction of buoyage from seawards.
P Tikus Fl.3s10M
Fort Cornwallis Fl.R.2s16M
Marina is lit on extremities F.R/F.G for outer protective pontoons and Q.R/Q.G at entrance.

VHF Ch 72 for harbourmaster at Penang Yacht Club.

Dangers
1. The tide flows strongly in the immediate approach to the yacht club marina.
2. There is a considerable amount of traffic in the approaches and a good lookout must be kept.

Mooring
Data 130 berths. Visitors berths. Max LOA 160ft. Depths 8m+.

Berth Where directed or wherever there is a berth free. Finger pontoons.

Note The tidal stream flows strongly within the marina and causes tidal swirls and eddies. Some care is needed over berthing as the current makes manoeuvring difficult and there is not a lot of space to get in and out of some berths. You should have all fenders and lines ready before entering.

Authorities Harbourmaster. Customs is at Georgetown near the Penang Yacht Club and immigration is at Butterworth on the other side of the channel. Charge band 2.

Penang Yacht Club, No 3, Lebuh Penang, 10200 Pulau Penang. ☎ (04) 261 8860 *Fax* (04) 261 6902.

Facilities
Services Water and electricity at or near every berth. Shower and toilet block.
Fuel Fuel quay near the entrance.
Repairs Small yard with 100-ton travel-hoist. Some yacht repairs can be arranged including mechanical, engineering and electrical work. Some chandlery and good hardware shops. Sealants, paints and antifouling. With a bit of looking most things can be found here and there are specialist workshops scattered around Georgetown.
Provisions Good shopping for all provisions. Several large supermarkets in Georgetown. Ice available.
Eating out Restaurants of all types in Georgetown. You can choose from basic street stall food right up to very expensive cuisine in up-market surroundings.
Other PO. Banks and ATMs that take *Visa* and *Mastercard*. Laundry. Taxis and rickshaws although the latter now charge prodigious amounts and are more of a tourist side-show. Hire cars and motorbikes. Rail connections at Butterworth. Buses to most places from Butterworth. Ferry connections to Langkawi. Domestic and some international flights from Penang Airport.

General
Georgetown is a special place and well worth a stopover. It is slowly being submerged under high rise development, but there is still more than enough of the old town to see and really the best thing to do here is just wander around and poke your nose into shops and markets. The sights and smells of the predominantly Chinese community are everywhere from steaming soup and noodle shops to stalls selling market produce to stalls selling cheap radios to joss and incense shops to vast department stores. This is a prosperous community dedicated to the dollar of whatever origin.

Other Anchorages
North Bay Anchor off the Mutiara Hotel in the large bay on the N. The anchorage is really only suitable in calm weather as the NE monsoon blows straight in. Restaurants and bars and other facilities ashore. The Mutiara Hotel has been hospitable to visiting yachts in the past.
Monkey Beach On the SW side of Muka Head. Sheltered from the NE monsoon.
South Bay The large bay on the S has gently

sloping depths and reasonable shelter during the NE monsoon. The wreck of a cement ship that was run aground here is conspicuous in the bay.

Pulau Rimau There is a cove on the NE side that could be useful in southerlies.

Pulau Payar Marine Park

The isolated group of islands lying approximately 14M SE of Pulau Enggang in the SE approaches to Langkawi. The relatively high islands (Payar is 88m) are easily identified from the S or N. The islands are a marine reserve and there are moorings for yachts off the SE side of Pulau Payar. Although an open anchorage it is normally comfortable enough in the NE monsoon. Report to the reserve rangers on arrival.

The islands provide the best diving, in fact just about the only decent diving, in the vicinity, with good visibility and a wide range of fish and coral. Fishing is prohibited and the area is for diving and looking with or without tanks under the control of the authorities. There is also an observation platform moored off the rangers buildings with an underwater observation tank.

Pulau Langkawi

Situated on the west coast of Malaysia just under the Thai border, Pulau Langkawi is an archipelago of islands of which there are said to be 100, but like all similar claims this depends on how small you go when you are counting. In fact there is one large island, Pulau Langkawi, and several other significant islands on the S and E, notably Pulau

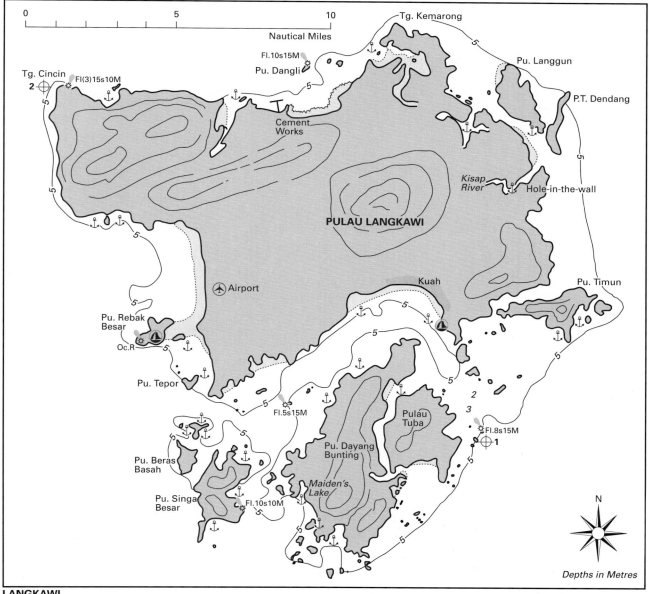

LANGKAWI
1 ⊕ 06°14'·5N 99°52'.6E Pu. Enggan Light 2 ⊕ 06°26'·3N 99°38'.8E Tg. Cincin Light

Dayang Bunting, Pulau Tuba and Pulau Singa Besar on the S, and Pulau Timun and Pulau Langgun on the E. It is a spectacular area with high cliffs, steep-to islands and lush tropical forest. The islands and anchorages are spectacular with jutting pillars of rock, fjord-like inlets dripping with vegetation, and deserted white sandy beaches. Ashore things vary between chic exclusive hotels with hot and cold running everything to simple fishing villages. Kuah on Langkawi island is the closest you get to a town after Penang.

There are numerous anchorages all around the archipelago and two marinas. Perusing the chart just turns up more anchorages and depending on the season there are lots of places where a yacht can anchor with care. A few are suggested here or are noted on the plan of the group. The area is mostly fairly shallow and approaches to anchorages require some care over navigation. A number of rivers empty into or near the Langkawi group and this makes the water a milky green and the bottom difficult to see. Out amongst the islands the water is clearer in parts, but for the most part you must still rely on the depthsounder when entering or leaving anchorages and avoiding shallow areas. It can be nerve-wracking sailing over large areas of water with just 3–4m under the keel until you get used to it. The anchorages are for the most part in fairly shallow water and you will have no problem with the holding which is predominantly mud or sand.

Kuah (Bass Harbour)

Charts BA *843*

Approach

The approach can be made from the SW through the islands or from the SSE through Selat Kuah. Care is needed over patches of shoal water in the approaches in both channels.

Conspicuous From either channel the islands can be identified with care. From the SSE the light structure on Pulau Enggang will be seen. Once into the SW channel the modern lighthouse (an inverted white cone shape) on Pulau Kedera stands out well.

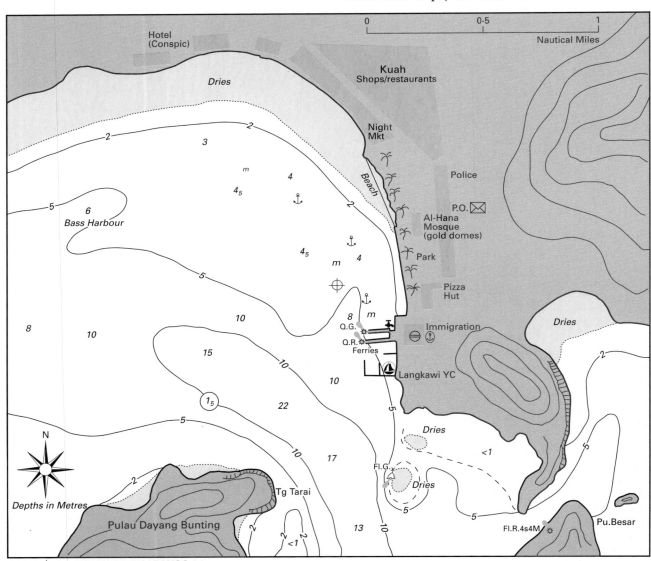

KUAH ⊕ 06°18′·58N 99°50′·9E WGS 84

From some distance off the modern developments around Kuah waterfront will be seen. Closer in the mosque with gold domes, the large statue of an eagle, and Kuah pier will be seen.

By night Although a night approach is possible it is not recommended for a first time entry. Use the following lights.

Pulau Enggang Fl.8s15M
Pulau Kedera Fl.5s15M
Beacon off Pulau Besar Fl.G.2s6M
The end of Kuah jetty is lit Fl.R.5s/Q.G/Q.R

VHF Ch 16 for port authorities. Ch 69, 72 for Langkawi Yacht Club and other yachts in the vicinity.

Dangers
1. There are numerous patches of shoal water in the approaches and care must be paid to your navigation.
2. High speed ferries come and go frequently and a good lookout must be kept.
3. Local fishing boats lay nets in the channels and a good lookout should be kept. They are usually attended by a longtail boat.

Mooring
Anchor off to the N of Kuah pier where convenient in 4–8m leaving the approaches to Kuah pier clear for the ferries. The bottom is mud and excellent holding. There is a pontoon on the pier for yacht tenders.

Shelter Good shelter although occasional squalls come off the mountains.

Authorities Immigration, customs and harbour-master are all conveniently located at Kuah pier.

Facilities
Water Either near Kuah pier or at Langkawi Yacht Club.
Fuel At Langkawi Yacht Club. For large amounts there is a fuel barge moored in the anchorage for which arrangements must be made in advance. Fuel can also be obtained at the fishing village on the NW side of Bass Harbour.
Repairs Some mechanical and electrical repairs. Hardware shops and a chandlers at Seaspeed in Kuah town. Langkawi is a duty-free zone and spares can be imported without duty. Most yachts choose to use Seaspeed as they are used to handling packages arriving for yachts. Seaspeed Boat and Yacht Supplies SDN, 51, Jalan Pandak Mayah 5, Pusat Bandar Kuah, 07000 Langkawi. ☎ (60)(4) 9660681 *Fax* (60)(4) 9669224 VHF Ch 69. Duty-free outboards and generators can also be obtained here.
Provisions Supermarket at the NW end of town. Other supermarkets in the town. Fresh fruit and vegetable market in town. Provisioning for basics is not too bad. As a duty-free port alcohol is very cheap and most yachts stock up here. To go shopping some yachts take the tender across to the village tide permitting – however do not stay in town too long drinking duty-free beer or you may have to

push the dinghy out through glutinous mud.
Eating out Adequate places in town. The night market on the waterfront has numerous stalls with local cuisine at cheap prices although there is no alcohol.
Other Banks including some ATMs which take foreign credit cards. PO. Courier services including DHL. Gas bottles can be filled. Ferries to Penang, Kuala Perlis and Kuala Kedah. Internal flights from Langkawi Airport with some international flights planned in the near future with the airport extension.

General
Kuah has grown in recent years from a ramshackle ferry and fishing port into a prosperous tourist and duty-free zone. It still straggles all the way around the waterfront making it a bit of an expedition to get to places, but mini-buses run frequently from Kuah pier into town. The front has some bizarre embellishments. Most prominent is the huge ferro-cement eagle painted somewhat extravagantly in eagle colours. The sea eagle is the symbol of Langkawi although you can't help thinking this huge edifice looks a bit like an advertisement for Langkawi fried eagle in competition with the KFCs around the place. Nearby is one of the most spacious Pizza Huts in the world complete with courtyards. Much of the waterfront is a landscaped park and further into town is a modern mosque (with the two gold domes) also in spacious landscaped grounds. In Langkawi itself there are some large extravagant hotels including one with turrets like something out of a Victorian Gothic novel. No doubt the future will bring additional expansive building programmes and sadly the clapboard and corrugated iron buildings that originally made up Kuah will disappear.

Langkawi Yacht Club

Approach
The pontoons of the club are situated immediately S of Kuah pier.
VHF Ch 69, 72.

Mooring
Data 50 berths. Visitors berths. Max LOA 50m. Depths 3–8m.
Berths Where directed. There are finger pontoons for most berths. Large yachts on the outside use their own anchors.
Shelter Good shelter during the NE monsoon. The ferries using Kuah pier set up a significant wash on the pontoons although efforts are being made to reduce the speed of the ferries in the immediate approaches to the marina and Kuah pier.
Authorities Harbourmaster and staff. Immigration, customs and harbourmaster nearby at Kuah pier.

Facilities
Services Water and electricity (220 and 415V) at all berths. Shower and toilet block.

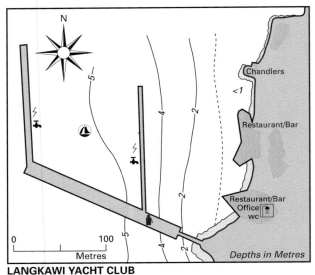

LANGKAWI YACHT CLUB

Langkawi Yacht Club just S of the pier at Kuah.

Fuel On the S pontoon.

Repairs Some basic repairs can be organised. A chandlers is to be built.

Provisions In Kuah town.

Eating out Restaurant and bar at the yacht club.

Other Phone and fax facility at the club. Laundry. Swimming pool to be built.

Langkawi Yacht Club, Kuah, 07000 Langkawi. ☎ (60)(4) 9664078 *Fax* (60)(4) 9665078.

Rebak Marina

Charts BA *843*

Approach

The marina is situated on the S side of Pulau Rebak Besar. The entrance to the marina is difficult to see even when quite close to. It is situated at 06°17'·44N 99°41'·68E WGS 84.

Conspicuous A building with a red roof to the E will be seen. Close in the breakwater protecting the channel will be seen.

By night The entrance and channel are lit and a night approach should be straightforward. Entrance Fl.G.5s/Fl.R.5s. Channel beacons Q.R/Q.G.

VHF Try Ch 16 or 69.

Dangers Yachts drawing 2m plus should wait for a rising tide before entering. There are 2·5–2·8m depths at MLWS and around 4·5–5m at high tide.

Mooring

Data 124 berths. Visitors berths. Max LOA 36m. Depths 2·5–2·8 at MLWS.

Berths Where directed. Finger pontoons.

Shelter All round.

Authorities Harbourmaster and staff.

Rebak Marina, Pulau Rebak, Langkawi. ☎ (04) 966 9941 *Fax* (04) 966 9944.

Facilities

Services Water and electricity at all berths. Showers and toilets.

Fuel Fuel quay inside.

Repairs Yard to be established at a future date.

Approach to Rebak Marina.

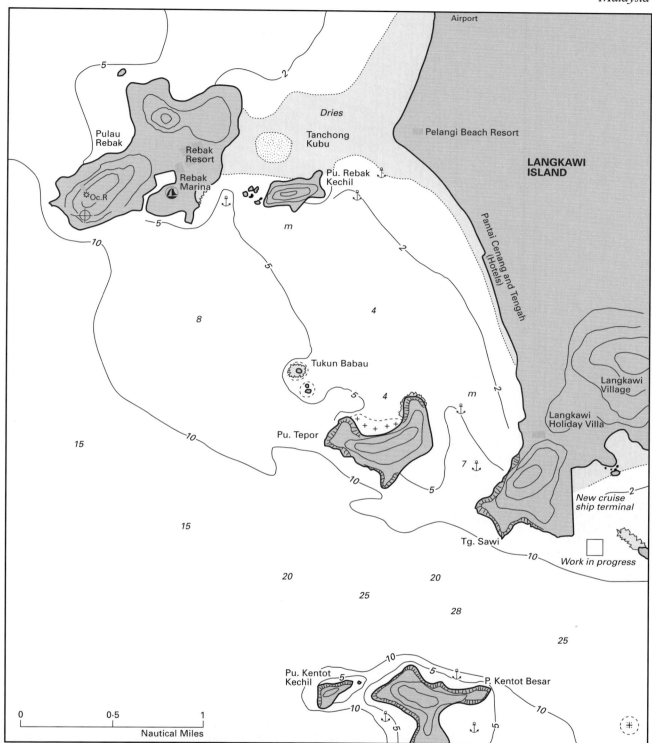

REBAK MARINA TO PULAU KENTOT BESAR ⊕ 06°17'·5N 99°41'·5E

Provisions Mini-market to be established.
Eating out Restaurant and bar.
Other Telephone and fax facilities. Swimming pool.
Ferry to the main island.

General

The marina and shoreside apartments and hotel are still being completed, but all basic facilities are in place. The marina and resort are very much an upmarket place where it was envisaged everyone would arrive from seawards whether on their own yacht or by the ferry service. It is now planned to

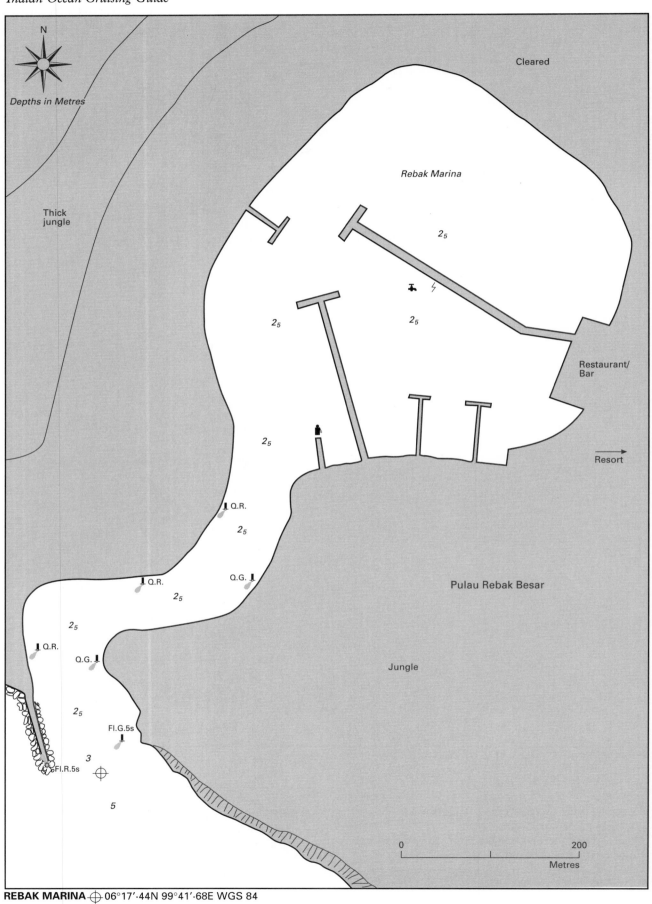

N

Depths in Metres

Cleared

Thick
jungle

Rebak Marina

2₅

2₅   2₅

2₅

Restaurant/
Bar

2₅

Resort

Q.R.

2₅

Q.R.   Q.G.

2₅

Pulau Rebak Besar

2₅

Q.R.

Q.G.

2₅

Jungle

Fl.G.5s

2₅

3

Fl.R.5s

5

0   200

Metres

REBAK MARINA ⊕ 06°17′·44N 99°41′·68E WGS 84

Rebak Bay anchorage.

build a causeway across to the island from Langkawi Island, presumably because there were just not enough people arriving here.

Anchorages around Langkawi archipelago

Proceeding from the NW corner and going anticlockwise.

Burau Bay In the NW corner of the large bay with the airport extension (Airport Bay) there are two coves on either side of Pulau Anak Burau which give good shelter with the NE monsoon. Anchor in 3–5m on either side of the islet. Ashore there are restaurants and bars at the resort.

Airport Bay The extension of Langkawi Airport runway into the bay necessitated the construction of two breakwaters to protect the runway proper. There are rumours that this may be developed into a mega-marina with 6000 berths. No-one seems to have carried out the necessary research to see if even one tenth of the berths could be filled and even if the marina was built, who would want to berth directly under the flightpath into the airport.

Pelangi Beach Resort A sympathetic resort in traditional Malay style in the NE corner of Rebak Bay on the S side of Pulau Rebak. You cannot get too close because of the shallows but there are a number of moorings in around 2m or anchor off. Good protection from the NE monsoon. Restaurant and bar ashore.

Rebak Bay Between Pulau Tepor in the S of the bay and the coast of Langkawi there is good shelter from the NE monsoon at 06°16'·89N 99°43'·67E WGS 84. Anchor in 4–10m on sand and mud. Several beach bars and restaurants ashore.

Cruise Ship Terminal Directly under Tungu Sawa, the SW tip of Langkawi Island a new cruise ship and ferry terminal is nearly complete. This is for the use of large ships although immigration and customs will have to be stationed here and might prove a useful alternative to Kuah. Care is needed of a nearby coral patch just ESE of Pulau Selang in the channel proceeding into Bass Harbour which can be difficult to discern on BA 843. There have been a few yachts which on cutting the corner through the channel have come to an abrupt halt.

Pulau Beras Basah There is a good sheltered anchorage from NE and SW on the E side of the island.

Pulau Singa Besar There are good anchorages on the NE and E sides of the island. Small beach restaurants sometimes open. The wide bay on the bottom makes a good lunch stop. In the approach from the S the small white light tower on the SE corner stands out well.

Telok Dayang Bunting (Fresh Water Lake anchorage) The long enclosed bay on the W side of Pulau Dayang Bunting. Anchor in convenient depths. The jetty at the head is used by speedboats bringing tourists over. In the evening the tours finish and it is a peaceful spot. Good shelter from the NE monsoon. Ashore there is the fresh water lake which, as local myth has it, restores the fertility of maidens who may have lost it.

Fjord anchorage A spectacular anchorage behind Pulau Gabang Darat at 06°11'·14N 99°47'·30E WGS 84. Entrance can be from the N or SW. Anchor in 6–12m on mud. Good all round protection. The steep slopes around abound in birdlife and troops of monkeys.

Telok Ayer Taban The large bay around the corner from Fjord anchorage. Adequate shelter from the NE monsoon only.

Surrounding islets The several islets around Fjord anchorage and Taban make a wonderful area just to potter. Most are limestone rising precipitously from the sea and undercut in places. They have numerous caves and prolific birdlife amongst the vegetation sprouting from all sides.

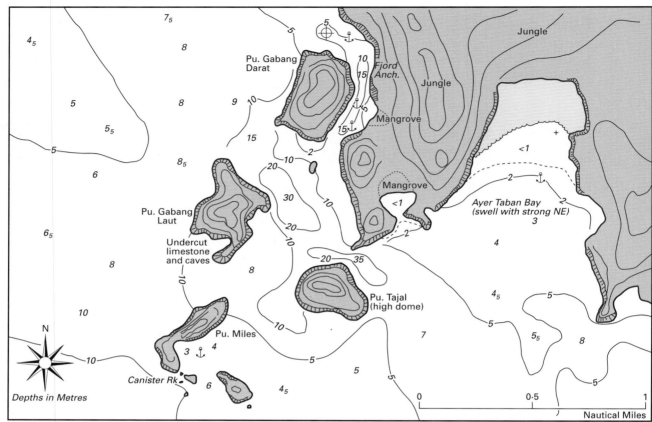

FJORD ANCHORAGE ⊕ 06°11'·54N 99°47'·13E WGS 84
(Gabang Darat)

Dayang Bunting NW side There are several good
anchorages along the NW side of the island which in
fact provides better shelter from the NE monsoon
than might appear from the chart. Due E of Pulau
Kedera and the islet after it are several coves with
sandy beaches. At one of these there is a fresh water
creek used by yachts to water up.

Bumbon Besar Bay The passage from Kuah
between Pulau Bumbon Besar and Langkawi Island
is easily negotiated. During the NE monsoon yachts
anchor in the large bay NNE of Bumbon Besar.
Care is needed of a shoal patch in the bay. A floating
restaurant sometimes operates here.

Hole-in-the-Wall Actually the Kisap River on the
E side of Langkawi Island. Care is needed of two
isolated rocks in the entrance after which navigation
is straightforward with good depths. Yachts can
navigate up to the corner where the river abruptly
turns N and which is marked by a charcoal factory.
Anchor anywhere. All round shelter. Wild
surroundings.

Kelawar River The next river N of Kisap. Some
yachts have reported it navigable.

Tanjung Rhu The inlet on the NE of Langkawi
Island. The Radisson Plaza Suite Resort is located
on the S side of the inlet.

Datai The bay on the N side of Langkawi close to
the NW tip is used by some yachts even during the
NE monsoon. The Datai Resort is located at the
head of the bay.

Thailand

Current situation

Thailand has long been a stable democracy with little internal or external dissent. There have been squabbles with Burma and Laos on the exact definitions of where the border is and a few confrontations on the eastern side between the Thai navy and the Vietnamese over where their respective territorial and exclusive economic zones begin and end. For the most part this has little impact on visitors.

Thailand does have its share of corruption, but for the most part this does not affect visitors. You may have to pay a few *baht* extra when you clear in and out to immigration and customs and if you intend to leave a yacht here for longer than one month then some greasing of local palms at immigration and customs is necessary to get the requisite paperwork through.

Documentation and visas

Normal boats papers and a valid passport for all crew members must be carried. You may also be asked for a radio licence and a certificate of competence of some sort although if you do not have either of these there appear to be few problems. A visa for one month will be issued when you clear in. It is important to know that this visa is different to the tourist visa normally issued when you arrive by plane and this can cause complications if you want to leave other than by the boat you arrived on. (See below.) You may be asked for a vaccination book but this is rare.

Entry formalities

The authorities are fairly relaxed about entry into Thailand. On entering territorial waters you must proceed to the nearest port of entry and clear in within 24 hours. Yachts do not normally fly a Q flag but a courtesy flag should be flown. Most yachts clear in at Phuket but it is possible to clear in at Krabi.

For Phuket most yachts go to Ao Chalong and then get a bus or *tuk-tuk* into Phuket town. You must bring the following documents: ship's papers, all crew passports, last port clearance papers, crew and passenger list, and, optional, radio licence and captain's papers or certificate of competence.

With these papers proceed to Phuket town where immigration and customs are located on Phuket Road going towards the harbour. It is usually best to get a *tuk-tuk* there although ensure that the driver does know where you want to go. At immigration you will be stamped in and a visa issued. You then go to customs to pay stamp duty. In the past it has been necessary to then go to the harbourmaster in Phuket Commercial Port for final clearance. In recent years this has not been necessary although check locally on the situation. Clearing out simply entails going back to immigration and then to customs to get your port clearance papers.

Although in theory you get one month only when clearing in, in practice most yachts spend two weeks to a month getting up to Phuket and another two weeks to a month leaving, usually to Langkawi. Always remember that technically you should leave within 24 hours after clearing out and that I only mention the practice common in these waters: I cannot endorse it here!

If you want to leave a yacht in Thailand and fly out of the country, then each person who has cleared in on the yacht as crew must put up a bond. In 1997 this was 20,000 *baht*, approximately $800. What happens in theory is that you deposit 20,000 *baht* in a Thai bank, get the bank to issue a letter of guarantee, go to immigration with this letter and have your visa amended. The amendment must be stamped when you exit the country and you should allow time for the relevant customs official to do this, usually at Bangkok Airport. When you return the letter of guarantee is redeemed and you get your 20,000 *baht* back. In practice the procedure normally requires some oiling of the cogs at immigration and my advice is to employ help from an agency to carry out the procedure.

One useful tip if you intend leaving the boat is for only one person to clear in as crew with any others listed as passengers. The bond does not apply to passengers with the catch being that passengers only get a 15 day visa.

Data

Area 514,000km^2 (198,457M^2)
Frontiers 4863km (2626M). Burma 1800km (972M). Cambodia 803km (434M). Laos 1754km (947M). Malaysia 506km (273M).
Coastline 3219km (1738M)
Maritime claims Territorial 12M. Exclusive economic zone 200M.
Population 56,100,000
Capital Bangkok
Time zone UT+7
Language Thai. English spoken in cities and tourist areas.
Ethnic divisions Thai 75%, Chinese 14%, Other 11%.
Religion Buddhism 95%, Muslim 3·8%.
Public holidays
  Jan 1 New Years Day
  Feb 17 Chinese New Year
  Apr 6 Chakri Day
  May 1 Labour Day
  May 5 Coronation Day
  May 11 Harvest Festival Day
  Jul 28 Asalaha Bupha Day
  Aug 12 Queen's Birthday
  Oct 23 Chulalangkom Day
  Dec 5 King's Birthday
  Dec 10 Constitution Day
  Dec 31 New Year's Eve
Variable
  Makha Bucha, Songkram, Visakha Bucha, Buddhist Lent.
Government Constitutional monarchy. Chief of state King Bhumbibol Adunlayadet (since 1946). Heir apparent Crown Prince Wachiralongkon. Democratically elected representatives.
Disputes Border disputes with Burma (Myanmar) and Laos. Maritime dispute with Vietnam over their adjacent waters.

Crime Crime against visitors is generally low although actual murder and violent assault figures for the Thais are high. Thailand has a homicide rate of 9·7/10,000 compared to 8·6/10,000 for the USA, usually considered one of the highest, although they kill each other and rarely kill visitors. Theft occurs in the cities and large tourist resorts but is rare from yachts. Many do not bother to lock up and there is little chance of anything being stolen. The most likely items are dinghies and outboards and the solution is to padlock the outboard to the dinghy and use some stainless steel cable or chain to padlock the dinghy to an immovable object such as a tree or metal piling. Ashore pickpockets and confidence tricksters operate in the tourist areas. Always wear a bumbag ashore to keep passports and cash secure and keep the bag to the front. If you are offered gems, antiques or other items at prices that are very low, it is likely you are being offered fakes. Fake gems are big business in Thailand.

Travel
Internal
Good air, rail and road links. Small ferries link some of the islands. Car and motorcycle hire in tourist areas.

Air Internal routes are efficient and safe. The most useful link is Phuket to Bangkok and there are 6–8 flights a day. There are also flights to Surat Thani and Trang in the S.

Rail From Bangkok the railway line runs S down the E side of the country through into Malaysia and on to Singapore. It is clean and relatively cheap, not to mention civilised.

Coach Most places in Thailand are connected by coach and the air conditioned coaches are cheap and efficient. Local services run shorter trips between towns and villages. In most places you can get about for comparatively short distances (such as around Phuket Island) by simply wandering out onto the main road and flagging down any buses or mini-buses going in the direction you want.

Hire cars and motorcycles In the tourist areas (such as Phuket) there are numerous hire car and motorcycle companies. Rates are fairly cheap. It should be borne in mind that Thailand in general, and Phuket in particular, has one of the highest accident rates in Southeast Asia and that motorcycle accidents are the most common cause of injury to tourists.

Taxis and tuk-tuks Around the cities and towns there are numerous conventional taxis or the three-wheeler kamikaze conversions known as *tuk-tuks*. Taxis will have a meter although you may have to persuade the driver to turn it on. For *tuk-tuks* agree a price beforehand. There are also numerous small vans which operate as taxis and on longer routes where you should also agree on a price beforehand. On longer routes there are share-taxis which may be anything from a pick-up truck to a minibus.

International
Connections by air and land.

Air Most international flights are from Bangkok. From here it is possible to fly to almost anywhere in the world. There are regular scheduled flights to Europe, the USA and Australasia. In Bangkok it is possible to find reasonably priced flights with a bit of looking around. An alternative is to fly out of Kuala Lumpur or Singapore which are easily reached by land or air from Phuket. There are some international flights and some charter flights out of Phuket, mostly to European destinations.

Land There are good rail and coach connections to Malaysia and Singapore.

Practicalities
Mail Not always lightning fast but reliable. You can send letters to Poste Restante but it is better to use a private address such as an agent or a marina.

Telecommunications IDD system. Country code 66. Phuket code 076. Digital mobile phones with a GSM card work if your supplier has an agreement in Thailand. The telecommunications system is adequate, but it can take some time dialling out of some places because of the demands on the lines. Likewise anyone dialling in may not always get through on the first go. There are a number of phone and fax bureau's in large towns and tourist resorts or use the phone/fax of an agent such as Big 'A' or Phuket Yacht Services.

Currency The unit is the Thai *baht* which is divided into 100 *satangs* although only 50 and 25 *satang* coins will occasionally be seen. The *baht* used to be tied to the US dollar but is now part of a basket of Asian currencies and is relatively stable although it nose-dived with other Asian currencies in 1997. There is effectively no black market and it is best to do transactions at a bank in case confidence tricksters do some sleight of hand with the number of notes you think you are getting.

Banks and exchange In any city or tourist resort there are banks which will change cash or travellers cheques. A number of banks will give cash advances against major credit cards. There are also ATMs which will take major credit cards. Many shops and restaurants will accept credit cards.

Medical care Is generally good. There are well-staffed and equipped hospitals in the cities and large tourist resorts and the doctors are generally well trained, often in Europe or the USA. The cost of care is medium, but it is advisable to have private medical insurance. The pharmacies are generally well stocked although drugs may be under different brand names.

Opinions on the water in Thailand vary. Some people like to treat it before use and others do not bother. If in doubt treat water before using it. Bottled water is widely available in restaurants and bars. Where the ice comes from is another matter.

Electricity 220V 50Hz AC.

Curiosities and culture
Keeping face and head to foot Losing your temper and getting angry with a Thai person is considered a loss of face and diminishes you in the

eyes of the other person. Amongst Thais *jai yen*, literally a 'cool heart', is considered an admirable quality and calmness and coolness in dealings with others is the cultural norm. A *farang* (non-Thai) should never lose his temper in dealings with Thais, even when recalcitrant officials are being awkward and demanding, implicitly or explicitly, a bribe. Look at it this way. Not only do you diminish yourself in the eyes of a Thai, but invariably dealings will take longer and paperwork will, inexplicably, get more complicated.

When in the presence of Thais it should be remembered that the body is assigned degrees of holiness or dirtiness. Not surprisingly the head is the holiest spot and the feet the dirtiest. Never point at anything with your foot as this is regarded as an insult. Likewise do not touch the head of anyone as this is the holiest and most spiritual part of the body. Although things are changing in the tourist areas, Thais frown on open displays of affection including kissing and holding hands in public. Men may hold hands in public and this is simply a sign of affection and nothing else that *farangs* might assume it signifies.

Buddhism Buddhism in Thailand is Theravada Buddhism which was imported from Sri Lanka in the 13th century. In this sense it relies on the teaching of the elders and the received lore of Buddhist colleges, although in other ways its has a very Thai aspect to it that, at a superficial level, gives it a charm and appeal of its own. In practice Thai Buddhism is fused with Brahmanism, animism and ancestor worship to give it a popular 'feel' all of its own. Outside most buildings you will see a Brahmanistic spirit house on which fruit, something to drink, rice and maybe a few flowers are laid every day. On some of the more remote islands you will see animist statues and shrines, some of an explicit phallic nature, and most Thais wear amulets and charms to keep away evil spirits. This bringing together of various religious elements is not seen as contradictory and gives Thai Buddhism a joyful aspect, a placating of all the gods so that things go right. I go along with this sort of syncretic approach.

Thais follow the Law of Karma whereby meritorious acts reduce suffering. This gives a daily impetus to Buddhist practice because this reduction applies to daily life as well as any future life. Thai *wats* (monasteries) are peopled by monks going about everyday life laughing, drinking, chatting and just getting on with the reduction of misery. It is not uncommon for young Thai men to spend a short period in a *wat*, anything from a year to five years, to gain merit for the family and also to prepare for a responsible life. And he gets to learn to read and write as well if he comes from a remote village.

Sin City and Aids Around Phuket the name Patong is pretty much synonymous with sin-city. At night parts of it come to life with a surprising variety of sexual choice. There are girlie bars everywhere and a few lady-boy bars as well. Not for nothing is Thailand known as one of top sex tourism destinations in the world and it has the unenviable reputation as a place where the girls (and boys) are easy and cheap. Along with this reputation has come the modern scourge of the late 20th century and estimates of those who are HIV positive are currently 600,000 with the World Health Organisation estimating a total of 8–9 million at risk. Figures such as 50% of prostitutes being HIV positive have been bandied about. In 1991 Thailand started an HIV awareness programme and began promoting safe sex. Despite this very public campaign it is likely large numbers will still be infected and for anyone on the razzle in Patong or elsewhere it is imperative that safe sex is practised. You have been warned.

Thai massages On most beaches you will see makeshift beds with Thai masseurs sitting patiently by them waiting for clientele. This has nothing to do with the nudge-nudge, wink-wink notions of massage parlours in the west and a Thai massage can do wonders for muscle tone and even things like whiplash neck and tennis elbow. It is a variation on Chinese and Indian massage techniques and identifies problems from certain *chakras* or energy points. It is to be recommended for long standing muscle complaints or just a pick-me-up.

Useful books

Thailand has significant English speaking readership and there are a number of English language daily newspapers and some monthly magazines on a variety of topics. I mention a few of the many books available below.

Sail Thailand Thai Marine & Leisure. ed. Collin Piprell. Artasia Press. Available locally or in the UK from Imrays. Covers all the western coast with plans of harbours and anchorages.

Thailand and Burma Handbook ed. Joshua Elliot. Footprint Handbooks. The best of the general guides by miles.

Rough Guide to Thailand Penguin. Adequate guide but doesn't cover out-of-the-way places.

Lonely Planet: Thailand Joe Cummings. Covers all of Thailand so not detailed on out of the way places.

God's Dust Ian Buruma. Vintage. Observations on Southeast Asia.

Geography and climate

The coast The west coast of Thailand is one of the most impressive coasts in Southeast Asia. It is nearly everywhere high and steep-to. Most of the coast and islands are limestone which has been eroded into weird and wonderful shapes and to describe the islands and islets as steep-to is nearly a misnomer: many of them are precipitous and close to vertical. Only around some of the river deltas is there flat land and a few of the islands have a gentler more rolling aspect to them in the south of the area. The limestone islands and islets are spectacular to say the least. Anywhere that tropical plants can get a hold is covered in green foliage and in places trees grow out of the slopes at impossible angles. Being limestone there are extensive cave and sinkhole systems as well

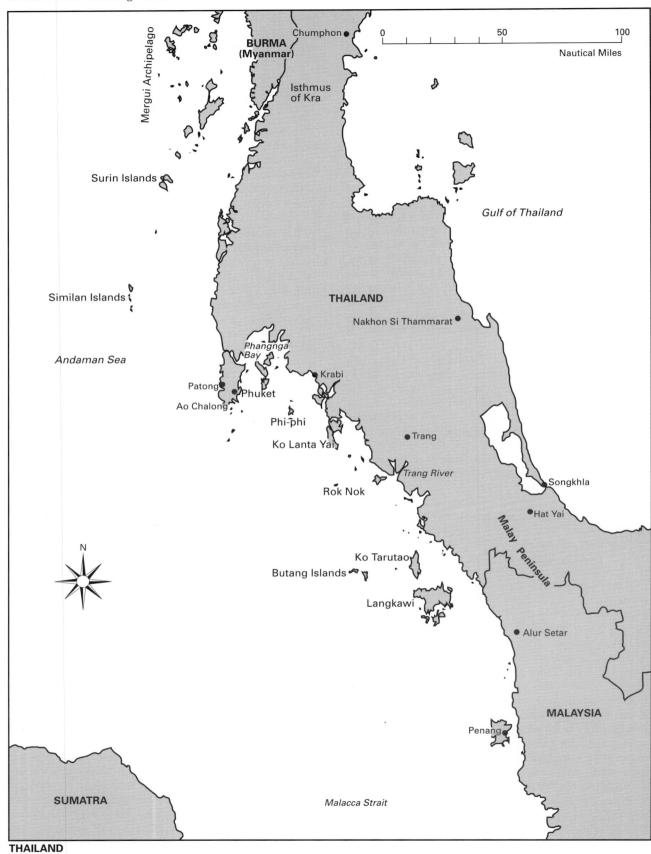

as the *hongs*, cave systems where the top of the cave has collapsed leaving a steep crater in the island which is often only accessible from caves at low tide.

Coastal waters The waters vary according to where you are. In Phangnga Bay and around the waters close to the coast the visibility is much reduced by silt brought down by the numerous rivers. Visibility is often less than 2m and snorkelling is not an option and the swimming not all that appealing. The water is not dirty as such, just a milky green from river sediment, although around the towns and tourist resorts there is pollution both from sewerage, the detritus of tourism most evident as plastic flotsam, and a sheen of spilt diesel from tripper boats. Only around the outer islands and away from major rivers on the coast nearer the Andaman Sea does the water get clearer and here snorkelling and swimming is a joy in warm tropical water.

For the most part the waters are fairly shallow and around the coast and islands you get to consider deep water as anything over 20m. It takes a little time to get used to these shallow depths but after a while taking on passages with 3–4m in them and crossing 2–3m patches becomes the norm. The bottom is mostly mud so if you do go aground it is not too much of a problem except if you do so at low water springs.

The silt rich waters around the coast attract lots of fish although the Thais are pretty good at scooping most of them up in trawl nets, set nets and fish traps for the huge tourist industry around the nearby coast. One of the hazards of cruising in the area is abandoned or lost fish traps which can be up to 2m long and of fairly heavy construction. As they usually float just below the surface a good lookout needs to be kept for them around the coast and even offshore. Another hazard is water-logged trees and branches brought down by the rivers which can be of substantial size and can do serious damage to a yacht should you collide with one at speed.

Climate There are two distinct seasons corresponding to the two monsoon periods although some divide the year up into three periods with the cool dry season from November to February, the hot season from March to June and the rainy season from July to October. The favoured season is during the northeast monsoon between November and April and the less favoured is the southwest monsoon between May and October.

The northeast monsoon is from November to April. This is the dry season and consequently the least humid season. Average temperatures range from around 31–32°C in November and December to 34–38°C in April. Temperatures are only a few degrees less at night around Phuket. The average humidity at midday is around 50–58% over the season. The northeast monsoon will have settled down by mid-November and lasts through until mid-April with a consistent pattern. The best months are reckoned to be December, January, and February.

The southwest monsoon is from May to October. This is the wet season and those unused to the tropics will find the humidity difficult to handle. Average temperatures range from 34–38°C in May to 31–32°C in October although temperatures will often reach 39–40°C. The average humidity is around 58–70% over the season. The worst months are reckoned to be July, August and September.

On the western coast of Thailand around Phuket there is a double rainy period with most rain falling in May and again in October. On average it will rain for more than 20 days in the month during these two months.

At Victoria Point	Av max °C	Av min °C	Relative humidity	Days rain 2·5mm
Jan	30	23	70%	1
Feb	31	23	66%	<1
Mar	32	24	70%	2
Apr	32	25	66%	7
May	30	24	85%	19
Jun	29	24	86%	22
Jul	28	24	86%	23
Aug	28	24	86%	22
Sep	28	23	87%	22
Oct	29	24	84%	19
Nov	29	24	82%	11
Dec	29	24	73%	5

Note The figures above are for Victoria Point 09° 58'N 98°35'E which is in southern Burma. In fact Victoria Point is on the N side of the Pakchan River which forms the boundary between Thailand and Burma and the figures are typical for the W coast of Thailand.

Weather
Prevailing winds near the coast The winds near the coast are basically determined by the NE or SW monsoon. However there is a lot of variation depending on the topography and the strength of the monsoon winds.

During the NE monsoon the wind is basically NE but can be channelled to blow anywhere from the N to the E off the land. When the NE monsoon is not blowing strongly and in the transitional periods on either side, a land and sea breeze blows or affects the prevailing NE winds. What will often happen is that the NE wind is augmented through the night by a land breeze effect and around mid-afternoon the NE wind will be stopped by the onshore sea breeze producing a calm or a light onshore wind. When the NE wind is augmented by the land breeze there is normally anything between 10–20kn of wind. In the afternoon there will frequently be a calm or a light onshore breeze up to 10kn or so. Depressions passing to the N of the area may also cause variations on the normal patterns.

During the SW monsoon the wind often lifts near the coast and there will be little wind during the night and stronger winds in the afternoon when the SW monsoon is augmented by the sea breeze. Overall the land and sea breeze effect is much less because of the greater cloud cover over the land. When the SW monsoon is blowing strongly there

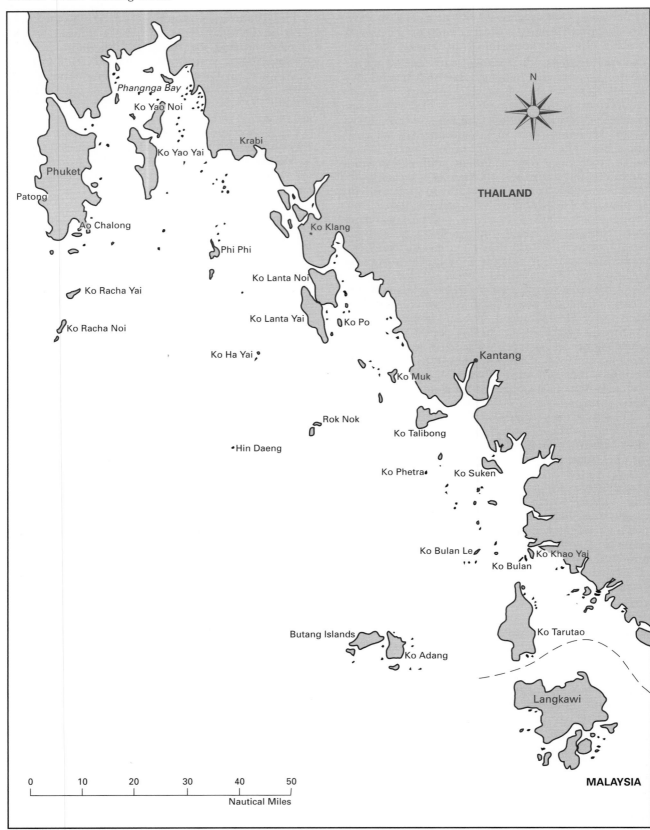

N

Phangnga Bay

Ko Yao Noi

Ko Yao Yai

Krabi

THAILAND

Phuket

Patong

Ao Chalong

Ko Klang

Phi Phi

Ko Lanta Noi

Ko Racha Yai

Ko Lanta Yai

Ko Po

Ko Racha Noi

Kantang

Ko Ha Yai

Ko Muk

Rok Nok

Ko Talibong

Hin Daeng

Ko Phetra

Ko Suken

Ko Bulan Le

Ko Khao Yai

Ko Bulan

Ko Tarutao

Butang Islands

Ko Adang

Langkawi

MALAYSIA

0   10   20   30   40   50
Nautical Miles

LANGKAWI TO PHUKET

will be consistent SW winds over the area, often with associated squalls.

At Victoria Point	Prevailing winds 0800	Prevailing winds 1700
Jan	NE–E/67%	NE–E/75%
Feb		NW/34%
Mar	NE–E/71%	NW/39%
Apr	NE–E/63%	NW/32%
May	SE–E/31%	SW–W/50%
Jun	SE–SW/56%	SW–W/70%
Jul	SW–W/45%	SW–W/74%
Aug	SW–W/46%	SW–W/65%
Sep	SE–SW/41%	SW–W/51%
Oct	NE–E/43%	NE–E/34%
Nov	NE–E/60%	NE–E/62%
Dec	NE–E/64%	NE–E/79%

For more information on wind direction and strength see the charts in *Technical Information* page 30-31.

Gales During the NE monsoon there are few non-tropical depressions that affect the area. There may be occasions as in late November 1996 when strong winds are generated as the spin-off from a tropical storm in the Bay of Bengal, but this is rare. On other occasions a non-tropical depression may pass to the N or S bringing gale force winds though this is also rare. Squalls may pass through the area, often in mid to late afternoon, but again winds are rarely gale force.

With the onset of the SW monsoon the incidence of gale force winds increases to around 5% in July. The effects are lessened near the coast although there can be a higher incidence of localised squalls bringing gale force winds for a short period.

Tropical storms It is rare for the W coast of Thailand to be hit by a tropical storm although it can get a peripheral effect in the form of unsettled weather and heavy seas setting onto the coast. Occasionally a tropical storm will pass close by as in November 1924 and 1989 when *Typhoon Gay* affected the area. There are however numerous places a yacht can find shelter in the comparatively shallow waters as heavy seas do not build up in the enclosed waters.

For more information see *Technical Information*, page 35.

Thunderstorms and waterspouts Thunderstorms and associated squalls occur although they are most common during the SW monsoon and the transitional periods on either side. They can also occur during the NE monsoon, although the squalls do not carry a heavy weight of wind and they are usually short lived affairs. During the SW monsoon squalls may reach 35kn for short periods but rarely more.

Waterspouts occur most commonly during the SW monsoon and the transitional periods.

Tides
Around Phuket the spring range is in the vicinity of 2·3m (7ft 6in). This is considerable enough to be taken into account as the comparatively shallow waters and channels mean that tidal streams can be significant at springs. In places tidal streams may be 3–4kn for an hour or two, enough to make your coasting very slow or lightning fast. For most of the area tidal streams are not this savage and are more usually 1–2kn. Away from shallow channels and the islands tidal streams are much less. The varying direction of the tidal streams around the islands and channels also means that some care is needed over navigation. The Admiralty charts give an indication of the direction and rates of tidal currents around the coast.

One other consequence of the tidal range in these shallow waters is that at low water there may be a significant stretch of mud exposed between the beach and the anchorage. This makes things very messy getting to and from the shore and in such anchorages it is wise to plan going ashore or returning to the yacht for a time before or after low water.

Currents
Currents around the coast are variable in rate and direction, but are generally weak and easily reversed. Currents are nowhere more than ¼kn except around the mouth of large rivers. Tidal streams as described above are the most important feature around the coast.

Navigation
The coast has been surveyed in recent years around the major harbours, but on the whole surveys for most of the area are from some time ago, probably late 19th-century surveys. The Admiralty and other charts have corrections of between 0·10 and 0·20 minutes to be applied to the charts, but these corrections are not systematic (for example some apply a correction E and others a correction W for longitude) suggesting that there are substantial random errors from old surveys. By my rough estimates using GPS I have found errors of between 0·25 to 0·40 minutes in some places. This means that considerable care must be used when navigating close to dangers to navigation and when approaching anchorages. This applies particularly to inland waters where visibility is low and it is difficult to see dangers such as the edge of a reef or the sea bottom. Where possible I have given GPS co-ordinates using WGS 84 datum. Other co-ordinates are schematic and should be treated with caution.

Harbours and anchorages

This section does not include anywhere near all the possible anchorages and for more detailed information you should consult *Sail Thailand* by Thai Marine Leisure which is available in Phuket and a few other places locally. A brief perusal of the charts will also turn up a lot of anchorages usable in the NE monsoon.

The description of anchorages is from the S to the N.

Butang Islands

A group of two major islands and a number of minor islands lying off the NE corner of Langkawi making them an easy day hop from the W side of Langkawi. The approach from the SE is straightforward although Hin Takon Chet is difficult to spot until close to.

There are numerous anchorages around the islands.

1. ***Ko Lipe S side*** Anchor in the bay on the S side in 10–20m. The depths come up quickly to the fringing reef which is irregular so it pays to have a

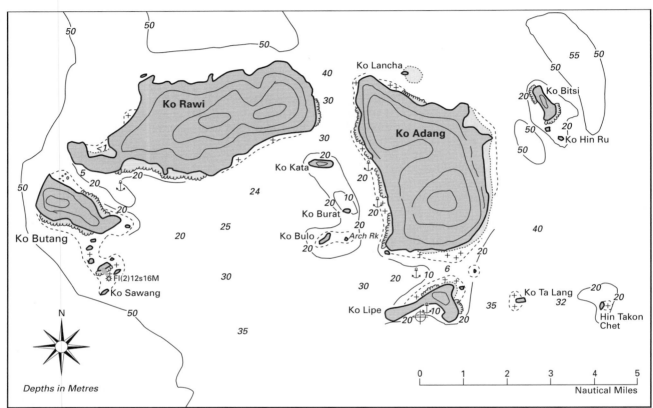

BUTANG ISLANDS ⊕ 06°29′·1N 99°18′·5E WGS 84

Butang Islands. Ko Lipe south side anchorage.

lookout aloft. The bottom is sand with some coral patches. There is also a current running around the bay. Good shelter from the prevailing NE winds although some ground swell works its way around into the anchorage. Open to the SW. Ashore there is a small village and primitive bungalows. Simple fare available ashore at the bungalows. Fish from the fishermen or there is good fishing around the reef.

2. *Ko Lipe N side* Anchor between Ko Lipe and Ko Adang in the channel in 8–15m on mud and sand. Keep a lookout for moorings used by the local fishing boats. Good shelter in the NE monsoon and reported to be adequate in the SW monsoon. A significant current runs through this channel. Simple fare ashore.

3. *Ko Adang W side* There are several anchorages on the W side that can be used in idyllic surroundings. Care is needed of the fringing reefs in places but with a little exploration there are several coves that can be used. Some ground swell may penetrate at times but on the whole it is peaceful if tucked close in. The slopes drop down steeply to a number of beaches and there are no facilities available.

4. *Ko Rawi SW corner* Anchor off the reef here in 20–25m. Some current flows through the channel. Reasonable shelter in the NE monsoon. A heavy swell penetrates into the anchorage with the SW monsoon. Good fishing around the reef.

Ko Tarutao

The large island directly N of the NW corner of Langkawi. Like the Butang Islands it can be reached in a day sail from the W coast of Langkawi. The island is a national park and fishing in the vicinity of the island is prohibited although this does not seem to deter Thai trawlers which fish intensively all around the island. In fact the trawlers are so thick on the sea at times that you will have to zigzag your way around them to get between Tarutao and Langkawi. Rangers are stationed on the island but do not object to yachts anchoring off or to parties going ashore, in fact they appear to welcome company from visiting yachts.

There are a number of anchorages around the island.

1. *Ao Talo Udang* Anchor in 4–7m off the W side of Ko Panan. The bottom is mostly mud and good holding. Good shelter from the NE monsoon but open to the SW monsoon. Ashore there are reported to be the remains of an old penal colony.

2. *Ao Pante* Anchor on the S side of the off-lying rocks in 5–10m. The bottom is sand and good holding. Good shelter from the NE monsoon although some ground swell penetrates. Open to the SW monsoon. The jetty on the shore is for the Tarutao National Park headquarters ashore. Limited provisions and a simple restaurant here. There is also a visitors centre and turtle breeding

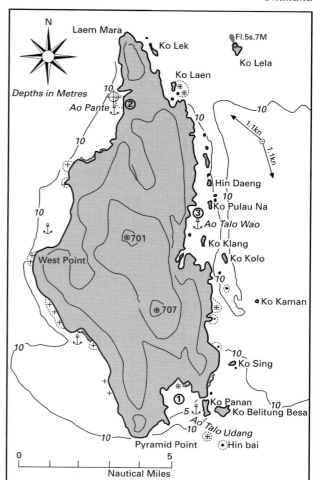

KO TARUTAO ⊕ 06°42′N 99°39′E

ponds. The rangers are welcoming to visiting yachts and helpful on walks and sights around the island.

There are also anchorages further down the W coast which can be used with care. Suitable depths can be found for anchoring although there always seems to be some ground swell around with the NE monsoon.

3. *Ao Talo Wao* An anchorage on the E coast between the islets and rocks. A pier on the shore is left over from when a prison was sited here.

Ko Bulan

The skinny island lying alongside the larger Ko Khao Yai off the mainland coast. The anchorage is in between the two islands and should be approached from the S. Anchor in 3–6m on a gently shelving bottom. Good shelter from the NE monsoon. The two islands are pretty much deserted except for local boats. Spectacular surroundings which repay the effort of exploration by dinghy.

Ko Phetra

07°06'·4N 99°28'·6E WGS 84 off S end of island

Anchor off the SE tip of the island in 6–10m. The bottom comes up quickly from 9–10m to 2–3m and less. There is a lot of current here and you will probably lie to the current even when it is blowing strongly from another direction. The island is also subject to strong squalls when it is windy. Good holding and adequate shelter in the NE monsoon. The island is a spectacular precipitous ridge of limestone covered in jungle and resounding to bird cries. It is a major bird nesting island and some of the ropes and paths can be seen.

Rok Nok

07°12'·88N 99°03'·9E WGS 84 (Channel anchorage)

An anchorage in the channel between the islands of Rok Nai and Rok Nok or off the NE corner of Rok Nok. If possible anchor in the channel in 5–15m trying to keep out of the main fairway. The best place is under the S end of Ko Rok Nai. Care is needed of coral patches closer in. Alternatively anchor off the NE side of Ko Rok Nok in 10–20m taking care of the reef off the beach which extends for 100–150m off. The bottom is sand and good holding. At times the ranger on Ko Rok Nai will tell boats anchored in the channel to move as they obstruct the passage for fishing boats.

Reasonable shelter in the NE monsoon but with any unsettled weather producing a swell the anchorage is most uncomfortable. In fact with any swell rolling in from the Andaman Sea the anchorage in the channel is a bit like being in a washing machine. The anchorage is a favourite stopover for yachts heading to or from Phuket with brilliantly clear water for swimming and sandy beaches.

Ko Lanta Yai

07°29'·5N 99°07'·1E WGS 84 (Under Ko Kluang)

On the E side of this island/peninsula there are several good secure anchorages. In the approach the high island/peninsula is easily identified and the light structure on the end (Fl(3)15s15M) is easily recognised. During the NE monsoon anchorage can be obtained in a number of places.

1. ***Ko Kluang*** Anchor off the S side in 4–6m taking care of the fringing reef which extends out from the S corner. Good shelter and a small beach ashore with oysters on the rocks. There is a sea gypsy village at Lek opposite where a few provisions may be found.

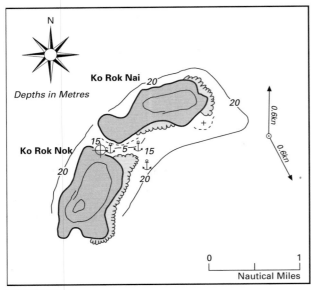

KO ROK NOK

Rok Nok. The anchorage in the channel.

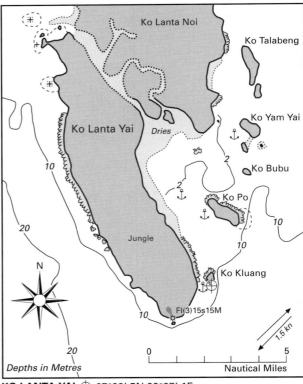

KO LANTA YAI ⊕ 07°29'·5N 99°07'·1E

Ko Lanta Yai S end. The light tower stands out well.

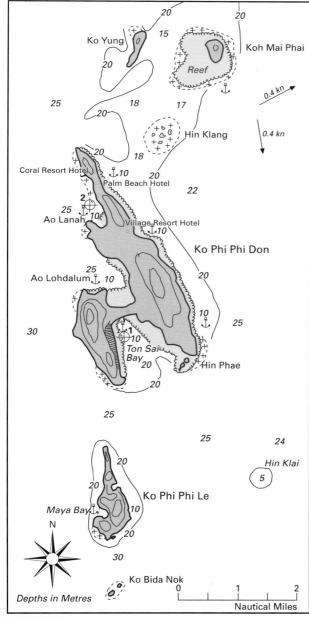

KO PHI PHI

2. **Ko Po** Anchor off the NW side in 4–6m taking care of the reef off the island. Good shelter from the NE monsoon in tranquil surroundings.

3. There are numerous other anchorages around here which can be explored with care and some appear to provide shelter from the SW monsoon. The bottom is mostly mud and good holding. The water is not very clear for swimming but the surroundings are spectacular with high land on the peninsula and everything covered in jungle.

Phi Phi

The large island of Ko Phi Phi Don and its smaller sister Ko Phi Phi Le are probably known to most people who visit Phuket. The large island is the most developed and after some of the other islands it is a bit like arriving at an offshore metropolis of Phuket. The island is said to be one of the three most beautiful islands in the world although the source of these judgements is not known, probably a glossy magazine or a travel brochure through which the

Ko Phi Phi Le, the smaller sister to Ko Phi Phi Don.

Ton Sai Bay on Phi Phi.

comment has since become enshrined in Thai tourist literature. In fact there are many other islands off the east coast which are every bit as beautiful or more so than Phi Phi, especially when the water around the islands are stained by a sheen of diesel from the tripper boats and from discarded rubbish and the air is punctuated by the staccato sound of unsilenced longtail motors. Still, it is a spectacular spot and Ton Sai Bay provides some of the nightlife absent on other islands.

The islands are easily identified from the distance, being high and steep-to and stuck out on their own. From the N care is needed of the reefs around Ko Mai Phai and especially of Hin Klang. The 5m patch off the E side of Phi Phi Le does exist as was verified by a super yacht recently which had its centreboard drawing more than 5m down. In the closer approach the numerous tripper boats from the mainland coast and Phuket and those operating out of Ton Sai Bay will be seen everywhere.

Most craft make for Ton Sai Bay.

Ton Sai Bay

Approach
Straightforward by day and possible at night with care. Make for the W side of the bay to avoid the reef and rocky outcrops on the E side. The reef fringing the W side of the bay is fairly even for most of its length and easily identified by day. At night care is needed of craft anchored in the bay, many of which do not have anchor lights.

Mooring
Anchor where convenient in the NW corner of the bay keeping clear of the jetty the tripper boats use and any of the permanent mooring buoys for the tripper boats. The anchorage can get crowded at times, but then it is possible to anchor further out. The bottom is sand, reasonable holding once your anchor is dug in.

Shelter Good shelter in the NE monsoon and reported adequate in the SW monsoon. It is only uncomfortable from the wake of the hordes of tripper boats charging in and out.

Facilities
Water From a tap near the tripper boat jetty. It should be treated before use.

Fuel There is a fuel barge used by the tripper boats where it may be possible to get fuel. Most yachts go elsewhere for fuel.

Provisions Adequate shopping for provisions in the shanty town on the isthmus.

Eating out Numerous restaurants of all types in the shanty town and around the adjacent coast. The restaurants on the N side of the isthmus have wonderful views out across the water or have a sundowner here and go into the shanty town to eat. Good seafood available in non-fiery dishes tailored to the European palate.

Other PO. Moneychangers who can change travellers cheques as well as hard currency. Telephone and fax agents. Ferries to the mainland and Phuket.

General
The anchorage under the precipitous slopes on the W side of the bay is beautiful and spectacular. Unfortunately the water often has a diesel sheen over it making it uninviting to swim in. There have been threats to remove the shanty town and install upmarket hotels around the foreshore, a pity as the shanty town has a good deal more interest than many of the hotels nearby offering bland international standards and cuisine.

Other anchorages around Phi Phi

1. *Ao Lanah* 07°46'·0N 98°45'·5E WGS 84. Anchor in 10–15m keeping clear of the coral reef filling much of the bay. Adequate shelter in the NE monsoon although some ground swell may penetrate.
2. *Ao Lohdalum* The large bay on the N side of the isthmus cutting off Ton Sai Bay. The large bay is

beset with coral heads and the reef and should not be used. It is possible to anchor in the cove on the NW side of the large bay keeping clear of the fringing reef. Anchor in 15–20m on sand. Adequate shelter only.

3. ***Resort Hotels NE side*** In calm weather it is possible to anchor off the resort hotels on the NE side keeping clear of the fringing reef. These anchorages are not normally good overnight stops being exposed to any wind and swell from the N.

4. ***Phi Phi Le/Maya Bay*** On the SW side of Phi Phi Le it is possible to anchor off Maya Bay in 20–25m. Most of the lagoon inside is encumbered by a shallow reef. By day large numbers of tripper boats come here so it is not a tranquil spot. The anchorage is not really a safe one for an overnighter. To see the other sights around Phi Phi Le potter off in the yacht and use the dinghy or take a longtail from Ton Sai Bay. Most people go to look at the Viking Cave where there are prehistoric pictures of Viking-like boats, Maya Bay, and a *hong* (collapsed cave system) on the E side. Just don't expect it to be tranquil.

5. ***Bamboo Islands*** The two smaller islands to the N of Phi Phi Don can be visited although there is no secure anchorage. Care is needed of Hin Klang. Anchor off where convenient and return to Phi Phi Don for the night.

Racha Yai

The island lying W of Phi Phi and S of Phuket Island. On the NW of the island there is an anchorage at Ao Racha Yai providing good shelter from the NE monsoon. Anchor in the outer part of the bay in 10–15m on sand. The surroundings are wonderful with a fine sand beach at the head of the bay and clear water over coral and sand in the inner part of the bay. The bay is popular with tripper boats so it is not exactly a peaceful spot. Ashore there are several restaurants with good seafood.

On Ko Racha Noi, the long thin island to the S of Racha Yai, it is possible to anchor off on the middle of the W side. This is not really a good overnight anchorage, but is a beautiful spot with good snorkelling in clear water.

Ao Chalong

Approach

The approach is a bit unnerving the first time because of the shallow depths and large extent of coral and mud-flats fringing the bay and Ko Lon, but on subsequent approaches it is straightforward. There are two passages into Ao Chalong on the W or E sides of Ko Lon.

Conspicuous The islands in the approaches are fairly easy to identify. The large Phuket Island Resort Hotel on the W side of the W channel is easily identified and the buildings around the NW side of the bay and the numerous yachts on moorings will be seen. On the E side the Fisheries Institute on the E side of the E channel which usually has a large ocean going trawler berthed off the pier is easily identified. The fairway buoy for Phuket Commercial Harbour is also easily identified along with the other channel buoys leading up the E side of the headland. Ko Thanam is easily identified and the buildings at Ban Nit will be seen once into the channel. Two pairs of small R/G buoys mark the channel from just N of Ko Thanam to Ao Chalong pier.

By night A night approach should not be made for the first entrance. Once familiar with the bay a night

Phuket Fishing Lodge and Jimmy's Lighthouse in Ao Chalong.

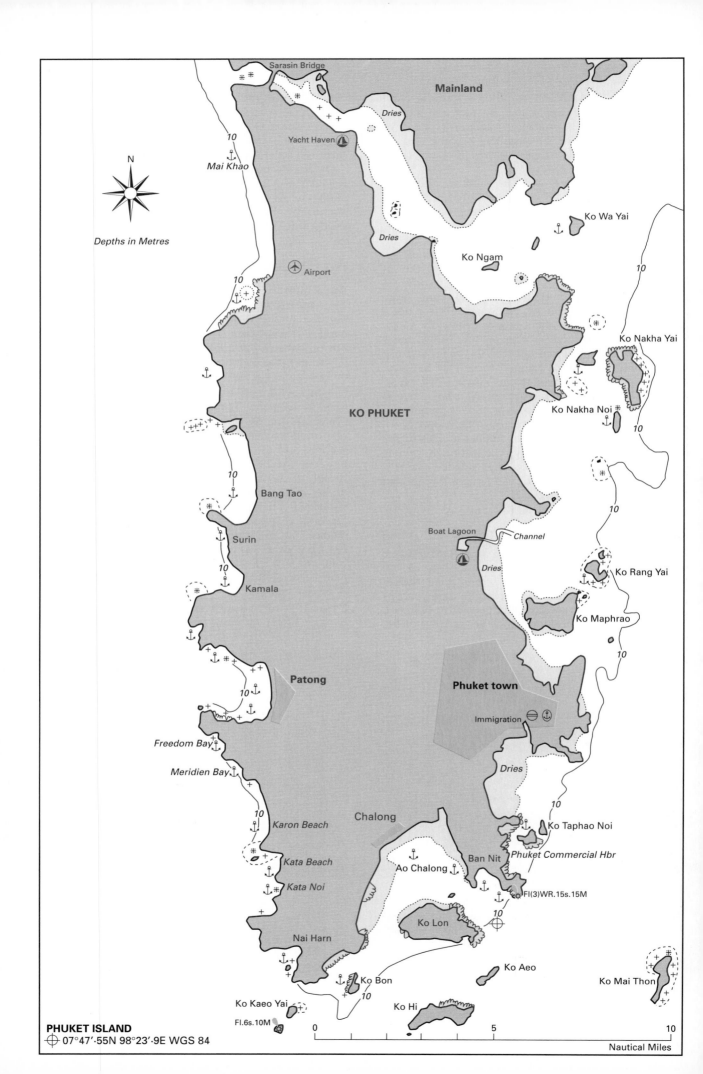

Sarasin Bridge

Mainland

Dries

Yacht Haven

Mai Khao

Ko Wa Yai

N

Depths in Metres

Ko Ngam

Dries

10

Airport

Ko Nakha Yai

KO PHUKET

Ko Nakha Noi

10

Bang Tao

Boat Lagoon

Channel

Surin

Dries

Ko Rang Yai

Kamala

Ko Maphrao

Patong

Phuket town

Immigration

Freedom Bay

Meridien Bay

Dries

Karon Beach

Chalong

Ko Taphao Noi

Kata Beach

Ao Chalong

Ban Nit

Phuket Commercial Hbr

Kata Noi

Fl(3)WR.15s.15M

Nai Harn

Ko Lon

Ko Aeo

Ko Mai Thon

Ko Bon

10

Ko Kaeo Yai

Ko Hi

Fl.6s.10M

PHUKET ISLAND
⊕ 07°47′·55N 98°23′·9E WGS 84

0   5   10

Nautical Miles

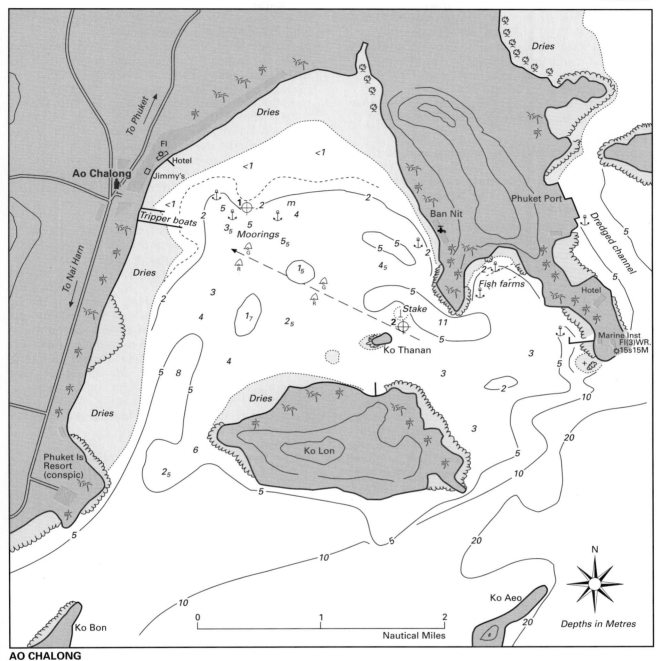

AO CHALONG

approach can be made with care. Off the fisheries on the end of the headland a light is exhibited Fl(3)WR.15s15M. The fairway buoy is lit Mo(A)6s. Off the Phuket Fishing Lodge a strong fixed white spotlight is exhibited until around midnight. The small buoys marking the main channel into Ao Chalong to the N of Ko Thanam are lit Q.R/Q.G although they should not be relied upon. Many of the moored yachts do not exhibit an anchor light.

VHF The general calling channel for yachts is Ch 69 and someone at the Phuket Boating Association based in the Fishing Lodge may be listening in. This is not an official service and you rely on the goodwill of others here for information or help.

Dangers

1. Care is needed in general of several shoal areas in the bay shown on the plan. Other shoal areas have been reported although not confirmed. For the most part the bottom is mud should you go aground. There is some fringing coral on the W and E sides of the bay as well as around Ko Lon.

2. Care is needed of the mud bank on the W side of the bay which is deceptive. It is easy to underestimate how close you are to the coast when the bank is covered by the tide. Head for the centre of the bay before making for the yacht mooring area.

3. In the E channel off Ko Thanam a set net is sometimes extended from the coast to a pole in

the position shown (p.a. 07°48'·35N 98°22'·83E WGS 84). The pole can be difficult to see and does not always appear to be in position. Care is needed with a good lookout forward for the pole and any fishermen in the vicinity who will wave a red flag and jump up and down.

4. Care is needed of numerous tripper boats including fast water taxis zooming in and out.

Mooring

There are numerous yellow mooring buoys to which a line can be taken. The moorings appear to be secure. Alternatively anchor where convenient, mostly in 3–5m depths. The bottom is mud and excellent holding.

Shelter Good all round shelter. With a strong NE monsoon there is a considerable chop in the bay which can make the anchorage uncomfortable although never untenable. With a strong SW monsoon there can also be a chop although it is generally less bothersome than the strong NE monsoon.

Authorities In Phuket. (See section on Entry Formalities.) Get a bus or taxi to Phuket from the roundabout on the main road. There has been talk at times of making a charge for the use of the mooring buoys, but to date they have been free.

Dinghies Are usually left on the beach in front of Jimmy's Bar where they appear to be safe enough. Make sure you tie it off. At low water springs there can be a fair expanse of mud exposed and a not inconsiderable number of yachties tend to spend their time in Jimmy's or elsewhere rather than wading through the viscous goo which is exposed. This only happens for a few days over low water springs and can be avoided by judicious timing for trips in and out.

Facilities

Water Call the water barge on VHF Ch 69 or by jerrycan from the shore and private sources. Large 20L containers of treated drinking water are available in Chalong village.

Fuel Call the fuel barge on VHF Ch 69. For small amounts and for petrol there is a service station close to the roundabout on the main road heading into Phuket.

Repairs Mechanical and engineering repairs in Chalong and Phuket. You can source them yourself or use the Big A Agency. For many repairs such as GRP, wood, electrical and electronic work it depends on what skills are available on yachts more or less permanently based here. There are some skilled folk around but you will need to find out by word of mouth. Rolly Tasker Sails can make and repair sails using the latest laser cutting equipment and also provides a rigging and spar service. Canvas-work can be carried out by Cobra and Sea Sports in Chalong. Most hardware and some chandlery can be found in Phuket town with G C Huat (pronounced 'Wat') justly famous for stocking a large range of spares. Some second-hand boat items can be found at the group of chalets on the Rawai

Road about 1½ miles from Chalong. See the addresses at the end of this section.

Provisions Some groceries and fresh fruit and vegetables can be found near the roundabout on the main road where there is a supermarket and a greengrocers. Ice from a factory on the road to the roundabout. For better shopping go into Phuket town where there are a number of large supermarkets including Robinsons which stocks many imported items. The buses usually stop and leave from the market which always has an impressive array of fresh fruit and vegetables and fresh fish and creatures of all shapes and sizes. It is worth a wander around even if you intend to buy little.

Eating out Most yachties spend a bit of time at Jimmy's Bar on the waterfront where reasonable food and cold beer is served by girls in sailor suits. Good Thai food, including good seafood can be found at other restaurants on the road to the roundabout or in the complex of stalls to the E, although at the latter make sure you ask for the chillis to be left out, even if you like hot food.

Other PO on the road going S from the roundabout. Banks and money changers in Phuket including ATMs which take *Visa* and *Mastercard* for cash advances. Laundry at Big A or other shops in Chalong. Telephone/fax service at Big A or in Phuket. Hire motorbikes at Chalong and hire cars and motorbikes in Phuket.

Addresses

Big A, Next to Jimmy's Bar. Can arrange most boat repairs, stocks Thai charts, laundry service, telephone/fax service and will hold mail.

Big A, Next to Jimmy's Lighthouse, Chalong, Phuket. ☎/*Fax* (66) (76) 381 934

Rolly Tasker Sails, 26/2 Chaofa Road, Chalong, Phuket, Thailand 83130. ☎ (66) (76) 280 347 *Fax* (66) (76) 280 348

G C Huat, 18 Rassada St (near the market), Phuket town, Phuket. ☎ (66) (76) 211 098 *Fax* (66) (76) 211 097

Spares can be ordered if they are not in stock.

Ban Nit on the E side of Ao Chalong.

General

Most yachts end up in Ao Chalong at one time or another. It is not only a secure anchorage, but a meeting place for cruising yachts with good facilities and easy access to Phuket town and the airport. It is a secure place to leave a yacht although it may not be a bad idea to get someone to keep an eye on it if you are going to be away for a long time. It is not the quietest place around with tripper boats and water taxis roaring in and out, but it is not too noisy either and some yachties have been known to settle down here for months.

Jimmy's Lighthouse is a well known watering hole for yachties and the service is friendly and the food reliable. The bay is unfortunately not a good place for swimming being a bit murky, but if you go over to the eastern side under Ban Nit the water is clearer.

Anchorages around Ao Chalong

1. **Ban Nit** On the E side of the bay where shown on the plan. This anchorage is more comfortable in the NE monsoon as there is little fetch, but with the SW monsoon a considerable chop can build up across the bay and roll into the anchorage. Pick up a mooring if one is free or anchor in 4–6m. A reef fringes the beach through which an access channel has been cut for dinghies. At low water springs a fair amount of mud is exposed. Ashore there are restaurants and bars. Water is available from a buoyed water hose off the water mooring buoy just off the reef. Call up on VHF Ch 69 (Ban Nit Marina) for the water to be turned on. It is reported to be potable. Fuel can be delivered and some minor repairs organised. There is a bus service into Phuket from the road on top of the ridge.
2. **Fish Farm Bay** In the bay around the corner from Ban Nit which has a number of floating fish farms in it there is good shelter from the NE monsoon. You can anchor inside the fish farms with care. Clearer water than in the bay proper.
3. **Aquarium** Next to the fisheries there is an aquarium which is open to the public. Anchor off in 5–7m on mud. Good shelter from the NE monsoon but there is usually a lot of wash from craft using the E channel at speed.

Nai Harn

07°45'·95N 98°17'·69E WGS 84

The bay on the SW tip of Phuket Island. It is easily recognised by the wind generators on the ridge above and once into the bay the white buildings of the Phuket Yacht Club on the N side. With care it would be possible to enter at night although it is not recommended. Anchor off the Phuket Yacht Club or other convenient depths in the bay in 5–15m. The bottom is sand and good holding. Good shelter from the NE monsoon although any swell in the Andaman Sea works its way in. There can often be a light surf on the beach which makes it interesting

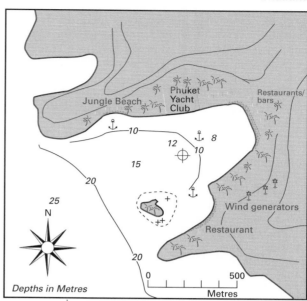

NAI HARN ⊕ 07°46'·37N 98°18'·1E WGS 84

King's Cup boats in Nai Harn.

getting ashore in the dinghy. Open to the SW monsoon. A yacht should not be left unattended here as if the wind turns it is a lee shore and every year there is usually a yacht which ends up on the beach.

Ashore there are the very upmarket facilities of the Phuket Yacht Club or a good selection of beach restaurants around the shore. To the W of the Phuket Yacht Club there is a small beach known as Jungle Beach with a simple but good seafood restaurant. It is possible to anchor close off here with good swimming in clear water off the beach.

In early December this is the base for the King's Cup with the committees and race office billeted in the Phuket Yacht Club. The place buzzes with dinghies going back and forth and parties ashore or on boats. It is an enviable location for a week of racing and should not be missed.

Patong looking out into the bay from the resort.

Patong

The large bay on the W coast of Phuket Island with a foreshore lined by hotels and buildings of all shapes and sizes and heights. It is difficult to miss. This is a popular NE monsoon anchorage with good shelter, although like Nai Harn care is needed with onshore winds. Anchor in 5–15m on a gradually shelving bottom. The bottom is mostly sand and good holding once you ensure your anchor is well in.

Ashore there are all the facilities of a large tourist resort. There are numerous banks and ATMs which will give cash advances on *Visa* and *Mastercard*. Telephone and fax services. Travel agents. There are enough restaurants of all types including Italian,

French, Mexican, English pubs, fast food, just about anything you might desire. There are more bars and night-clubs than almost any other square mile in the world. This is sin-city with a deserved reputation for sexy shows and sexy girls. Just remind your crew there are a lot of lady-boys around and that the slickest sexiest shows are usually of the lady-boy variety. Patong is popular with yachties over Christmas, New Year and Songkran when there is usually a lot of festivity at Patong and impressive fireworks.

West coast of Phuket. From bottom to top: Kata Noi, Kata, and Karon.

Other west coast anchorages

Between Nai Harn and to the N of Patong there are numerous other bays which can be used during the NE monsoon which have a number of hotels and restaurants on the foreshore, often a large number of hotels and restaurants as the whole Phuket W coast is a popular tourist destination. Access to the bays is mostly straightforward. The following are popular anchorages going N from Nai Harn.

Kata Noi, Kata Beach, Karon Beach, Meridien Bay, Freedom Bay, Kamala, Surin, Bang Tao, Mai Khao.

Boat Lagoon

A marina built inside the mangroves with a 2km long winding channel from the sea marked by beacons. For most craft drawing more than 1·5m it

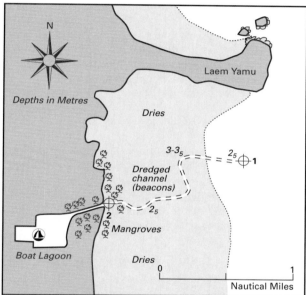

APPROACH TO BOAT LAGOON
1 ⊕ 07°58'·67N 98°24'·95E WGS 84
2 ⊕ 07°58'·05N 98°23'·9E WGS 84

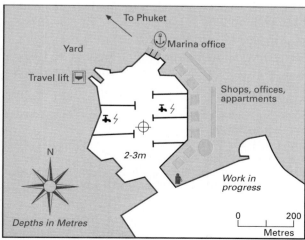

BOAT LAGOON ⊕ 07°57'·8N 98°23'·2E WGS 84

Boat lagoon tucked up inside the mangroves

is best to go in on a rising tide. Craft drawing up to 2·5m can enter although it is planned to dredge the channel so that deeper draught craft can enter.

Approach
The seaward end of the channel is located under Laem Yamu and NW of Ko Rang. The beacons are not easy to make out, but closer in will be easily identified. If you are waiting for a rising tide there is a pleasant anchorage off the beach on the SW side of Ko Rang.

Conspicuous The islands of Ko Rang, Ko Maphrao and Ko Mali are easily located. The beacons are difficult to spot at first but closer in will be seen. The entrance to the channel is at 07°58'·67N 98°24'·95E WGS 84.

By night A night entrance must not be attempted.
VHF Ch 71 for the harbourmaster. He will advise you on the state of the tide and on whether it is practical to enter.

The channel marked by poles into Boat Lagoon.

Note At 0755 local time the harbourmaster at the Boat Lagoon broadcasts on Ch 71 a weather forecast, tide times and ranges, and a list of faxes received in the office by boat name.

Dangers

1. There are a number of shallow spots in the channel which are dredged periodically. If you go aground it is all mud in sheltered waters within the bay.
2. If large craft, particularly large motor yachts are coming out as you go in, it can be a bit of a squeeze in the channel. Slow down and edge by.

Mooring

Data 120 berths. Visitors berths. Max LOA 100ft. Draught restricted to 2·5m by entrance channel.

Berth Where directed. There are finger pontoons for most berths.

Shelter All round shelter.

Authorities Harbourmaster and marina attendants. Charge band 2. Sliding scale for longer term stays.

Facilities

Services Water and electricity at every berth. Shower and toilet block. Phone and cable TV connections possible.

Fuel Fuel quay with diesel and petrol at the entrance.

Repairs 60-ton travel-hoist. Large area of hard standing. Good range of services. Mechanical and engineering repairs. GRP and wood repairs. Electrical and some electronic repairs. Sail repairs can be arranged. Canvas work. Chandlers. Phuket Yacht Services are a long established company that can carry out or arrange most repair jobs. See address at the end of this section.

Provisions Limited provisions available in the marina. There is a small supermarket at the land entrance to the marina or it is a short distance into Phuket town.

Eating out Limited in the marina. Go into Phuket town.

Other Exchange facilities. Telephone and fax service. Taxis available into Phuket or walk out to the main road and flag down a bus or *tuk-tuk*.

Addresses

Phuket Boat Lagoon, 22/1 Thepkassatri Road, PO Box 500, Phuket, ☎ (66) (76) 239 055 *Fax* (66) (76) 239 056

Phuket Marina Services, Phuket Boat Lagoon, 22/1 Moo 2 Thepkassatri Road, Phuket 83200, ☎ (66) (76) 238 944 *Fax* (66) (76) 238 943 *E-mail* marserv@phuket.ksc.co.th

General

Although it sounds a bit odd, it is pleasant if a little bizarre to wend your way up what was an old creek through the mangroves and suddenly come upon a Mediterranean style marina development with stucco apartments around the edges. It is even more odd to be able to get on and off your yacht without dinghying ashore. The marina was the first to be developed on the west coast of Thailand and because it provides secure berths and good yacht facilities it has prospered. It can be a bit still in here out of the wind during the humid summer period, but there is little else like it except for the Yacht Haven development on the north of Phuket Island. There are plans to expand the number of berths for the second stage of the development and dredge and widen the entrance channel.

Yacht Haven

A new marina and condominium development on the N of Phuket Island just E of Sarasin Bridge which connects Phuket Island to the mainland.

Approach

The entrance in from Phang-Nga Bay looks difficult, but in practice it is straightforward. The islands and islets in the approaches are easily identified and the only tricky bit is in the immediate approaches between the mud bank fringing the coast of Phuket Island and the isolated sand bank on the NE side. Both of these dangers can usually be seen and at low tide they dry. A course of around 320°M on the tall electricity pylon on the mainland side at Sarasin Bridge from Ko Ngam leads more or less clear to the marina as shown on the plan. There is some tidal current in the enclosed waters running pretty much NW–SE along the channel, but it poses no real problems.

Conspicuous The condominium development around the marina and the marina itself are easily identified.

By night A night approach should not be attempted unless totally familiar with the area. A transit light is to be established at the marina Iso.RWG.4s.

VHF Ch 72 for the harbourmaster.

Mooring

Data 300 berths. Visitors berths. Max LOA 90ft. Max draught 5m at the marina.

Berth Where directed. Finger pontoons.

Shelter Good shelter although there can be a bit of a chop when winds blow freshly up and down the channel.

Authorities Harbourmaster and marina attendants. Charge band 2/3.

Facilities

Services Water and electricity at every berth. Phone and cable TV can be connected. Shower and toilet block.

Fuel Fuel quay.

Repairs Small slipway and workshops. Some repairs can be organised from here.

Provisions Mini-market. Ice.

Eating out Several restaurants.

Other Exchange facilities. Laundry. Car hire and taxi service. Phuket Airport is around 15 minutes away.

General

The Yacht Haven has experienced a number of teething problems during the building programme, but is now up and running. Not all services are

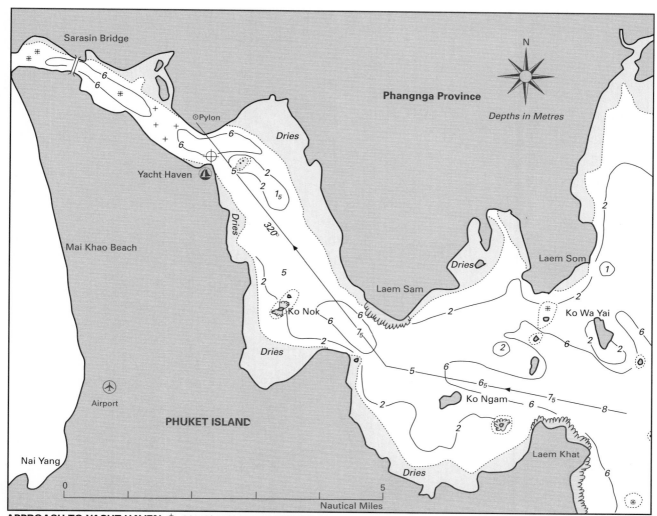

APPROACH TO YACHT HAVEN ⊕ 08°10'·34N 98°20'·4E WGS 84

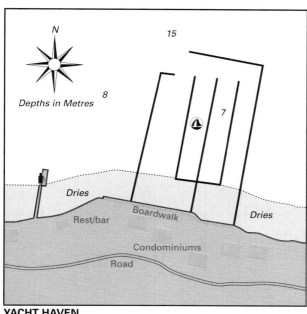

YACHT HAVEN

available at the time of writing, but it is likely most facilities will be in place in the near future.

Phang-Nga Bay

Phang-Nga Bay is the large area between the east coast of Phuket and the mainland coast around to Krabi. The whole bay is peppered with islands and islets and most of the water is comparatively shallow making anchoring an easy prospect. The islands and islets are simply spectacular, tall limestone pinnacles covered in jungle and surrounded by green waters. Many of the islands have *hongs*, the collapsed cave systems which are accessible from the sea at low tide. Wandering along a dark tunnel until you get to where the roof has collapsed and it is open to the sky is an experience you should not miss – a bit of claustrophobia is worth it for the entrance to the steep-to hole at the end. The water in Phang-Nga Bay, fed by numerous rivers, has a lot of river silt in it making it fairly murky, although quite clean for swimming.

The tide as expected flows up into Phang-Nga Bay on the flood and out on the ebb. Tidal currents

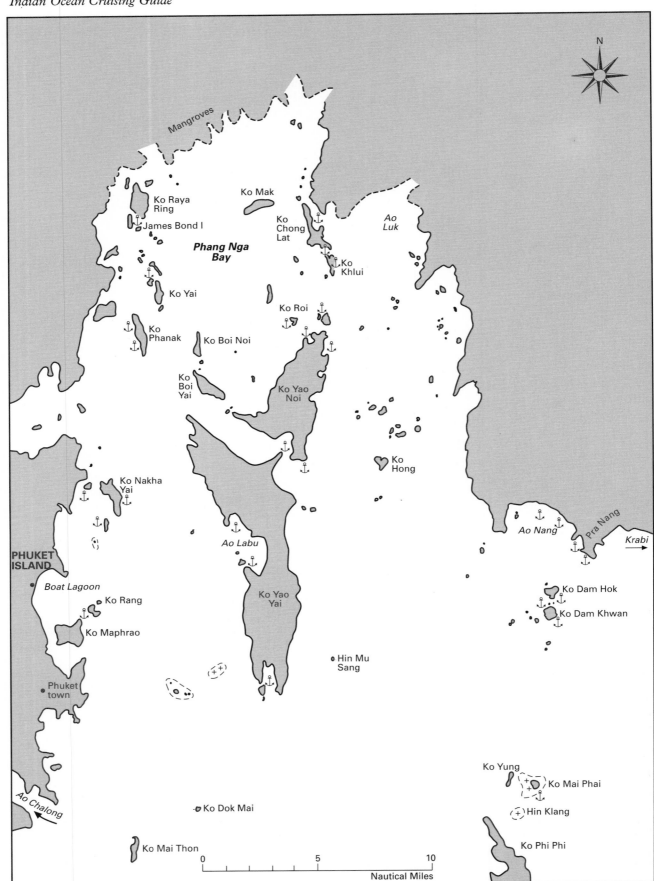

PHANG NGA BAY TO PHI PHI

often exceed 2kn at springs so a bit of planning for the tide does not go astray. The sheltered waters are rarely rough and although squalls can come through, they are usually less than 30kn and fairly short-lived affairs. They may be accompanied by torrential rain which drastically reduces visibility.

I will only mention a few of the numerous possible anchorages here. A perusal of the chart and reference to the plans and instructions in *Sail Thailand* should sort out an itinerary and suitable anchorages.

Ko Yao Yai The largest island in the bay lying off the E coast of Phuket. There are several anchorages with Ao Labu half way down the W side being easy of access and well sheltered in the NE monsoon. It is also possible to anchor in the bay at the S end although most of it is encumbered by a reef.

Ko Yao Noi The large island above Ko Yao Yai. Anchorages on either side of the N end of the island.

Ko Phanak Convenient depths around the island in settled weather. During the NE monsoon anchor in the SW or NW bays. Several near the NW bay.

James Bond Island The small islet of Ko Phing Kan at the S end of Ko Raya Ring. It was used in the filming *of The Man With The Golden Gun* and consequently is visited by hordes of tripper boats every day. In reality the scenery around other islands is better than the location here. Visit it by tripper boat if you must.

Ko Chong Lat The thin island with Ko Khlui under it. Good anchorage in the channel between Chong Lat and the coast or around the N end of Ko Chlui. Strong tidal streams in the vicinity.

Ko Hong Group The cluster of islands between Ko Yao Noi and the mainland coast. More for lunch stops than an overnight stay. Visit here and go to Krabi for the night.

Ao Nang (Krabi)

Yachts do not actually go to Krabi itself, but to Ao Nang or to Laem Nang.

Approach
Straightforward. The islets in the approaches are easily identified.

Mooring
Anchor in the middle off Ko Sam or in the SE corner. Anchor in 3–6m on a sandy bottom.
Shelter Good shelter in the NE monsoon. Open to the SW.

Dinghies Off Ko Sam you can get into the river and leave the dinghy at the jetty to get into Krabi. The road is nearby and buses and taxis run into town. In the SE corner there are a number of places where you can get the dinghy ashore off either the Krabi Resort or Pra Nang.

Authorities Immigration and customs in Krabi town.

You only need to see them if you are clearing in or out of Thailand.

Facilities
Around the beach there are numerous restaurants and bars with some more upmarket ones at the flashy resorts. Good seafood available. Limited provisions available. In Krabi there are banks, provisions and telephone and fax agencies. You can get a bus or taxi into Krabi from the main road running around the shore.

General
The bay is spectacular under high limestone cliffs covered in jungle. Palms line the beaches and the water is clean and clear for swimming and snorkelling. The anchorage is popular in the summer for both its beauty and a modest choice of facilities ashore.

Laem Nang

Anchor in the bay N of the reef, or if there is room, in the cove S of the reef running out to the islets off the SW side of the headland. Good shelter in the NE monsoon. There are beach restaurants and bars around the beach and the upmarket Dusit Rayavadee Hotel across part of the peninsula. The location is superb with clear water and good snorkelling. There is no road access to Krabi.

Similan Islands

This group of islands lies just over 50M NW of Patong on the W coast of Phuket. With clear seas between Phuket and the islands the best policy is to leave around midnight arriving sometime in the morning. This has the advantage of picking up the offshore land breeze and NE monsoon to give a close reach to the group. A light is exhibited on Ko Similan, Fl(3)20s17M.

The islands are a national park and the water around them is exceptionally clear. Not surprisingly they are popular with diveboat parties and during the NE monsoon there are a lot of diveboats around. Good diving and snorkelling all around the islands.

Ko Similan There is really only one useful overnight anchorage on Ko Similan itself. On the NW tip of the island is a bay affording good shelter from the NE monsoon. Pick up one of the visitors moorings if one is free or a diveboat mooring if not in use. You may find diveboats return late in the day to reclaim the mooring you are on. If you have to anchor off it will be outside the moorings area in 15–30m as the bottom drops off quickly. Good shelter from the NE monsoon. The anchorage is not as tranquil as might be wished with the coming and going of diveboats, generators and compressors buzzing away all over the place and diveboat parties going on late into the evening. The bay itself is beautiful and there are good walks ashore.

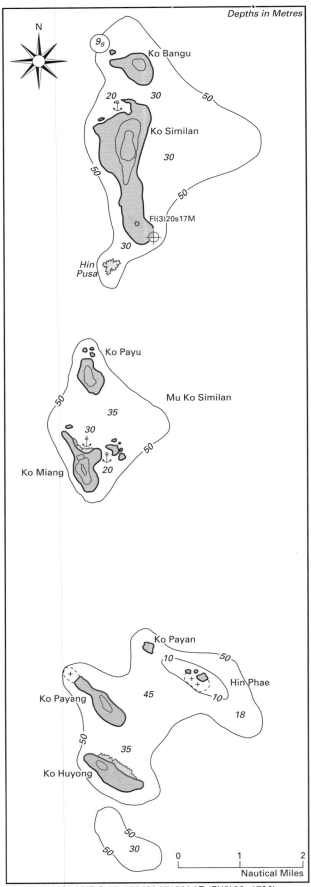

Depths in Metres

N

Ko Bangu

20   30   50

Ko Similan

30

50

50

Fl(3)20s17M

30

Hin Pusa

Ko Payu

Mu Ko Similan

50

35

30

20

Ko Miang

Ko Payan

10   50

Hin Phae

Ko Payang   45   10

18

50

35

Ko Huyong

50

50   30

0   1   2

Nautical Miles

SIMILAN ISLANDS 08°37′·9N 97°39′·1E (Fl(3)20s17M)

Ko Miang The best anchorage here is off the E side under the islet lying just off the coast. Anchor in 15–20m on sand, good holding. In settled weather this is a possible overnight anchorage, although the tidal streams running down the E side of Ko Miang are quite strong. Idyllic surroundings and good snorkelling in clear water.

It is also possible to anchor off the national park headquarters to the NW although this is not a good overnight anchorage. Restaurant and bungalows ashore.

Surin Islands

The group of islands lying just under the Thai-Burmese border. A light is exhibited on Ko Chi, the northernmost of the group, Fl.10s15M.

At the time of writing it is prohibited for pleasure craft to enter Burmese waters and it is essential you observe this restriction on navigation.

There are two useful anchorages during the NE monsoon on the W and E sides of Ko Surin Nua. The best anchorage is reported to be on the SW side of Ko Surin Nua tucked into the cove where the two islands nearly meet. Anchor in 15m taking care of coral heads. Alternatively there is an anchorage under the headland running out from the SE end of Ko Surin Nua.

National Park headquarters on Ko Surin Nua.

Burma
(Myanmar)

Burma has been promoting its tourist potential for a number of years with 1996 officially 'Visit Myanmar Year'. At the time of writing this promotion of its tourist appeal does not include visits by yachts and it is prohibited to enter Burmese waters in a private yacht. The archipelago of islands and indented mainland coast extending from the Thai border to the mouth of the Irrawaddy and the Cheduba archipelago down from the Bangladesh-Burma border makes a mouth-watering cruising prospect. The Chergui archipelago, in particular, is as extensive as the islands off the W coast of Thailand and the cruising possibilities immense. Set against this is the political situation in Burma which must be weighed up against any future opening up of Burmese waters.

Burma is one of the most politically repressive regimes in Southeast Asia. Prior to the Second World War Burma was one of the richest countries in the region. It is now the poorest. In 1962 General Ne Win staged a coup d'etat which ushered in a period of political and social repression which continues to this day. In 1988 riots and demonstrations by the population against the government were brutally repressed. Ne Win ordered the streets to be cleared with bullets and estimates put the casualties at 12,000 with 3000–4000 killed. A military junta was set up, the State Law and Order Restoration Council (SLORC), which has continued to rule the country with all the repression and disregard for human rights that Ne Win used to keep order. In 1990 elections were held and Aung San Suu Kyi's National League for Democracy (NLD) won 82% of the vote despite the fact that Aung San Suu Kyi had been under house arrest since 1989. SLORC had miscalculated and immediately imprisoned the leaders of the NLD and arrested many of its activists. Others fled to Thailand as a period of violent repression and atrocities by the military was mounted to contain the threat of democracy triumphing against the junta. In 1995 Aung San Suu Kyi was released only to be put under house arrest again where she remains. Meanwhile SLORC promotes the tourist potential of the country and has tendered contracts to large multinationals for oil, gas and mineral rights.

If you are intending to visit Burma by land I suggest you weigh up the moral legitimation that tourists give to this corrupt regime. If you do visit I suggest you avoid government (SLORC) sponsored hotels and tours which are in any case very expensive by Southeast Asian standards. Spend your money at local hotels and restaurants and after your visit write to the tourist office expressing your concern over repression by SLORC of the population. The violence to the population is evident with a bit of sniffing around although the locals are usually reluctant to talk for fear of informers and the secret police. Organisations like Amnesty International have extensive files on the repression in Burma and much has been documented elsewhere. If pressure on SLORC leads to a situation where the democratically elected NLD and Aung San Suu Kyi come to power, it will lead to a country which will be a joy to visit and to the eventual possibility of cruising around its extensive coastline and islands by private yacht.

Further reading
Thailand and Burma Handbook Footprint Guides/Trade & Travel.
Freedom from Fear Aung San Suu Kyi. Penguin
Outrage: Burma's struggle for democracy Bertil Lintner. White Lotus. Documents the 1988 uprising and is banned in Burma.

Andaman Islands
BA *825, 1419, 1398*

The Andaman Islands are an archipelago running more or less in a N–S direction for 200 miles between 13°40'N and 10°30'N. There are said to be over 200 islands in the group, although the three largest islands, North, Middle and South Andaman, lie close together and overlap at the edges to effectively make up one very large landmass called Great Andaman. At the bottom of the group is Little Andaman.

The Andamans are governed by India and it is necessary to get an Indian visa with a permit to visit a restricted area before arriving at Port Blair. An Indian visa can be arranged in Bangkok or Kuala Lumpur and is in any case necessary if you are continuing on to India. For further details on visas see the relevant section under India. A number of yachts have arrived in Port Blair without a visa and while some have been allowed to stay a week or so, most have been given three days and restricted to Port Blair itself.

The islands have extensive fringing and barrier reefs and great care is needed within 10 miles of the coast. There are also significant tidal currents around the islands and through the channels, some of which give rise to overfalls and can run at 3–4kn at springs. Anyone on passage to or from the Andamans will find patches of disturbed water and overfalls all around the Andaman Sea, even 50 miles or so from land. It can be quite disconcerting to run into an area of disturbed water from a virtual calm or long ground swell when there are depths of well over 1000m and no land in sight.

Yachts must head for Port Blair on the SE side of South Andaman and not stop elsewhere in the group. The islands were once off limits as there were a number of Soviet military bases here and much sensitive monitoring equipment remains.

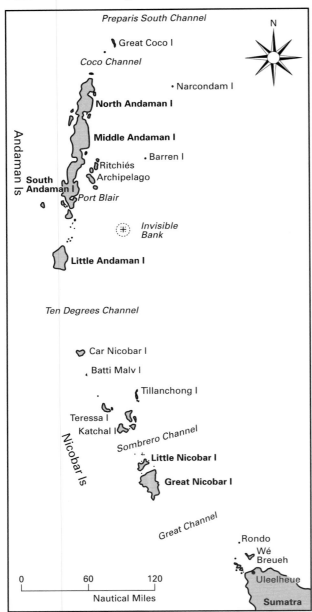

ANDAMANS AND NICOBARS

Port Blair

BA 514

Approach

Most boats will make the approach from the SE. The only danger in the outer approaches is Invisible Bank. In the final approach Ross Island should be left to port. Once up to the entrance the approach is straightforward and clear of dangers until up to Phoenix Bay.

Conspicuous Ross Island can be difficult to make out, but closer in the light structure on the N end will be seen. The hinterland and coast is heavily wooded and it can be difficult to distinguish buildings and structures.

By night Although the approach is reasonably well lit, a night approach is not recommended.

North Point Fl(2)12s20M
Ross Island N end Fl.15s8M
Perseverance Point Fl.10s8M
Southern entrance Fl.5s6M
Command Point Fl(2)20s5M
Blair Reef beacon Fl.R.6sm6M.

VHF Ch 16 for coastguard and navy.

Dangers Care is needed of Blair Reef in the final approach to Phoenix Bay.

Mooring

Anchor where directed or in convenient depths in the SE of Phoenix Bay. You may be directed onto the quay to clear in and in some cases it has been possible to stay on the quay.

Shelter Reasonable shelter with the NE monsoon although it can get a bit rolly in the bay sometimes.

Authorities Police and naval authorities. There are no standardised procedures for clearing in and you will have to let the navy and police sort things out.

Facilities

Water Near the quay.
Fuel Can be organised.
Repairs Basic mechanical and engineering repairs only.
Provisions Most of the basics can be found in Aberdeen.
Eating out Local restaurants in Aberdeen with excellent seafood and venison – mostly South India style, but also Chinese and Burmese styles. As more tourists arrive it is likely more restaurants will open.
Other PO. Bank. Hospital. Taxis. Ferries and flights to mainland India.

General

Aberdeen has seen some development in the last couple of decades, but it remains essentially a small colonial town. Doubtless things will change as more hotels are built. For the moment it is small enough to be able to see just about everything there is in half a day. From Aberdeen you can organise excursions to the farms, the saw mill on Chatham Island and get to the beach resorts at Corbyn Bay.

Most yachts have been given permission to anchor off Ross Island and also the islands of Wandour Marine Park around the S end of South Andaman Island. The diving and fishing here is reported to be nothing short of superb.

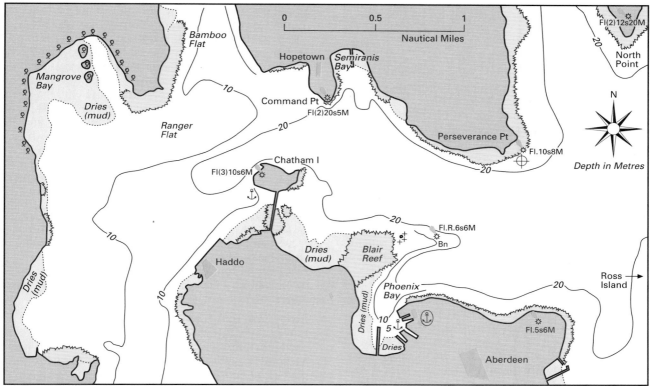

PORT BLAIR ⊕ 11°41'·3N 92°44'·8E

Nicobar Islands

The Nicobar Islands are administered by India in conjunction with the Andamans. Unlike the Andamans, the Nicobar Islands are not open to yachts and it is prohibited to navigate close to the coast or anchor off the coast anywhere. There have been odd rumours that the islands will be opened up to tourism and be accessible to yachts, but at the time of writing the islands are definitely off limits to yachts. In 1997 a yacht which anchored off in the Nicobars was arrested and detained before being requested to leave. Other yachts have in the past related stories of cruising in the Nicobars, but I would counsel caution over many of the stories which are apocryphal accounts usually fourth or fifth hand and related after a good number of beers in a bar.

It is a shame that the Nicobars cannot be cruised as there are a wealth of natural harbours and bays as can be seen from a brief perusal of the chart. In the past, and the not too distant past, the islands had a reputation for piracy and cut-throat inhabitants. The Nicobarese were said to practice cannibalism and to this day there are still a number of indigenous tribes (reckoned at about 15% of the population) on the Nicobar Islands. While the Indian government would have you believe that prohibiting cruising around the coast is to do with protecting the native peoples, it also certainly has something to do with the Russian military installations on the islands which are now in the hands of the Indian military. There is air and naval surveillance of the coast and surrounding seas which will be evident if you are near the coast or on passage through Ten Degree Channel, the Sombrero Channel or Great Channel. However there is no problem using these channels on passage E or W, although care may be needed in Sombrero Channel.

Sri Lanka

Current situation

Since 1983 when anti-Tamil riots erupted in Colombo and left hundreds of Tamils dead, there has been increasing violence leading to a civil war between the predominantly Singhalese Sri Lankan military and Tamil resistance groups. One of these groups, the Liberation Tigers of Tamil Elam, or Tamil Tigers for short, soon gained ascendancy as the dominant resistance group and has fought a guerrilla war in the north of the island since the mid-1980s. Despite proclamations by the Sri Lankan military that the group would be wiped out (in 1987, 1991 and 1995–96) very soon, it continues to fight on. All the actual fighting is concentrated in the N and NE of the island, but the Tigers use suicide bombers and frogmen to mount attacks elsewhere, notably in Colombo.

The on-going violence means there is considerable internal security and this applies to any yachts visiting the island. In effect there is only one harbour, that at Galle, used by yachts, and here your yacht will be searched (a fairly cursory procedure) by the navy and at night small depth charges are randomly dropped into the harbour to deter Tamil frogmen from entering and placing explosives on craft. If you happen to be coming from India to Sri Lanka, a fairly unusual route which I used going eastabout, you may well be subject to additional searches, in my case by an armed party and an apologetic officer. While this might all seem dramatic, you get used to it surprisingly quickly.

Inland there are few problems travelling around and most areas in the S and middle of the island are considered safe from Tamil attacks. You are more likely to be worried by the police who have a reputation for corrupt practices and the general advice is not to go to a police station unless you really need to. If you do, go with a friend and if possible report any incident to your consular office. I should add that on the one occasion I went to a police station inland in Kandy I encountered no problems apart from a general lack of interest in my plight.

Documentation and visas

Normal boats papers and a valid passport for all crew members must be carried. A visa can be issued on arrival and need not be obtained in advance.
Evidence of immunisation against yellow fever may be asked for, especially if you have come from Africa.

Entry and exit formalities

Entry is straightforward. Arrival should be timed for daylight hours as it is prohibited to enter the harbour at night and in any case it is hardly worth the risk of being mistaken for a Tamil boat making a surprise night attack on the harbour. If you arrive off the harbour at night, as I did on the trip eastabout, this means pottering up and down between the large numbers of fishing boats operating off the coast which becomes less nerve-

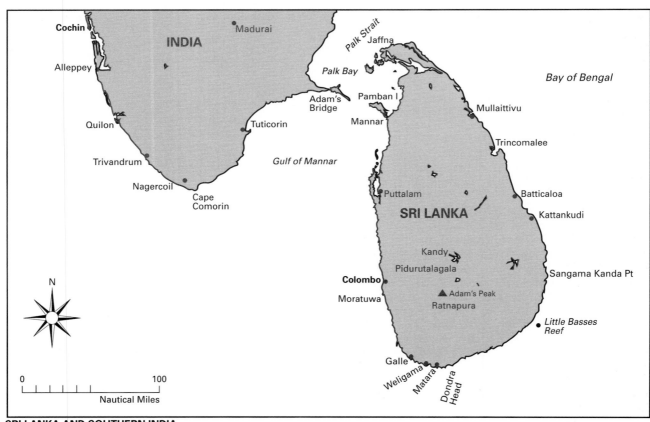

SRI LANKA AND SOUTHERN INDIA

wracking as the night wears on when the positions of the fishing fleet are established.

Because of the ongoing civil war with the Tamils in the north there is much security in evidence. Recently security has been tightened and yachts must now wait at the entrance until a navy cutter comes out to clear you into the harbour. This entails either a cursory search of the yacht and/or just taking the names and passport numbers of those on board and a few details on the yacht. You can then enter the harbour.

When you have moored the procedure is as follows:

1. You will be visited by the harbourmaster or his representative who will inform the clearing agent (the Windsors) of your arrival or will authorise you to go ashore to clear in. Clearing in can only be done through the Windsors. You will be dealing with one of the late and legendary Don Windsor's sons, either Santosh, Vinney or Indra. There always seems to be some discontent over this, but in fact the Windsors are the only ones who have lodged a bond with the government to carry out the requisite paperwork.
2. You must clear with the port health officer either on board or in the company of a 'guide' from the Windsors.
3. You clear with customs and immigration, usually with a 'guide' from the Windsors.

The basic cost is $140 which covers the paperwork dealing with customs and immigration and one month's mooring in the harbour and the Windsor's fee. For additional months charges are $66 plus an agency fee. You have to pay for one month's mooring even if you intend staying only a few days so it makes sense to plan for up to a month in Galle. There is much to see and do.

The Windsors can be contacted in advance and mail can be held there.

Don Windsor & Co Ltd, 6 Closenburg Road,
Magalle, Galle, Sri Lanka, ☎ (94) 9
22927/34592 *Mobile* 072 31213
Fax (94) 9 34592

Once you are cleared in there is no obligation to use the Windsor's for other services although many yachts choose to do so.

Exit formalities are included in the fee above and involve notifying the Windsors of a departure date. Although formalities usually only take a few hours for clearing out it is best to notify the Windsors several days in advance in case of holidays or other difficulties. You will need to give them your passports and ships papers.

You must clear in and out of Sri Lanka at every port which effectively proscribes cruising between ports. This is not, in any case, practical as although the ports below are listed as possible yacht harbours which can legitimately be visited, at least according to the handout attributed to the Secretary of Defence, only Galle and Colombo are equipped to handle pleasure yachts and several of the harbours listed lie within the war zone. If the civil war ends in the future then other ports may be suitable destinations for yachts and it may be possible to cruise around the island again.

Permitted ports for yachts: Colombo, Galle, Trincomalee, Jaffna, Kankasanthurai.

Data

Area 65,610km² (25,332M²)

Coastline 1340km (724 M)

Maritime claims Territorial 12M. Exclusive economic zone 200M. There may be sea and air patrols up to 100–150M off the coast and you may be buzzed by an aircraft or helicopter.

Population 17,800,00

Capital Colombo

Time zone UT+5½

Language Sinhalese and Tamil. Around 10% of the population speak English.

Ethnic divisions Sinhalese 74%, Tamil 18%, Moor 7%.

Religion Bhuddist 69%, Hindu 15%, Christian 8%, Muslim 8%.

Public holidays Most holidays are organised around the lunar calendar and vary from year to year. *Poya* days are full moon days. There can be 'normal' *poya* days and *poya* days on which there are special celebrations. The largest *poya* celebrations are in May (*Wesak*) and July (*Esala*). On any *poya* day no alcohol is sold and places of entertainment are closed. In practice this does not apply to hotels.
Feb 4 National Day
May 1 May Day
May 22 National Heroes Day
Jun 30 Bank Holiday
Dec 25 Christmas
Dec 31 Special Bank Holiday

Government Democratic Republic. There is much rumoured and some recorded evidence of fairly hefty corruption involving the various parties, but especially the anti-Tamil JVP, in the killing and disappearance of people and involvement with the criminal fraternity.

Disputes Internal civil war between the Sri Lankan military and the Tamil Tigers who want to establish an independent homeland, Tamil Elam, in the N of the island. See preceding *Current Situation*.

Crime The crime level is low. Despite the poverty evident in many places, actual theft and violent crime to visitors is very low. You will be overcharged by the locals and conned by touts, but it is very unlikely you will be the victim of theft via pickpockets or muggings. The yacht harbour at Galle is within the customs enclosure for the port and there are no known reports of theft in the harbour.

Touts Sri Lanka has some of the most persistent touts in the world. You will be followed for hours by touts offering to change money, sell gems, lace and seashells, take you to yet another Bhuddist temple, sell you illegal substances and questionable services, indeed find anything you need. If an apparently affable young man enquires if he can help you, the chances are he will expect a fee in return for finding you things that you can easily find for yourself. It can become irritating even to the most tolerant of us and I can only counsel patience and a brisk walking pace.

Travel
Internal
Rail and coach links to most of the major towns and cities. Also mini-bus and driver and hire cars and motorcycles.

Rail The trains are fairly basic and rattle along at a bone-shaking pace, but are cheap and adequate for the comparatively short distances covered between towns.

Bus The buses are basic and the driving erratic. Buses connect to most places but they are usually crowded to overflowing and the better option is to take a train if possible.

Mini-bus Most yachties will elect to take a mini-bus from one of the agents and this is the sensible option. Make your choice on cost and an intuitive choice of driver. The driver will understand that excessively erratic driving will cause dissent and you get to more or less make up your own itinerary with advice from the driver. It pays to do a bit of research beforehand in case there is anything you would really like to see.

Hire cars and motor bikes Hire cars and motorbikes available at Hikkaduwa and Colombo. We hired motorbikes at Colombo and played biker boys around the highlands. On the main roads there is a lot of traffic pumping out poisonous diesel fumes and it pays to remember that it often rains for a bit in the afternoon. Once you get off the main roads there is not too much traffic to worry about and the welcome in small villages off the normal route is often embarrassing – you feel like royalty riding around and returning the locals waves and smiles. It turned out to be the best thing we did in Sri Lanka and I recommend it if you feel like a bit of adventure.

International
There are a few international flights to Southeast Asia and India and onwards to Europe with Air Lanka. A number of other carriers like Air France also have flights to and from Sri Lanka, but with the troubles there are not a lot of flights overall.

Practicalities
Mail Is slow and inefficient, but generally reliable. Mail can be sent to the Windsors who will hold it for you at the address above. Several courier services at Colombo including DHL.

Telecommunications IDD system. Country code 94. The telecommunication system is adequate. There are IDD bureau's in most major towns or use the telephone and fax system of someone like the Windsors.

Currency The unit is the Sri Lankan rupee. Sri Lankan rupees are not interchangeable with Indian rupees and in fact are not interchangeable with very much after you leave Sri Lanka. The rate is fairly stable, but there is little point to hold Sri Lankan rupees before or after your stay in the country.

Banks and exchange In Galle there are several banks that can exchange cash and travellers cheques for rupees. There are also money changers and touts offering to change cash. The Bank of Ceylon will give cash advances on *Visa* cards. Banking hours are 0900–1300 Mon-Fri.

Medical care Is generally good with a recommendation in private hospitals. Many of the doctors have trained in the UK or Europe and will nearly always speak English. Ask at the Windsors for a recommendation. A wide range of drugs can be bought over the counter at pharmacies.

The water is generally safe to drink but if in doubt treat it before using it or filling the boats tanks. Bottled water is available.

Electricity 230–240V AC. The current is variable.

Curiosities and culture
Buddhism Sri Lankan Buddhism is of the Hinayana form which declined in India with the ascendancy of Hinduism. The Hinayana form, or Little Way, emphasises the monastic way of life as the route to nirvana. In fact Sri Lankan Buddhism has been much modified over the years and has for a long time been closely intertwined with secular affairs and matters of state. In Sri Lanka there is an ongoing debate over whether Buddhism should be actively supported by the state as opposed to the more ascetic and self supporting forms found elsewhere, and this debate is actively picked up by the main political parties who try to identify themselves with Sri Lankan Buddhism. The institutionalised nature of Sri Lankan Buddhism is much in evidence with large temples, monasteries and statues of the Buddha scattered around the landscape. For me it does not have the softened edges and more gentle form of Buddhist practice of whatever form found elsewhere. There is a definite presence and mode of worship of the Buddha somehow at odds with other more ascetic forms. Then again what would an old agnostic like me know about these things?

The Highlands If you are in Sri Lanka it would be inexcusable not to go up into the highlands. Huge tea plantations with delightful old-fashioned names like *Wilderlands* and *Hightree* are graced by 19th- and early 20th-century colonial buildings. Thick jungle clings to the slopes and waterfalls drop a hundred feet and more down rocky slopes. There are enough Bhuddist temples and shrines to satisfy anyone and the highland soil grows some of the largest and brightest vegetables I've seen anywhere. Many of the villages have old colonial guesthouses and at six and seven thousand feet it gets cold at night – a welcome respite from the humid heat on the coast. Most yachtsmen hire a minibus and driver from one of the agents in Galle and get a semi-organised tour staying in guest-houses where recommended. However there is no reason why you cannot travel on public transport as a good rail system connects main centres and buses run to smaller places. Alternatively hire a motorbike.

Useful books
Sri Lanka Handbook Footprint Guides. Excellent guide.
The Reef Romesh Gunesekera. Granta

Geography and climate
The coast Sri Lanka is geologically an extension of the Indian Peninsula separated by the narrow and shallow Palk Strait. Most of the land around the coast is flat with numerous fresh and salt water lagoons close to the coast. Nearly all of the coast is covered in high coconut palms and just behind there is invariably thick jungle. Behind the coastal plain the land rises steeply to the central highlands which are mountainous with the valleys folded in on themselves forming steep-to precipitous slopes. It is a spectacular landscape with the highest peak at Pidurutalagala (2524m), although the lower Adams Peak (2260m) is the more conspicuous from seawards.

Coastal waters Around the E, S and most of the W coast of Sri Lanka there is deep water a short distance off. Only in Palk Bay and Palk Strait is there shallow water where until 10,000 years ago Sri Lanka was joined to India. The steep drop-off from the coast and the position of the island at the bottom of the Indian peninsula means that the coast is constantly battered by large seas depending on the monsoon season. Around much of the coast there is always some ground swell which usually breaks as surf on the coast. Many of the beaches have dangerous tidal rips and strong undertow and there are usually a few tourists drowned every year when swimming off some beaches.

Visibility is generally good around the coast, although it is reduced where rivers flow into the sea and where heavy surf stirs up the bottom. Coral grows around much of the coast and there is some good diving although strong currents make many places dangerous.

The position of the island dividing the sea areas E and W of it also means that it is rich in fish stocks, the last geographical barrier for fish migration W or E. Along the S coast there are always numerous fishing boats, large and small, during the NE monsoon and in places it is positively crowded. During the SW monsoon heavy seas largely prevent fishing on the exposed coasts.

Palk Bay and Palk Strait This area of shallow water littered with reefs and shifting sandbanks is little used today, in fact I can find no references to yachts using it at all in recent years. This is partially because of the troubles in the N of Sri Lanka and partially because of the very real difficulties of the passage anyway. The old passage used at one time is at the W end of Pamban Island where you have to wait for a railway bridge to open. The approach is very difficult and pilots used to be available for the passage. MacPherson on *Driac* made the passage before the war and had this to say about it.

'Don't think I would like to tackle it with a yacht drawing more than 8ft.

Experienced a light land and sea breeze and anchored off Shingle Island, covering the south approach to Pamban, on February 1st. The channel from here to the Pass is fairly well marked with perches, but we nearly got ashore trying to creep through next morning, so we dropped the hook half-way and waited for a pilot. Pilotage is compulsory, and the railway bridge (on the Indian side) isn't lifted till the dues have been paid.'

After Pamban Island the passage across the shallow Palk Strait is not at all straightforward with banks of 5·5–9m (18–30ft) and shoal patches of 2·45–2·75m (8–9ft).

Climate Like India the climate is dominated by the NE and SW monsoons and reference should be made to the notes for India. The island, sitting down closer to the ITCZ, is generally wetter than the bottom of India. Climatically the island is divided into the dry zone of the N and E and the wet zone of the S and W, but all things are relative and the dry zone is actually quite wet. Even in the dry season of the NE monsoon it is common to have a short period of heavy rain in the afternoon when the cloud builds up over the highlands.

At Colombo	Av max °C	Av min °C	Relative humidity	Days 1mm rain
Jan	30	22	67%	7
Feb	31	22	66%	6
Mar	31	23	66%	8
Apr	31	24	70%	14
May	31	26	76%	19
Jun	29	25	78%	18
Jul	29	25	77%	12
Aug	29	25	76%	11
Sep	29	25	75%	13
Oct	29	24	76%	19
Nov	29	23	75%	16
Dec	29	22	69%	10

Weather
Prevailing winds near the coast During the NE monsoon winds are deflected down the E coast of Sri Lanka so that they blow from the NNE–N down the coast curving around to blow from the ENE along the S coast. In the Gulf of Mannar the wind is channelled and blows out of the gulf with considerable strength. Around the SW corner winds are mostly variable with a sea breeze sometimes being the prevailing wind.

During the SW monsoon the strong SW winds blow directly onto the W and S coasts raising considerable seas.

Gales During the NE monsoon there are no gale force winds to speak of apart from localised thunderstorms. One local anomaly is in the Gulf of Mannur where the NE monsoon is channelled through the gap between peninsular India and the top of Sri Lanka which effect can give rise to gale force winds over some of this sea area.

With the SW monsoon gale force winds increase and although the recorded percentage is low at around 1–2%, the actual incidence is locally reported to be much higher. Heavy seas set onto the

Month	Prevailing winds 0900	Prevailing winds 1500
Jan	NE/56%	NW/38%
Feb	NE/46%	W–NW/78%
Mar	NE/26%	W/42%
Apr	SW/30%	SW–W/77%
May	SW/56%	SW/61%
Jun	SW/61%	SW/63%
Jul	SW–W/86%	SW–W/91%
Aug	SW–W/85%	SW–W/92%
Sep	SW–W/79%	SW–W/91%
Oct	SW–W/56%	SW–W/75%
Nov	NE/29%	W–NW/58%
Dec	NE/53%	W–NW/50%

Notes Winds for Colombo on the W coast of Sri Lanka. Prevailing winds show a definite sea breeze effect in the afternoon during the NE monsoon. The sea breeze effect will alter the gradient wind to different onshore directions depending on location. Thus at Galle the wind is more SW than at Colombo. Other winds blow for the remaining percentage.

For more information on wind direction and strength see the charts in *Technical Information*, pages 30–31.

W and S coasts of Sri Lanka during the SW monsoon making it a difficult and in places dangerous coast, even if gale force winds are not blowing locally.

Tropical storms Because tropical storms usually breed at around 10° above the equator, Sri Lanka rarely experiences tropical storms. However there are incidences of tropical storms passing over Sri Lanka from the Bay of Bengal and an incidence of a storm breeding in the Gulf of Mannur. This, I would emphasise, is a rare phenomenon.

Thunderstorms and waterspouts Thunderstorms are fairly common in this region where the ITCZ covers or touches the area.

During the NE monsoon these thunderstorms are of fairly short duration and the associated squall is not usually of any consequence. Occasionally there will be strong winds around 30–35kn for an hour or so.

During the SW monsoon there are exceptionally violent and prolonged thunderstorms at the onset of the SW monsoon and to a lesser extent during the SW monsoon. Many of the associated squalls are very strong at up to 40+kt and can be of some duration.

Waterspouts occur in this area at times but in general it is rare to see one, especially during the NE monsoon.

Tides

The tidal range around Sri Lanka is on average less than one metre at springs. Tides are mostly diurnal. Tidal streams are of less importance than the effects of currents converging around Sri Lanka, with the exception of tidal streams in Palk Bay and Palk Strait. Here the Admiralty mentions tidal streams of ¾–1kn setting in irregular directions according to the marine topography and the effects of ocean currents deflecting or augmenting the tidal stream.

Currents

Currents around Sri Lanka are generally stronger than many other places in the northern Indian Ocean. Rates of 1–2kn are common and currents up to 4kn (100M per day) are not uncommon. Sri Lanka is the point of confluence for the current systems in the Arabian Sea and Bay of Bengal and the currents in these two seas are all pushed away from or towards Sri Lanka at the bottom of peninsular India.

As elsewhere in the northern Indian Ocean the currents result from the circulation caused by the NE and SW monsoons. Around Sri Lanka these currents are deflected and accelerated as they hit the coast. Mostly the current flows parallel to the coast in one direction or other, but close inshore strong counter-currents and variable sets are common with an onshore set frequently occurring. The variable and often onshore sets close to the coast mean some vigilance is needed when coasting to or from Galle. The traffic separation scheme for ships runs some 5M off the coast at Dondra Head and yachts frequently keep inside the traffic separation scheme when on passage from Thailand or Malaysia to Galle. A close eye needs to be kept on the GPS for cross-track error as well as on the fishing boats all over the place.

Current direction and rates can be obtained from the charts in *Technical Information*, pages 48-49 but the following notes may be useful.

Along the S coast the current is WSW–SW going from November to March. Rates are strongest in December and January with average rates of 1·25 and 0·8kn respectively. However rates of 4kn have been recorded at intervals. In April and May the direction is variable, although usually SE going. From June to October the current is E–ESE going. The rate is strongest in June with an average rate of 1·25kn.

Along the E coast the current is mostly S–SSE going. Rates are mostly 0·5–0·7kn with the exception of November to January. During these three months the current is sucked around the SE corner so it closely follows the contours of the coast. Rates average 1–1·25kn at this time and rates of 3·5–4kn have been recorded. From February to April the current is NW–NNW going and averages over 0·4–0·5kn.

On the W coast currents are less determinate until some distance off the coast where the general monsoon pattern predominates.

Galle
Charts BA *819*

Approach

In the approach there will be lots of fishing boats off the coast and as most yachts will be making part of the approach along the coast at night, some care and attention is needed. The final approach through the buoyed channel is on 003°. Yachts should wait at the harbour entrance until a naval cutter comes out

Sri Lanka

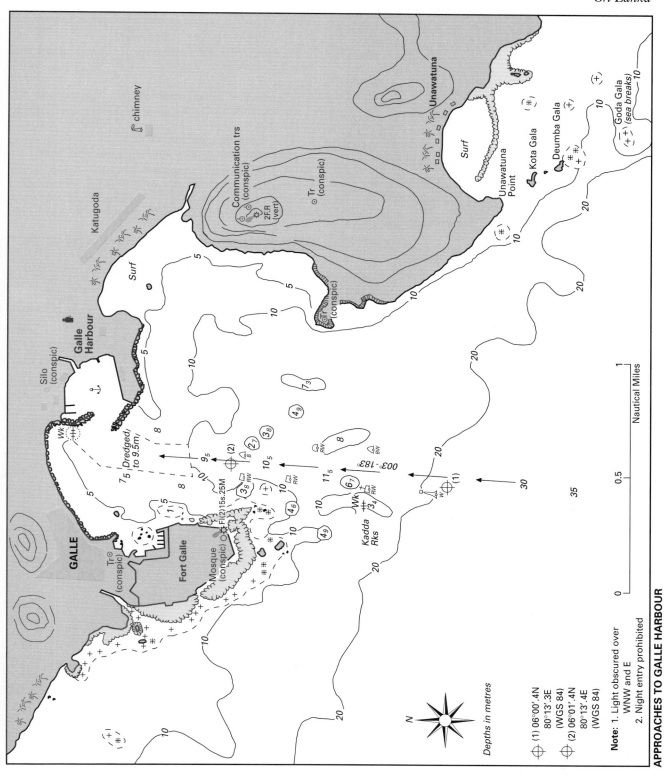

APPROACHES TO GALLE HARBOUR

127

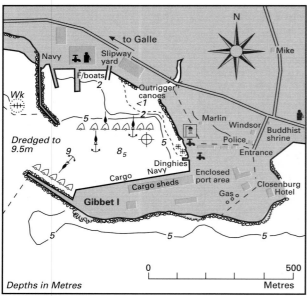

GALLE HARBOUR ⊕ 06°02'·01N 80°13'·91E WGS 84

There is a 2F.R on the communication tower on the E side of the bay. No. 1 pier 2F.R.

VHF Ch 16/12 for port control. Don't worry too much if there is no answer.

Dangers

1. There are numerous fishing boats in the approaches along the coast and a good lookout is needed.
2. There can be a considerable swell rolling in onto the coast making the approach uncomfortable.

Note The buoyed channel has some unorthodox buoys marking it. See the approach plan for details. In practice the approach is more straightforward than it looks and there is no problem by day. The

Fishing proas. Most use outboards for power, but a few still use sails. One of the big advantages of these craft is getting out through the surf and back in again – they just slice through the surf with ease.

Stitched wooden boat in Galle.

to carry out a preliminary check before entering and mooring up.

Conspicuous Fort Galle on the headland is easily identified and a white mosque on the SE corner is conspicuous. The lighthouse is easily located and a lattice communication tower near Galle town is conspicuous. Two communication towers on Edwards Pillar on the E side of the bay are also conspicuous. Closer in the buoys marking the channel will be seen. The entrance to the harbour is difficult to make out until close to, but a silo and a number of storage tanks will be seen making location straightforward.

By night A NIGHT ENTRANCE IS PROHIBITED. The best thing to do is potter around 3–4 miles off waiting for day-break. In the approach use Point de Galle light Fl(2)15s25M. The light is obscured from the E and W approaches.

Netting from a proa in Galle harbour. I have to say they never seemed to catch very much.

Approaches to Galle with the mosque and lighthouse in Fort
Galle conspicuous.

waypoints given for the approach channel are to
WGS 84 datum.

Mooring

Once cleared in by the navy proceed into the
harbour. Mooring is between your own anchor and
a stern line from the mooring buoys laid out from
the east side of the harbour. When the harbour is
crowded, as it can be in January and February,
yachts also moor under the end of the breakwater
with an anchor out and a long line to the shore. The
bottom is mud and good holding once your anchor
has dug in, although some like to lay a second
anchor just to be on the safe side.

Shelter Good shelter in the NE monsoon and some
yachts have been left here for the SW monsoon as
well. During the NE monsoon some ground swell
enters the harbour but it is quite comfortable inside.

Authorities Naval personnel, harbourmaster,
customs, immigration. See notes on entry
formalities for details on clearing in.

Note The harbour is 'bombed' every night by a dory
from which small depth charges (or more usually a
stick of gelignite) are dropped into the water to deter
Tamil Tiger frogmen from swimming into the
harbour and sabotaging naval boats. The
underwater explosions initially disturb people's
sleep, but most get used to the sharp crack of the
detonation and after a few days it is not worrying.
The navy personnel who cruise around in the dory
can occasionally be a nuisance themselves coming
over to ask for cigarettes and alcohol.

Facilities

There are several agents apart from the Windsors
whose addresses follow at the end of this section.

Water By jerrycan from a tap near the dinghy jetty.
There are showers in a fairly ruinous block just N of
the dinghy jetty. It is also possible to go alongside
the fisheries quay when there is room to take on
larger quantities of water. The water is generally
considered potable, but if in doubt add bleach or
tablets to it.

Fuel By jerrycan from the fisheries quay or go
alongside to take on larger quantities. Care is
needed to get the tides right as depths off the quay
are tight.

Gas Filling station on the E end of Gibbet Island.
Most gas bottles can be filled and the station is an
agent for some international companies like
Camping Gaz.

Paraffin In Galle town or get one of the agents to fill
cans. The quality is reported to be mediocre.

Laundry Any of the agents take in laundry which is
cheap and will be returned neatly folded and
smelling of the sun.

Repairs There is a slipway with cradles running on
rails at the Fisheries quay. The yard can carry out
basic work but nothing more. Bottom cleaning by a
diver with bottles can be arranged. Mechanical
repairs are possible but results have not been
outstanding for an engine rebuild on a Perkins, for
example. Some engineering repairs. Minor electrical
and electronic repairs. Most of the good facilities for
repair work are in Colombo, but in practice it is
probably best to arrange work through one of the
agents and the Windsors are the ones who can
facilitate getting workers and spares into the harbour
area. Duty-free spares can be imported via an agent
although the procedure is not always trouble-free.
Sail repairs and canvas work locally although the
repairs to my cruising chute were inadequate.
Canvas work locally. There is reported to be a large
Hood sail loft in Colombo which can do first class
repairs and of course make new sails. Hardware
shops in Galle with a basic stock of paints and
sealants and better hardware and tool shops in
Colombo.

Provisions Most yachts use Mike Yacht Service
Centre to provision. He has a good stock of basic
items including many imported goods. Good
canned and basic staples. For fruit and vegetables
there is a good market in Galle and despite the usual
warnings that you will be 'ripped off' I found that
after a little familiarity the stock was adequately
priced and generally fresher than elsewhere. There
are also good general provision shops in Galle which
can be used with no hassle – again despite the
rumours advising against going there. Sri Lankan

tea in various blends including Earl Grey is available everywhere and is of course excellent. Sausages and bacon available. Excellent bakers in Galle and Fort Galle – the plum cake keeps reasonably well on passage. Ice from the Fisheries but said to be non-potable for drinks.

Eating out For a night out most head for Unawatuna by auto rickshaw where the Hot Rock Café is a favourite with good food including seafood and cold beer at reasonable prices just back from the surf on the beach. There are also other restaurants at Unawatuna. Above the harbour at Galle is the Closenburg Hotel which serves mediocre food but has a great view from colonial surroundings. In Galle there are several restaurants of varying quality and in Fort Galle several wonderful old fashioned tea rooms for an afternoon cuppa.

Other PO. Banks. The Bank of Ceylon will do cash advances on *Visa*. Telephone and fax from the Windsors. Mail can be sent to the Windsors. Small hospital and dentists. If possible go to Colombo. Hire cars. Bus into Galle town. Auto rickshaw. Bus and train to Colombo.

Don Windsor & Co Ltd, 6 Closenburg Road, Magalle, Galle, Sri Lanka ☎ (94) 9 22927/34592 *Mobile* 072 31213 *Fax* (94) 9 34592

Marlin Yacht Service, 9/1 Gibbets Lane, Magalle, Galle, Sri Lanka
Good cheap courtesy flags, laundry and minor services, may start a 'restaurant'.

Mike Yacht Service Centre, Udugama Road, Magalle, ☎ (94) 9 34054
Provisions, tours, laundry and minor services.

General
Galle is a convivial place to visit and few people leave with a bad taste in their mouth. Galle town is a pleasant if rambling place where most facilities can be found. Fort Galle is nearby surrounded by the sea and full of colonial Portuguese, Dutch and British architecture. Above the harbour the colonial splendour of the Closenburg Hotel is somewhat faded but it is as good a place as anywhere to sip a cold beer in the evening. Unawatuna is a short auto rickshaw ride away and a favourite with yachties out for an evening on the razzle.

Fort Galle is worth at least a day for a wander around and a visit to the gem shops there. A word of caution: it is best to make your own arrangements with the gem workshops as the touts and agents are tied into a cut for their introduction and in my experience that can be as much as double the price you should pay. Just feel free to visit any of the gem shops and don't be pressured to go to just one because you have been told the others will rob you blind. Sri Lanka produces large numbers of semi-precious stones such as sapphires, star sapphires, garnets, amethyst and the like and these can be incorporated into some fine silverwork at very reasonable prices.

The natural harbour at Galle has a long pedigree. It is claimed by some to be the ancient harbour of Tarshish which traded with the Egyptians and Persians and with the Levant in Greek and Roman times. It was visited by that great traveller Ibn Battuta in 1344 and later the Portuguese, Dutch and British made it their own as evidenced in the architecture in Fort Galle. It declined when the large commercial port at Colombo was built and is only used by a few small coasters and the navy today. There are plans to build a small yacht marina at Fort Galle under Point de Galle, but things never seem to happen with any haste in Sri Lanka and it remains to be seen if it ever comes to fruition.

Colombo

Charts BA *1655*

Approach
Straightforward. The high rise buildings of Colombo will be seen and a white Buddha on the S side of the harbour is conspicuous.

By night
A NIGHT APPROACH IS PROHIBITED WITHOUT PRIOR AUTHORISATION.
Main light Fl(3)10s25M
NE breakwater F.R.10M
Fisheries harbour F.R.5M
NW breakwater Fl.R.3s10M; DirF.WRG.7-5M
  S head Fl.G.3s10M
SW breakwater head Oc.G.5s13M **Spur**
  Q.G.8M**Head** Fl.G.3s5M
There are numerous other lights on the piers and quays within the harbour.

VHF Ch 16/12 for port control.

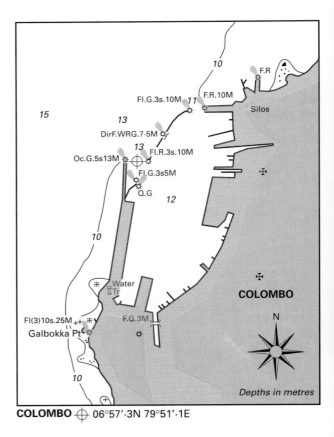

COLOMBO ⊕ 06°57'·3N 79°51'·1E

Mooring

Berth where directed. Yachts are usually directed to the S of the harbour.

Shelter Reported to be uncomfortable with the NE monsoon from a reflected ground swell within the harbour.

Authorities Naval personnel, harbourmaster, customs, immigration.

Facilities

Water and fuel from within the harbour area. Good shopping for provisions and numerous restaurants of all types. International flights.

General

No yachts I know of have visited Colombo recently, but it is possible to stop here en route or as the first port of call in Sri Lanka.

India

Current situation

India has been a stable democracy, in fact the largest democracy in the world, since independence in 1948. However some of the problems of secession unresolved at the time remain to this day. There are still numbers of minority groups in India, principally in Kashmir and the Punjab. The stand-off between Pakistan and India also causes some internal friction and it may surprise some to know that there are still large numbers of Muslims and Christians in a predominantly Hindu society. In some places they make up a majority. In Mangalore Muslims are in the majority and in Kerala Christians (predominantly Catholic) are the dominant group. For most intents and purposes this has little effect on visiting yachties except that internal state security is strong and much in evidence. The police and the naval authorities keep a tight control on all movement on the water and internal security is a national watchword. The following tale is meant to be cautionary only and it should be remembered that many, including myself on two separate occasions, have visited India by yacht without problems.

At the end of 1995 the French catamaran *Galathee* (registered in Mauritius) was intercepted by the coastguard and searched. The catamaran had been surveying the sea-bed in the approaches to Cochin. The search turned up an impressive array of equipment: two side-scan sonar's, two magnetometers, and two computers with programmes to analyse the data. The six crew members were arrested and imprisoned and the catamaran impounded by the coastguard. Later the Indian sponsor was also arrested. The French national who had chartered the catamaran and the captain stated that they had been surveying the sea-bed in the approaches to Cochin for aquaculture and tourism projects. The case took a curious twist when the charterer and the captain stated that they believed they had permission to survey after meeting a local MP. Things got even murkier when it was revealed that the Frenchman had tried to erect a high frequency antenna on a church in Fort Cochi which would have enabled them to transmit directly to the land. Once naval intelligence got hold of the data in the computers all sorts of spying accusations hit the newspapers. The naval authorities believed the data would be useful for submarine operations. They denied that the data had any use for aquaculture purposes or tourism. The gossip amongst the yachties was that the catamaran was being used in a survey for a Portuguese wreck in the approaches to Cochin. Certainly it seemed a clumsy operation and hardly a furtive one as the catamaran regularly chugged in and out of harbour for water, fuel and provisions. When I left Cochin the crew had just been released on bail after a year of incarceration and were awaiting trial. The moral of the story is clearly not to do anything which could be

remotely construed as contrary to the security of a country anywhere, but especially in India.

Documentation and visas

Normal boats papers and a valid passport for all crew members must be carried. A VALID VISA MUST BE OBTAINED BEFORE YOU ARRIVE IN INDIA. A visa cannot be obtained on arrival although extensions to a visa can be organised. Visas are issued as follows.

Tourist visa. Valid for up to one month after the date of issue and valid for one month in India.

Tourist visa for 3 months. Valid from the date of issue.

Tourist visa for 6 months. Valid from the date of issue.

Tourist or business visa for 1 year. Valid from the date of issue.

Visas can be obtained in Malaysia (Kuala Lumpur), Thailand (Bangkok), or Sri Lanka (Colombo).

Evidence of immunisation against yellow fever may be asked for. There have been some instances of visitors being required to produce proof that they are HIV negative although no visiting yachts have been required to do so.

Entry and exit formalities

Entry into India is labyrinthine in what can only be described as Dickensian surroundings. It can take a swift 4 hours or may take a day if the requisite officials cannot be seen in normal working hours (0900–1700). You should have a small amount of rupees set aside for the harbourmaster's fees (around 500 rupees should do it) as these cannot be paid in foreign currency. The procedure is time consuming, but it is all carried out pleasantly and politely.

In the approach to any major port call up the coastguard on VHF Ch 16 or port control on Ch 16 (changing to Ch 12) when 10 miles off. You will be asked for the yacht name, registration, number and names of crew and your ETA at the entrance to the harbour. When at the entrance call up again to get permission to enter.

Customs will come out to the yacht where valuables, navigation gear, firearms, etc. will be itemised. You will be asked to sign various forms to state you have no firearms (other than those declared) and no class A drugs on board. You can then proceed ashore to the harbourmaster who will fill in a number of forms and make a small charge (to be paid in rupees only). You must then go back to customs where your boats papers will be locked away and a receipt for them issued. You must then go to immigration and be stamped into the country.

If you have to move within the harbour written authorisation must be obtained from the harbourmaster. This basically entails you writing him a note of your intentions and he will then issue permission.

To exit is basically the reverse of this procedure.

For every port in India you must enter and leave in this manner. You cannot cruise 'between' ports once you have cleared into the country and clear out at the last port.

Data

Area 3,287,590km² (1,269,346M²). Includes the Lacadive, Nicobar and Andaman islands.

Frontiers 14,103km (7,615M). Bangladesh 4053km, Bhutan 605km, Burma 1463km, China 3380km, Nepal 1690km, Pakistan 2912km.

Coastline 7000km (3780M).

Maritime claims Territorial 12M. Exclusive economic zone 200M.

Population 900,000,000 (2010 projection 1,172,101,000)

Capital New Delhi

Time zone UT+5½

Language Hindi and English. 14 other official languages. 24 languages commonly used. Numerous regional dialects. In most large towns and tourist areas it is an easy enough matter to find someone who speaks English and in larger towns the English is impeccable. Think of how many modern novelists writing in English are Indian or of Indian extraction. There are well stocked English language bookshops in the major cities and several national English daily newspapers.

Ethnic divisions Indo-Ayran 72%, Dravidian 25%, Mongoloid and others 3%.

Religion Hindu 82·5%, Muslim 11·5%, Christian 2·5%, Bhuddist and Jains 1·2%.

Public holidays
  Numerous Hindu and Moslem holidays which can vary from state to state.
  Jan 1 New Year
  Jan 26 Republic Day
  Aug 15 Independence Day
  Oct 2 Mahatma Gandhi's Birthday
  Dec 25 Christmas

Government Democratic Republic, the largest democracy in the world. The Congress party dominated by the Nehru dynasty has been the key political party since 1948. The opposition is mostly made up of coalitions of national parties. The civil service inherited from the British plays an important part in political life although it has recently been seen to be corrupt at higher levels.

Disputes With Pakistan over Kashmir. Border disputes with China and Bangladesh. Riparian disputes with Pakistan over the Indus and Bangladesh over the Ganges. At the time of publication India had still refused to sign the Nuclear non-proliferation Treaty.

Crime The crime level is low. Although there are beggars on the streets and locals will try to overcharge tourists, actual crime is very low by any standards. In Bombay and on train journeys a little more vigilance is required for pickpockets and baggage thieves. Common advice is to take a chain and padlock so your luggage is securely attached to the rack, but I and many others have travelled safely without this precaution.

In Cochin there are no reported losses from yachts, even those left unattended while the crew were on extended excursions ashore. In Bombay you may need to be a little more vigilant, but certainly nothing like you would be in any of the so-called civilised countries of the world.

There have been reports of fishing boats off the

bottom of India coming up to yachts and stealing items, in fact at one time the advice was to stay 80 miles off. This is the rumour-mill working at its worst and the fishing boats which approached me and others off the coast were after cigarettes, food or money and although they came close to the boat they were not hostile or threatening. If you are really worried remove loose items from the deck and leave the VHF volume turned up loud on channel 16 which is busy most of the time.

Travel
Internal
Good air, rail and coach links throughout the country. A car and driver is also well worth considering.

Air Indian Airlines is the main internal carrier although there are now a number of private companies operating internal flights. Internal flights are nearly always fully booked and you need to make a confirmation well in advance. Queue jumping occurs and you need to be persistent on popular flights.

Rail India has a well developed rail network which now has computerised booking in most places which works well. Train travel is relatively cheap and if possible it pays to go 1st class air-conditioned if it is available. If you go 2nd class sleeper do not try for more than 12 hours at a stretch. The only train available from Bombay to Cochin for example, is 2nd class sleeper and that is a 38 hour journey and not to be recommended in one go. Food and drink are available on board and at stations from roaming vendors.

Coach and bus It is possible to get everywhere by bus and to most places by coach. The latter is to be preferred with air conditioning and reserved seats. Ordinary buses are overcrowded, stop frequently, break down, and are to be avoided except for short journeys.

Car and driver It is possible in most places to hire a car and driver at comparatively low rates. The car will usually be the ubiquitous Morris *Ambassador* of the 1950s which are still made in India, although some Japanese cars are now made under licence. In 1997 the rate was around 6 rupees per km for a round trip although you can and do get lower rates in some places after haggling a lot. You will soon know what the bottom rate is. For two or three people this is recommended, especially if you are doing a round tour inland. The driver will sleep with the car (by choice) so will not need a hotel room for the night.

Taxis Operate in the cities and towns. Fix a price in advance as meters are often 'not working sir'. Bombay is the worst place for overcharging.

Auto rickshaws The motorised three-wheelers that are the best way of getting around most towns and villages. Again meters will often not be working (except in Mangalore where all auto rickshaws use their meters) and so a price should be agreed in advance or offer two or three rupees over the meter price at journey's end.

International
There are international flights to most countries in the world from New Delhi and Bombay. There are also international flights from Madras, Calcutta, Trivandrum, Tiruchirappali, and Goa. All cities will have a competent travel agent who can arrange flights.

Practicalities
Mail Is slow and inefficient and will often not arrive. If you are sending letters from India ask to see the stamps franked at the PO. Important letters arriving in India should be sent by registered mail. Postcards sent from India will often not arrive. Parcels sent from India must be taken open to the PO so the contents can be checked. Outside the PO there will be a number of 'parcel-men' who will wrap it up in the approved fashion. To send parcels is time consuming and quite simply a hassle. I would suggest that you do not have parcels sent to India or if you must, have them sent by a courier firm to a major city.

Mail can be sent to Poste Restante at any post office where it will be held for one month before being returned. Putting 'please hold' on mail does not work.

Telecommunications IDD system. Country code 91. The telecommunication system is poor although you can generally get a line out without too much bother from a bureau in a city or large town. In the country it will be more difficult.

To telephone out use a bureau which will charge less than a hotel. Any city and large towns will have a bureau with 'PCO-STD-ISN' sign and here there will be a cubicle where you dial out and the time is metered at the desk. Typical costs are $2–$3 per minute for Europe and a bit more for the USA.

Some bureau's will have a fax service where the fax is sent for you. Any bad connections or error transmissions must be paid for. Typical costs are $4–$5 per page to send a fax and 40¢–50¢ per page to receive faxes. Again errors in transmission must be paid for. Faxes may not get in or out because of the numerous power cuts which occur in some areas and anyone sending a fax should be asked to try again after 3–4 hours in case there has been a power cut.

Mobile phones working on the GSM system will work in some major cities if your supplier has an agreement in India.

Currency The unit is the Indian rupee. Now that the rupee has been floated there is little difference between bank rates and black market rates. It is also illegal to change money on the black market with the possibility of stiff penalties.

Banks and exchange In any city or large town there will be several banks which can change cash or travellers cheques for rupees. There are also exchange agencies which will change cash or travellers cheques in some places. Always try to get an encashment certificate which enables you to change rupees back into hard currency if you need

Ernakulam. Indian trucks are often lovingly decorated.

Local markets around the Indian Ocean are a source of both the familiar and unfamiliar. Experiment with unfamiliar fruit and vegetables and spices and herbs for that nouveau boat cuisine.

Fishing canoes at Cannonore.

Off the bottom of India the local fishing boats will come up to you looking for alcohol and cigarettes. Their boat handling is a bit erratic but they are hardly pirates.

Indian Ocean NE monsoon sunset. Sometimes the skies can look a bit angry, but rarely does anything come of it.

Yemeni fishermen off the coast near Mukalla. They look like extras from a Hollywood pirate movie, but are simply curious and a cup of tea and biscuits will usually satisfy them.

Langkawi in Malaysia. Telok Dayang Bunting (Fresh Water Lake an looking in from the channel.

King's Cup competitors fly spinnakers on the Phi Phi to Nai Harn race. You can catch races all the way from Darwin to Thailand on the SE Asia Regatta circuit.

Around Malaysia there are numerous anchorages up large rivers as here in the Dinding River. Those who have cruised extensively around the coast say there are countless anchorages around once you get used to chugging up rivers and tributaries.

Limestone outcrops characterise the Langkawi archipelago making it a spectacular place to cruise around.

Fishing boat towing a bamboo raft off Langkawi. I'm not quite sure how you catch fish this way, but it at least has the merit of being easy to spot and avoid by day.

Langkawi in Malaysia. Fjord anchorage behind Pulau Gabang Darat.

Thai trawler. In places there c...
lot of trawlers around and a go...
lookout must be kept for the e...
the trawl lines.

Above Longtails in the Butang Islands. *Below* Thailand. Anchorage off the SW side of Ko Rang near the entrance to Boat Lagoon.

India. Throw-netting in the anchorage off the Bolghatty Hotel.

Butang Islands. Ko Adang west side anchorage.

Ton Sai Bay
Phi Phi Don.
alaysia.
rage at
hong Bahru.

Above Galle harbour on the SW corner of Sri Lanka.
Left Kerala backwater. The only way to get around the smaller canals is by a poled canoe.

Above India. Cargo canoe in Co[
Below Aden. The Prince of Wale[

Above India. Sulphur canoe-barges being towed through the anchorage off the Bolghatty Hotel.
Below Red Sea sunset. If you get a chance to look at it through the spray coming on board, the night skies really are that blue velvet studded by diamonds out of the *Arabian Nights*.

Left Balihaf in Yemen.

Top right Panjim in India. The Portuguese and Catholic influence is everywhere. If you like old churches head for Old Goa.
Left Suez Canal. A desert landscape with ships trundling through it.
Right Mukalla, a sort of mini-Manhattan on the Yemeni coast.

Port Sudan has a surprisingly good fresh fruit and vegetable market.

Port Fouad Yacht Club looking across the west branch of the Suez Canal to Port Said town.

Right Hanish Islands. The fishermen are as piratical a looking lot as you could wish for on their leaky *sanbuq's*.

Below Coco Island.
Below right Parc de Ste. Anne looking W to Mahe and Port Victoria. *Seychelles Tourist Office*

to and can also be used to pay in rupees where payment must usually be made in foreign currency such as some large hotels.

Credit cards can be used in some banks to get a cash advance although it is a time consuming process in most places. Credit cards (*Visa* and *Mastercard/Access*) are increasingly being taken by large hotels, upmarket restaurants and some shops. Charge cards (*American Express* and *Diners*) are not widely accepted. One thing to check is that sterling is not changed at the lower US dollar rate. Indian rupees are difficult to exchange at a good rate outside of India and if you are coming from Sri Lanka, Sri Lankan rupees are difficult to exchange in India.

Medical care Is generally better than most people think in the cities when you can pay for it. There are good doctors and dentists, trained in Europe and Australasia/USA, with modern equipment. Standard western practices such as using disposable needles are followed in the good clinics. Ask for recommendations and go to a private practice if

Auto rickshaws get you around cities and towns in an emphatic manner. Agree the price beforehand if the meter is 'not working'.

possible. In the country outside the cities medical care is poor. A wide range of drugs can be bought over the counter at pharmacies although brand names for common drugs may differ. For major problems fly to Europe or Australasia if possible.

For those interested in alternative medicine India has a lot of it. Kerala is the centre for Ayurvedic medicine, a naturalistic system which offers diagnosis of the body's 'humours' (blood, mucous, wind, and gall) and treatment using herbs, minerals, oils and water. Ayurvedic massage using various oils is well worth exploring even if you have little interest in the theory and is advertised in numerous places in Kerala including Cochin.

Care must be taken with water in India and it is wise to treat any water you put into the boats tanks. Bottled water is available in most places.

Electricity 220–240V AC. There are frequent power cuts in many states and a lot of the shops will have generators for the power cuts. A street full of generators fills the streets with exhaust fumes and can be most unpleasant.

Curiosities and culture

Begging In most of the large cities (with the notable exception of Cochin which has banned begging on its streets) you will see and be pestered by numerous beggars. Many of them are badly deformed and the sight is distressing to say the least. Sad-eyed children are especially appealing to the visitor. I would suggest you refrain from handing money over to beggars for the simple reason that once seen to do so, you will immediately be surrounded by many more and they are difficult to shake off. If you would like to give money, give it to an organisation. There are also syndicates of beggars operating which obtain money by presenting a letter, often in English, telling a tale of woe and asking for help.

In some places confidence tricksters operate with the ploy of way-laying you and telling a tale of

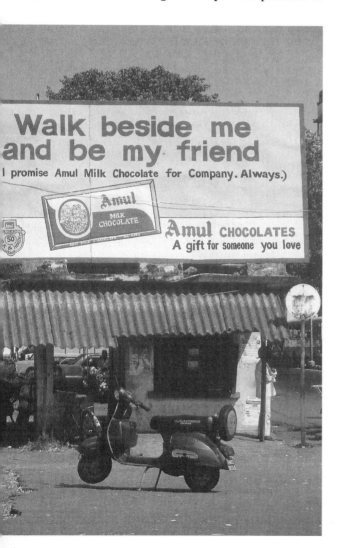

The English have left their mark in tangible ways including some wonderfully old-fashioned advertising.

distress and need and, of course, ask for money. In places they can be very persistent and if you show interest it is unlikely you will easily get rid of them. One other ploy to watch out for is the request for a penfriend and your address. You may find that your name is used as a reference for an exit visa or passport application.

Having outlined the ploys around I should add that poverty is very real in India, there is a lot of need, and only the callous could not react to it. Just use some judgement for individual cases.

Karma Cola This biting book by Gita Mehta details the clash of east and west in India. Many westerners have come to India, some by yacht, looking for an alternative to what they perceive as their own arid and sterile western way of life. Some of them are deluded, some genuinely puzzled by the spiritual vacuum of the west, some are seeking an easy-fix enlightenment, and some just come for a good time in a country where the cost of living is relatively cheap. While India has a long and varied tradition of enlightenment and practices towards that goal, most of those I have encountered looking for it have little idea of the traditions and belief systems to be found here and tend to gloss over things like the relationship of the belief systems to the appalling caste system and to the poverty to be found on every street corner. To those enlightened visitors who regard me as a cynical and unsympathetic soul damned to be reincarnated as the lowest form of insect (and no doubt an obvious product of this age of *kaliyuga*) I commend *Karma Cola* and its attempt, tritely summarised here, to unravel the striving of the west to get into India's heart and soul and the east to emulate the material success of the west.

Trains India has one of the largest railway networks in the world and it is still expanding. Rail travel in India is a delight where you will encounter people of all types travelling to all sorts of places. Workers returning from long stints in other parts of India, travelling salesmen, sons going home to see mum, students, beggars and itinerant musicians. The railway stations are a microcosm of life in India and on slow trains you can jump off to buy a *thali* (rice and *puri* with a sauce of some description wrapped in a banana leaf), pots of curry and rice, sweet cakes and sticky buns, fresh fruit and fresh fruit juice. The train clatters along at a sedate rate (mostly) allowing you time to gaze out at the landscape of the Indian sub-continent without an organised itinerary of things you should see. Travelling by train is to be recommended although in 2nd class, and you can only get 2nd class to some destinations, restrict journeys to 10 hours or so unless you are particularly masochistic.

Cars and motorbikes For the mechanically minded India is a bit like a living motor museum. The 1950s Morris *Ambassador* is still manufactured here although it is being replaced by Japanese joint venture products like Suzuki and Toyota cars. The

350cc single pot Royal Enfield *Bullet* motorcycle of the 1950s is also still made and much in evidence. The *Bullet* has special significance for me, bringing back memories of teenage years when I bought one, stripped it down and rebuilt it. Never did get the clutch quite right. The hollow 'poom' of the exhaust of the Indian *Bullet* is like a sound-bite back to those years although sadly, like the *Ambassador*, it is being replaced by soulless modern bikes made under licence to Yamaha and Honda.

You can hire a car and driver, which will inevitably be a Morris *Ambassador*, at relatively low rates, and it is a wonderful experience, a bit of post-colonial nostalgia, to be driven around the country in one of these cars. You can also hire a Royal Enfield *Bullet* with a bit of looking around and take yourself off on a thudding ride around the country.

Useful books
India has a wide English speaking readership and there are good bookshops stocking titles from the UK and a prolific local press publishing newspapers, magazines and books in English. I mention only a few of the many books available below.

India Handbook ed. Robert Bradnock. Footprint Handbooks. The best of the general guides and streaks ahead of other popular titles.

Rough Guide to India RKP. Adequate but sketchy in places.

Lonely Planet: India Adequate.

Chasing the Monsoon A Frater. Penguin. Interesting account following the arrival of the SW monsoon as it sweeps over India.

A Passage to India E M Forster. Available in Penguin.

Midnight's Children Salman Rushdie. On India and independence. I won't mention any other titles.

An Area of Darkness V S Naipaul. Penguin. Harsh criticism partially revised by his later and softer *A Million Mutinies*.

Karma Kola Gita Mehta. Penguin. Already mentioned above. She has written other books about India like *A River Sutra* also well worth getting hold of.

Geography and climate
The coast Peninsular India is mostly bordered by low coastal flats behind which are the Western Ghats, the N–S ridge of the peninsula that was pushed up by the movement of the land away from Africa. The Ghats are bordered by coastal flats varying from 5 miles to 60 miles wide. Most of the coast is low-lying and covered in jungle. In some areas, S of Bombay and around Cannanore for example, there is higher land and a few low cliffs and hills near or on the coast. The low-lying coast and the haze from cooking fires and light and heavy industry means that the coast is mostly difficult to make out until closer to and from seaward it suddenly materialises out of the haze. There is some sort of human activity along just about all of the coast, although some bits are surprisingly sparsely inhabited.

Coastal waters Surrounding India is a shallow muddy shelf deposited by the silt brought down by the numerous rivers flowing off the peninsula. Most of the harbours are in fact built within the estuaries of rivers. The fresh water brings down a good deal of silt with it and consequently much of the sea near the coast is murky with limited visibility. Only on the coast away from major rivers will you find comparatively clear water and only here will there be limited coral growth. For most of the coast the bottom is mud, good for anchoring but not that great to swim around in. Elsewhere the bottom is a mixture of sand, coral rubble and occasionally gravel.

The silt-rich waters around the coast attract lots of fish and consequently lots of fishing boats. Fishing is largely confined to the NE monsoon when the sea is calm and to the transition periods, although fishing boats can be caught out as happened in 1996 off Bombay when upwards of 50 boats were lost in a sudden storm. The approaches to major and minor ports are cluttered by fishing boats of every description from large trawlers (pair trawling is often practised) to dugout canoes and proas. Larger fishing craft are well lit, but smaller craft will flash a light or splash some oil onto a brazier to alert you to their presence.

Climate The climate over peninsular India is largely determined by the monsoon season. Monsoon is used as a term to describe a season but really means the actual change from one season to another.

The NE monsoon is the dry and cool winter season from November to March. The NE monsoon winds are comparatively gentle affairs and in fact most of India is sheltered from the worst effects of cold winds by the bulk of the Himalayas. The relatively still conditions encourage polluting haze to build up and it is not uncommon for the airport at New Delhi to be closed because of poor visibility. Along the coast the visibility is much reduced and it is often difficult to make out otherwise salient features.

The SW monsoon is the hot rainy season, and also the more turbulent season. It runs from April to October. The SW monsoon is heralded by dramatic thunderstorms with spectacular lightning displays. The summer SW monsoon is also the season for tropical storms although the E coast of India is the only area likely to be affected. The heat during the SW monsoon can be oppressive with high temperatures and high humidity. Because of the ferocity of the SW monsoon few yachts sail in this period around the Indian coast and in any case many harbours are closed during this period, so it is unlikely that most yachtsmen will experience the discomfort of the summer.

At Bombay	Av max °C	Av min °C	Relative humidity	Days 2·5mm rain
Jan	28	19	61%	0·2
Feb	28	19	62%	0·2
Mar	30	22	65%	0·1
Apr	32	24	67%	0·1
May	33	27	68%	1
Jun	32	26	77%	14
Jul	29	25	83%	21
Aug	29	24	81%	19
Sep	29	24	78%	13
Oct	32	24	71%	3
Nov	32	23	64%	1
Dec	31	21	62%	0·1

Weather

Prevailing winds near the coast During the NE monsoon, when yachts cruise the W coast of India, land and sea breezes prevail. Up to 20–30 miles off the coast the land and sea breeze effect is well developed and consistent. The sea breeze normally fills in around 1200 and blows onto the coast at around 10–15kn. A short sea is set up but it is not problematic. The sea breeze normally dies around 2000 at night and the land breeze blowing off the coast sets in around 2200–2400. It generally blows at around 8–12kn. At times there may be calms through some of the night. The exception to this pattern is around the Gulf of Mannar where the NE monsoon is funnelled through the gap between the bottom of India and the top of Sri Lanka and fans out over the adjacent sea area. The wind here will often blow at between 20–30kn and raises a considerable sea.

On the E coast of India the NE monsoon blows directly onto the coast and is turned to a more northerly direction. The wind strength here is often around 10–20kn and a heavy swell is pushed down onto the coast. This is most evident for the southern half of India with wind speeds decreasing towards the N around Calcutta.

During the SW monsoon winds on the W coast of India are consistently from the SW–W in the day and night and can blow with some force. During June and July winds are often 20–25kn and regularly

Month	Prevailing winds 0800	Prevailing winds 1700
Jan	E–NE/84%	W–NW/81%
Feb	E–NE/81%	W–NW/88%
Mar	E–NE/78%	W–NW/91%
Apr	E–NE/73%	W–NW/79%
May	E–NE/61%	W–NW/65%
Jun	E–NE/38%	W–NW/69%
Jul	E–NE/33%	W–NW/82%
Aug	NE/19%	W–NW/83%
Sep	NE/25%	W–NW/86%
Oct	E–NE/60%	W–NW/65%
Nov	E–NE/74%	W–NW/61%
Dec	E–NE/85%	W–NW/74%

Notes Winds for W coast of India at Cochin. Prevailing winds are for the morning land breeze and afternoon sea breeze and any gradient effect on the SW monsoon winds. Other winds blow for the remaining percentage.
For more information on wind direction and strength see the charts in *Technical Information*, pages 30/31.

blow at 30kn plus. A heavy swell is pushed onto the coast and squalls of 30–40kn are encountered from time to time. As a consequence many of the harbours along the W coast are closed during the SW monsoon and radio and light facilities literally do not run at this time.

On the E coast the SW monsoon blows fairly consistently off the land from the SW to WSW. Land and sea breezes tend to slow or augment the SW monsoon winds by small amounts only.

Locally named winds

Bhoot small dust storm
Challiho strong southerlies, often squally, preceding the SW monsoon as it proceeds north
Elephantas southerly squalls marking the end of the SW monsoon
Thar hot dry wind in Rajasthan

A bit of trivia. In the Sanskrit *Vedas* there are two major deities. One of these is Dyaus, the sky father, who was imported into Greek mythology as Zeus, creator of the wind and weather in the ancient world.

Gales During the NE monsoon there are few non-tropical depressions that affect the area. Non-tropical depressions may move across from Arabia to Pakistan and northern India with associated warm and cold fronts. These can cause squally disturbed weather in the north, but the further south you go the less the effect. Apart from localised thunderstorms there are virtually no gale force winds to speak of south of 15°N during the NE monsoon.

With the onset of the SW monsoon the frequency of gale force winds of Force 7 and above from non-tropical depressions increases dramatically. In July at the height of the SW monsoon there are winds of Force 7 and above 40% of the time in the middle of the Arabian Sea and off the W coast of India for between 4–8% although like all recorded data the actual incidence of gale force winds seems higher. The sea state off the coast is usually rough with surf over the shallow coastal area from the high incidence of gales further out to sea. The incidence of gale force winds drops dramatically in September in the intervening period between the SW and NE monsoon.

Tropical storms On the W coast there are two main periods for tropical storms. The first is at the beginning of the SW monsoon from late May to June. These tropical storms normally originate in the Arabian Sea around latitude 10–14°N and move in a N–NW direction. They may curve towards the NE and Pakistan. The second period is from October to November and these tropical storms originate in the Bay of Bengal and move across to the Arabian Sea. By the time they arrive in the Arabian Sea the wind strength is much diminished. Overall the incidence of tropical storms on the W coast of India is low at around 1 per year. If a full blown cyclone develops there is considerable danger

in the coastal region from storm surges which can cause coastal damage and flooding.

On the E coast of India there is a higher incidence of tropical storms and a considerably higher incidence of full blown cyclones. Tropical storms developing at or below 10°N in the Bay of Bengal will often head in a NW direction in October to November and to a lesser extent in December to March towards the E coast of India. In November 1996 two cyclones hit the E coast of India around Andhrapradesh causing great loss of life and property. The average incidence of cyclones in the Bay of Bengal is around 2 per year but it does seem that in recent years the average has been consistently higher.

Thunderstorms and waterspouts Thunderstorms and associated squalls are common at the onset of the SW monsoon and indeed the W coast has been described as a solid wall of lightning at this time. Many of the associated squalls are very strong at up to 40+kt and can be of some duration. Thunderstorms also occur around the ITCZ during both the SW and NE monsoons, although these are not usually accompanied by vicious squalls.

Waterspouts occur although with no greater frequency than elsewhere in this area.

Tides

Along both the W and E coasts of India the tidal range varies from N to S with a greater range in the N and less range in the S.

On the W coast the spring range is around 3·5m at Bombay decreasing to around 2m at Mormugao and to 1m or less at Calicut, Cochin, and down to Cape Comorin and the E coast of Sri Lanka. The tides are diurnal and although in the S the range is not great, the tidal streams can be very strong in confined channels as at Cochin where the tidal range is augmented by the rivers flowing out into the harbour.

On the E coast the picture is pretty much the same with a spring range of around 2·5m at the mouth of the Ganges (this range is increased during the wet season to 4m) becoming around 1·5m at Madras and less than 1m further S.

In general the tidal streams are from the N–NW on the flood and S–SE on the ebb. However the bottom contours and any geographical features like capes or islands can dramatically alter the direction. Also the tidal streams can be amplified by large rivers flowing out over a shallow delta as at Cochin where there is generally 9 hours ebb to 3 hours flood.

Currents

To a large extent currents around the W and E coasts of India result from the current circulation caused by the NE and SW monsoons. However the circulation set up in the Arabian Sea and the Bay of Bengal causes some counter-currents which may be contrary to the general current circulation. Tidal streams in the comparatively shallow water also cause local effects.

On the E coast the picture is not too complicated with basically a SSW-going stream following the coast with the NE monsoon and a NE-going stream with the SW monsoon. The only place where it gets a little complicated is off the mouth of the Ganges where the tidal streams may reverse or augment the main currents.

On the W coast the predominant current is SE-going following the coast from February to September. In February the current is fitful and easily reversed while in April to September rates may be as much as 0·6kn in April and 0·75kn in July. From October to January there is generally a weak NW-going current. In January there is a weak circulating current between 8–10°N. Around the Laccadives there are variable currents which you need to keep an eye on when in the vicinity of the islands.

In general currents around the coast appear to be stronger than generally indicated and it is wise to keep an eye on cross-track error to get some idea of what is happening locally.

Navigation

The coast has been surveyed in recent years around the major harbours and in general the approaches to major ports are accurately charted. Away from the major ports the coast has not been adequately surveyed for some time and care is needed in the comparatively shallow coastal waters, especially in areas likely to silt. Most modern charts are referenced to Indian datum. Most GPS receivers do not have this datum listed (it is not Indian-Bangladesh or Indian-Thailand) and generally carry a warning that the datum for the chart cannot be adequately determined and that GPS co-ordinates should be plotted with care. Where possible I have given GPS co-ordinates using WGS 84 datum. Other co-ordinates are schematic and should be treated with caution.

Harbours and anchorages

Note Except for Bombay, Panaji (Goa) and Cochin, other harbours and anchorages are covered by brief notes only as yachts normally clear out of India when leaving a port before entering another port and clearing back into India. This makes it difficult to cruise to ports and anchorages where the authorities are unfamiliar with the formalities for pleasure yachts. A few yachts have cruised to ports and anchorages other than Bombay, Goa and Cochin and so brief details of ports and anchorages other than the main three on the west coast are included as a starter for those interested in doing some more research.

The order of harbours is from S to N.

Quilon

08°52'·7N 76°34'E (Tangasseri Point lighthouse)
An open anchorage under Tangasseri Point. Can be used in the morning before the sea breeze gets up. A channel leads into the backwaters although the entrance channel shifts and depths vary.

Alleppey

09°29'·5N 76°19'·3E (Alleppey lighthouse)
An open anchorage, although with the NE monsoon it can be used in the morning before the sea breeze gets up.

Cochin

Charts BA *65*

Approach
Visibility along the coast and in the approach to Cochin is reduced by industrial haze and the smoke from charcoal burning and cooking fires. A buoyed channel (dredged to 11–12·5m) leads into the harbour.

Conspicuous There are always a number of ships anchored in the roadstead at the outer end of the buoyed channel. The fairway buoy at the beginning of the channel will be seen and the other buoys marking the channel can then be followed in. Closer in the high buildings of Ernakulum and the lighthouse just N will be seen.

By night
Cochin main light Fl(4)20s28M
Ldg Lts on 078°36' *Front* Q.11M *Rear* Iso.4s11M
Ldg Lts on 107°15' *Front* Q.11M *Rear* Iso.4s11M
Channel light buoys Fl.R.5s/Fl.G.5s
Inner harbour light buoys Fl.R.3s/Fl.G.3s
A night approach can be made with care.

VHF Ch 16/12 for port control. Call up when 5M off and give ETA. You will be asked to call up again when off the entrance to the harbour.

Dangers

1. There are fishing boats everywhere in the approach up to 30M off. Some will have surface

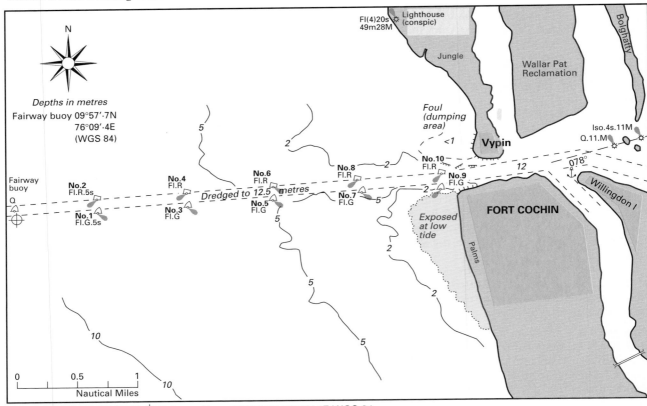

APPROACHES TO COCHIN ⊕ Fairway Buoy 09°57'·7N 76°09'·4E WGS 84

nets for prawns. These are usually laid in a V with a fishing boat stationed at each corner. At night they are lit by a quick flashing white in the middle and a Fl or F.G/R at either end. There are boats long-lining and trawlers either trawling alone or pair-trawling. The latter pose the greatest danger and every care is needed at night. In general the fishing boats are well lit with the exception of some smaller craft which will flash a torch or show an oil lamp.

Cochin. Approach to the anchorage off the Taj Malabar Hotel where you clear in. The building on the left is the new port office.

2. Large commercial ships use Cochin and have right of way in the approach channel.

Note The coastguard often patrol the approaches to Cochin and may come over to check you out.

Mooring

Taj Malabar Proceed into the outer harbour and anchor off the Taj Malabar Hotel where indicated in 2–7m. The bottom is mud and good holding. The current swirls around here creating strong eddies but it is quite secure. Formalities for clearing in will be carried out here as follows. It may take as little as 3–4 hours or as long as 24 hours depending on arrival time. Office hours are 0900 to 1700 with some offices closed for lunch. The relevant officials are all, in my experience, polite and friendly.

1. Customs will come out to the boat with the relevant paperwork and will make a cursory check of items on board.
2. You will then go ashore to the harbourmaster on the waterfront and pay a small fee. The fee can only be paid in rupees so have a small amount handy.
3. You must then go to customs just back from the waterfront and hand over the ships papers for which a receipt will be issued.
4. You must then go (by auto rickshaw or taxi) to immigration. It is easiest if all crew go to immigration.
5. You must then go to the harbourmaster and compose a letter asking permission to move to the anchorage off the Bolgatty Hotel.

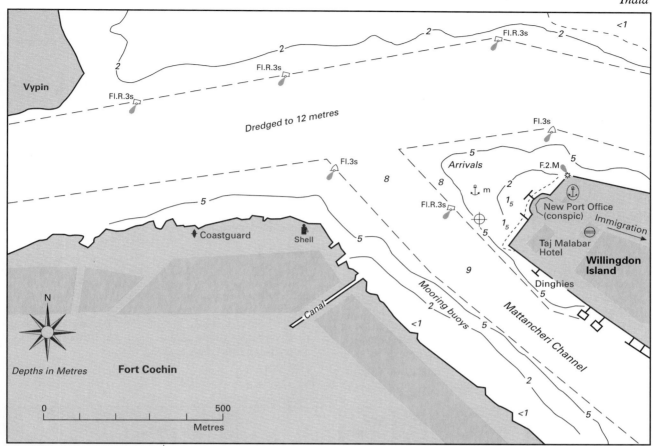

TAJ MALABAR ANCHORAGE ⊕ 09°58'·14N 76°15'·4E WGS 84

The exit procedure is the above in reverse order.

Bolgatty Hotel Once you have completed formalities and obtained permission from the harbourmaster you can then proceed to the anchorage off the Bolgatty Hotel. The channel to the anchorage presents a few problems for deeper draught craft. It is not marked and the temptation is always to head directly for the yachts moored off the hotel. Follow the channel indicated on the plan and leave about halfway through the flood. If you do touch the bottom it is all soft mud and you should be able to plough your way back into the deeper part of the channel. A local boat will usually come to help out if you get stuck. To my knowledge the deepest draught craft to get through the channel was 2·80m. A bit of keel dredging was necessary to do this. Once into the anchorage anchor in 3–3·5m. The bottom is sticky mud and good holding.

Cochin. Looking out to the approach channel from the Taj Malabar anchorage with the fishing fleet coming in.

Cochin. Ernakulum waterfront. The arched footbridge runs
over the canal leading to the market.

Shelter Excellent all-round shelter. This is pretty
much a hurricane hole and yachts have been left
here for extended periods. The current is strong but
the holding excellent and so no problems will be
encountered. In general there is 9 hours ebb to 3
hours flood in the anchorage. It does have a
significant resident population of mosquitoes.

Authorities Harbourmaster, customs and
immigration on Willingdon Island.

Facilities

A number of bumboats operate ferrying people to
and from the Bolgatty Hotel and they will also
provide some services to yachts. For fuel, gas,
laundry, etc. a small amount will be added on, but
we are really talking about small amounts. Use your
own discretion when making a choice.

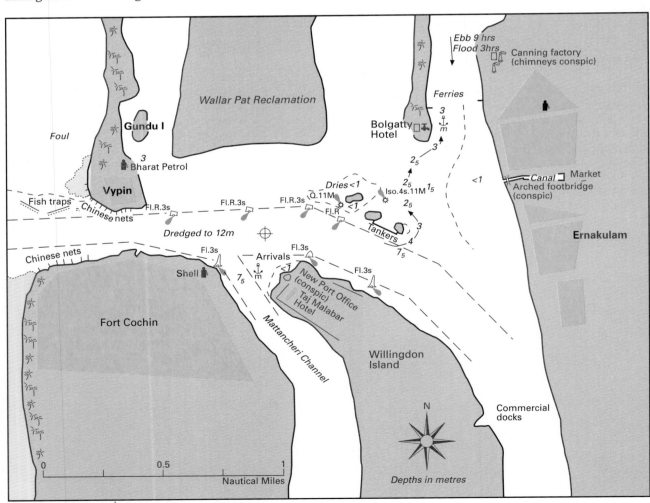

COCHIN HARBOUR ⊕ 09°58·24N 76°15·4E WGS 84

Water By jerrycan from the Bolgatty Hotel or get one of the bumboats to fill jerrycans. The water should be treated.

Fuel By jerrycan from Ernakulum or one of the bumboats will fill jerrycans for you. There is a fuel station at Vypin, Bharat Petrol, with 3m off the quay, and the Shell station at Fort Cochin with 2·5–3m off the quay. At either of these remember that the Chinese nets overhang the water a fair way off and care is needed not to get tangled up in the net. This is not as silly as it sounds as your natural inclination is to concentrate on getting into the quay and it is all too easy to keeping looking dead ahead rather than up. (No, it wasn't me that got tangled up).

Gas Most gas bottles can be filled at Ernakulum although there may be problems with some fittings such as *Camping Gaz*.

Paraffin Ashore in Ernakulum.

Laundry On Bolgatty Island or in Ernakulum. Alternatively ask one of the bumboats.

Repairs A few yachts have been hauled at the Norwegian run docks in the commercial port S of Ernakulum. Hauling is on a slipway. There is talk of setting up a small boatyard for yachts here. Ashore there are good facilities for mechanical and engineering repairs. Good mild and stainless steel work can be carried out. Galvanising. Electrical and minor electronic repairs. Basic refrigeration repairs. Some wood repairs although usually not to yacht standards. Canvas work. Some basic spares like seals, bearings, impellers and outboard parts. Good hardware shops with paints and sealants. Most of the workshops are in Ernakulum.

Provisions Most basics can be found although there are significant holes for the basics. Supermarket near the waterfront. Excellent fresh fruit and vegetable market a short way up the canal with the conspicuous arched footbridge over it. The selection of good quality fruit and vegetables is astounding even by Indian Ocean standards. It is possible to take a dinghy up the canal for major loads but it is filthy and the dinghy will be covered in grime afterwards. Good shopping for dried fruits and nuts, especially cashews. Freshly ground spices. Also try the plum-cake sold in some of the bakeries.

Eating out Range of restaurants in Ernakulum. The Taj Malabar has more westernised fare and also does an excellent Sunday lunch buffet with the use of the swimming pool if you eat there – recommended. Several other hotels also do good food at reasonable prices.

Other Banks. Grindleys will do a cash advance on *Visa* cards. PO. Telephone and fax bureaus. Mail can be sent to the Bolgatty Hotel, Bolgatty Island, Ernakulum, Cochin, Kerala. Hospital and dental services. Dr Sujit Vasudevan, Ojus Clinic, Mullassery Canal Rd, Ernakulum ☎ 370 0303 has been recommended. Hire cars. Bus services along the coast and trains across to Madras. Internal flights to Bombay.

General

There are few people who do not enjoy their stopover in Cochin. It is a friendly low-key place with good facilities and a suitable base for expeditions inland. To date there has been no theft from boats of any consequence and many, myself included, have left yachts in the Bolgatty anchorage unattended for several weeks and travelled inland. If you feel better about it hire a boatman to keep an eye on the yacht while you are away. In some cases yachts have been left for months and in one case for years.

Cochin itself has much to excite the senses. The city is a watery one split by the estuarine canals into different parts and connected by small ferries which run all day and late into the night ferrying the inhabitants around. Long sailing canoes with patchwork sails carry local produce to the islands and spits of the city and rowing boats powered by impossibly thin arms connect the lesser parts of Cochin. Ernakulum is the commercial hub and the place to go for shopping and services. Willingdon Island houses the harbour offices and freight

Delivering fuel in Cochin. It costs a little more for boat service, but in the scheme of things the amount is relatively little

agencies. Fort Cochin is off on a limb and has a bit of everything from small hotels to the offices of sugar and spice houses. Vypin and smaller places like Bolgatty Island are largely residential.

At the very least you must take a tour of the Kerala backwaters from Cochin. Stretching south down the coast are interlinked waterways surrounded by thick jungle. You will be poled around the canals with the jungle just a handspan away and it is a thoroughly relaxing way to get acquainted with the flora and occasionally the fauna. I will never again take black peppercorns for granted now I know they grow on vines around the trees and must take hours to pick. Half day backwater tours are easily organised in Ernakulum from the main ferry terminal or a travel agent. You can spend another half day just hopping on ferries and exploring the different parts of Cochin around the perimeter of the estuary. The Kerala backwaters are a largely unknown waterways system with ferry services connecting the parts further south and with more time you can travel down to Quillon and Alleppey.

Like Goa further north, there is a distinct Portuguese element to Cochin. Much of the population is Catholic and there are churches everywhere. Scattered around in-between are Hindu temples and on Fort Cochin there is a Jewish synagogue. At the entrance to the harbour and around the channels are huge Chinese drop-nets suspended on counter-balanced poles and around Bolgatty fragile canoes manned by wizened fishermen with throw-nets balance gracefully as they follow the tide-line in and out netting shrimp and small fish. Cochin is a patchwork of sights and sounds and a few smells that you won't forget, a gentle introduction to a vast country and not a bad place to linger despite the mosquitoes that plague the anchorage.

Laccadive Islands

The chain of islands lying some 200 miles off the W coast between 08° and 12°30'N. The islands are all coral atolls and consequently are relatively low-lying with the palm trees on the islands the first thing you will see. The islands are a part of India and are off-limits to yachts. It may be possible to get permission to visit them, but that is unlikely. Foreign tourists are allowed on only two of the islands, Bingaram and Suheli, and then only as part of an organised package tour.

The name Laccadive literally means one hundred thousand islands and was used to cover the Maldives as well as the present day Laccadives. The southernmost island, Minicoy, still retains a strong Maldivian character. The islands are divided into a N and S group. The N group is known as the Amindivi Islands and is composed of Amini, Kadmat, Kiltan, Chetlat and Bitra Par. Amini is the main island in the group with a significant population. The S group is known as the Cannanore

Islands and is composed of Minicoy on the S side of Nine Degree Channel and Suheli Par, Kalpeni, Kavaratti, Pitti, Agatti and Androth on the N side of the channel. Bingaram is part of the Agatti group.

Several yachts have thought about anchoring off one of the islands close to Nine Degree Channel to dive to clean up the bottom, but I have yet to come across anyone who actually has. There look to be several places where yachts could anchor off the smaller less populated atolls and on the larger atolls there are good lagoons with passes marked across the barrier reef. It should be remembered that whatever you do, the Indian navy does not mess about when it comes to enforcing maritime regulations and consequently if you do decide to stop without permission, don't expect leniency if apprehended.

When on passage near the islands in Nine Degree Channel or between the islands currents seem to be irregular in direction and strength. On one occasion I have had N-going current of between ½-¾kn in January when coming down through the islands above Nine Degree Channel. In February I had ½-¾kn of W-going and then later E-going current. It is likely that the tidal streams amongst the islands produce significant currents that are variable in direction depending on the prevailing ocean current and the submarine topography. Just keep an eye on the cross-track error on the GPS.

Beypore

Charts BA *3461*

Approach
Beypore light and the rocky breakwaters protecting the river entrance will be seen. With onshore winds there is a confused swell at the entrance.

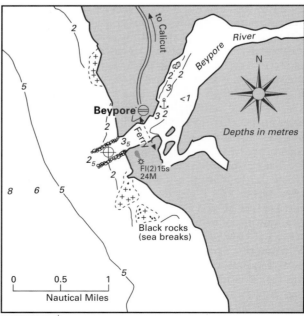

BEYPORE ⊕ 11°09'·5N 75°48'E

By night Main light Fl(2)15s24M. Entrance F.G/F.R.2M. A night entrance should not be made.

Mooring
Proceed into the river and anchor off the fishing quay in convenient depths. Good shelter but there is a significant current.

Facilities
Water and fuel on the fishing quay. Limited provisions in Beypore nearby and a few restaurants. Calicut is about 20 minutes away by auto rickshaw.

General
Beypore is the port for Calicut and a pleasant enough place. The harbour is packed with fishing boats.

Mahe
11°42'N 75°31'·8E (Fl(2)10s12M light)

Local fishing boats anchor under the headland off the village. Shelter appears good. Idyllic surroundings.

Tellicherry
11°44'·8N 75°29'·2E (Fl(3)9s10M light)

An anchorage under a small bight. Care needed of reefs and shoal water in the approach. Anchor at the S end of the above- and below- water reef between the jetty and rocky islets. Reasonable shelter. Town nearby.

Cannanore
11°51'·5N 75°21'·4E (Fl.10s17M light)

St Angelo Fort is conspicuous. Anchor off outside the fishing port with a stern anchor to hold you into the swell. It may be possible to get into the fishing harbour but reconnoitre first by dinghy. This is an attractive place with a fine beach fringed by palms. About 5 minutes into Cannanore town by auto rickshaw.

Cannanore: Launching fishing canoes through the surf.

Mangalore
12°50'·8N 74°50'·3E (Fl.3s11M N side of river)

A small cargo dhow and fishing port on the confluence of the Gurpur and Netravati Rivers. The entrance is beset by shifting sandbanks and strong currents. Dhows go up a backwater to Mangalore old port. This is picturesque but rather seedy and has a definite menace to it with some local heavies around.

New Mangalore Harbour
Charts BA *3461*

Approach
New Mangalore harbour is a large all-weather commercial port N of Mangalore proper. The cranes and gantries at the port and oil storage tanks and a large steelworks near the harbour are all conspicuous. The entrance channel (dredged to 12·5m) is buoyed.

By night
Suratkal Point Fl.10s31M
Airfield Aero Al.WG.7·5s28M
Lg Lts on 078°56' *Front* Q.6M *Rear* Oc.10s6M

VHF Ch 16/12.

Mooring
Where directed.

Authorities Harbourmaster and customs. Immigration in Mangalore.

Facilities
Water and fuel can be arranged. The port is within an easy taxi ride of Mangalore proper.

General
The harbour is not somewhere you would choose to visit, being grimy and polluted, but it could be useful in an emergency if a harbour with easy access in all weather was needed along this bit of coast.

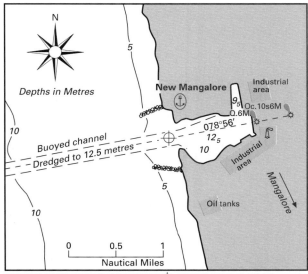

NEW MANGALORE HARBOUR ⊕ 12°55'·5N 74°48'·5E

Coondapoor

13°37'·3N 74°40'·4E (F.4M S side of river)

The mouth of the Chakra and Haladi Rivers. Approach from the SW to avoid reefs and shoals to the N. There are reported depths of 2m over the bar into the river where there are 5–6m depths. A local pilot is advised. In the river shelter looks good.

Belekeri

14°43'N 74°12'E
Charts BA *3464*

Anchorage possible in the W cove on the N side of Belekeri Bay.

Karwar Bay and Baitkol

Charts BA *3464*

Approach

A yacht should head for Baitkol harbour. Although the anchorages on the S side of Karwar Head look like they could be sheltered with an offshore wind, in fact surf breaks along most of the S anchorages. The deep water channel (dredged to 10m) into Baitkol harbour is buoyed.

By night
Oyster Rocks Fl.10s26M
Baitkol E side Q.R.6M

Mooring

Anchor off NE of the harbour entrance in 3–6m. There is usually flat water here during the NE monsoon. You may be able to find a berth alongside in the small commercial harbour.

Authorities Harbourmaster and customs.

Facilities

Water and diesel nearby in the commercial harbour. Limited shopping for provisions. Local restaurants/cafés.

General

Karwar Bay is a quite beautiful spot, fringed by palms and with the jungle always nearby. Karwar Head is a high steep-to headland covered in dense jungle. Baitkol harbour hardly seems to dent the surroundings and is a small low-key affair compared to other larger commercial harbours along the coast.

Panaji (Panjim)

(Goa/Mandovi River)
Charts BA *492*

Approach

An anchorage in the Mandovi River off Panaji town (referred to locally by its old name of Panjim). The entrance to the Mandovi River is between two sandbanks where the Mandovi River empties into Aguada Bay. Ideally the approach should be made around late morning when the sandbanks are more easily identified. Once into the channel head for the small lighthouse on the N side and from there to the anchorage indicated in Verem Bay.

Conspicuous The white lighthouse and signal station on the headland on the N side of Aguada Bay are conspicuous. A large hotel on the slopes further E is also conspicuous. In the immediate approach to the river the small fort and lighthouse on the W side of the channel are conspicuous. The buildings of Panaji town are easily identified on the S side of the river.

By night The lighthouse on the N side is lit Fl(3)G.20s27M. Under it closer to the shore is a Fl.R.3s12M.

The small lighthouse in the channel is lit Fl.G.1·5s3M. The two channel buoys are lit Fl.3s (occas).

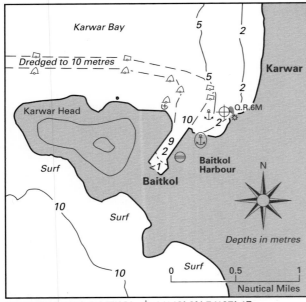

KARWAR BAY & BAITKOL ⊕ 14°48'·2N 74°07'·4E

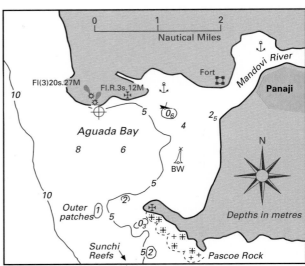

PANAJI APPROACHES ⊕ 15°29'·4N 73°46'·5E

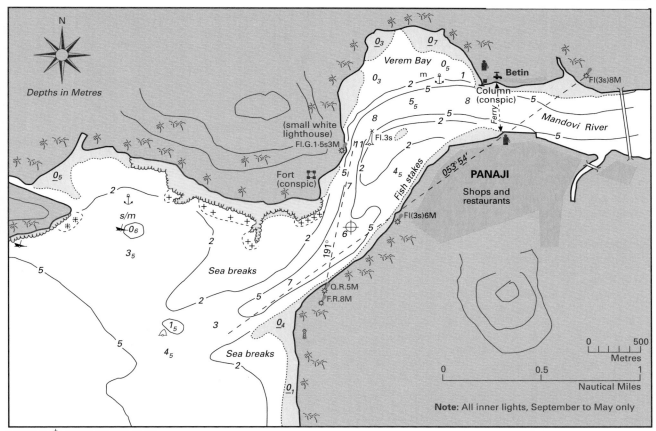

PANAJI ⊕ 15°29·5N 73°48·7E

There are leading lights for the channel on 053°54': *Front* Fl.3s6M *Rear* Fl.3s8M. The leading lights used as a back-bearing once into the river on 191° are: *Front* Q.R.5M *Rear* F.R.8M.

Note The inner lights operate from September to May only during the NE monsoon. The lights are not in operation in the SW monsoon. A night entrance is not recommended.

VHF Port control on Ch 16/12.

Dangers
1. Entrance should not be attempted during the SW monsoon when heavy surf often breaks across the entrance and in the approaches.
2. Entrance between the sandbanks to the N and S of the entrance must be made with someone conning you through. The sea generally breaks on the sandbanks and at low tide part of the sandbanks are above water.

Goa (Panjim). The anchorage in the Mandovi River off Panjim town.

147

3. A current is generally flowing out of Mandovi River and care is needed of cross-currents, especially just inside the sandbanks.
4. Workboats and barges regularly use the river and yachts should keep well out of their way.

Mooring

Anchor due W of the conspicuous column where shown in Verem Bay in 2–5m. The bottom is mud and good holding.

Shelter Good shelter. You are mostly out of the land and sea breeze effects here and you are also out of the worst of the current.

Authorities Harbourmaster, customs and immigration at Panaji near the town quay.

Anchorage It is also possible to anchor on the N side of Aguada Bay in 3m. Good shelter from the prevailing winds in flat water.

Facilities

Water From local sources on the N side at Betin.
Fuel Diesel and petrol from the petrol station on the N side at Betin and on the S side at the ferry quay.
Gas Most gas bottles can be filled in Panaji.
Paraffin Available ashore at Betin.
Laundry At Betin or Panaji.
Repairs It should be possible to haul out in an emergency. Mechanical and engineering work at Panaji. Electrical repairs. Good hardware shops ashore with a range of paints and sealants. Good selection of tools made in India.
Provisions Good shopping for all provisions in Panaji. Fruit and vegetable market near the bus station at Patto. Limited shopping for basics in Betin.
Eating out Excellent selection of restaurants serving good Indian food, variations on Indian food and western/Goan fare. Good seafood. Try the *Venite* on rua 31st Jan Rd for a treat.
Other Banks will exchange travellers cheques. Andhra Bank or Bank of Baroda do cash advances on credit cards. PO. Telephone and fax bureaus. Hospitals. Hire cars and motorbikes. Buses to most parts of India or connections to other buses and the rail system. The new Konkan Railway to Bombay is now open. Internal and international flights from Dabolim Airport about 30 minutes away.

General

Goa has become a synonym for long sandy beaches inhabited by pot-smoking hippies who got caught in a time warp. In fact most of them have long disappeared to beaches further south because the beaches along this bit of coast are now lined by huge hotels full of northern Europeans here for the winter sun. The province of Goa has a large tourist industry and charter flights fly here direct bringing thousands in every day. Panaji itself, not being on the beach, has few of the European imports and is surprisingly untouristy given it is the capital and hub of the region. It is a fine old city with most facilities and some excellent restaurants.

Panaji was originally a suburb of the old capital, now called Old Goa, a bit further up the river. The Portuguese influence is evident everywhere from old buildings of the period with high ceilings and all-round verandahs, porticoed arcades, fine squares, and Catholic churches all over the place. Old Goa upriver is now overgrown with jungle, its many churches and other buildings melding into the undergrowth, a touching reminder of how quickly colonial splendour can disappear. The tomb of St Francis Xavier, built by one of the last of the Medici family, is kept in good repair and the saint's body is taken out every ten years and displayed to the public. The next time is 2004. All around the old town centre are the remains of many fine churches and it is well worth a trip up the river to see Old Goa. There are numerous trips arranged from Panaji.

Panaji is not the easiest place to be in a yacht because you are stuck out on the N side of the river away from easy access to facilities. It is a safe anchorage and worth the inconvenience for the charm of Panaji and is also a safe place to leave the boat for short trips inland.

Note The sea breeze is often turned NW–NNW between Bombay and Goa.

Port Redi

15°45'N 73°44'E
Charts BA *3464*

Care needed of reefs in the approach. Shelter reported adequate under the headland.

Vengurla

15°51'·2N 73°37'E

Anchorage possible under the headland on the N. Care needed of reefs in the bay. Shelter reported to be good.

Devargh Harbour

16°23'·3N 73°22'·6E

It is reported there are 5m plus depths up to the headland (Fort Point) sheltering the inlet running SW and that in the inlet depths shelve gradually. Anchor behind the headland where convenient. Shelter looks good.

Vijayadurg Harbour

16°33'·7N 73°20'E

The entrance to Vaghotan River. Anchorage under the N side. The river proper has a shallow bar at the entrance.

Rajapur Bay

16°36'·5N 73°19'·3E

At the entrance of Rajapur River. The cove under the N side of the bay appears to offer good protection in the NE monsoon.

Ratnagiri Bay

16°59'N 73°16'·4E
Charts BA *3460*

Anchorage in convenient depths under the headland. Shelter appears to be good in the NE monsoon. The town of Ratnagiri is nearby.

Mirya Bay

17°01'N 73°16'E
Charts BA *3460*

Large bay under Mirya Head. Harbour works reported.

Jaigarh Bay

17°18'·2N 73°12'E

The mouth of the Shastri River. Straightforward access. Anchor in the NE corner or under the W entrance point. Shelter looks adequate.

Dabhol

17°33'·9N 73°08'·5E

The mouth of Vashishti River. There are reported to be depths of 3m in the entrance channel towards the S side. Shelter inside looks good.

Janjira

18°18'N 72°57'·8E

The mouth of Rajpuri Creek. There are reported depths greater than 5m into the river following a more or less central channel. Anchor off under Janjira Fort on its rocky islet and the coast E where depths are convenient. Shelter looks good during the NE monsoon.

Revandra

18°32'·3N 72°54'·5E

The mouth of the Kundalika River. A sand bar obstructs most of the entrance with a black buoy marking the extremity (NE monsoon only). There are reported 2m depths in the entrance channel although local sources say 3m. Local knowledge needed. Inside shelter looks all-round.

Bombay

Charts BA *1487, 2621*

Approach

Visibility in the approaches from some distance out is generally bad from local industry, cooking fires and the general air pollution in Bombay from motor vehicles and other sources.

Conspicuous There are numerous oil rigs in the approaches from 80–90M off the coast in the case of the Bombay High Oilfield Development Area. The approach route for commercial vessels is either due E to Bombay or around 20M off the coast from the NNW and 10–15M off the coast from the SSW. BA 1487 should be consulted. In the immediate approaches there are numerous ships at anchor waiting to unload or load cargo and the skyscrapers in the Colaba area will be seen. The lighthouse on Prongs Reef on the N side of the entrance, a tower with white, red and black bands is conspicuous and the light tower on Sunk Rock can also be identified. The main channel for commercial ships into the harbour is buoyed. Closer in, the small lighthouse on Dolphin Rock will be seen as will the monumental Gateway of India and the high-rise Taj Mahal and Intercontinental hotels.

By night The harbour and approaches are well lit, but a night approach should be made with due caution for unlit fishing boats up to 20 or more miles off.

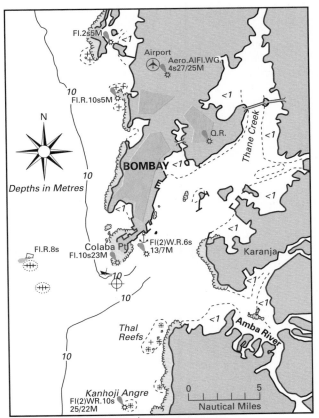

BOMBAY APPROACHES ⊕ 19°51'N 72°48'E

Bombay. Anchorage off the Bombay Yacht Club under the
Gateway of India.

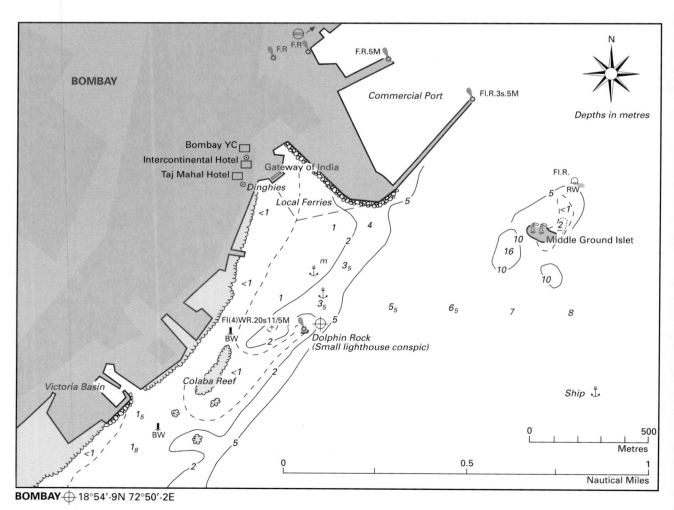

BOMBAY ⊕ 18°54'·9N 72°50'·2E

Bombay Airport Aero AlFl.WG.4s27/25M
Bombay LtF No.2 Fl(2)10s10M
Prongs Reef Fl.10s23M
Gull Islet Fl.5.s7M
Sunk Rock Fl(2)WR.6s13/7M
Dolphin Rock Fl(4)WR.20s11/5M 147°-R-236°-W-270°-R-000°
Tucker Beacon Oc.WR.5s13M
Kanhoji Angre Island Fl(2)WR.10s25/22M 336°-R-001°-W-201°

There are numerous minor lights around the commercial and naval dockyards for which *Admiralty List of Lights Vol. F* should be consulted.

VHF Ch 16/12 for port control and pilots. Call up when 10 miles off and follow any instructions. You will usually be asked to anchor off the Bombay Yacht Club if you manage to get through.

Dangers
1. There will be numerous ferries, large and small, charging about at speed. Special care is needed as you get closer to the Bombay Yacht Club.
2. There are always numerous local craft in the approaches and within the port area itself. Most of these are fishing boats large and small although there will also be local craft ferrying goods around.
3. Care must be taken of commercial ships entering or leaving port which have right of way.
4. The tidal streams are strong in the approaches and in the harbour proper. At springs rates of up to 4kn have been recorded. The tide is generally easterly on the flood and westerly on the ebb but can be ENE turning N on the flood and WSW on the ebb. The direction is to some extent variable within the harbour depending on the depths and there can be tidal swirls in places.
5. Fishing stakes and unmarked nets may be found some distance off the coast in the approaches.

Mooring
Proceed into the anchorage off the Bombay Yacht Club and anchor 2–5m N of Dolphin Rock wherever there is space. The bottom is mud and good holding.

Shelter Good shelter during the NE monsoon. The discomfort here is from the wash from local ferries, fishing boats, bum-boats and shipping using the channel.

Authorities Harbourmaster, customs, immigration.

Entry On arrival call up port control and inform them you want to clear in. Customs will then come out to visit you and you must then fill in the requisite paperwork detailing everything concerning the yacht and its occupants and various forms stating you are not carrying illegal drugs or firearms. You must then visit the harbourmaster, customs again, and finally immigration. You will need a small amount of rupees to pay the harbourmaster who will not (usually) accept other currencies.

Exit Basically the above procedure in reverse. You will need to notify the coastguard on VHF Ch 16 of your intention to leave.

Note It may be useful to contact the Bombay Yacht Club in advance announcing your arrival. They may be able to help with entry and exit procedures.

Facilities
Note The Bombay Yacht Club may extend a helping hand to visiting yachtsmen. You can only ask.
Water There is a tap on the quay ashore. It may be possible to obtain larger amounts within the commercial harbour. Check with reliable locals on water purity, but in general it is advisable to sterilise any water taken on here.
Fuel By jerrycan from the shore. You can engage a local boatman to ferry it out. There must be a small-craft fuel quay within the harbour complex – enquire at the Bombay Yacht Club or to the local ferries and tripper boats operating off the quay.
Gas Most gas bottles can be filled ashore although there may be difficulties over some bottles such as *Camping Gaz* bottles.
Paraffin Available ashore.
Laundry A number of laundries in the vicinity.
Repairs There are slipways and repair yards within the port complex. It may be possible to haul at one of these. With a bit of research facilities for engine repairs, mechanical and engineering work, electrical repairs and basic canvas-work will be found. Obtaining spares for marine engines and equipment is next to impossible and importing spares is difficult. Numerous hardware shops with a good range of paints and sealants.
Provisions There are several supermarkets in the local area and numerous small grocery shops and greengrocers. Alternatively go to Crawford Market a little distance N for a wide selection of fresh fruit and vegetables, dairy products, meat and fish.
Eating out There is everything to choose from. Nearby in the Taj Mahal and Intercontinental there are western-style restaurants. In the streets nearby there are numerous other restaurants and you can wander around and find all sorts of restaurants from the humble to the more up-market. In general it is possible to eat well for little.
Other Banks and ATM machines which accept foreign credit cards. *American Express*, Bank of America (*Mastercard*) and Grindleys ANZ (*Visa*). PO near Victoria Terminus and in the Intercontinental. Telephone and fax services from agencies. Buses and taxis. Hospitals. Ask in the Intercontinental for advice. 24-hour pharmacies. Rail services all over India from Victoria Terminus nearby. Ferry service to Goa. Internal and international flights from Sahar International and Santa Cruz about an hour by taxi from Gateway of India.

General
Bombay is smelly, polluted, noisy, dirty and crowded beyond belief. If you can't cope with the hubbub of a big city where hundreds of people seem to want to inhabit the same patch of ground you are on, then Bombay is not for you. If you like a bustling and vibrant city then Bombay is not to be missed.

You don't have to walk very far before commerce of every type, from small food stalls to emporiums full of a diverse assortment of goods, assault your senses. Only those with no curiosity at all will fail to be enchanted by the streets of Bombay.

The city itself is heir to some wonderful architecture mostly bequeathed by the British. There is Victoria Terminus, the Victorian Gothic train station still used to connect Bombay to the rest of India. Around Horniman Circle are the Venetian Gothic Elphinstone buildings and nearby is the Town Hall with Doric columns shipped out from England. Off the anchorage the monumental Gateway to India is in Indian-Saracenic style and was built to commemorate the visit of George V and Mary in 1911. The Bombay Yacht Club is housed in an old colonial building with a wonderful sense of calm to it after the hustle and bustle around the Gateway to India. Large fans revolve lazily overhead and there is a library, trophies and models of yachts, a reading room, everything a proper gentleman's club should have including peace and quiet.

You will be pursued everywhere in Bombay by beggars, touts and the mildly curious. It is something you have to get used to and my tip of the day for a visit here is not to give money to beggars. It's not that I am mean-minded, but as soon as you donate so much as a rupee you will be surrounded in a flash by many more beggars and the only way to shake them off is to duck into a shop where hopefully the shopkeeper will keep them out. The alternative is to walk around looking like the Pied Piper with a string of voluble urchins tagging along imploring you to give them a few rupees.

Maldives

Current situation
The islands have been a republic since 1968 when the sultanate was abolished. It is a stable country even though there has been discontent amongst the young. In 1988 a coup was put down with help from the Indian government.

Documentation and visas
Normal ships papers and a valid passport for all crew members must be carried. Most foreign nationals do not need a visa and will be given 30 days on arrival. Yachts must go to Male first to clear in where a permit will be issued.

Entry formalities
On arrival at Male call up on VHF Ch 16 and the marine police will come out to the yacht. Most people then use an agent who will come out to you with the other requisite officials: health, customs and immigration. An agent whose name often crops up is 'Fifo' and in 1997 charges were around $40 US a day. Other yachts have reported a flat $90 fee for clearing in. It may be that some negotiation is in order for the agents fee although you can be sure it will increase in the future.

Once cleared in a yacht can cruise the North and

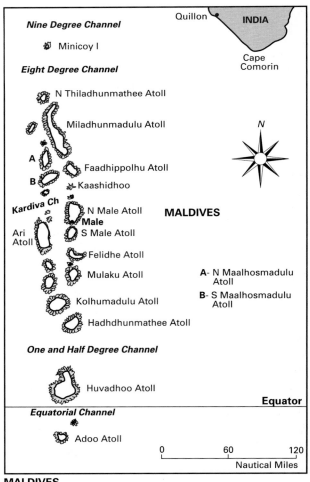

MALDIVES

South Male Atolls for two weeks. After this period a charge of $5US per day is levied for the next one month and for any periods over this length of time a charge of $8 per day is levied. There seems to be some discrepancy over these charges and they may well be reviewed.

Some yachts stop at one of the northernmost islands, usually Turakunu Island (Ihavandiffulu Atoll), with engine or other mechanical 'problems' and there appear to be few problems with this, although I cannot recommend it. What normally happens is that the island headman will get in touch with Male to get clearance and then as long as it is a brief stopover (1–3 days) there appear to be few problems. I will add that this leniency should not be over-exploited or it may be withdrawn.

Data
Area 300km^2 (116M^2) (The smallest member of the UN)
Coastline 644km (348M)
Maritime claims Territorial 12M. Exclusive economic zone 35-310M.
Population 222,000
Capital Male
Time zone UT+5
Language Divehi (Sinhala dialect). Some English spoken.
Religion Sunni Muslim. The Muslim religion on the island is a very gentle form.

Public holidays
The Muslim holidays vary from year to year.

Jan 1	New Years Day
Feb 5	Martyr's Day
Jul 26/27	Independence Day
Aug 29/30	National Day
Nov 3	Victory Day
Nov 11/12	Republic Day

Government Democratic Republic

Crime Low levels of all crime. This is a safe place.

Travel
Internal
For short trips between the islands *dhonis* (local boats) will ferry you around. Air Maldives has flights to 2 southern and 1 northern atoll. A hovercraft connects some islands from Male. Maldivian Airtaxis operate sea-planes. On the islands you get around on foot or sometimes by bicycle.

International
There are numerous scheduled flights from Male to Southeast Asia, India, Europe and the USA. There are also a number of charter flights from Europe.

Practicalities
Mail Mail is quick and reliable. Mail can be sent poste restante to Male.

Telecommunications IDD system. Country code 960.
Telephone and fax from the post office at Male. Alternatively use the telephone and fax of the agent. Some hotels and shops will allow you to use the telephone and fax for a charge. Phonecards available.

Currency The unit is the *ruffiya* divided into 100 *laari*. The currency is reasonably stable at the present time.

Banks and exchange Banks will exchange hard currency (US dollars preferred) and travellers cheques (US dollars preferred). The Bank of Ceylon in Male will give cash advances on *Visa*. Although technically all transactions must be in *ruffiya*, the US dollar is usable for most transactions. Remember it is technically illegal. Some shops and many of the hotels will take the major credit and charge cards.

Medical care Rudimentary. Specialist care is not available. In the event of major illness head for Europe or Australasia. The water is generally potable but can often be brackish and tastes awful. Collect rainwater whenever possible for consumption.

Electricity 220V 50Hz AC

Useful books
Sri Lanka Handbook Robert Bradnock. Footprint Handbooks. Includes the Maldives.
Common Reef Fishes of the Maldive Islands Charles Anderson & Ahmad Hafiz. Novelty Printers. Available in Male.
Living Reefs of the Maldives R C Anderson. Novelty Printers. Available in Male.

Geography and climate
The coast The Maldives is made up of some 19 major atolls which encompass approximately 1200 coral islands. Many of these are very small and generally no more than 2·5m (8ft) above sea level. This has caused the Maldivians to be much concerned about global warming as if the sea level continues to rise, even at very small rates, the effect on the islands will be catastrophic. If present predictions are correct and a rise of 1m occurs by the year 2100, most of the Maldives could be uninhabitable. It is not so much the loss of actual land, but the effect of storm surges, which will likely cause much damage, as in 1987 when high tides and a storm surge caused severe damage to the airport on Hulule and to the island of Male.

The word we use to describe the sort of islands that make up the Maldives, an atoll, comes from the Maldivian word, and the atolls are textbook examples of coral-based islands surrounded by a circular barrier reef enclosing a lagoon. Like all atolls, the high palms will be the first thing you see although from the distance the afternoon clouds gathering over an island are a useful though not infallible clue to the presence of an atoll.

Coastal waters In true atoll fashion the reefs are surrounded by very deep water with only a few shallow areas off some of the islands. Around the barrier reef on the drop-off depths are typically 200–300m. Within the lagoons the depths are also considerable, often 40–50m until close to the island. This makes anchoring difficult and typically a yacht must anchor in anything from 15–40m. Anywhere there are more convenient depths will invariably be off a resort hotel and as the island is usually leased to the resort, yachts are often asked to move on. The considerable depths in which a yacht has to anchor means that you need to pay every attention to anchoring tackle and to the anchor winch which will be struggling at these depths.

The bottom is typically sand or coral. In many places there will be coral heads which easily snag anchor chain and it is prudent to rig a trip-line. The reefs have abundant marine life over them and indeed most of the resorts cater for diving holidays. There is frankly not a lot else to do.

Climate The climate is equatorial and although the islands are influenced by the NE and SW monsoons, the influence is less pronounced than further N. As further N, the dry season and calmer period is during the NE monsoon from November to April. During the SW monsoon rain is more likely, although because the islands sit across the ITCZ, rain, often heavy, can fall at any time.

Temperatures range from 25°–30°C throughout the year. Mean sea temperatures are 28°–29°C throughout the year.

Weather
Prevailing winds near the coast Prevailing winds are pretty much determined by the NE and SW monsoons although the position of the Maldives just above the equator means that winds will often be variable and weaker in the more southerly islands than in the northern islands of the group. Generally winds are NNE–NE turning to N–NW around April for the NE monsoon. During the SW monsoon winds are typically westerly. Wind speeds are typically around 15–20kn although there are often days of calm or little wind.

Gales The pattern of gales associated with the SW monsoon found further N does not strictly apply to the Maldives, especially the southern atolls. May is the month with the highest average of gales at around 5% in some years. Squalls associated with thunderstorms pass through and wind speeds can exceed 40kn at times. Because the islands lie between the equator and 8°N, they are not affected by tropical storms, although the storm surge from cyclones can affect anchorages.

Tides
The tidal range around the islands is nowhere more than 1m at springs. For some of the shallow passes into the lagoons this range can be critical allowing you to just scrape in, so it is necessary to keep a record, even a mental one, of the state of the tide and its likely range.

Currents
Close to the atolls the currents are unpredictable in direction and strength and are often in contrary directions to the equatorial counter-current or to current patterns in the Arabian Sea. As a general rule currents set either E or W through the large navigable channels between the atolls for Eight Degree Channel, One and a Half Degree Channel and Equatorial Channel. For the smaller channels and passes into the lagoons the current set depends on the marine topography and shape of the atoll. Although variable, the currents close to the coast can be considerable and rates of between 1 and 4kn have been recorded.

The moral is simple: keep an eye on cross-track error on the GPS and a lookout up the mast or forward when traversing a pass into a lagoon. The 'reef-sucking' phenomenon applies to most places in the Maldives.

Navigation
In general the Maldives are well charted and most modern British Admiralty charts can have GPS positions plotted directly on to them. This does not apply when within 1–2M of reefs or land as there are random errors incorporated into what are basically still 19th-century charts. All navigation within the atolls must be first and foremost of the eyeball variety backed up by prudent use of the GPS and any other aids to navigation.

Harbours and anchorages
Below are details on Male where yachts must go to clear in before cruising around the atolls. While it might seem restrictive to be granted permission for just the North Male and South Male atolls, in practice there are more than enough anchorages here to keep any coral-hopping cruiser happy.

Male
Charts BA *3323*

Approach
The normal approach to Male is through Male Channel (Gaadhoo Koa) on the SE corner of Male Atoll.

Conspicuous Several radio masts on the SE corner of Male Island and a communications tower near the middle of the island will be seen. The control tower and radio masts on Hulule Island will also be seen. From the distance planes making the final approach to the airport on Hulule Island are a good pointer to where it is.

By night There are no useful lights for a night approach. The loom of the lights on Male and the lights at the airport will be seen. The radio masts carry F.R lights. The communications tower on Male has an Oc.R. Stand off until the morning before making a final approach.

VHF Ch 16 for the marine police. Call them up when you are making the final approach through Gaadhoo Koa.

Mooring
Anchor off the N side of Male. The anchorage is very deep and you will usually be anchoring in 30–35m. The bottom is sand and coral and some

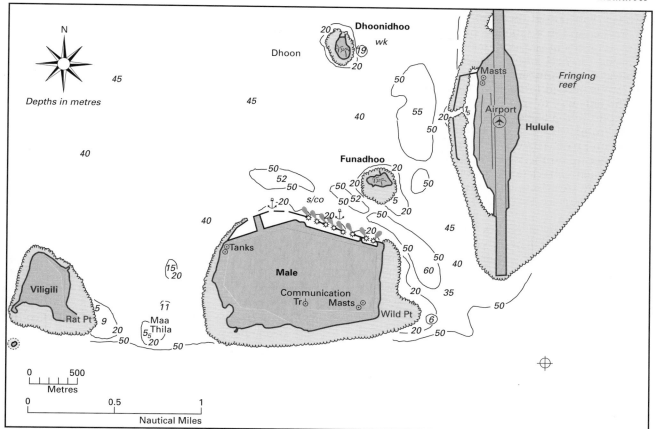

APPROACHES TO MALE ⊕ 04°10′N 73°32′E

yachts have reported coral patches which can snag the chain. Use a trip line.

Shelter Reasonable shelter although there is some wash from passing craft.

Authorities Marine police, customs, health, immigration, harbourmaster.

Note Some yachts have used the new harbour on the NW corner of the island. Berth Mediterranean-style stern or bows-to the wall or anchor inside the breakwater. Depths are reported to be mostly 3–5m.

Facilities

Water From various sources in the town. The water comes from a desalination plant and is potable.

Fuel The agent can arrange for fuel to be ferried out in drums with a pump and hose for small amounts. A delivery charge is made.

Laundry Can be arranged ashore at a price.

Repairs Minor mechanical and electrical repairs. A diver can be arranged for bottom cleaning.

Provisions Most staples can be found and there are several small supermarkets. Fruit and vegetables are limited. Fish from the fish market.

Eating out Indian fare at a number of local establishments. European style food at the hotels at a price. Good fresh fish available although it is not often cooked imaginatively.

Other PO. Banks. Cash advance on *Visa* at the Bank of Ceylon. A visa for India can be obtained quickly and easily here. *Dhotis* to nearby islands and internal and international flights from Hulule.

General

The capital is a small place and it will take you only 20 minutes to walk it from end to end. Around one quarter of the total population of the Maldives lives here and it has a transient population of those visiting to sell and buy, get medical treatment, and just visiting to see the sights. Take some time out to visit the fish market on the waterfront to identify good eating fish and marvel at the skill of the locals gutting and filleting the fish.

The old inner harbour dates from the 17th century when the Dutch considered the Maldives a protectorate and an extension of their rule in Sri Lanka. Like many of the other structures around it is built of coral blocks, the only available building materials on the islands. There are a number of mosques and a small museum in Male, but really it is a place just for wandering around before relaxing in the shade with a cool drink.

Anchorages

There are numerous anchorages around the Male Atolls. Depending on draught yachts can enter some of the lagoons and find a secure anchorage within. Alternatively it is possible to anchor on the lee side of some islands. The following notes may be useful.

1. Many of the passes into a lagoon are fairly shallow. Typically some passes are around 1·30–1·50m and this effectively locks out many yachts with deeper draught. Some passes are deeper at around 4–6m and these will usually

have substantial beacons marking the pass. Smaller and more shallow passes may be marked by sticks or brushwood or not at all. It is always useful to check out the pass first by dinghy and always have someone aloft to con you in.

2. Care is needed in many of the atolls of bombies. The only way to spot these is from aloft.

3. Depths in the lagoons are usually 5–10m making anchoring easy. Use a trip line if there appear to be coral patches around that might snag chain.

4. Anchoring on the lee side of an island will be in the usual considerable depths of anything from 30–40m. At times it is useful to put a stern anchor out to hold the bow into any ground swell.

5. The reception at resorts on the islands varies. Some just do not want you around and do not allow anchoring in their 'own' bit of water – usually the bit that has convenient depths. Some resorts will allow you to anchor but generally expect you to eat ashore. The local fishermen are friendly and you can often get crayfish or fish from them.

Pakistan

Few yachts bother to make the detour up to Pakistan and I would probably not have included it but for meeting one person who had made the trip. Yachts should head for Phitti Creek to the E of Karachi if they are headed this way and not to Karachi Port itself.

While there is considerable internal dissent and a lot of internecine violence in cities like Karachi, most travellers will not be affected by it. Nonetheless it would pay to monitor the BBC World Service and if possible avoid Pakistan when elections are being held.

Phitti Creek

Charts BA *1284*

Approach

Phitti Creek leads to Port Muhammad bin Qasim. The entrance to Phitti Creek is through the Ashan Channel. In the approaches ships will often be seen anchored off the entrance waiting to go into the port. Ashan Channel is well buoyed with a least depth of 10m up to the port area. The surroundings here are all low-lying.

By night A night approach should not be made. Buddo Island is lit Oc.6s16M. There are leading lights into Port Muhammad bin Qasim on 032°26' front Q.11M rear Buddo Island light. Ashan Channel is lit by lightbuoys Fl.R to port and Fl.G to starboard.

VHF Ch 16, for port authorities. Call up when 12M off Ashan Channel and request permission to enter. Call up again when at the entrance to Ashad Channel for permission to proceed.

Tides Around 3m range at springs and neaps.

Note With the SW monsoon a heavy swell sets onto the entrance to the channel.

Mooring

Berth where directed to clear in. This is a commercial port with no facilities for yachts. After clearing in you may be able to anchor off somewhere more convivial.

Shelter Excellent shelter in the delta. Tidal streams are strong here.

Authorities Harbourmaster, customs, immigration and health at Port Muhammad bin Qasim.

Facilities

At the port there is water and electricity. It is likely that you will be able to organise fuel. There is a small settlement at Korangi and Karachi should be easily accessed from the port. Either get someone to organise a taxi or more likely you will be able to arrange a lift into Karachi with someone from the port.

Cruising Association HLR Mr Qureshi, c/o Muhammad Ibrahim & Co (PVT Ltd), 500/14 M. PKRY Ani Rd., Saddar, Karachi 0302, Pakistan. ☎ 568 3511, 568 1400.

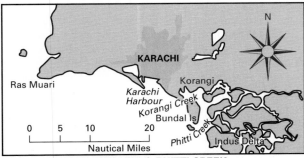

APPROACHES TO KARACHI & PHITTI CREEK

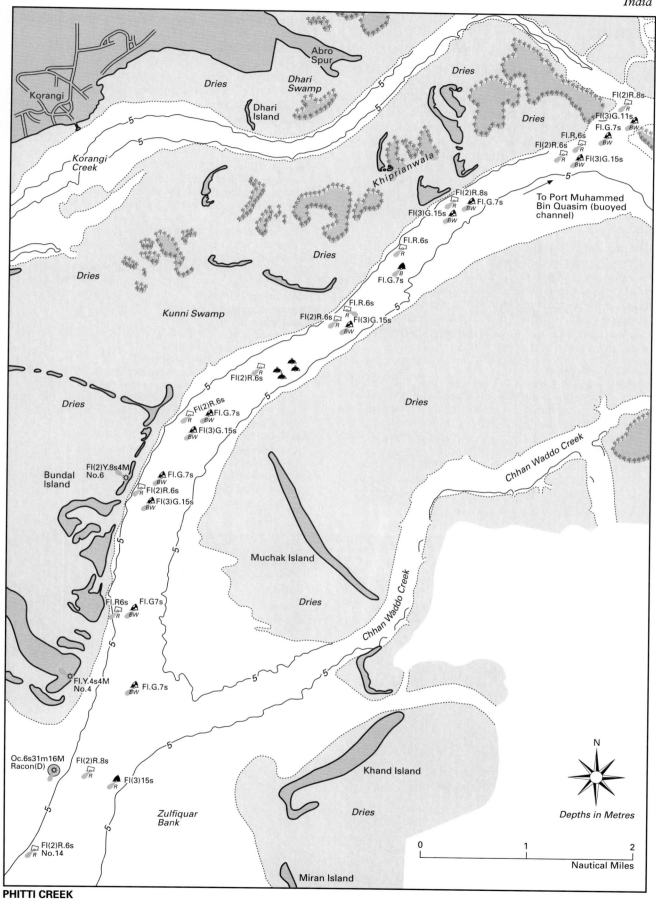

Korangi

Abro
Spur

Dhari
Swamp

Dries

Dhari
Island

Dries

Fl(2)R.8s
R

Korangi
Creek

5

5

Dries

Fl(3)G.11s
BW

Fl.R.6s
R

Fl.G.7s
BW

Khiprianwala

Fl(2)R.6s
R

Fl(3)G.15s
BW

5

Fl(2)R.8s
R

Fl.G.7s
BW

To Port Muhammed
Bin Quasim (buoyed
channel)

Fl(3)G.15s
BW

Dries

Fl.R.6s
R

Fl.G.7s
B

5

Dries

Kunni Swamp

Fl.R.6s
R

Fl(2)R.6s
R

Fl(3)G.15s
BW

5

Dries

Fl(2)R.6s
R

5

Dries

Fl(2)R.6s
R

Fl.G.7s
BW

Fl(3)G.15s
BW

Chhan Waddo Creek

Fl(2)Y.8s4M
No.6

Bundal
Island

Fl.G.7s
BW

Fl(2)R.6s
R

Fl(3)G.15s
BW

5

Muchak Island

Dries

Chhan Waddo Creek

Fl.R.6s
R

Fl.G.7s
BW

5

5

Fl.Y.4s4M
No.4

Fl.G.7s
BW

5

Khand Island

Oc.6s31m16M
Racon(D)

Fl(2)R.8s
R

Fl(3)15s

Dries

Zulfiquar
Bank

5

5

N

Depths in Metres

Fl(2)R.6s
No.14
R

Miran Island

0   1   2
Nautical Miles

PHITTI CREEK

Oman

Current situation

From 1965 the Dhofar rebellion in the south made things unsettled in Southern Oman, but the conflict was effectively brought to an end in 1982 when Yemen and Oman established diplomatic relations and Aden effectively stopped bankrolling the rebels. The British army played a covert role in all this as well. Today Oman is a settled country under Sultan Qaboos and despite being sealed off from the western world for a long period, it is a surprisingly forward-looking country. There have been one or two incidents in recent years, but nothing of consequence to bother visitors.

Documentation and visas

Normal boat's papers must be carried and a valid passport for all crew members. A visa is not required when you arrive by yacht at Mina Raysut where the ships papers and passports are retained by the authorities and a shore-pass issued. Your passport can be redeemed for things like changing money and then given back to the authorities.

Entry formalities

In the approach to a port call up on VHF Ch 16 when 2–5M off. You will be asked for a few details and directed to enter the harbour. Here you will be visited by health, immigration, customs and the harbourmaster. The ships papers and passports will be retained until your exit. You must not go ashore or receive visitors until you are cleared in. There is no clearance on the Muslim weekend (Thursday and Friday) and outside office hours on Saturday to Wednesday you will have to wait on board until the next day.

Exit procedures are basically the reverse of entry except you must go ashore to do the paperwork. Go to immigration who will provide you with four copies of the clearance papers. Take these in order to the harbourmaster, port office, immigration police to collect your passports, customs, and finally the port office to collect the ships papers.

Data

Area 212,460km^2 (82,031M^2)

Frontiers 1374km. Saudi Arabia 676km. UAE 410km. Yemen 288km. Note: Oman has a separate territory on the Musandam Peninsula controlling the Strait of Hormuz and 17% of the world's oil production transits this point going from the Persian Gulf to the Arabian Sea.

Coastline 2092km (1130M)

Maritime claims Territorial 12M. Exclusive economic zone 200M.

Population 1,588,000

Capital Muscat

Time zone UT+4

Language Arabic. Some English spoken in Muscat and Salalah.

Ethnic divisions Mostly Arab.

Religion Ibadhi Muslim 75%. Remainder mostly Sunni and Shi'a Muslim. It is courteous to dress correctly when going ashore and dealing with officials. For men that means long trousers and a shirt, for women a dress which covers the arms and legs.

Public holidays
The Muslim holidays vary from year to year.
18–19 Nov National Day

Government Monarchy. The current ruler is Sultan Qaboos bin Said Al Said.

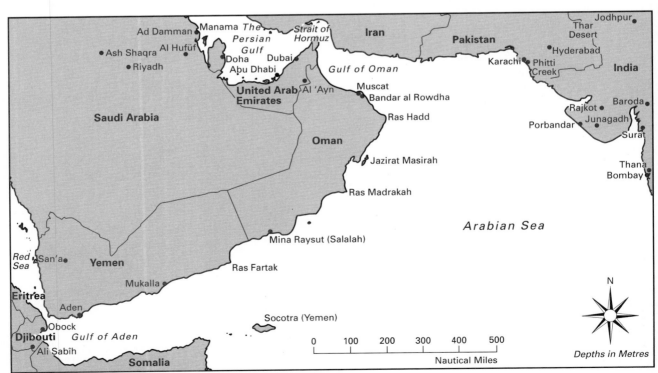

RED SEA TO INDIA

Disputes Border dispute with Yemen over where the border lies.

Crime Low level of petty crime. The harbour at Mina Raysut is a secure area and there have been no reports of theft.

Travel
Internal
Public transport is limited. In Salalah there are no buses and you either hitch-hike or get a taxi. Hitch-hiking is quite easy and accepted. There are flights and coach services between Salalah and Muscat.

International
From Muscat there are flights to Southeast Asia, Europe and the USA, and to the other Gulf states. Flights out of Oman are very expensive and there are no bucket shops.

Practicalities
Mail Is quick and efficient. Mail can be sent to Salalah c/o of the Salalah Holiday Inn, Salalah, Oman.

Telecommunications IDD system. Country code 968.

In Muscat telephone and fax from a hotel. In Salalah there is the central GPO (0730–1230 Sat-Wed/Thurs 0900–1100) for telephone calls. Holiday Inn for telephone and fax.

Currency The unit is the Omani *riyal* (OR) divided into 1000 *baisa*. It is a convertible currency and quite stable. At the time of writing £1GBP = 0·58 OR.

Banks and exchange Banks will change hard currency (US dollars and sterling GBP preferred) to *riyals*. There are also money changers in Muscat and Salalah.

Medical care Is generally very good. Hospitals are modern and many Omani doctors have trained in the UK or USA.

For the most part the country is free of infectious diseases with just a few places where malaria remains a threat. Hygiene in the towns and cities is good. The water is potable and need not be treated although you should take local advice.

Electricity 220V 50Hz AC.

Useful books
Middle East Lonely Planet. Has an adequate section on Oman.

Arabian Sands Wilfred Thesiger. Penguin. Thesiger ended up in Salalah after crossing the Empty Quarter.

Travels in Oman – On the track of the early explorers Phillip Ward. Oleander.

For information on
Geography and climate
Weather
Tides
Currents
Navigation
see the relevant sections covering the NE coast under Yemen.

Harbours and anchorages

Muscat/Marina Bander al-Rowdha
Charts BA *3522, 3518*

Approach
Yachts should head for the marina. The fairway buoy is located at 23°35'·4N 58°37'·8E, WGS 84.

By night The buoyed channel and marina entrance are lit.

VHF Ch 16/9. Call sign *Marina Control*.

Mooring
Data 140 berths. Depths 5·5m MLWS.

Berth Where directed.

Shelter All round shelter.

Authorities Harbourmaster and marina staff.

Facilities
Services Water and electricity at all berths. Shower and toilet block.

Fuel On the quay.

Repairs A travel-hoist is to be installed. Mechanical and engineering repairs.

Eating out A restaurant and several bars at the marina.

Contact: Marina Bander Al-Rowdha ☎ (968) 737 288 *Fax* (968) 737 285.

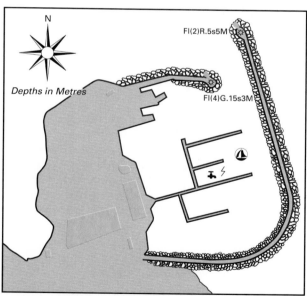

MARINA BANDER AL ROWDHA (MUSCAT)
23°35'·4N 58°37'·8E WGS 84 (Fairway buoy No.5)

Mina Raysut

(Salalah)
Charts BA *2896*

Approach
Straightforward by day or night. There are no dangers in the direct approach from the E.

Conspicuous A communications tower and storage

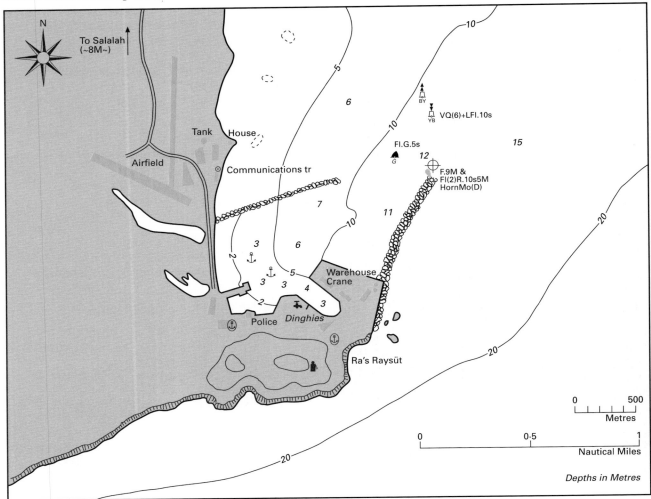

MINA RAYSUT ⊕ 16°56′·6N 54°02′E

tanks N of the harbour will be seen and the breakwaters are readily identified. The breakwaters are reported to show up well on radar.

By night E breakwater F.9M and Fl(2)R.10s5M. Lightbuoy on starboard side of channel VQ(6)+LFl.10s and closer in light buoy Fl.G.5s.

VHF Ch 16. Call up port control when 2–5M off and give ETA. You will usually be asked to proceed into the harbour on arrival.

Mooring

Anchor where indicated on the plan in 3–5m. The bottom is mud and good holding.

Shelter Good shelter during the NE monsoon despite the fact it looks open to this direction. Shelter is reported to be good during the SW monsoon.

Authorities Harbourmaster, customs, health, and immigration. For entry and exit formalities see notes above.

Facilities

Water By jerry can from the shower block on the quay. For larger amounts you will need to make arrangements to go alongside and get the 'waterman' to unlock a water point. A charge is made for this.

Fuel Diesel is available from the Shell depot on the hill S of the harbour. You pre-pay for the amount you want and a tanker delivers it to the quay. Obviously the Shell office is none too pleased if you only want a small amount. For small amounts of diesel and for petrol take jerry cans to the service station in town.

Laundry In town at one of the hotels.

Repairs The naval workshop within the harbour can help out. Enquire first and don't presume you can just wander in at will – it is a naval secure area. Some minor mechanical and engineering work in town.

Provisions Most provisions can be found in Salalah including staples and fresh fruit and vegetables. The new souk near the town centre is probably the best place for meat and fruit and vegetables.

Eating out Restaurants in Salalah. Most of the restaurants offer Chinese or Indian food, or variations on them. For European style meals you will have to go to the Holiday Inn on the coast which is also the only place that sells alcohol.

Other PO. Banks and money changers. Telephone

The desert coast.

and fax services from the GPO and at the Holiday Inn. Mail can be sent to the Holiday Inn where it will be held for collection (Salalah Holiday Inn, Salalah, Oman ☎ 235333). There are no buses from Mina Raysut to Salalah and most people hitch-hike. Taxis at the New Souk. Buses to Muscat from Salalah. Internal flights from Mina Raysut to Muscat.

General

Salalah has a temperate climate in contrast to almost everywhere else in the Arabian Peninsula, friendly locals, and a secure harbour. The latter is the real attraction for yachts providing an easy landfall on the Arabian Peninsula with diesel and water easily available. It is a pleasant first bite at the Arab world and although there is not really a lot to do and see, the surroundings under the steep slopes are spectacular, and the seascape down to Yemen attractive in that desolate desert way.

There is a small museum in Salalah and the site of the ancient city of Zafar is near the Holiday Inn, but few bother to visit either and in truth you are not missing too much. Most opt for a visit to the Holiday Inn and a cold beer in relaxed surroundings looking out over the sea.

Yemen
Current situation

North and South Yemen have had a number of civil wars over the last ten years. With the collapse of the Soviet Union the north has sought to unify with the once communist but now more liberal south. The last confrontation was in 1994 and during the fighting Aden was bombed. Foreign nationals, including yachtsmen, were evacuated. Two yachts were damaged in the fighting and sunk in the harbour. There were no casualties. When the fighting was over efforts were made by the harbour authorities to raise the yachts. This was accomplished successfully in both cases. Since 1994 yachts have again used Aden and things are back to normal, although evidence of the various civil wars litters the harbour. A number of yachts have cruised the coast of Yemen, including myself in 1995/96 and 1997, and the authorities have been nothing but helpful.

There are undercurrents of dissatisfaction evident between the north and the south, particularly where northerners have been given positions of authority in the institutions of the south such as customs, police, the army, etc. On the whole you will not be affected by this except for a little surliness and requests for larger than usual 'gifts'. It would be wise to monitor the airwaves in case trouble brews again.

Documentation and visas

Normal boats papers must be carried and a valid passport for all crew members. Evidence of vaccination from yellow fever and cholera has occasionally been asked for. A visa can be easily obtained for Yemen and if you intend to travel inland this is worth getting. Crew arriving in Yemen to join a boat must have a visa before arriving.

If you intend to stay on board every night a visa is not required and instead your passport will be retained by immigration and you will be issued with a shorepass. Your passport can be redeemed for things like changing money and then given back to immigration until your departure.

Entry formalities

In the approach to any major port call up port control on VHF Ch 16 or 13 when 10 miles off. You will be asked for an ETA and asked to call up again when 2 miles off. Night entrance is prohibited so time your arrival for daylight hours. In practice some (myself included) have arrived at night and anchored off to clear in in the morning.

On arrival you must go ashore to customs, health, and immigration. If you do not have a visa your passport will be retained by immigration and a shorepass issued. Small 'gifts' ranging from a few dollars or a few packets of cigarettes (preferably *Marlboro*) may be asked for.

Data

Area 527,970km² (203,850M²). Includes Perim, the Hanish Islands and Socotra. Note the Hamish Islands are now occupied Eritrea.

Frontiers 1746km (931M). Oman 288km. Saudi Arabia 1458km.

Coastline 1906km (1029M).

Maritime claims Territorial 12M. Exclusive economic zone 200M.

Population 10,395,000

Capital Sa'na

Time zone UT+3

Language Arabic. Some English spoken in the south, especially in Aden.

Ethnic divisions Predominantly Arab. Small Indian influence along the coast. Tribal divisions are marked with the two predominant groups being the Hashids and the Bakils. Inland there is the possibility of being caught up in tribal disputes, but near the coast this is unlikely.

Religion Muslim. As the north effectively won the last civil war in 1994 there has been a tightening of the loose secularism formerly evident in the south. Men should dress correctly and women should wear clothing that covers most of the body or they will be regarded as available and subjected to much attention by the male population.

Public holidays

In addition to Muslim holidays the following secular holidays are observed.

May 1 Labour Day

May 22 Day of National Unity

Sep 26 Revolution Day

Oct 14 National Day

Nov 30 Independence Day

Government Democratic Republic. During 1990 the unification of the Yemen Arab Republic (YAR) with the People's Democratic Republic (PDRY) took place. In 1994 after a brief civil war between the north and the south legal government has again been established with a bias towards the policies of the less secular north.

Disputes Border dispute with Oman over where the border lies. Border dispute with Saudi Arabia over where the exact border lies is now exacerbated by the discovery of oil deposits in the disputed region. Armed dispute with Eritrea over the Hanish Islands. Eritrea invaded Greater Hanish in December 1995 and yachts are advised to keep well clear of this area. Overall the Yemeni government is in disfavour with many of the Middle East states because it sided with Iraq in the Gulf War. Large numbers of Yemenis who formerly worked abroad have now returned as they find it mysteriously difficult to renew work and residence permits.

Crime Low level of petty crime. As stated to me by one Yemeni, 'you will have nothing stolen from you here, but you can be killed over a question of honour'. Large numbers of the males carry automatic rifles (often customised Kalishnikovs), sidearms and the traditional *jambiya*, the curved dagger usually worn in an ornamental sheath on the belt. However you are unlikely to feel threatened by this once you have become accustomed to the sight of men wandering around with lethal hardware. There have been some reports of fishing boats harassing yachts, but I believe in most of these cases that the object is food and curiosity. After encountering numerous fishing dhows I have not once felt threatened. These fishermen live wretched lives and a few small gifts will enhance that life significantly. And you may get a sizeable fish in return for modest gifts.

Travel

Internal

Getting around Aden or Mukalla is best done by taxi. The rates are generally very reasonable. Buses and share-taxis operate around Aden and Mukalla. There are internal flights from Aden to Sa'na.

International

Yemen Airways (Yemenia) has connections from Sa'na to Cyprus, Frankfurt, Amsterdam, London, Paris and Rome. However there are only a few flights a week and the air fares are very high. Air France flies once a week to Sa'na. There are also flights to Ethiopia and Egypt and these are more reasonable. Probably the best thing to do is fly to Egypt and get a cheap onward ticket from there to Europe.

Practicalities

Mail Is surprisingly quick and efficient out of the country. It is possible to have items couriered into Aden. Post can be sent to the post office at Steamer Point although the reliability varies.

c/o Post Office, Steamer Point, Aden, Yemen.

Telecommunications IDD system. Country code 967.

In Aden and Mukalla there are numerous bureau's offering telephone and fax services. Indeed these agencies seem to be one of the few growth areas in Yemen along with money-changers. Typical charges vary but are generally around $3 a minute for calls to Europe, $4–$5 to send a one page fax to Europe and 30¢-50¢ per page to receive faxes.

Currency The unit is the Yemeni *riyal*. The bank rate is typically 25–30% below the black market rate. It is illegal although widespread to change money on the black market.

Banks and Exchange Banks will change US dollars to Yemeni *riyals*. The bank in Aden will also change travellers cheques in US dollars to US dollars cash. The US dollar is really the only currency accepted for changing into Yemeni *riyals*. There are numerous official and unofficial money-changers who will give you a substantially better rate than the bank. Only US dollars in good condition will be accepted and damaged or even creased bills may be rejected. $100 bills are the favoured denomination and those later than 1990 with the anti-counterfeit strip are preferred.

Medical care Is generally poor. If you are seriously ill try to get to your home country or to Europe as quickly as possible and if necessary use your health insurance to get repatriated. Some drugs are available over the counter in the pharmacies but do not rely on specific drugs to be available.

Immunisation is suggested for typhoid, hepatitis A and polio. The water supplies in Aden have been affected by the shelling in 1994 and water should be treated. Malaria is prevalent throughout the country except for Aden and its environs. AIDS has been reported.

Electricity 220V 50Hz AC. There are frequent power cuts and all shops usually have a generator sitting outside for when cuts occur. In larger urban areas there are often sectored cuts with one part of the town being turned off for 6 hours or so and then another part of the town at another time. Because of this be wary of frozen products.

Curiosities and culture

Qat Pronounced 'gat'. This is the national narcotic of Yemen and it seems that the majority of the male population indulge in it. It is a small evergreen bush, *Catha edulis*, cultivated in the highlands and trucked down daily to the markets on the coast. The leaves are chewed to produce a mild stimulant effect and every afternoon you will see Yemenis sitting around chewing *qat*. The stated attributes are a peaceful disposition, heightened sexual prowess and even more heightened sexual prowess. The leaves are chewed into a mulch and by the end of the afternoon the user will have a large pulpy ball of the stuff distending the cheek pouch. It has no immediate effect and it was explained to me that the couple of leaves I tried were not enough and I should continue chewing for a few days until a cumulative effect kicked in. It is not cheap and it would appear that a good deal of the income of the average Yemeni goes on the stuff.

Women Yemen is a male dominated society and except for a few, all women are clothed top to bottom in black with a full veil leaving only the eyes exposed. The eyes are probably the most beautiful encountered anywhere. It is probably unwise to gaze overlong at a Yemeni woman and certainly unwise to approach or even point a camera at them without prior permission. Whenever I sought permission to take a photo it was denied except for one bizarre instance in Mukalla. Remember you may be breaching the code of honour in Yemen by pointing a camera at a Yemeni woman and for that the consequences may be harsh. Foreign women should wear loose-fitting garments that cover the whole body and may feel more comfortable wearing a scarf over the hair as well.

Jambiya The ceremonial curved dagger worn in a special belt. Simple *jambiyas* can be bought cheaply in shops in Mukalla and Aden. Ornate *jambiyas* and the more expensive *dhuma*, a slender version of the *jambiya*, can cost upward of $200–300 depending on how ornate they are. The most expensive are those with handles made from African rhinoceros horn and in fact Yemen is the main consumer of rhinoceros horn, sadly endangering the survival of the species because of poaching to satisfy the Yemeni demand for the stuff.

Rifles and sidearms By right males can carry a rifle and a sidearm in Yemen. Many do not but a fair number wander around with automatic rifles, usually Kalishnikovs, many of them with customised stocks and fancy engraving on the chamber and barrel. Lesser numbers carry sidearms. It is not uncommon in a hotel or restaurant to find at the

Transporting dinner home in Mukalla.

reception a collection of rifles that have been handed in. Strangely enough you get used to the sight of men walking around with an automatic rifle slung over the shoulder and most people do not feel overly threatened.

Alcohol With the victory of the north in 1994 there have been strict controls on alcohol and it is not commonly for sale. There is a black market in Aden and alcohol is available in a few of the luxury hotels at inflated prices, typically $4–$6 for a small can of beer. If Aden becomes a free port as intended then it is likely controls will be relaxed within the free port area, though not elsewhere along the coast. Because alcohol is strictly controlled you will get numerous requests to supply it. Whether you do or not depends on the situation and the recipient, but remember what you are doing is illegal.

Boatbuilding Most traditional boatbuilding takes place along the Red Sea coast in the Timahah region. There are basically two types of craft constructed. The *huri* is transom sterned with a high bow and anything from 5–6m up to 15m. The *sanbuq* is double-ended, of heavier construction and usually around 15 to 20m. The *huri* is normally powered by twin outboards and is used for coastal fishing, although they can often be seen some distance offshore even in bad weather. The *sanbuq* is used for fishing and transportation along the coast. The *sanbuq* is usually powered by an inboard diesel and will have some loosely defined living accommodation. They all leak and it is not uncommon for *sanbuqs* to have one or two auxiliary engines to drive large pumps in order to stay afloat. I've seen them pumping continuously from one pump with the other pump started at odd times to help out and the hose bores are big. I estimated one *sanbuq* had to be pumping out 30+ gallons a minute. The boats are built by eye with no plans although a few formers may be used. Timber is imported, mostly pine, spruce and *zinjil*, a red hardwood from

Fish in abundance. A local fisherman drags his catch ashore at Mukalla.

Indonesia. No doubt steel and GRP will take over in the future, but for now the leaky but beautiful *sanbuqs* and *huris* are still built.

Useful books

Lonely Planet: Yemen. Yemen in detail.
Lonely Planet: Middle East. Covers all the Middle East with enough detail on Yemen to be useful.
Motoring With Mohammed Eric Hansen. Abacus. Good read about a yacht being wrecked off the Red Sea Yemen coast and the author's return to recover his notebooks.

Geography and climate

The coast The desert coastline of Yemen is nothing short of spectacular. It embodies all those old stereotypes of Lawrence of Arabia and the Bedouin with rolling sand dunes coming right down to the water and the occasional tight green splash of an

oasis. What is surprising is just how volcanic the whole area is. Between the rolling sands old volcanic peaks and lava flows look like chocolate coating the sands. Aden itself is a cluster of old calderas and all along the coast others will be seen. In the region between Oman and Yemen, in ar-Ruba'al-Khali (the Empty Quarter), some of the hottest temperatures on earth have been recorded.

Coastal waters Varies from area to area. The water is mostly very clean with exceptional visibility, in places to 10–15m. The littoral area is often of volcanic origin, typically basalt, with some fringing coral depending on the location. The bottom is most often sand. When approaching the coast some care is needed of isolated rocky projections, but for the most part the approaches are free of the extensive coral reefs common in the Red Sea. The area has abundant marine life and fishing becomes mostly a matter of whether you want fish today or not. Several species of tunny and dolphin fish will go for trolled lines without hesitation.

Climate The climate varies considerably with the NE monsoon being dry and the SW monsoon bringing rain. Rain can at times be substantial along the coast, although in some years there may be little rain at all. Although the monsoon is regular, the rain-bearing clouds can pass the coast by. There may also be isolated rain during the NE monsoon depending on depressions passing to the N and rain clouds often circle around the peaks at Mukalla and Aden. The Empty Quarter receives no rain. Temperatures range from 30°C in the winter to 40°C in the summer. Nights are slightly cooler along the coast although inland temperatures can plummet dramatically.

At Aden	Av max °C	Av min °C	Relative humidity	Days 1mm rain
Jan	28	22	63%	1
Feb	28	23	65%	0
Mar	30	24	66%	0·3
Apr	32	25	66%	0
May	34	27	66%	0
Jun	37	29	51%	0
Jul	36	28	49%	1
Aug	36	28	50%	0·7
Sep	36	28	56%	0·2
Oct	33	24	58%	0·2
Nov	30	23	61%	0·2
Dec	28	23	62%	2

Weather

Prevailing winds near the coast Prevailing winds are pretty much determined by the NE and SW monsoons and the topography of the Gulf of Aden. The high land masses along the coast channel winds into or out of the Gulf.

The NE monsoon is deflected by the coast down into the Gulf of Aden where the wind blows from the E and is then channelled around up into the Red Sea from the SE and S through Bab El Mandeb. The wind strength tends to increase with the funnelling effect of the Gulf of Aden so that while there is 10–15kn along the eastern coast, at Aden there may be 20kn, and at Bab El Mandeb the wind can be blowing at 30kn and even gale force as far up as the Hanish Islands.

The SW monsoon is deflected so it blows from the SW off the African coast turning to the S along the eastern Yemen coast. It keeps a fairly true SW direction over the open sea. Typically the SW monsoon is stronger than the NE monsoon and there are often associated squalls, especially during the first month of the SW monsoon. When established the SW monsoon will be blowing at 20kn from the W–WSW in the Gulf of Aden, turning more SW at the entrance where the wind force increases to 30kn and can often reach gale force in July and August. A heavy sea is set onto the eastern Yemen coast.

Aden	Prevailing wind 1	Prevailing wind 2
Jan	E/71%	SE/27%
Feb	E/75%	SE/24%
Mar	E/66%	SE/29%
Apr	E/58%	SE/37%
May	SE/43%	E/37%
Jun	SW/60%	SE/19%
Jul	SW/80%	S/6%
Aug	SW/80%	SE/11%
Sep	SW/45%	SE/32%
Oct	SE/50%	E/29%
Nov	E/67%	SE/29%
Dec	E/74%	SE/23%

Notes Winds for Gulf of Aden at Aden. Prevailing winds 1 and 2 give percentage of the two most prevalent winds. Other winds blow for the remaining percentage.

For more information on wind direction and strength see the charts in *Technical Information*, pages 32-33.

Locally named winds

Asifati Tropical storm in the Arabian Sea
Belat Strong N–NW wind which can reach gale force. Blows off the land and brings dust and sand. It is strongest in eastern Yemen and particularly in Kuria Muria Bay in the Oman. Typically lasts 1–2 days.
Kharif Katabatic wind off the south side of the Gulf of Aden which reinforces the SW monsoon. Most common in June, July and August.

Gales Are rare during the NE monsoon except for the funnelling effect through Bab El Mandeb. With the SW monsoon gale force winds are common and there can be associated squalls of considerable strength. The average wind strength in June and August is some 25kn and in July the average wind strength is 30kn plus. This of course means there is a high percentage of gale force winds estimated to be some 20% of all winds. This high percentage of gales means that most native craft are laid up during this time and even small coasters do not put to sea. Many of the harbours and anchorages along the Yemen coast are untenable in the SW monsoon.

Tropical storms The incidence along the Yemen coast is very low and virtually unheard of in the Gulf of Aden. Most tropical storms deflect NE before hitting the Arabian peninsula or have declined to below tropical storm intensity when they reach the coast. Tropical storms occur in April-June and September to November, but overall the incidence is low with only 5 storms over Force 8 reaching the coast in a 50 year period.

Thunderstorms and waterspouts Localised thunderstorms are recorded although in my experience with the NE monsoon they are short-lived and the associated squalls are not prolonged. Waterspouts are recorded but principally during the SW monsoon.

Tides

The tidal range in the Gulf of Aden is around 2·5–3m at springs becoming less in eastern Yemen. The tides are diurnal becoming less so towards eastern Yemen and again less so towards Bab El Mandeb. Tidal streams are pretty much overcome by the prevailing current except at Bab El Mandeb where the tidal stream compressed through the narrow straits can run at 3+kt over any underwater shelf. In the Small Strait on the E side I managed to do only 0·1kn over the ground for nearly an hour when going S according to the GPS (and my long observation of the lighthouse on Perim Island) while the speed over the ground was 5·5kt. A large part of this is current (see below), but the tidal stream component is significant and can augment or decrease the normal N-going current during the NE monsoon.

Currents

Currents along the Yemen coast are dependent on the SW and NE monsoons.

During the NE monsoon currents are westerly into the Gulf of Aden with given rates of around 1/4–1/2kt in the Gulf of Aden and off Socotra and northern approaches to the gulf. In my experience these rates are appreciably greater up to 10 miles off the coast and commonly run at 1kt or more in a westerly direction following the contours of the coast. Off headlands the rate can be as much as 1 1/2kt. The current only decreases to a rate of 1/4–1/2kt when just E of Socotra. Having spent a long time beating out of the Gulf of Aden the rate of current was assiduously monitored on the GPS and plotted to give rates often over 1kt in December and January.

During the SW monsoon the current flows out of the Gulf of Aden in an easterly direction fanning out at the entrance to the gulf. Rates are given at around 1kt in the Gulf of Aden, 1 1/2kt around Socotra, and 1/2–3/4kt off the eastern coast. If average rates correspond to those given for the NE monsoon then current up to 10 miles off the coast can be expected to be appreciably greater.

Navigation

The coast has not been adequately surveyed since the 19th century. Many of the capes and islands and islets are known to be out of position by up to 4M or more. However the new metric charts have corrected some of the errors and generally navigation off the coast is not a problem with due

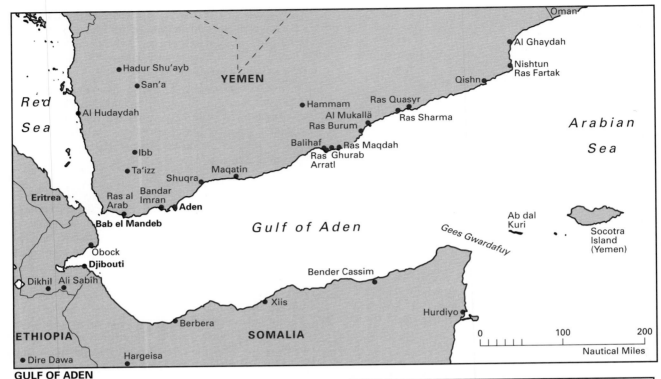

GULF OF ADEN

care and attention. When closing the coast to anchor or enter a harbour it is essential that basic coastal navigation techniques are employed and that the final approach is made with someone conning you in. GPS should not be used as the final reference when closing the coast or dangers to navigation. Where possible I have given GPS co-ordinates using WGS 84 datum. Other co-ordinates are schematic and should be treated with caution.

Harbours and anchorages

Nishtun

Charts BA *3784*

Approach
Straightforward by day. The oil tanks and installations at the port are easily identified.

By night Can be made with care. The light on the promontory is Fl.9s18M and the end of the pier is lit Fl.R.3s.

VHF The port authorities and pilots listen out on Ch 13, 16 (0700–1400).

Mooring
Anchor in the NE of the bay in 2–5m under the lee of the promontory. A swell works its way around into the bay so it may be worthwhile putting out a stern anchor to hold the bows into the swell.

Shelter Good in NE monsoon only.

Authorities Harbourmaster, police and military who will want to see your papers.

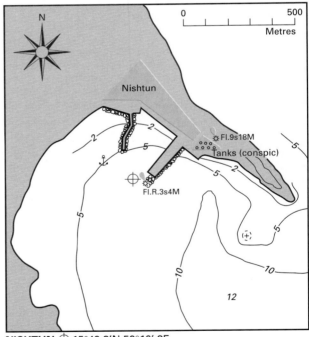

NISHTUN ⊕ 15°49·3′N 52°12′·3E

Facilities
Water. Fuel may be available. Limited provisions.

General
Not often used by yachts on passage between Mina Raysut and Mukalla/Aden although it could be useful in an emergency.

Ras Fartak

This prominent cape is usually mentioned as the point to head for to pick up a good slant during the NE monsoon when making a passage eastabout towards India and Sri Lanka. Here the NE monsoon will be more NNE–NE, rather than E–ESE, and there is also the chance of N or NW winds. MacPherson picked up a solid NE here and N at night at the end of December and so shaped his course to the Laccadives from Ras Fartak.

Khaysart on the S side of Ras Fartak is used by trading dhows. It was at one time the pre-eminent slave trading port on the coast.

Qishn Bay

Charts BA *3784*

A large bay located under Ras Sharwayn. Ras Sharwayn has two conical peaks on it called Conical Peak (581m) and more imaginatively Asses Ears (551m). Asses Ears are two distinct projections like a pair of asses ears and are easily identified when coasting towards the ENE. The bay looks to offer good shelter during the SW monsoon, but it is likely that a swell will penetrate into the bay. It is not suitable in the NE monsoon when a heavy swell sets in. Depths for anchoring are convenient and the bottom is reported to be sand and some coral patches.

It should be borne in mind that this is a fairly remote area.

Ras Quasyr

Ras Quasyr is a low rocky cape bordered by scattered rocks and coral. Care is needed using the plan and the approach must be by day only. 23 miles E of Ras Quasyr lies Palinurus Shoal, a rock and coral reef with least depths of 4·5m reported over it.

In the NE monsoon anchorage can be obtained in the cove to the NW of the cape. Care is needed of

the reefs on either side. Shelter in here is reported to be adequate with a stern anchor to hold the bows into the ground swell which works its way around the cape. It may also be possible to anchor closer to the extremity of the cape tucked under the twin islets on the plan although care would be needed to get through the rocks and reefs in the immediate approach.

The anchorage off the village is not suitable in the NE monsoon and looks like it would be subject to swell with the SW monsoon.

In this vicinity basalt effusions from past volcanic eruptions scar the coast. The old lava flows of black basalt are in striking contrast to the base white limestone of the region in a more dramatic version of the Yemeni coastline elsewhere. Rainfall is very low and in the words of the Admiralty Pilot, '. . . the heat in May is almost unsupportable'.

Ras Sharma

The cape is a limestone promontory not easily distinguished from the rest of the coastline. The village of Al Qarn lies on the W side and it is possible to anchor off here. However the best anchorage is in the cove just under the W side of the tip of the cape where shown. Here there are convenient depths in flat water with the NE monsoon. The approach should be made by day when the islet of Jazarit Sharma will be easily identified when close to the cape and from there the approach to the cove is straightforward.

Limited supplies may be available in the village at Al Qarn.

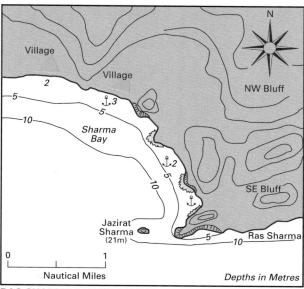

RAS SHARMA 14°50′N 50°01′E

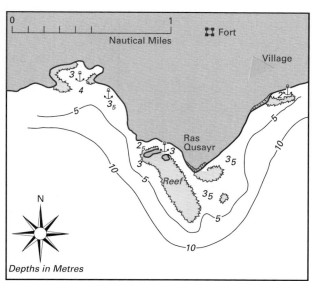

RAS QUASYR 14°54′N 50°17′E

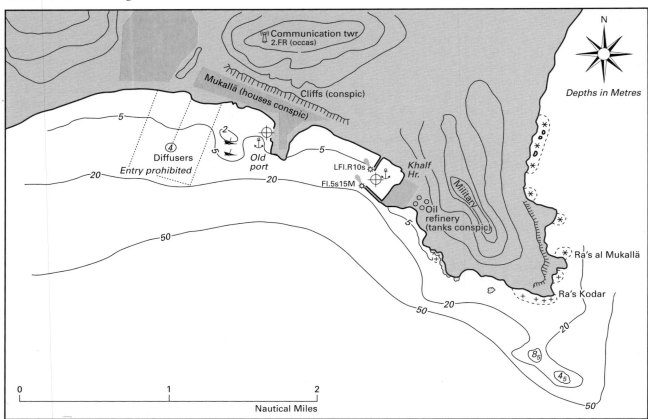

APPROACHES TO MUKALLA

⊕ 14°31'·4N 49°08'·9E **(KHALF HARBOUR)**

⊕ 14°31'·6N 49°08'E **(OLD PORT)**

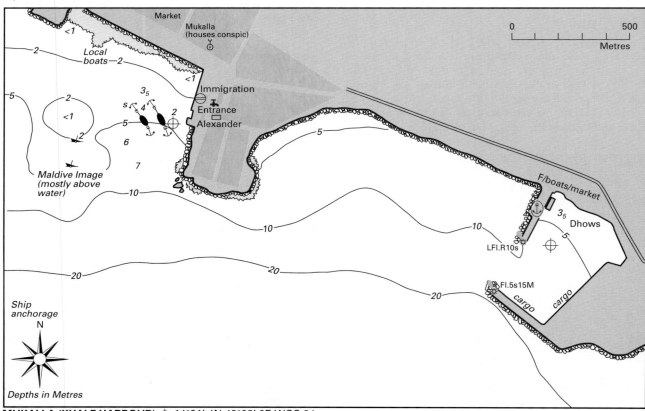

MUKALLA (KHALF HARBOUR) ⊕ 14°31'·4N 49°08'·9E WGS 84

(OLD PORT) ⊕ 14°31'·6N 49°08'E WGS 84

Mukalla

Charts BA *3784*

Approach

The headland ending in Ras Kodar under which
Mukalla sits is easily identified. The steep-to grey-
red cliffs on either side of the headland are
conspicuous. In the evening dark clouds often sit
over the high land.

Conspicuous There are a number of communication
towers on the ridge of the headland. From the S the
white houses of the town are conspicuous. From the
N a scattering of white houses will be seen on the E
side of the headland. Closer in the breakwaters of
Khalf harbour are conspicuous as is the outermost
wrecked cargo ship (*Maldive Image*) off the old
harbour. There are often cargo ships anchored in
the roadstead.

By night A night entrance is possible, but a yacht
should proceed into Khalf Harbour and then go to
the old harbour in daylight. The Fl.5s15M at Khalf
Harbour shows up well. A 2F.R on one of the
transmitter towers on the ridge has a good range.
The Fl.R on the inner breakwater at Khalf will be
seen when closer in. A number of the mosques have
green lights on the minaret – green being the
Muslim holy colour.

VHF Ch 16 for the harbourmaster 0700–1600
Mon–Fri. You will not always get a reply.

Dangers

1. Care is needed of the rocky patch off Ras Kodar
   although at 4m least depth it should not be a
   problem. It is easily identified by the disturbed
   water around it. By day it is surrounded by small
   fishing craft and there seems to be an abundance
   of fish off the headland.
2. The military has a presence along the ridge
   complete with artillery. Do not take photos. They
   have some powerful radar or other scanning
   equipment which wiped out my GPS in the
   vicinity of the headland.

Blacksmith in Mukalla.

Approaches to Mukalla.

Mooring

Anchor in Khalf Harbour in 4–6m on the N side. There are usually cargo dhows at anchor here. In the NE monsoon yachts should proceed directly to the old harbour by day. Anchor in 4–10m and put out a stern anchor to hold the bow into the ground swell. The bottom is sand and a bit of rubble, reasonable holding. There are usually cargo dhows at anchor as well.

Shelter Good shelter in the NE monsoon in the old harbour. The ground swell is not really uncomfortable once you have a stern anchor out. Khalf Harbour could be used during the SW monsoon although I suspect there would be a worrying surge inside.

Authorities Harbourmaster. Immigration. Police. The harbourmaster can supply a weather forecast if asked.

Agent Iskender (Alexander) who has his office near the port gates. He will approach you when you come ashore and is the general Mr Fix-it for Mukalla. His rates for services are slightly more than the norm, but he can find things that would otherwise be difficult to get and it is quicker and more efficient than spending days doing it yourself.

Facilities

Water From a tap near the port entrance or Iskender will ferry jerrycans out.

Fuel A permit from customs is required. By jerrycan from one of the petrol stations outside town. Although it costs more it is much easier to let Iskender get it and have it ferried out to the boat by jerrycan. There seems to be a general shortage of diesel and it can be difficult to find without help.

Repairs At least one yacht has been hauled out by the harbourmasters office. Basic engineering and mechanical repairs. Some electrical repairs possible.

Provisions Good shopping for basic provisions. Supermarket in the suburbs with reasonable selection of basics. Excellent shopping for fresh fruit and vegetables in the market near the old harbour.

Also a good fish market close to the fruit and vegetable market.

Eating out Several good restaurants near the old harbour with excellent fresh seafood, grilled chicken and excellent pilaff. In the market there is a rough and ready canteen that does excellent fish in a pit oven with *roti*. Nearby you can get a pudding of *roti* mashed up with banana – recommended.

Other PO. Moneychangers who are only interested in US dollars. Laundry. Telephone and fax bureau's. Taxis. Hotels. International medical clinic. Some flights to Aden and Sa'na.

General

Mukalla is a wonderful place and some time, at least two or three days, should be spent here just looking around. The old mini-skyscraper houses perched precariously beneath the limestone cliffs behind make a wonderful backdrop to the old harbour. On closer inspection some are crumbling and as ever the Yemenis seem to have a predilection for discarding garbage in the streets, but it is a fascinating place to wander around. The people are friendly and there are all the sights and sounds of the Arabian Peninsula.

Close by on the waterfront is the blacksmiths 'market' with the blacksmiths squatting over mini-charcoal forges making everything from knife-blades to large iron nails. The dexterity of the smiths using simple equipment is a joy to watch and conceivably they could make basic repairs to small items if given a pattern or the original. By the fruit and vegetable market is the fish market with everything from large tunny and shark to dolphin fish, snapper, swordfish, and a few poor undersized crayfish. In the fruit and vegetable market there is an abundance and quality of produce seemingly mocking the arid sands and lack of rainfall to the north and east. And of course there is *qat* without which Yemen would probably grind to a standstill.

One excursion worth making is to the fresh water swimming hole in the desert. This is an underground aquifer into which the roof has

The wreck of the *Maldive Image* looking out from the old harbour at Mukalla.

Ras Burum looking SW.

collapsed. It is one of those special and bizarre experiences to swim in clear sweet fresh water in the middle of the desert and should not be missed. Get Iskender to take you and take his advice on which day to go as it is popular with the locals on weekends and holidays.

Ras Burum

The cape is easily identified and from the N the town in the crook of the bay will be seen. The anchorage looks like it would provide adequate protection in the SW monsoon with more of an enclosed bay than appears on the chart. With the NE monsoon it is often calm down this stretch of coast from Mukalla to Ras Burum.

Care is needed of the islet and reef off Ras Burum, although it is easily identified in daylight.

Ras Maqdah

The anchorage under this cape which is easily identified when coasting. Barraquah Island off the cape looks like it has white stripes (guano) on it. Anchor under the W side of the cape taking care of

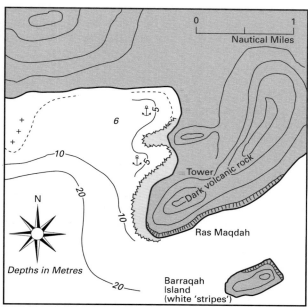

RAS MAQDAH 13°59′N 48°26′E

the fringing reef and a finger of reef which extends out from the coast. The water is very clear and by day it is easy to identify all dangers. The bottom is sand with some isolated coral and rock patches. Good shelter from the NE monsoon in flat water.

You will be visited by local fishermen in outboard powered *huris* who will be curious and may have fish for sale.

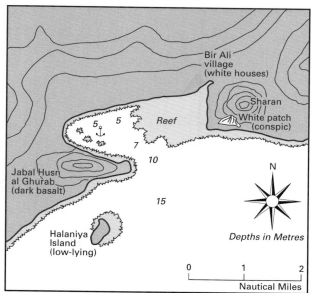

GHURAB 14°00′N 48°20′E

Ghurab

An anchorage under Ras Ghurab. Sikha Island is a double-humped island easily identified when coasting. Closer in it is difficult to identify the low-lying islands of Halaniya and Ghadarayn which appear to be rough basalt and coral extensions of the reefs and rocks off the coast. Great care is needed in the immediate approaches as it is not at all apparent that everything is where it should be. The white houses of Bir Ali are easily identified but the approach into the anchorage should be made in the morning with someone aloft conning you in. Shelter is not the best in the anchorage and not as good as at Ras Maqdah and Balihaf.

Ras Ar Ratl

An indifferent anchorage under this round volcanic cape. The crater on the cape is easily identified with white limestone or guano covered cliffs off it. Anchor in the cove in 6–10m on sand and coral patches. A swell works its way around into here with the NE monsoon and frankly you are better off going to Balihaf nearby.

Balihaf

Approach
Sikha Island and Ras Ar Ratl crater are readily recognised from the E and the conical peak on the end of Balihaf headland is conspicuous from some distance off. Once around the headland the fort and the tower N of the village will be seen and the few crumbling buildings of the hamlet are easily located. Further around the bay the oil terminal at Rudum will be seen with the storage tanks visible. The oil terminal is brightly lit at night.

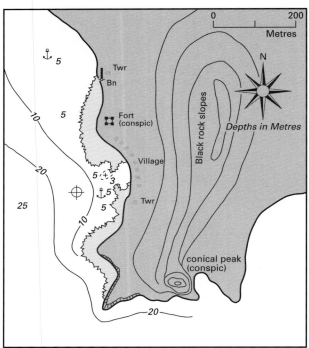

BALIHAF ⊕ 13°58'·5N 48°10'·5E WGS84

Mooring

Have someone up front to con you in as the coral extends some way out, especially on the N side of the cove. Anchor in 6–10m on sand, good holding.

Shelter Good shelter from the NE monsoon with little swell finding its way around into the cove. The wind sometimes blows lightly from seawards, but this is probably a swirling effect from the high land around. You can anchor further N of Balihaf cove but there is more swell there. Open to the SW monsoon.

Facilities

None really. The local fishermen may offer to get you diesel. You can also buy fish from the fishermen

if you so desire. The coast road to Mukalla runs close by.

General

This is an enchanted little place and I spent an enjoyable 3 days over Christmas here. The water is very clear, there are fish everywhere and oysters on the rocks around the cove. The locals are very curious and can be a bit of a nuisance coming by to say hullo, to ask for things, or just to look at you. Life is hard here and the fishermen stroked the canvas dodgers as if they were made of velvet, marvelled at the stainless steel fittings and would have died for the multiplait rope. Yet not once did I feel threatened and nor did a single item go missing despite the apparent poverty all around. The hamlet was evidently once a military outpost with the fort still standing, but it is no longer used and the only inhabitants are the fishermen and their families.

Maqatin

An indifferent anchorage on the W side of the islets off a blunt promontory. The islets show up better than you would expect when coasting. There is a ruined tower ashore, but there are also several other towers along the coast to confuse the situation. If the NE monsoon is not blowing strongly the anchorage can be used, but with even a moderate breeze from the E–SE it is advisable to go on to Aden.

Shuqra

A reef-bound anchorage. The approach is difficult and I have yet to come across anyone who has braved the approach and anchored here.

Christmas view at Balihaf, a *Beau Geste* location along the Yemeni coast.

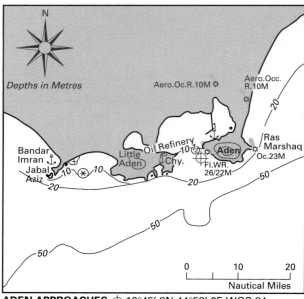

ADEN APPROACHES ⊕ 12°45'·8N 44°58'·2E WGS 84

Aden looking NW.

Aden

Charts BA *3660, 3662*

Approach

The lumpy jagged outcrop that is the Aden Peninsula is easily recognised from some way off.

Conspicuous From the E the white houses of Krater will be seen. Once around the headland the most conspicuous thing is the huge oil refinery at Little Aden. The chimneys (some with flares) and tanks are easily identified. The large fairway buoy will be seen and after that the buoyed channel is easily identified. Closer in the light tower on the breakwater is clearly visible. There are always numerous ships anchored in the roadstead waiting to enter the port.

By night The harbour is well lit but a night entry is prohibited. Lights are as follows:
Elephants Back main light Fl.WR.2·5s26/22M 306°-R-322°-W-061°-R-119°
Ras Marshaq Oc.5s23M
Breakwater LFl.G.5s10M
Fairway buoy Q. **Channel buoys** Fl.R/Fl.G
Little Aden Oil Harbour Iso.G.2s10M/Iso.G.2s10M/ LFl.R.5s10M

VHF When 10 miles off call port control on VHF Ch 13/16. You will be asked to call up again when 2 miles off. Details of the following will be required: boat name, port of registry, registration number, GRT, LOA, owner, skipper, number of crew, nationalities.

Dangers
1. There are two wrecked ships outside the buoyed channel. These are clearly marked by isolated danger buoys. It is not strictly necessary to stay within the buoyed channel as long as you have located the approximate position of the two wrecks and have a large scale chart of the approaches.
2. Just inside the breakwater there is a wreck above water.

Mooring

Proceed into the harbour and anchor off the Prince of Wales Pier where shown. The bottom is mud and excellent holding. The tidal streams through here can be quite strong, but once your anchor is well in there should be little problem.

Shelter Good shelter from the NE monsoon and probably from the SW monsoon.

Authorities Harbourmaster, customs, immigration, and police.

Entry On arrival go ashore to the Prince of Wales Pier where you will be cleared through customs and immigration. There is a small charge at customs and a small 'gift' may be asked for. A few dollars or a packet of cigarettes should suffice and are not strictly necessary. Immigration is just across the road and here a shorepass will be exchanged for your passport (which is locked away in a safe) if you do not have a visa. If you have a visa your passport will be stamped and returned to you. If you have given details to the harbourmaster by VHF it is not necessary to go there. If not go to the harbourmasters office on the small hill at the root of the breakwater and provide details.

Exit Buy the requisite stamps from the post office or from Omar or Hussein and go to immigration. They will provide a note to take along with the stamps to the harbourmaster. Here you will receive clearance and you can then return to immigration to collect the passports. Once you are ready to leave call the harbourmaster on VHF Ch 13/16 to get permission to leave harbour.

Note
1. On arrival at the Prince of Wales Pier you will probably be contacted by Omar or Hussein, the two local drivers who cater to yachts. They are worth every dollar and will help you clear in and out as well as a myriad other things.
2. The harbour is prone to heavy oil pollution at times. This probably comes from damage to the bunkering stations during the 1994 conflict or to spillage when ships are bunkering. Suggestions such as waxing your hull have been made and probably work, but the majority usually opt to wash the filth off with petrol and in my case this worked fine. The problem is that the wash from workboats tends to splash heavy oil up the topsides and the result is just appalling. You may be lucky as in the three week period I was here there was no oil around for the first week.
3. Only go ashore at the Prince of Wales Pier. Dinghies are normally left on the W side of the pier where there are several unused bum-boats. If you go ashore elsewhere you will probably receive a visit from the military as I know to my cost.

Facilities

Note Omar and Hussein, the two drivers usually on the quay to greet new arrivals, can considerably smooth the way for yachties. They know where to get most things, where the best fruit and vegetables are, where reliable repair shops are, and where you can get the cheapest (such as it is) beer in Aden. They can also take you on tours around the nearby

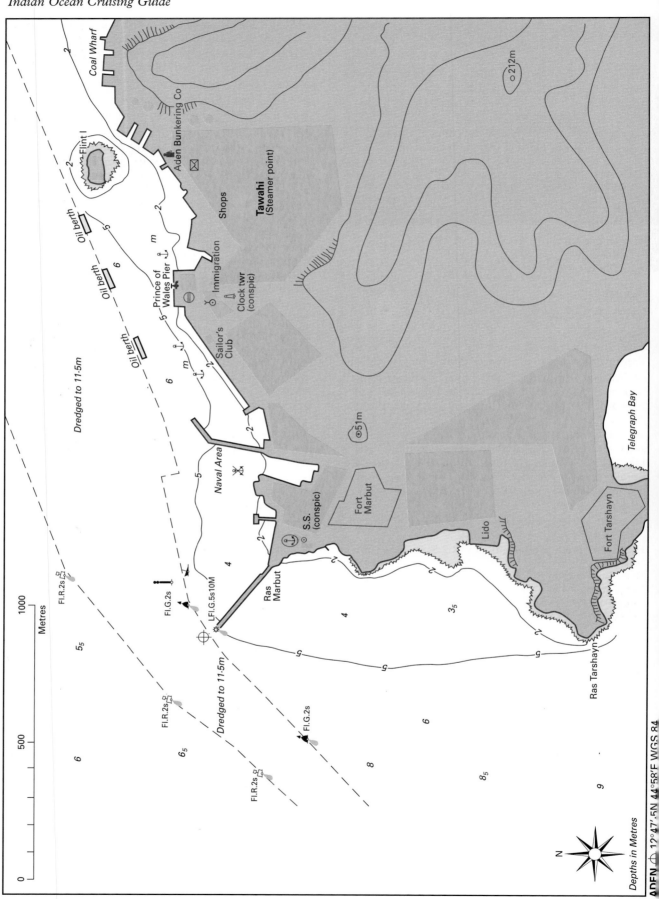

The yacht anchorage at Aden looking out from The Sailor's Club.

Aden dhow harbour E of the yacht anchorage looking down from the road to Krater.

coast and if nothing else you should go to Krater for half a day.

Water On the Prince of Wales Pier. You can take it off by jerrycan or you may be able to go alongside for a brief spell to fill up. A small charge is made. There have been reports that the water may have been contaminated after the 1994 bombing but numerous yachts have taken on water here since then with no reports of bad water. Still it might be worthwhile sterilising the water with bleach or proprietary purifiers.

Fuel At the Aden Bunkering Company about ½ a mile E of the Prince of Wales Pier. You must make arrangements with customs to go there and fuel must be paid for in hard currency or in riyals with a bank receipt to show the requisite amount of hard cash has been changed. It is possible to get small amounts by jerrycan with Omar or Hussein although this is illegal and you may have to provide a 'gift' for customs to get it to the boat. At times customs can be sticky about this.

Gas Most gas bottles can be filled at Little Aden. Arrange with other yachts to have Hussein or Omar take them there and ensure you leave at least 24 hours for filling.

Paraffin Hussein or Omar can usually find it. Like diesel or petrol it is illegal to carry it in jerrycans to the boat so some 'arrangement' will have to be made.

Laundry A number of laundry-men on the Prince of Wales Pier seem to have the concession for laundry.

Repairs It should be possible to haul out here in an emergency, but there are no dedicated facilities. Basic mechanical and engineering repairs are possible. Few spares for anything. Some electrical repairs can be made and at least one yachty has had an alternator rewound here and purchased new batteries. In Krater there are several hardware shops that stock a limited range of items useful on a boat.

It is possible to have items sent by courier to Aden.

Provisions Basic staples in Tawahi and Krater. There is a supermarket at Khormaksar where a wider range of goods is available including frozen produce. Always check the sell-by date of any items including those in the supermarket. Fresh fruit and vegetables are plentiful and can be obtained in Krater or better still in the Arab market. Ask Hussein or Omar to take you there.

Eating out The Sailors Club nearby is usefully located and serves up excellent food. Unfortunately it is sometimes heir to a loud live band that plays interesting Yemeni music and bad western music. In Tawahi there are numerous small restaurants serving good food at bargain prices. Much of it will be cooked over a flame that resembles the afterburner of a jumbo jet. Eating with the hands is *de rigeur* in these smaller establishments and normally food is mopped up with delicious *rotis*. Several of the large hotels have restaurants and these are the only places you will get alcohol, though at much inflated prices. A small can of beer is usually $4–$8 depending on the hotel. Hussein and Omar will know where the cheapest beer is. There is also a Chinese restaurant in Khormaksar and a number of restaurants in Krater.

Other Money-changers in Tawahi and Krater. Alternatively Hussein or Omar can help out at close to the best rate. Travellers cheques in US dollars can be changed to cash dollars US at the bank in Khormaksar. PO. Telephone and fax bureau's in Tawahi which will hold faxes for you. Buses and shared taxis around Aden. International medical clinic. Flights to Sa'na. Taxi to Sa'na.

General

Most people do not retain a deal of affection for Aden. The disgusting oil pollution that covers your pride and joy in the harbour, the dust and rubbish ashore, the general lack of facilities should you need to effect repairs, and on top of it all the virtual absence of alcohol to smooth over all this, casts a

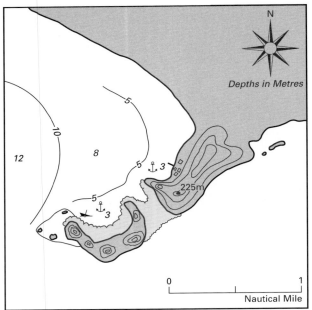

BANDAR IMRAN 12°44'·5N 44°44'·5E

gloom over perceptions of Aden. Set against this is the friendliness of most of the locals you run across, good seafood, the strange mish-mash of colonial and local architecture that is Aden, and the willingness of Omar and Hussein to ease your way. These two gents make life easy in Aden with their helpfulness and spry wit and it is worth engaging their services to take you out of the place for a days tour of the country inland and the adjacent coast. If nothing else look around Krater and wander down to the fishing harbour on the end of the peninsula.

Bandar Imran

Ten miles W of Little Aden is the headland of Ras Imran with the island of Jabal Aziz off its extremity. The headland and Jabal Aziz are high and bold and stand out well. Closer in a number of rock pinnacles around Jabal Aziz stand out well. Approach to the anchorages behind the headland and island should be around the outside of the island and rocks as coral and rocks are to be found closer in.

Anchor in the bay behind the island taking care to avoid the reef around the shore or behind the headland where local boats are anchored. Good shelter in the NE monsoon in flat water. This anchorage is often used by yachts to stop and clean off the oil that has besmirched the topsides in Aden before proceeding to the Red Sea. There are few facilities ashore and in any case, technically, you will have cleared out of Yemen when leaving Aden so it is best not to go ashore so close to Aden. Local boats will come out to say hullo and for 'favours', but pose no menace.

Ras al Arah

It is possible to anchor on the W side of this stubby cape where there is some protection in the NE monsoon. However the wind is usually SE around here and protection under the cape is not the best. Care is needed in the approach of the reef and shoal water extending S from the cape proper for some 2M. Make the approach on a course of due N.

Bab el Mandeb

A number of anchorages are possible around the Small Strait between Mayun (Perim Island) and the Yemen coast. The best anchorage during the NE monsoon is on the N side of Ras Bab El Mandeb. It should be remembered that the wind has turned to the SE–SSE through the Straits of Bab El Mandeb and often reaches 25–30kt. If you arrive in a comparative lull it is likely that before too long the wind will pick up again so plan to be able to leave or make sure you are securely anchored should the wind pick up.

Mayun (Perim Island) is a military area and yachts are prohibited to navigate within the sectors shown on the chart and are not allowed to anchor off the island.

Somalia

Somalia today is in a state of anarchy with at least 12 different groups ruling different parts of Somalia as war lords. In 1991 the US Operation *Restore Hope* initially seemed to bring the two most dominant war-lords, General Aidid and Ali Mahdi, to an agreement. This broke down within a matter of days and US attempts to restore order added fuel to Somali discontent. In 1994 a bungled attempt by US marines to capture Aidid in Mogadishu led to the death of a number of marines and hundreds of Somalis. The US withdrew and a state of anarchy prevails to this day. UN aid workers do their best to keep starvation at bay for the civilian population, but when an estimated 80% of aid is looted and aid workers are themselves kidnapped at times, the situation is nothing short of desperate.

The country should not be visited by yachts and in fact yachts should stay well off the coastline because of the risk of piracy. See section iiv in the Introduction.

Red Sea

Geography and climate

The coast Typically the Red Sea coast is low-lying land and islands with fringing reefs. There are also numerous isolated reefs. The coast does have some higher land in places and some of the islands such as the Hanish group and Muhabbaka Islands are high islands which can be readily located in contrast to most of the low islands along the coast. In places such as in the Gulf of Suez and around Safaga in Egypt and along the Yemen coast there are high mountains close to the coast. The low-lying parts of the coast can be difficult to identify and here GPS really comes into its own. Likewise low-lying islands can be difficult to spot and judicious use of GPS helps out immensely. Parts of the coast and some islands have scrubby trees that somehow survive the savage summer temperatures.

Coastal waters The waters around the coast are typically fairly shallow, often less than 20m, although depths usually come up quickly from 10–15m to the fringing reef. For this reason it is imperative that navigating through the reefs and into anchorages on the western side should be carried out around midday and preferably no later than 1400 so the sun is not too low to make identification difficult. Most yachts will have been cruising in tropical waters and through reefs already, but for some reason the Red Sea claims more than its fair share of victims each year. Rather than opting to race for an anchorage each day, it can be better to go outside the reef and sail through the night to arrive at an anchorage around mid-morning if practicable.

Anchorage is typically on sand or mud with some coral patches in places. In general the holding is good in most anchorages and I encountered no real problems anywhere.

The Red Sea is a rich marine environment, especially around Sudan, Eritrea and Yemen, where little commercial fishing takes place. In some places it is like a marine soup and the phosphorescence at night beats anything in any other sea. It can be positively spooky at times. Underwater there is such an abundance of fish that you hardly have to move to see them. In the south there are significant numbers of sharks, especially hammerheads and silver and white tips. While normally found in deeper water on the drop-off, I have often seen them in very shallow water off the reefs and if like me you are not too keen on them, it is best to dinghy into the lagoon and then go snorkelling. Marine growth on the hull is prolific and impeller logs must be cleaned fairly frequently as barnacles and coral worm grow at an alarming rate. On two occasions my log was stopped completely by growth after just a week in Massawa and five days in the Hanish group.

Climate

The climate varies considerably and winter temperatures in the northern Red Sea can come as a bit of a shock to those used to tropical temperatures. In the south temperatures are mild in the winter and very hot in the summer. In Massawa summer highs of 40°C are not uncommon. In the north summer temperatures are less and winter temperatures on the face of a cold front can be very cold with a savage wind chill factor. In the Suez Canal I had not only a wool jersey but full wet weather gear as well to keep warm.

At Cairo	Av max °C	Av min °C	Relative humidity	Days 1mm rain
Jan	18	8	40%	1
Feb	21	9	33%	1
Mar	24	11	27%	0·8
Apr	28	14	21%	0·4
May	33	17	18%	0·2
Jun	35	20	20%	0
Jul	36	21	24%	0
Aug	35	22	28%	0
Sep	32	20	31%	0
Oct	30	18	31%	0·3
Nov	26	14	38%	0·8
Dec	20	10	41%	1

At Port Sudan	Av max °C	Av min °C	Relative humidity	Days 1mm rain
Jan	27	20	65%	0·9
Feb	27	19	66%	0·3
Mar	29	19	63%	0·1
Apr	32	22	59%	0·2
May	35	24	51%	0·2
Jun	39	26	45%	0·1
Jul	41	28	44%	0·8
Aug	41	29	47%	0·6
Sep	38	26	51%	
Oct	34	24	64%	1
Nov	31	23	64%	4
Dec	28	22	66%	2

For data in the south see under *Yemen*.

Weather

Prevailing winds near the coast Prevailing winds near the coast are pretty much according to the patterns detailed in *Technical Information* page 32-33. For the most part winds blow up or down the Rift Valley with small amounts of sheer near the edges. Overall I found little discernible consistent difference when swapping from coast to coast, although there was a bit more easterly in the wind close to the Saudi coast. In general the wind speed closer to the coast is perhaps 5–10kt higher than the wind speed over the open sea where the wind is channelled by the land on the coast. Set against this is the fact that wave height is generally greater in the middle than on the western side.

There are a few pockets where the wind is consistently from a different direction. Around Massawa and the off-lying islands the wind is generally a sea breeze from the E and there are some calms. Around Hurgadha and down to Safaga the wind is often lighter than out to sea and there can be a sea breeze effect.

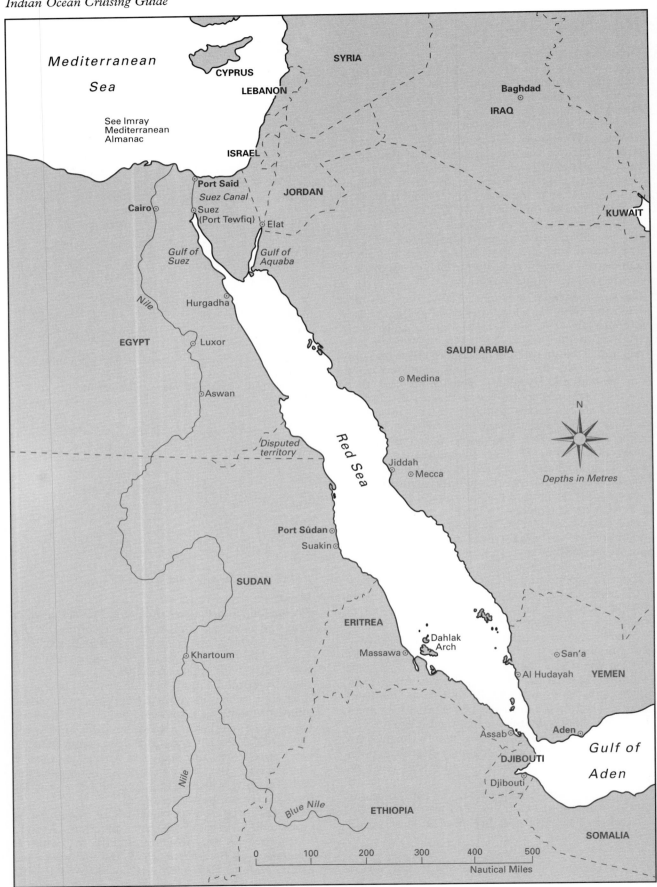

RED SEA

Port Suez	Prevailing wind 1	Prevailing wind 2
Jan	N/24%	S/18%
Feb	N/24%	S/22%
Mar	N/38%	S/20%
Apr	N/41%	S/20%
May	N/57%	S/13%
Jun	N/68%	NW/12%
Jul	N/65%	NW/11%
Aug	N/68%	NW/13%
Sep	N/75%	NW/13%
Oct	N/58%	NW/11%
Nov	N/49%	NW/15%
Dec	N/39%	NW/13%

Notes Winds for Gulf of Suez at Port Suez. Prevailing winds 1 and 2 give the percentage of the two most prevalent winds. Other winds blow for the remaining percentage.

Port Sudan	Prevailing wind 1	Prevailing wind 2
Jan	NE/48%	N/E/46%
Feb	NE/44%	E/30%
Mar	NE/41%	E/36%
Apr	NE/42%	E/36%
May	E/47%	NE/33%
Jun	E/49%	NE/36%
Jul	E/57%	SE/E/27%
Aug	E/54%	SE/23%
Sep	E/58%	NE/29%
Oct	E/60%	NE/21%
Nov	NE/44%	N/32%
Dec	NE/45%	E/30%

Notes Winds for Port Sudan. Prevailing winds 1 and 2 give percentage of the two most prevalent winds. Other winds blow for the remaining percentage.

At Assab	Prevailing wind 1	Prevailing wind 2
Jan	S/SE60%	NE/25%
Feb	S/SE/61%	NE/24%
Mar	S/SE/72%	E/8%
Apr	S/SE/76%	N/10%
May	S/SE/61%	N/12%
Jun	N/NE/58%	NW/18%
Jul	N/NE/62%	NW/21%
Aug	N/NE/66%	NW/18%
Sep	N/NE/66%	E/SE/24%
Oct	E/SE/68%	S/22%
Nov	SE/44%	E/43%
Dec	SE/60%	E/20%

Notes Winds for Bab El Mandeb at Assab. Prevailing winds 1 and 2 give percentage of the two most prevalent winds. Other winds blow for the remaining percentage.

Locally named winds

Dchaoui Another name for the Haboob in Sudan
Haboob Dust storm in Sudan. Winds can be violent and visibility severely reduced. Usually followed by rain.
Hawa Janubi Southerly in Arabian Peninsula
Hawa Shimali Northerly in Arabian Peninsula
Khamsin Sirocco in Egypt. From the Arabic for 'fifty' as it is said to blow for 50 days.
Nasim Sea breeze in Saudi Arabia.
Sharav Desert wind in Israel
Simoon Desert wind in North Africa. From the Arabic for 'poison'.

Sirocco Southerly off the desert.

Gales Gales resulting from depressions passing over are rare for most of the Red Sea. The exception is in the northern quarter of the Red Sea where depressions passing over the Mediterranean may dip down across North Africa or the effects of depressions in the Mediterranean passing close to the northern end of the Red Sea are felt. Although depressions are rare in most of the Red Sea, gale force winds are not uncommon. The prevailing northerlies can often get up to 35 plus knots for periods of 1–3 days. Generally after 3 days the winds will die down to a more typical 20kt and there may even be a day of calm. At Bab El Mandeb southerlies often blow at gale force, although more typically winds are 20–25kt. You may have to wait some time for strong southerlies at Bab El Mandeb to die down in the latter part of the year: one yacht waited for 22 days at Assab before the wind moderated enough for them to dash to Aden.

Tropical storms Are unknown in the Red Sea.

Thunderstorms and waterspouts Are rare for most of the Red Sea except around Suez in the winter. Waterspouts are also rare except around Eritrea.

Tides

The tidal system of the Red Sea is an independent one with a semi-diurnal nature. When it is low water at the N end of the Red Sea it is high water at the S end and vice versa. The spring range is not great and only at either end in the Gulf of Suez and at Bab El Mandeb are there strong tidal streams. In the middle of the Red Sea there is no appreciable spring range while at the N end the range is around 0·6m and at the S end around 0·9m.

Tidal streams around Bab El Mandeb are considerable although the effect is only to decrease or augment the prevailing current. In the Strait of Gubal tidal streams are 1–2kt with the N-going stream lasting longer than the S-going. Around the bays in the Gulf of Suez the direction of tidal streams varies and can often set towards reefs.

Currents

Currents in the Red Sea are a combination of prevailing currents and the effects of tidal streams. On both passages up and down the Red Sea the current pattern has not really conformed to the overall current pattern given in *Technical Information*, pages 48-9. Often the current has been contrary to the given current direction. Close to the coast and reefs current direction can be variable in both rate and direction. There does seem to be the dreaded 'reef-sucking' current around where the current sets towards the reef. In my experience I have sometimes needed to alter course by as much as 15°-20° to stay on a true course because the current was pushing me off by that amount. Within the reefs currents can be strong and when conning from the cross-trees it can be frightening to see the yacht going faster sideways than it is going forward.

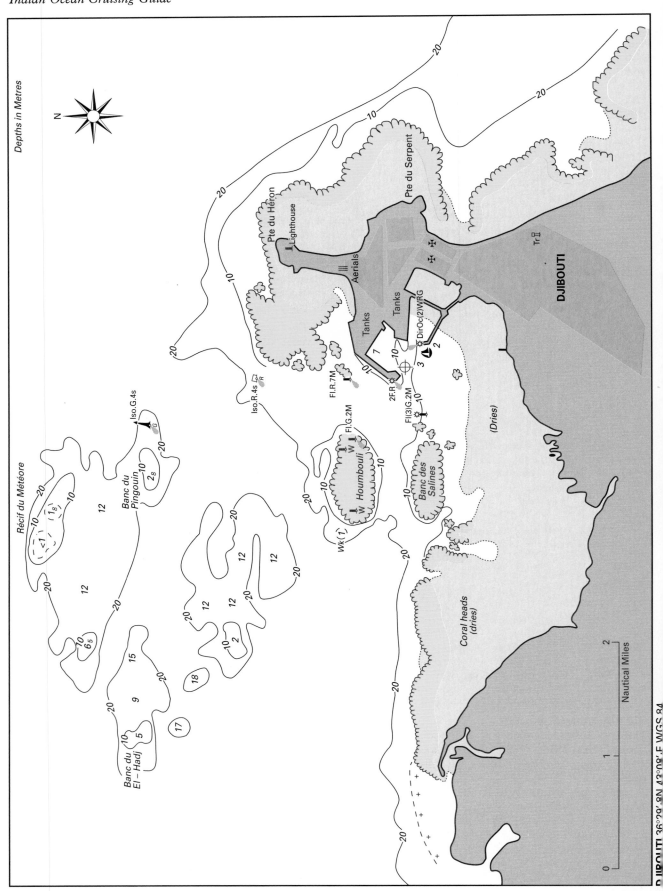

Depths in Metres

N

Pte du Héron

Lighthouse

Pte du Serpent

Aerials

Tr

Tanks

DirOc(2)WRG

Tanks

DJIBOUTI

7

Iso.R.4s
R

Fl.R.7M

2.F.R

Fl(3)G.2M

3

2

Iso.G.4s

Récif du Météore

*Banc du
Pingouin*

G

Fl.G.2M
W
W *Houmbouli*

W

Wk (*1*)

*Banc des
Salines*

(*Dries*)

*Banc du
El – Hadj*

*Coral heads
(dries)*

20

20

10

20

10

20

10

(1)

20

10

20

10

12

12

20

12

12

12

20

2

20

12

20

10

18

15

9

17

5

10

6

10

2

5

8

20

20

10

20

10

10

2

8

20

20

10

20

20

10

Nautical Miles

0   1   2

Navigation

The coast has not been adequately surveyed since the 19th century and there are serious discrepancies and errors even on the modern metricated charts. In general I allowed a circle of probable error around my GPS position of at least 1M and in some cases, for example on the coast of Sudan and Eritrea, a circle of error of around 1½M. There are also serious discrepancies over general descriptions such as whether or not an island has a reef around it, over the extent of reefs, over whether a reef is exposed at low tide or not, and over depths. It is unlikely many areas will be re-surveyed although some areas (North and South Massawa Channels for example) have been re-surveyed for geological and oil survey purposes. Whether or not this data finds its way onto hydrographic charts is unknown. The moral here is very clear: keep a sharp eye on the depth sounder and when close to land or dangers to navigation augment the GPS with eyeball navigation and any fixes you can obtain. The final approach to an anchorage must be made with someone conning you in. Where possible I have given GPS co-ordinates using WGS 84 datum.

Note For detail it is recommended you consult *Red Sea Pilot* by Elaine Morgan and Stephen Davies.

Country profiles

Djibouti

Current situation

Djibouti was a French *territoire outre-mer* until 1976 and in 1977 gained independence. Although the French granted independence to Djibouti, it remains essentially funded by France and there is a strong French military presence as well as commercial concerns. There is, after all, little to Djibouti except its strategic position as a port near Bab el Mandeb. The rest is desert. While the French retain a strong military presence here Djibouti is a stable country and the only danger is the sea area off nearby Somalia which is effectively in a state of anarchy. Yachts visiting Djibouti should keep well clear of the sea area off Somalia and make the approach and exit from a NE direction.

Documentation and visas

Normal ships papers and a valid passport for all crew members must be carried. A visa is issued on arrival and is free for up to three days. For longer periods a charge is made ($25 in 1997) per person. French nationals do not require a visa.

Entry formalities

A yacht should proceed straight to Djibouti town. When 10M off call up the *capitainerie* on VHF Ch 16 and request permission to enter. Once anchored off take the ships papers and passports to the *capitainerie* and to immigration. Passports are held until you leave.

When you are ready to leave go to the *capitainerie* to obtain clearance and then to the port office to pay harbour dues. Once you have your clearance papers and the receipt for dues, you can collect the passports from immigration.

Data

Area 23,200km² (8958M²)
Coastline 314km (170M)
Maritime claims Territorial 12M.
Population 417,000
Capital Djibouti
Time zone UT+3
Language French and Arabic. Some English spoken.
Religion Muslim (94%)
Government Republic.
Crime Some petty crime in Djibouti town. Outside there is some risk from groups (predominantly FRUD) committed to armed conflict against the government.

Practicalities

Mail Generally reliable. It can take some time to reach destinations. Poste Restante which is reliable.

Telecommunications International telephone and fax from the PO in Djibouti town. IDD code 253.

Currency The Djibouti franc divided into 100 centimes. US dollars are widely used.

Banks and exchange Cash and travellers cheques can be changed at a bank. Banking hours are 0700–1130 Mon to Sat. It is reported you can get cash advances on major credit cards. There are moneychangers who will change hard currency.

Harbours and Anchorages

Djibouti

Charts BA *262*

Approach

A number of reefs lie in the immediate approach and around the off-lying islands, principally Ile Moucha and Ile Maskali. The approach can be made from the E through Passe Est leaving Moucha and Maskali to starboard or from the N leaving the islands to port. The leading marks for the approach from the N are a black tower with a round top in the front and a BW tower with a triangle at the rear. Leading marks are in line on 184°.

Conspicuous The off-lying islands of Moucha and Maskali are relatively low-lying (11m and 9m respectively) and are difficult to spot from the distance. The buildings of Djibouti, especially the oil silos and the cathedral, stand out and a number of transmitter pylons will be seen be in the town.

By night A night approach is not recommended.
Ile Maskali W end Fl(2)6s24m10M
Ile Moucha NE end Fl(3)R.12s10M
Ldg Lts on 184° *Front* DirQ.17M *Rear* Q.19M
Banc Maskali light buoy Oc(4)R.12s
Banc du Pingouin light buoy Iso.G.4s
Banc du Heron light buoy Iso.R.4s

Reef entrance Fl.G.2M/F.R.7M
YC jetty Dir Oc(2)WRG.6s(occas).

VHF Ch 16 for *capitainerie*. Ch 06 for yacht club (variable times).

Dangers Care is needed of the various reefs in the approaches and it is recommended you make the approach in daylight before 1400 so that the reefs are easily spotted.

Mooring

Anchor off the yacht club where convenient in 3–4m. The bottom is mud and good holding. Dinghies can be safely left at the club pontoon.

Shelter Protection is good except for strong winds from the W.

Authorities The port captain, customs and immigration are located nearby. A charge is made for anchoring here.

Facilities

Water At the yacht club. Arrangements can be made to go alongside to take on water, but care is needed over depths.

Fuel Small quantities available in the town. Arrangements can be made for fuel to be brought to the boat and pumped on board or to the dhow harbour.

Repairs Some mechanical and engineering repairs, but prices are generally high for average work. Enquire at the yacht club.

Provisions Good shopping for all provisions although prices are not cheap. Nothing much is grown in Djibouti itself so nearly everything is imported. Wine is available at reasonable prices for this part of the world. Good market in the town.

Eating out Food is served in the yacht club. Elsewhere there is very good fare to be had in some up-market restaurants, but prices are high. Around the market there are some local and cheap Arab eateries.

Other PO. Banks. Telephone and fax services at the PO. Car hire. International flights.

General

Djibouti really exists because of its port and its position near the entrance to the Red Sea. Yachts visiting here have to make a bit of a detour, but it offers good services, communications and a bit of colonial luxury and choice of French wines. French yachts like it for obvious reasons. If Aden is not your cup of tea for whatever reasons, then Djibouti makes a good alternative.

Yemen

See separate entry under *Yemen*.

Eritrea

Current situation

The Eritrean People's Liberation Front fought a 30 year war against Ethiopia which they finally won in 1991. This was the longest civil war in Africa and a war which was largely unnoticed in the west. Part of the reason for this was that no-one imagined that a poorly armed band of guerrillas could defeat the might of Ethiopia's army which in the latter stages of the war was heavily supported by the USSR. Ethiopia had an airforce, navy and armoured divisions. The EPLF had only the weapons they captured from the Ethiopians and knowledge of the mountains. It is an incredible story of courage and endurance. In a referendum in 1993 the people voted for Eritrea to be recognised as an independent state and it joined the UN.

At the present time the country is ruled by a council made up of the EPLF elite although elections are promised for the near future. After 30 years of war there is understandably still some tension over borders and yachtsmen should play everything by the rules. It is imperative that yachts go directly to a port of entry, either Assab or Massawa, to clear in and do not stop anywhere en route. In 1996 two yachts were arrested after anchoring in a bay on the Eritrean coast. The crew were unceremoniously arrested and detained in Asmara before being released and allowed to continue. This was both unfortunate and badly handled by the Eritreans. However some 4 months previous I had cruised along part of this coast after clearing in at Massawa and and experienced no problems. Again in 1997 I was here and again experienced no difficulties.

In 1995 just five days after I had left the Eritreans invaded the Hanish Islands which had always been considered a part of Yemen up to then. Why Eritrea should do this is a moot point although it almost certainly includes the matter of extending the exclusive economic zone for oil and fishing rights. The fate of the islands is still unresolved and yachts should steer clear of the area around the Hanish Islands.

The recent clashes between Eritrea and Ethiopia in the SW mean it would be prudent to avoid Assab until the situation is resolved. At the time of publication Eritrean and Ethiopian forces are lined up either side of the border and it is difficult to know whether some accommodation can be reached or whether there will be a full scale conflict. Monitor the situation and adjust your itinerary accordingly.

At the present time the Eritrian authorities are uncertain about how to treat visiting yachts. There is a certain suspicion about cruising yachts and there may at times be what comes across as a belligerent attitude by some authorities. This is unfortunate because the population as a whole are some of the friendliest and most honest in this part of the world. My advice is to keep an ear to the ground and visit the place. For me it was one of the highlights of the Red Sea.

Documentation and visas
Normal ship's papers and a valid passport for all crew members must be carried. A visa will be issued on entry for which a passport-sized photo is needed. In 1997 a visa cost $25 per person. There is also $5 per day tourist tax which is usually applied on a per boat basis. Theoretically a cruising permit is needed to sail up through the Dhalak Islands, but in practice most yachts do not obtain one. The cost of the permit seems to be something of a lottery with prices varying between $50 and $250 quoted for the permit.

Entry formalities
A yacht must enter at Assab or Massawa. Do not stop anywhere in Eritrean territory before entering at Assab or Massawa.

When 10M off the port call up port control on Ch 16/12. You will be asked to call up again when 1M off and given permission to enter harbour. You will be asked to come alongside if there is room and you will then be visited by harbourmaster, customs and health. You must then go ashore to immigration where the visa and tourist taxes are paid and then to the port office where permission to stay will be granted. The entry procedure normally takes just a couple of hours in normal office hours. Outside office hours you may have to wait within the port area until the next working day. Do not go ashore until cleared in.

Exit formalities simply involve contacting the port office and signing the requisite papers to clear out.

Data
Area 93,680km² (36,170M²)
Coastline 1094km (591M)
Maritime claims Territorial 12M.
Population 2,500,000 (Difficult to assess because so many fled or were killed during the 30 years of war.)
Capital Asmara
Time zone UT+3
Language Tigrinya and Arabic. English widely spoken and is the official second language in schools.
Religion Predominantly Christian. Most of the balance are Muslim.
Government Revolutionary council. Democratic elections promised in the near future.
Crime Very low levels of petty crime.

Travel
Internal
Limited. From Assab and Massawa there are primitive buses to Asmara. Mini-buses available. Taxis. Limited flights between Assab and Massawa to Asmara.

International
Limited flights to Ethiopia, Egypt and several European destinations.

Practicalities
Mail Reliable. It can take some time to reach destinations. Packages can be flown into Asmara and transport by bus arranged to Massawa or Assab. Poste Restante which is reliable.

Telecommunications International telephone and fax from the PO in Massawa and Assab. The system is overloaded and it can be impossible to get faxes and phone calls through to Eritrea. Phoning and faxing out is normally straightforward. The normal procedure is to pre-pay a set amount for a phone or fax call and then the balance will be refunded after the call.

Currency The *nacfa* (named after the most famous battle in the long war). The Ethiopian *birr* is also used until the new currency is widespread. The rate is reasonably stable.

Banks and exchange Cash and traveller's cheques can be changed at a bank. A better rate can be obtained on the black market and although common practice remember it is illegal.

Medical care Hospitals are rudimentary. A few drugs including home grown antibiotics are available. The water should be treated although in places there are filter systems.

Useful books
Towards Asmara Thomas Kenneally. Faction account of the last days of the war. A must-read even if you do not go to Eritrea.
Guide to Eritrea Edward Paice. Bradt Publications.

Harbours and anchorages
For details on other harbours and anchorages see *Red Sea Pilot* Elaine Morgan and Stephen Davies.

Massawa
(Mits'iwa, Mitsawa)
Charts BA *164, 171*

Approach
Through either the North Massawa Channel or the South Massawa Channel. For these approaches BA 164 and 171 or similar are recommended. A yacht should not stop en route before clearing in at Massawa.

Conspicuous The islands and light structures in the approach channels are readily identified. Off Massawa the cement factory on the N side of Khor Dakliyat (often belching smoke) is conspicuous. The square signal tower on the N side of the harbour entrance and on the S side a water tower and the main lighthouse (BW bands) are conspicuous. The harbour breakwaters will be seen when closer in. There are usually a number of ships anchored in the roadstead off the S side of the harbour. There are leading marks on the N end of Talaud Island showing the entrance channel in, but these are not really necessary once you are up to the entrance.

By night A night entry must be made with caution.
Main light Iso.4s14M
Entrance Fl.R.3s7M/Fl.G.3s7M
Ldg Lts on 243°30' *Front* F.R.6M *Rear* F.R.8M.

VHF Ch 16/12 for Massawa port control. Call up when 10M off and again when 1M off.

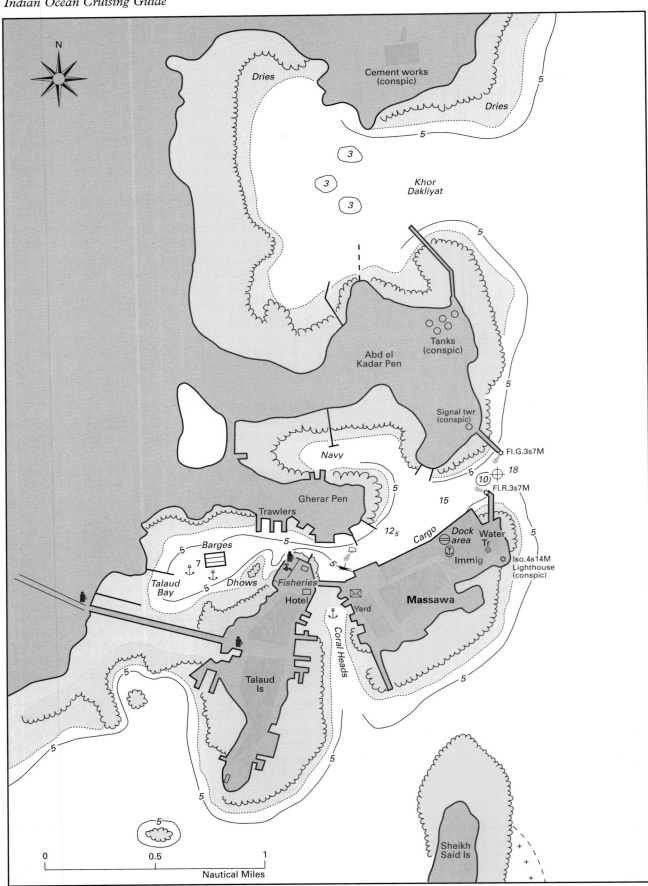

N

Dries

Cement works
(conspic)

Dries

5

③

③

③

Khor
Dakliyat

5

5

Tanks
(conspic)

Abd el
Kadar Pen

Signal twr
(conspic)

5

Fl.G.3s7M

5
⑩ ⊕ 18

Fl.R.3s7M

Navy

5

Gherar Pen

15

12₅

Cargo

Dock
area

Water
Tr

5

Trawlers

5

5

Iso.4s14M
Lighthouse
(conspic)

Barges

5

7

Talaud
Bay

5

Dhows

Fisheries

Immig

Hotel

Yard

Massawa

Coral Heads

Talaud
Is

5

5

5

5

5

5

Sheikh
Said Is

+

+

+

0   0.5   1

Nautical Miles

Note Once into the harbour you will usually be asked to go alongside the commercial quay to clear in. Care is needed to avoid the wreck at the W end of the quay. If the quay is full you may be asked to anchor off in the outer harbour.

Mooring

Once you have cleared in proceed to Talaud Bay. Care is needed of the reefs off the S side of the channel into Talaud Bay. Keep closer to the N side than to the S side. Just W of the fisheries quay there is an isolated reef which must be avoided as it is tempting to turn WSW into the bay which will take you across or onto the reef. Again stay close to the N side until the reef is identified and you can safely turn into the bay. Anchor where convenient in 4–10m. The bottom is mostly mud, good holding. Recently it has been reported you can anchor off in front of the Dahlak Hotel on the S side of the bridge connecting Massawa Island. Enquire on arrival. Care is needed of coral around the edges of the inlet and there are isolated coral patches further out.

Shelter Excellent all-round shelter. The water is clean enough to swim in.

Authorities Harbourmaster, health, customs and immigration at the commercial harbour.

Facilities

Water At the Fisheries quay. If you take a yacht over to the quay you will be charged (around $50) for berthing. If you jerrycan water back and forth by dinghy the cost of the water is nominal. The water here is filtered and good quality. However the filtration system often seems to break down. Water can also be delivered by tanker to the commercial quay. The water in town should be treated.

Fuel A yacht should be able to squeeze onto the outer end of the fuel quay on the Fisheries quay. Alternatively jerrycan fuel from the fuel quay. The fuel is sometimes contaminated with water so check your separator and filters carefully after running the engine.

Gas Most gas cylinders can be filled in Asmara. Use one of the 'agents' to help you.

Paraffin Can be obtained in town.

Laundry Mike the laundry man will do it and much else besides. See below.

Repairs There is really nowhere to haul. It may be possible to get craned out at the commercial harbour in an emergency. Maiks Boatyard on the SE side of Massawa Island has looked after several small yachts left here in the past. Some mechanical and engineering work can be carried out. Very limited hardware. Several yachts have had spares flown into Asmara and bussed down to Massawa using an agent.

Provisions Some staples and tinned goods available. Fresh produce is poor and expensive. Good Italian pasta available.

Eating out Several good and cheap restaurants. The Eritrean Restaurant has a good range of food including good pasta. The Salaam restaurant in the old town on Massawa does wonderful baked fish in a pit oven. The more up-market Adulis nearby also has good fish. The last two are Muslim restaurants and do not serve alcohol. Fresh fruit juices (guava, orange, mango) are widely available.

Other PO (telephone and fax). Bank. Buses and taxis to Asmara.

Agents There are no specific yacht agents as such, but a number of the big ship agents may approach you. One person who will introduce himself to you as 'Mike the laundry man' can do much else besides and is honest and helpful. He is a useful contact and will normally pedal up on his bike to greet you: Mike (Weldemichael H'Tzion) ☎ 552 467. Another big ship agent who may be helpful is Burhane Red Sea Fast Ship Chandler, PO Box 139, Massawa. ☎ 552 607. These two may often be found in their 'office' at the *Seghem* (Ostrich) Restaurant on the waterfront of Massawa Island.

General

Massawa is a useful stop on the way north as there will usually be southerlies at least this far up. It is also a fascinating introduction to a country most know little about. The Italianate port town is being gradually put back together after the intensive fighting which demolished so much of it. There is still much to do. Heavy calibre machine gun holes

The lighthouse on Shumma Island in the southern approach channel to Massawa.

The yacht anchorage in Talaud Bay. Here *Tetra* is anchored just inside the reef running parallel to the fisheries quay. Most yachts must anchor on the other side of the reef.

pock-mark many buildings. The bomb craters have not all been filled in. A couple of Soviet tanks have been left as a ready-made memorial to the 'Heroes of Massawa'. Much remains to be done but I was surprised at the progress made in a little over a year between my two visits here.

Massawa really consists of the old Turkish town on Massawa Island surrounded by the colonial buildings the Italians built during their time here. There is a very real Italian feel to the place. In the restaurants all sorts of pasta, from lasagne to linguini, are served alongside the Eritrean dish of choice, the hot *zinguini* stew commonly made from goat meat. The famous *Moretti* beer originally brewed by the Moretti family who built the wonderful art deco house on the end of Talaud Island is still made and is excellent. Some Italian wine is available although if stored badly in the heat of the summer it can be off. In most cafés there is a dilapidated expresso machine and occasionally you

will find one that works. Despite the heavy bombing of Massawa by the Ethiopians, many of the wonderful colonial buildings with wrap-around verandas remain and are being restored. This is a little Italy a thousand miles and more removed.

Despite the somewhat torturous bus trip, a visit to Asmara should not be missed. The mountain capital at 7500ft is wonderfully cool after the heat of the coast. Remember to take a pullover. Asmara was hardly damaged in the war as by this stage Mengistu knew he had lost to the EPLF and the troops just melted out of the capital into the mountains leaving it relatively undamaged. It is a vision of Italy locked away in the fastness of the East African mountains, an anomaly that makes you pinch yourself to realise that this is really Africa.

Sudan

Current situation
Sudan is a country riven by civil war and famine, governed by an Islamic party that has introduced shariya law, a country which has disputes with every country it borders and that includes Eritrea, Ethiopia, Kenya, Uganda and Egypt. It has surprised many that the government is still in power and given recent rebel advances in the south, it is imperative that the situation is monitored closely. What is surprising given the situation in most of the country is that Port Sudan exudes such an air of normality. In 1997 the port was open to visiting yachts and most services were easily accessed.

Despite the apparent air of normality in Port Sudan yachtsmen should take special care in Sudanese waters and follow the situation in the countryside carefully. It is worthwhile getting permission from Port Sudan to cruise along the coast if that is your intention. It would be wise at present to avoid all border areas although there have been no major problems in recent years.

Documentation and visas
Normal ships papers and a valid passport for all crew members should be carried. Certain passport holders such as Israeli, Egyptian and South Africans will not be permitted ashore and anyone with an Israeli stamp in their passport will likewise not be allowed to land. In 1997 there was a charter yacht in here with engine problems on which two crew members, one with an Egyptian passport and the other a USA passport with an Israeli stamp, had not been allowed ashore for a month. For most nationals a visa is not required and you will be given a shorepass to get in and out of Port Sudan. Two passport photos are required.

Entry formalities
When 1M off the harbour call up port control on VHF Ch 16. They will take a few details on the yacht and crew before allowing you to enter and anchor off. You may also be called by an agent at this point as they monitor the radio for inbound

yachts. Once at anchor you will be visited by one of several agents who will arrange entry formalities. It is possible to do the paperwork yourself, but most people choose to let an agent handle everything as they have the 'contacts' to get it all done quickly and smoothly. In 1997 the charge was $50 US for the agents fee plus around $8 per day for port fees.

Agent El Barbary, PO Box 31, Port Sudan, ☎ (249) 31 26338 *Fax* (249) 31 26558

Data
Area 2,505,810km² (967,499M²) (The largest country in Africa.)
Coastline 853km (461M)
Maritime claims Territorial 12M. Contiguous to 200m depths.
Population 26,477,000
Disputes With just about everyone including the US and Great Britain. Border disputes with Eritrea, Ethiopia, Kenya, Uganda and Egypt. The southern states are accused of helping the SPLA (Sudanese People's Liberation Army) which stands for secular rule. It has made significant military gains in the south in 1996 and 1997. The Egyptians have long disputed the border area with Sudan and have the extra beef that Sudanese terrorists tried to assasinate Mubarak on his visit to Sudan and are now protected by the Sudanese government. In 1997 there were Egyptian naval ships off the border area. Most of the countries around Sudan have closed their borders to trade and travel.
Capital Khartoum
Time zone UT+2
Language Arabic. Many other languages. Some English spoken.
Ethnic divisions Black 52%, Arab 39%, Beja 6%.
Religion Sunni Moslem 70%, Indigenous mostly Animist 20%, Christian 5%.
Public holidays
  Jan 1 New Year
  Mar 3 Unity Day
  Moslem holidays which vary from year to year.
Government Revolutionary Council which was installed by the army after the 1989 coup. Martial law has been imposed and the Council adheres to Islamic Fundamentalist principles including *shariya* law.
Crime Appears to be a low level.

Travel
Internal
Bus or share taxi to Suakin. In general internal travel is not advised.

International
Some flights to Egypt and Italy from Khartoum.

Practicalities
Mail Unreliable.
Telecommunications IDD system. Country code 249. Port Sudan 31.
  In general the system is poor. Calls in and out are rationed and it can be impossible to get incoming calls. Telephone office in Port Sudan where with persistence you can get out. El Barbary has a phone and fax but as the power is frequently off the fax is little use.
Currency Sudanese pound (£Sud).

Banks and exchange Banks and money changers in Port Sudan will change US dollars cash. $100 bills post 1990 preferred.
Medical Poor. Few doctors and few drugs. Get out quickly.
Electricity 240V. Frequent power cuts.

Harbours and anchorages
The *marsas* and reef anchorages north of Port Sudan have been much used by cruising yachts to coast up towards Egypt. See *Red Sea Pilot* by Elaine Morgan and Stephen Davies.

Port Sudan
Charts BA *3492*

Approach
Is straightforward from seawards and by day straightforward inside the reefs from the N and S. The light structures and moles at the entrance are reported to show up well on radar.

Conspicuous Saganeb lighthouse and island are conspicuous. The light structures on Wingate Reef do not stand out but will be seen. There are usually numerous ships anchored off in the roadstead around the Fl.G on the isolated reef. The light structure on the S fringing reef is conspicuous and further in the light structure marking the remains of the wreck on the S fringing reef is easily identified. The buildings around the harbour stand out well and a large square silo on the S side is conspicuous.

By night Possible from the seawards approach although care is needed. It should not be attempted without radar. On my night approach several of the lights were not working and I stood off until dawn.

Saganeb Reef Fl.5s19M
Wingate Reef (Silayet) Fl(3)15s6M S end Fl.G.3s6M. Neither of these two lights seem to have the stated range.
Fringing reef S side Fl(2)10s10M
Damma Damma Q.R.6M
Mole N side Fl(2)G.5s and F.G.3M
Mole S side Fl.R.3s5M

Note The lights should not be relied upon and in 1997 the entrance lights were not working.

VHF Ch 16 for port control. Call up when 2M off and you will usually be instructed to proceed into the anchorage on arrival. You may be asked to call up again on arrival at the harbour entrance.

Dangers Care is needed of the reefs in the approach and particularly of the fringing reef which comes up quickly from 60–80m in the immediate approaches.

Mooring
Anchor off in 3–10m in the inlet on the W side. The bottom is mud and good holding.

Shelter Good all-round shelter. Northerlies can blow with some force into the anchorage and if worried lay a second anchor. No sea penetrates the anchorage.

Authorities Harbourmaster, health, customs,

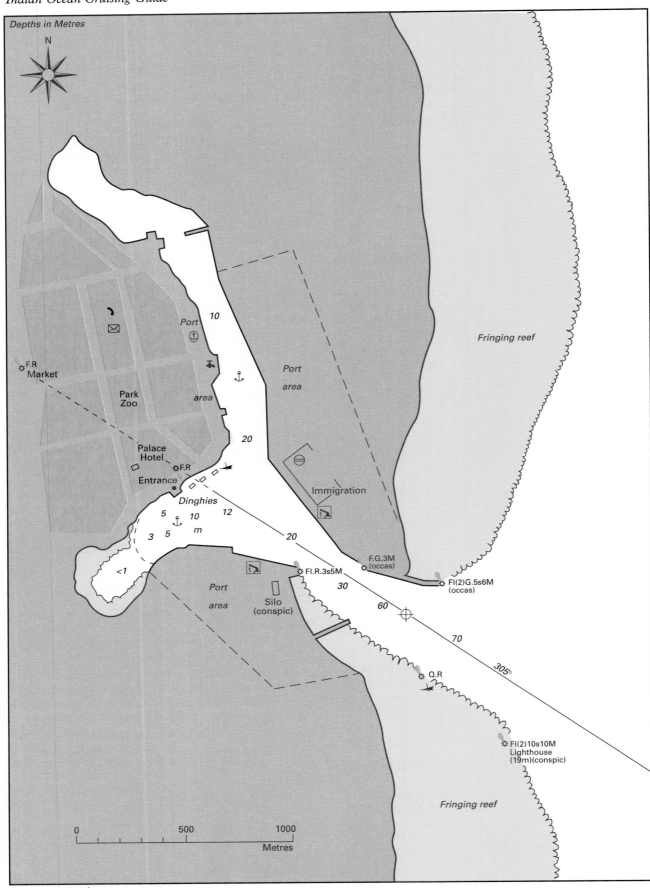

Depths in Metres

N

Fringing reef

Port area

10

Port area

20

20

Port

Market

F.R

Park
Zoo

area

Palace
Hotel

F.R

Entrance

Dinghies

5   10
m

3   5

12

20

<1

Immigration

F.G.3M
(occas)

Fl.R.3s5M

Fl(2)G.5s6M
(occas)

Port
area

Silo
(conspic)

30

60

70

305°

Q.R

Fl(2)10s10M
Lighthouse
(19m)(conspic)

Fringing reef

0   500   1000

Metres

PORT SUDAN ⊕ 19°36´·1N 37°14´·2E WGS 84

The yacht anchorage in the W inlet at Port Sudan.

immigration and harbour police. If you employ an agent (recommended) the various officials will be ferried out to the yacht by the agent. If you decide to clear in yourself allot at least one day as the offices are scattered all over the place. Some *baksheesh* may be demanded and normally a packet of cigarettes suffices. The ships papers and passports will be retained by the harbourmaster and shorepasses issued.

Facilities
Water Can be ferried out by the agent. Alternatively arrangements can be made to go to the water barge in the N part of the harbour. Water quality is poor and the water is brackish.
Fuel Can be ferried out in jerrycans for small amounts or for larger amounts arrange with the agent to go to the fuel quay in the N inlet. Power cuts often mean that the pump here is not working. The fuel is often contaminated with water.
Gas Most gas bottles can be filled by the agent.
Laundry Can be arranged by the agent at a price.
Repairs There is a dry dock with reasonable charges in the N inlet. At least one yacht I know of has used it. Minor mechanical and engineering repairs possible. Some basic paints can be found.
Provisions Limited basics. There are some imported items at a price. Check the sell-by dates. Excellent fruit and vegetable market in town with a surprising variety of produce.
Eating out Limited. There are some basic restaurants and a slightly better restaurant in the hotel near the harbour. There is of course no alcohol around.
Other PO. Banks and money changers. Duty-free shop. A few taxis. Ferry (irregular) to Jiddah and on to Suez. Flights to Khartoum.

General
Port Sudan exudes a remarkable air of calm for a country in turmoil. The locals go about their business in an orderly way and are friendly to strangers arriving in their port. The market hustles and bustles with local commerce. The roadside tea and coffee stalls do a roaring business all day. The port is even being expanded. There is a definite army presence and here and there you see the faces of refugees and outsiders marked by the strain of conflicts in the region, but overall I was knocked out by the air of normality that pervades the place.

Most yachts which stop here do so for some respite from the northerly winds and to take on fuel and water and fresh fruit and veggies. There is little to see inland that you cannot see from the various *marsas* up the coast (read desert vistas) and in any case internal travel is difficult and not recommended while the civil war rages. While it is unlikely that Port Sudan will be attacked, after all even the SPLA will need a working port if it takes power, it is only wise to monitor the situation closely before calling here.

Saudi Arabia
In general yachts are not welcome in Saudi territorial waters and most yachts choose to cruise up the western side of the Red Sea. Some yachts have visited Jiddah to take on fuel and water and supplies with varying degrees of success. If you must visit Jiddah it is imperative you call up port control on Ch 16 to request clearance to enter the port. For further information refer to *Red Sea Pilot* by Elaine Morgan and Stephen Davies.

Egypt
Current situation
Egypt is one of the most liberal and westernised of the Arab countries and for the most part the coast is a stable place to cruise along. It is only sensible to steer clear of the border area with Sudan and any military areas. While the coastal areas are stable, inland there is some terrorism from fundamentalist groups who want Egypt to become an Islamic country along the lines of Iran or Sudan which are accused of aiding the terrorist groups. There have been several attacks on tourists, mostly on coaches visiting areas around the Nile, and some deaths. This has severely dented the tourist industry and internal security by the army is now much in evidence everywhere. It is unlikely a yacht cruising along the coast will be targeted by terrorists and no incidents have occurred to date. When travelling inland it is probably wise to go by taxi although in real terms the risk on other modes of transport is low.

Documentation and visas
Normal ships papers and passports for all crew

members should be carried. A visa obtained in advance may be useful although in practice an agent can obtain one with little trouble. If you plan to cruise along the coast before getting to a major port then it would be sensible to have a visa in advance. Two passport photos are required for a visa obtained in Egypt. By law you must have your visa stamped by the police within one week of entering Egypt.

Entry formalities

You must clear in and out of every port. In most of the major ports an agent can do this for you at a price, often a fairly substantial price. If you complete formalities yourself some *baksheesh* is in order or you may, like me, end up waiting for a relevant official for half a day or so. Miraculously he will appear when a few packets of cigarettes are on offer.

Recently there have been reports that if you clear in at Hurgadha you will have to obtain a cruising permit at a cost of around $300 US. This does not seem to apply to Safaga or any other ports. If you anchor off Hurgadha en route from another Egyptian port there seems to be no problem. Keep your ears to the ground for future developments.

To clear in at any port (with the exception of Suez and Said where you will need an agent to transit the canal in any case) the procedure is as follows. You will be visited by the health officer, harbourmaster, customs and immigration. Sometimes you will have to go ashore to find one or several of these and this is where it gets messy if you are doing it yourself. Office hours are 0900–1400 and extra charges (and more *baksheesh*) are payable outside these hours and at the weekend and public holidays. Immigration can issue a visa and if you already have one it must be stamped within one week.

Most port areas are guarded by the harbour police who will want to check your passport – even upside down! Fees are payable to all the officials and port dues are also payable.

To clear out you must visit all the officials except health and obtain clearance papers to the next port. There seem to be few problems stopping over at anchorages although if there are army or police ashore they will usually want to check your passport.

For details on transiting the Suez Canal see the section under *Harbours and Anchorages*.

Data
Area 1,001,450km^2 (386,662M^2)
Coastline 2450km (1323M)
Maritime claims Territorial 12M. Contiguous zone to 200m depths.
Population 60,000,000
Time zone UT+2
Language Arabic. Some English and French spoken.
Ethnic divisions Eastern Hamitic 90%. Greek, Italian, Lebanese, Syrian stock 10%.
Religion Muslim (mostly Sunni) 94%, Coptic Christian and other 6%.
Public holidays
 Apr 25 Sinai Liberation Day
 May 1 Labour Day
 Jun 18 Evacuation Day
 Jul 23 National Day
 Oct 6 Armed Forces Day
 Muslim holidays which vary from year to year.
Government Democratic Republic
Crime Some petty theft in the cities and tourist areas. Most harbour areas are guarded and there is little likelihood of theft. If you report a theft relating to a government employee (such as a Suez Canal pilot in my case) it will be treated seriously if you persist and kick up a fuss.

Travel
Internal
There is an adequate coach system connecting major towns and cities and a limited rail network. Within towns there are buses or perhaps more useful, numerous mini-buses that stop just about anywhere on a more or less set route. There are also taxis. To go to the Pyramids, Valley of the Kings, or other famous sites it is probably best to take a taxi for the day as prices are reasonable and it is better to be driven in Egypt than to drive. There are some internal flights between Hurgadha and Cairo for example.

International
From Cairo it is possible to fly to most destinations in the world or at least to somewhere you can pick up a connecting flight. There are some scheduled and charter flights to Hurgadha.

Practicalities
Mail Slow and inefficient. Poste Restante although it does not work well in practice. If possible address mail to an agent to hold for you.

Telecommunications IDD system. Country code 20. Telecommunications are good on the whole with few delays for incoming and outgoing calls. Telephone calls can be made from the PO. Probably the best thing to do is to use the agent although you will pay through the nose for telephone and fax calls.

Currency The unit is the Egyptian pound (£E) divided into 100 *piastres*. The currency is reasonably stable at the present time.

Banks and exchange Banks will exchange hard currency (US dollars preferred but £GBP, Ffr and Dm accepted) and travellers cheques. In Hurgadha Thomas Cooks near the harbour will give cash advances (in $US or £E) on *Visa* and *MasterCard*. In Port Said there is at least one ATM which gives cash advances on *Visa*. In Cairo there are numerous ATMs which accept *Visa* and *MasterCard*. The large hotels, restaurants and travel agencies accept major credit cards.

Medical care Is adequate in the cities and large towns. Elsewhere medical care is rudimentary. In the event of a major illness fly to Europe. Pharmacies are adequately stocked with the standard drugs although many will be under a different brand name. Most chemists speak English. The water is generally potable, but if in doubt treat it.

Electricity 220V 50Hz AC

Useful books

Wonders of the Red Sea David Fridman and Tony Malmqvist. Isis. Published and available in Egypt.

There are numerous local guides and maps to diving sites and the fish of the Red Sea published and available locally in Egypt.

Egypt Handbook Anne and Keith McLachlan. Footprint. Excellent guide.

Egypt & the Sudan Lonely Planet Guide.

The Alexandria Quartet Lawrence Durrell. Faber. Read it again just for the pleasure.

Hashish Henry de Monfreid. Penguin. Intriguing and colourful tale of Henri's smuggling adventures bringing hashish from Greece to Egypt in his yacht in the 1920s. He also wrote *Secrets of the Red Sea* (OP).

Harbours and anchorages

Hurgadha

Charts BA *3043*

Approach

The approach through the reefs looks a little tricky, but in practice it is straightforward by day. The approach should not be made at night. Most of the isolated reefs can be identified by the cluster of dive-boats around them. If you are making the approach from the SE then around 1500 and later numerous dive boats will be on the return trip back to Hurgadha.

Conspicuous The islands and reefs in the approach are reasonably easy to identify from aloft. In the approach from the SE the Sheraton Hotel, an oval art deco building on 3 floors with large windows and a large white hotel immediately N of it will be readily identified. A course of around 295° on the Sheraton when into the approach channel leads you through the reefs to Hurgadha. Once close to Hurgadha the channel to the clearing in jetty is partly marked by beacons and is in any case obvious.

By night A night approach should not be attempted.

VHF Fantasea II Agency can be contacted on VHF Ch 16 if required.

Dangers There are numerous reefs, both isolated and fringing, in the approaches. It is useful to have someone up the mast conning you in.

Note There is a considerable amount of traffic with dive boats coming and going, but on the whole they do not pose too much of a problem.

Mooring

Berth Mediterranean style on the clearing in jetty. The bottom is mud, coral and weed, reasonable holding.

Shelter Adequate. The wind normally blows either down the N channel or off the land.

Authorities Health, harbourmaster, customs, immigration, harbour police. Fantasea II Agency can be used to clear in. The agents fee in 1997 was $100 although the introduction specifically mentioned that there would be none or only a small fee. Alternatively clear in yourself as most of the offices are close to the jetty. According to Fantasea II port dues were free for up to 10 days after which a cruising permit for 3 months will cost $100. This cost is now reported to be $US300 (1999).

Agent Samir Hares, Fantasea II, PO Box 44, Hurgadha ☎ (65) 443 675 *Fax* (65) 442 288. Note that you will be charged an agents fee (anything from $100 up) despite assurances when you arrive that that is not so and other services will cost more through the agent.

Anchorage After clearing in it is possible to proceed down the S channel and anchor off. Yachts have often anchored off the Sonesta Hotel where some facilities are available. An alternative anchorage is off the Marriot Hotel. Yachts en route in Egypt have reported no charges for just anchoring off. The bottom is mud with some coral and a few old moorings. Generally good shelter.

Facilities

Water Via the agent or close to the jetty there is a desalination plant from which water can be taken in jerrycans. Alternatively on the jetty at the Marine Sports Club or at the Sonesta Hotel in the S channel.

Fuel Fuel quay near the clearing in jetty or at the Marine Sports Club. Small amounts in jerrycans can be arranged by the agent.

Gas Most gas bottles can be filled although some types may cause problems.

Paraffin Can be obtained ashore.

Laundry Via the agent (expensive) or take it ashore yourself to one of the laundries near the clearing in jetty.

Repairs The boatyard near the clearing in jetty may be able to haul you out on a sledge although it mostly deals in dive-boats. The Marine Sports Club is reported to be investigating putting in a hoist of some sort. Mechanical and engineering repairs. Some electrical repairs. Several chandlers with imported gear. Hardware shops. Canvas work.

Provisions Good shopping for the basics although any imported goods are expensive. Adequate fruit and vegetables.

Eating out Numerous restaurants of all types. Several good and quite cheap fish restaurants near Thomas Cooks. Many of the large hotels (including the Marriot) have a buffet which is good value for money with a wide range of food.

Other PO. Banks. Thomas Cook near the clearing in jetty will give cash advances on *Visa* and *Mastercard*. Share mini-buses and taxis. Flights to Cairo. Some international flights, mostly to Europe, from Hurgadha.

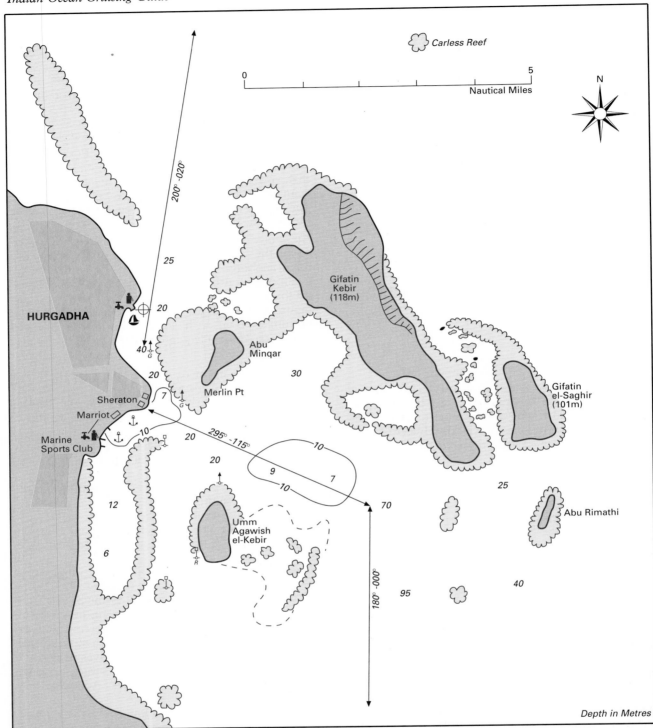

HURGADHA AND APPROACHES ⊕ 27°13′·8N 33°50′·6E WGS 84

General

Hurgadha is something of a brash high rise resort catering for northern Europeans looking for some winter sun and usually a bit of diving thrown in. Along with Sharm El Sheikh it is the diving mecca of the Egyptian Red Sea coast although for yachties who have sailed up through the Red Sea and dived over some of the reefs further south, it is a bit of a disappointment. Ashore the brash resort comes as a welcome breath of civilisation with all the amenities a large resort offers. Things like working telephones, cash advances on credit cards, cold beer, fast food joints and buffet dinners provide a strange and unreal glee after the wilderness to the south. Like all bright baubles, the fool's gold of Hurgadha soon shines out and you find yourself talking lovingly about places you were cussing a few weeks previously.

Suez

Port Tewfiq

Charts BA *3214, 233*

Approach

There are always numerous ships at anchor and entering or leaving the canal. The numbers of ships can be confusing and in the approaches they often obscure channel marks and conspicuous objects on the shore. When ships are entering the channel they at least show you where the deep water channel is.

Conspicuous The numerous ships at anchor will be seen and if you head for them you at least know there are sufficient depths. The channel light buoys will be seen closer to the deep water channel, although the ships at anchor often obscure them. The steel pylon tower of Newport Rock and Green Island are easily identified. The actual entrance to the canal can be difficult to identify from the distance but the channel is well marked and there are no difficulties following it. The short section of canal up to Port Tewfiq is marked by beacons which have deep water right up to the structure.

By night Confusing. The lights of the ships at anchor make it difficult to identify the channel light buoys and even major lights may be obscured by the bulk of large ships. Although confusing, if you take your time there are no problems in a night approach.

Newport Rock Fl.5s10M
Green Island Q
Shab 'Ataqua Fl.3s3M
Birket Misallat F.13s18M
Port Ibrahim F.R.4M/F.G.4M
Entrance to Suez YC Q.R/Q.G light buoys
The deep water channel into the Suez Canal is lit by light buoys Fl.G/Fl.R.

VHF Ch 16 for pilots and agents. The agents monitor Ch 16 and you will likely be contacted by the agent (usually Prince of the Red Sea) rather than the Suez Canal authorities. The Prince of the Red Sea monitors Ch 16, 24 (24/24).

Note You may be approached by a pilot boat or a chandlers boat pressing you to take the services of one or other agent before entering Port Tewfiq. The best policy here is to say you have already made arrangements and proceed without committing yourself beforehand.

Dangers
1. There are always large numbers of ships inbound or outbound from the canal or coming up to the big ship anchorages. Commercial ships have right of way at all times and you must keep clear of them.
2. There can be strong tidal streams running at the head of the Gulf of Suez which may accelerate or retard progress. Keep a careful eye on the cross-track error on the GPS.
3. North winds at the head of the Gulf of Suez usually blow strongest in the afternoon and into the late evening. It is not a bad idea to time arrival at dawn having come up through the night when winds are lighter and may even have been favourable at times. Although cautioned against, there seem to be few problems entering the canal in company with the N-going convoy as there is plenty of room to stay out of their way close to the edges of the channel. Do keep a wary eye aft for ships joining the convoy.

Port Tewfiq. The yacht moorings off the Suez Yacht Club.

The of Gulf of Suez is studded with oil platforms. Most are clearly marked on the chart but there can also be one or two new ones that haven't made it onto the chart yet.

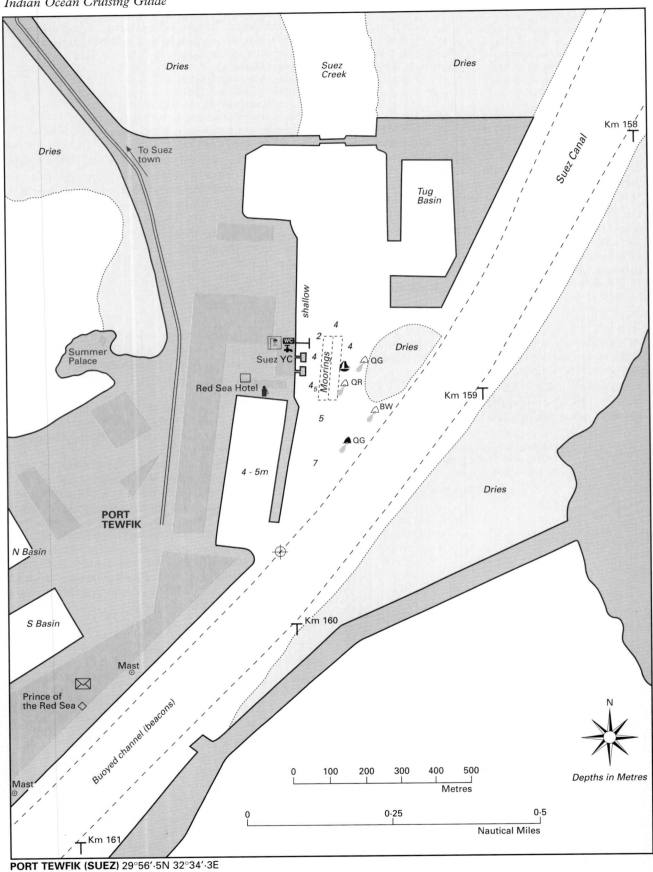

PORT TEWFIK (SUEZ) 29°56'·5N 32°34'·3E

Mooring

Moor fore and aft to the buoys off the Suez Yacht Club. A boatman will usually row out to help you.

Shelter Good all round shelter. Yachts have been left here for substantial periods.

Authorities Yacht club attendant. Health, harbourmaster, customs, and immigration. Often you will not have to see any of these if you use the Prince of the Red Sea as your agent.

The Prince of the Red Sea has established himself as the main yacht agent here for canal transits and on the whole he provides a good service at a fair price. Most yachts use his services. A mooring charge of $8 per day is made.

Mohamed F Soukar, Prince of the Red Sea Co, 40 Gohar El Kayed St, Port Tewfiq, ☎ (20) 62 222 126 *Fax* (20) 62 223 825

Facilities

Water On the jetty at the yacht club. If you do go alongside here to take on water do not go very far N past the jetty where it gets shallow.

Fuel On the quay in the basin nearby. Arrange a time with the agent to collect fuel. Smaller amounts can be brought out to you in jerrycans.

Gas Most gas bottles can be filled via the agent.

Paraffin Available ashore. Enquire to the agent.

Repairs Few available locally. Some mechanical and engineering repairs possible. Basic hardware shops in Suez town.

Provisions Most basics can be found in Suez town along with a just adequate selection of fresh fruit and vegetables.

Eating out Several good fish restaurants in Suez town. The Summer Palace on the W side of Port Tewfiq has food and alcohol.

Other PO and banks in Suez. Driver and car can be arranged for trips to the Pyramids or other sites. Buses and share taxis to Cairo.

General

Most find Suez a drab little place with not a lot going for it. I have to say after two visits here I have an affection for it and enjoy wandering around. The people are friendly, there are several good fish restaurants on the High Street, you can find most things and just take it easy after the slog up the Gulf of Suez. To get into Suez walk up to the main road and flag down a mini-bus which will whisk you into Suez town in five minutes. If you just want a quiet beer wander across the main road and a short distance up the obvious side street is the Summer Palace ('Samir Balis' in Egyptlish).

Tewfiq is a secure port to leave the yacht for a visit to the Pyramids which can be comfortably made in a single day. I can recommend Foaad Hessen as that rarity in Egypt, a calm and patient driver who will not give you white knuckle syndrome throughout the drive. He drives the ubiquitous Peugeot 405 and can be found at the address below. Although it sounds like a geeky touristy thing to do, I recommend hiring a horse or camel to ride around the Pyramids and sand dunes humming the theme tune from Lawrence of Arabia all the way and feeling vastly superior to the other tourists being disgorged by the coach-load.

Foaad Hessen, 14 Elgomhoriya St, A.R.E. Suez. ☎ 570061/326849.

Suez Canal

Charts BA *233*

I know of nobody who has arranged their own transit of the Suez Canal in the last five years or more. Everyone uses an agent and just about everyone uses The Prince of the Red Sea at Suez and Nagib Latif of the Felix Agency at Port Said. Despite mutterings from the odd few, both of these agents provide a good service at a competitive price. The transit from south to north costs less than the transit from north to south. On average the transit going N costs around $200 and the transit going south around $320 (1997 figures). This is to do with the pricing structure from the canal authorities and not an arbitrary decision by the agents.

The Prince of the Red Sea, (Mohammed F Soukar, although you will probably deal with his son Heebi), 40 Gohar El Kayed St, Port Tewfiq, ☎ (20) 62 222 126 *Fax* (20) 62 223 825. *VHF* Ch 16

Felix Agency (Nagib Latif), Al Gomhoria St, Post Tower Building, 4th Floor Office no. 12, Port Said, ☎ (20) 66 409 401 *Fax* (20) 66 402 443. *VHF* Ch 22

Transit of the Suez Canal normally takes two days. A yacht is required to be able to motor at a minimum 4kt. If a yacht can do 8kt plus it may be possible to transit in one day. Remember your engine will be working overtime for at least 10–12 hours to get you through so it needs to be topped up with oil and ready to withstand a good two

Felucca in the Bitter Lakes, Egypt. Sailing craft are losing ground to diesel power in the Indian Ocean, but are still used in Indonesia, India, Sri Lanka, Yemen, Sudan, Egypt, and in places down the coast of East Africa.

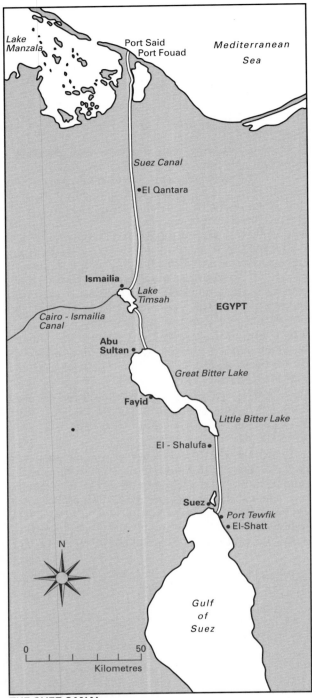

THE SUEZ CANAL

(though not always) speak some English. They will all, without fail, want *baksheesh*. Some cruising folk find the demands by turn funny, irritating, a strange cultural quirk, infuriating or downright insulting. It should be remembered that asking for *baksheesh* in Egypt is an institution and a perfectly normal process. For most of us it is antithetical to our norms and means of behaviour and often we do not know how to deal with it. I suggest that you delay payment until near the end of the leg and then offer the going rate (around $10–$15 for small yachts, $20 for larger yachts plus a discretionary number of packets of cigarettes in 1997) which will immediately be refused as an insulting amount by the pilot. Put the *baksheesh* below where it is visible and say: OK, if you refuse it I'll keep it. Ignore any further requests and it will be asked for before he leaves. One new development on the pilot agenda is that when you arrive in Port Said, the pilot will be taken off by the pilot launch and a new pilot put aboard for the trip out to the seaward end of the channel into the Mediterranean or for the one mile trip to Port Fouad Yacht Club. It is in order not to give him anything despite demands for a minimum of one carton of *Marlboro* and $20 etc.

Yachts usually leave Suez at the end of the north bound convoy or more often with the tail-end of the convoy. One thing to watch for is the shoal patch at the entrance to Port Tewfiq which some pilots like to cut across. I suggest you go out the way you came in through the buoyed channel as I have seen at least one tug go aground on the shoal patch and be left high and dry by the ebbing tide. There are usually good depths outside the markers so do not panic when the pilot takes you outside the channel. Whatever speed you do, the pilot will urge you to go faster. Just keep the engine revs at a figure you are happy with. The pilot will often helm the boat for you and in my experience they have all been careful about the job of conveying your pride and joy safely through the canal.

Occasionally the pilot will want to give a few packets of cigarettes (*Marlboro* being the preferred currency) to a pilot station. On my southbound transit this was insisted upon for a couple of pilot stations but for the northbound transit no demands were made. You will have to pass close to a number of the pilot stations to identify the yacht, say hullo to the pilot's friend and in some cases to hand over paperwork. You also need to keep the VHF open, normally on Ch 13, 12 or 11. If you appear to be having undue problems tell the pilot you are going to give the agent a call on the radio and this will usually circumvent apparent problems.

In Ismalia you will need to drop the pilot off at the pilot station where there are generally good depths (around 3–4m off the end of the jetties) and then proceed to the anchorage just WSW of the pilot station. Depths here come up quickly to 2m and less and generally you will anchor in 3–8m. The bottom is mud and the shelter good. In the morning the next pilot will be ferried out to you by the pilot launch – have some fenders ready.

consecutive days motoring. If you need to get a tug to give you a tow through the canal, figures in the vicinity of $3000 US have been bandied about although I have no hard evidence what the actual price may be. And in case you were contemplating it – you cannot be towed by another yacht.

Every yacht must take a pilot on board. The pilot from Suez to Ismalia will disembark there and another will join you in the morning for the passage to Port Said (and vice versa for a north to south transit). The pilots are generally friendly and usually

For the most part the pilots in the Suez Canal are courteous and diligent although they will always nag you to go 'faster-faster' and will always be offended at the meagre *baksheesh* you offer.

The passage through the canal is a pretty relaxed affair that most enjoy. The sides of the canal are littered with metal detritus from the Six Day War and discarded engineering equipment. Dredgers work in parts of the canal, but the channel clear of the area being dredged is obvious. The desert vista is mostly obscured by high banks along the sides of the canal, but up at the cross-trees you can see what is going on. Enjoy it.

Data
Distance 162km (100·5M)
Suez to Ismalia 84km (52·1M)
Said to Ismalia 78km (48·4M)
Depths In the main channel 13–20m
Convoy times
Northbound convoy 0600
Southbound convoys 0100 and 0700

Tides
Port Said 0·5m range at springs
Port Suez 1·5m range at springs
Tidal streams are strongest in the S half of the canal and can reach 3–3½kt at springs. This can significantly add or subtract to your speed although once N of the Great Bitter Lake the stream is much reduced. In the N part of the canal after Ismalia the stream is significantly less and rarely exceeds 1kt.

Port Said
Port Fouad
Charts BA *233*

Approach
From the canal you can choose to keep on going straight through Port Fouad after picking up the pilot and out into the deep water channel which is clearly marked. Alternatively the pilot will take you to Port Fouad Yacht Centre. From the Mediterranean the approach is reasonably straightforward to the buoys marking the deep water channel into Port Fouad. Where the channel divides take the westernmost channel and not the Port Said bypass channel on the east.

Conspicuous From seawards the oil rigs off the coast will be the first thing you see after which the numerous ships anchored off in the roadstead will be seen. Ships normally anchor just W of the outer buoys to the deep water channel. Stay within the channel as there are a number of wrecks outside it when closer to Port Said. The high rise buildings of Port Said will eventually be seen and the approach into the port is straightforward in the buoyed channel.

By night The oil rigs are well lit as are the ships anchored in the roadstead which will often obscure the main light. There will also be numerous fishing boats with set nets, trawling or purse seine fishing.
Main light Fl.10s20M (range appears to be substantially less)
El Bahar Iso.2s15M
E breakwater Oc.R.6s
Ldg Lts on 217°40' *Front* F.R.6M *Rear* Oc(2)R.10s7M
VHF Ch 16 for port control. Call up when 10M off and you will be instructed to proceed into the harbour. You will often be hailed by a pilot boat which is usually looking for *baksheesh*. It is not necessary to take on a pilot although you will probably be instructed to listen out on Ch 11 or 13. Call up port control when 2M off if requested to do so. You may also call up an agent if desired at this point. Felix Agency operates on Ch 22 but also listens in to Ch 16.

Dangers
1. There are numerous ships coming and going from Port Said at all times. A good lookout must be kept from at least 40M out. Commercial ships have right of way in the buoyed channel at all times.
2. Numerous fishing boats, especially trawlers,

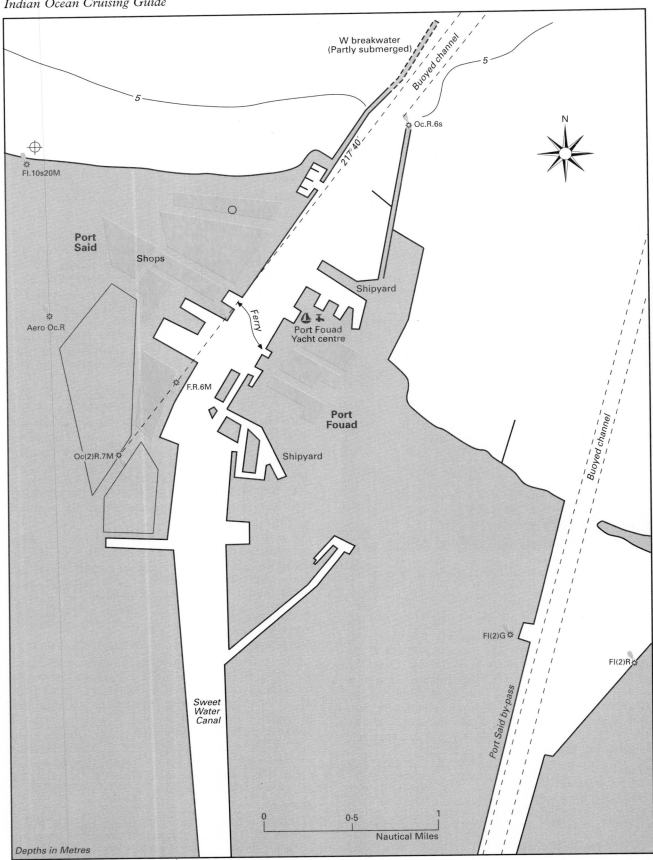

W breakwater
(Partly submerged)

Buoyed channel

5

5

☼ Oc.R.6s

N

☼
Fl.10s20M

217°40′

**Port
Said**

Shops

☼
Aero Oc.R

Ferry

Shipyard

Port Fouad
Yacht centre

**Port
Fouad**

☼ F.R.6M

Oc(2)R.7M ☼

Shipyard

Buoyed channel

Fl(2)G ☼

Port Said by-pass

Fl(2)R☼

*Sweet
Water
Canal*

0   0·5   1

Nautical Miles

Depths in Metres

PORT SAID AND PORT FOUAD ⊕ 31°16′·4N 32°17′·6E

Port Fouad Yacht Centre at Port Said.

operate around and in the deep water channel.
Care is needed to avoid them and their trawl. The
end of the trawl may be marked by a buoy of
some description, but is more often not marked
at all.

3. Care is needed of the partly submerged western
breakwater. Stick closely to the buoyed channel
in the immediate approaches to Port Said.

4. There may be fog or perhaps industrial pollution
cutting visibility in the approaches to a mile or so.
This makes a night approach particularly difficult
as I found out in mid-October 1995.

Mooring
Yachts proceed to Port Fouad Yacht Centre. Berth
Mediterranean-style to one of the wooden jetties.
There is also a large mooring buoy in the middle of
the basin to which a line can be taken. The bottom
is mud and reasonable holding although anchors
sometimes pull through it.

Shelter Good shelter although the wash from large
ships passing through and also from the pilot
launches and bumboats create an uncomfortable
wash.

Authorities Health, harbourmaster, customs,
immigration. Suez Canal officials. Your agent will
arrange for clearance into Egypt and for the relevant
canal officials to the visit and inspect the yacht. A
charge of $8–$12 per day is made according to
LOA.

Agent Nagib Latif, Felix Agency, Al Gomhoria St,
Post Tower Building, 4th Floor Office no. 12, Port
Said ☎ (20) 66 409 401 *Fax* (20) 66 402 443. *VHF*
Ch 22

Facilities
Water Good potable water on the quay. Hot showers
in the run-down block within the Yacht Centre.
Fuel Can be arranged by the agent. A tanker can
come down to the yacht centre or smaller amounts
are brought by jerrycan.

Gas Some but not all bottles can be filled via the
agent.
Paraffin Available ashore.
Laundry Via the agent or take it to Port Said
yourself, the latter being the cheaper option.
Repairs It may be possible to haul out in an
emergency. Some mechanical and engineering
work. Hardware shops in Port Said.
Provisions Adequate shopping for basics and fresh
fruit and vegetables in Port Said.
Eating out Restaurant at the yacht centre although it
mostly does lunches. Restaurants in Port Said. The
Galab on the High Street is good value and has
alcohol.
Other PO. Banks. ATM which accepts *Visa* and
Mastercard. Taxis and mini-buses. Coaches to
Cairo. Ferry to Cyprus.
Note To get to Port Said walk out of the yacht centre
gates on the S side and a short distance down the
road you will come to the ferry quay which crosses
to Port Said. This is a free service and you just walk
on to the ferry along with several hundred other
people trying to get on.

General
Port Fouad is a dirty garbage-filled hole of a place
that is constantly noisy and disturbed by the wash of
craft rushing around. If you are making a
southbound transit you must stop here. If leaving
the canal and the weather forecast is OK it is up to
you whether or not you stop here. On the other side
of the canal Port Said is a bustling city and although
ramshackle and run-down, I quite like the place.
There are interesting shops and several reasonable
restaurants. There are usually several cruise ships in
here on a stopover for the passengers to be delivered
to the Pyramids and other sites on the Nile. If
proceeding southbound, Suez is a better place to
leave the yacht for a tour inland.

II. Southern Indian Ocean

Australia

For general information and data on weather see *Australian Cruising Guide* by Alan Lucas.

Documentation and visas

Normal boats papers and a valid passport for all crew members must be carried. Valid yellow fever vaccination certificate for every person on board if arriving from a place where yellow fever occurs. Clearance papers from last port of call.

All non-Australian nationals (except for New Zealanders) MUST HAVE A VISA BEFORE ARRIVING IN AUSTRALIA. With a valid visa you will be given 6 months stay in Australia which can usually be extended for another 6 months.

Entry formalities

All yachts must go to a port of entry when clearing in. When in Australian territorial waters and 10–15M off call up coast radio on VHF Ch 16 or 2182kHz and inform the authorities of your arrival. You will be asked for the yacht's name, arrival port, ETA, last port, number of crew on board and if any animals are on board. When you arrive anchor off

and do not go ashore. Quarantine inspection will be carried out and then immigration and customs clearance can proceed. Australian quarantine regulations are stringent and it is likely certain foodstuffs will be destroyed. No animals on board will be allowed ashore and heavy fines and the possible destruction of the animal may result from infringing regulations (which usually results from the animal going missing or being allowed ashore). Immigration and customs will want to see your last port clearance papers and will issue postcards for you to post back to them from points along your itinerary along the lines of the system used in the USA. Departure must also be from a port of entry.

All or some of these procedures apply to subsequent stops at Australian dependencies which here means Ashmore Reef, Christmas Island and Cocos Keeling.

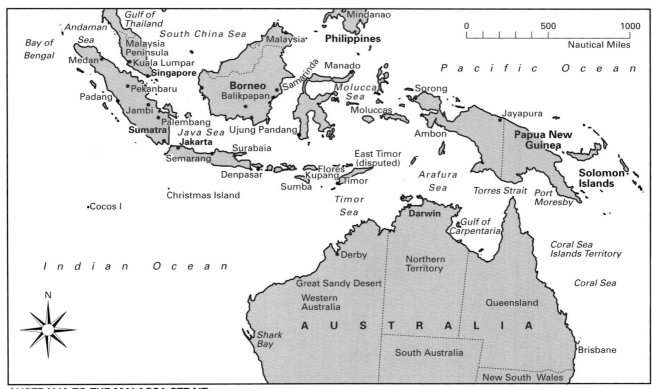

AUSTRALIA TO THE MALACCA STRAIT

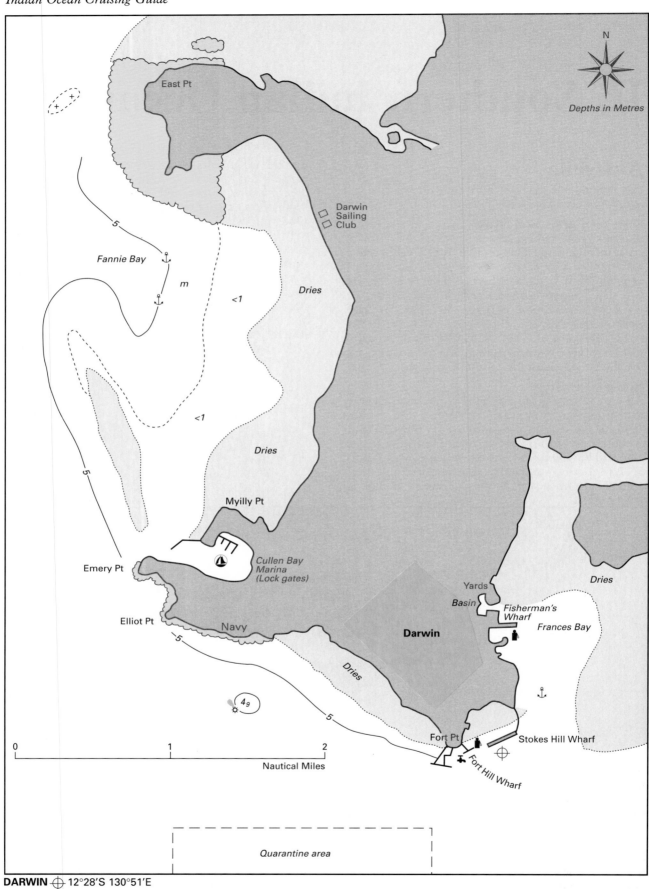

N

Depths in Metres

East Pt

Darwin
Sailing
Club

Fannie Bay

m

Dries

<1

<1

Dries

Myilly Pt

Cullen Bay
Marina
(Lock gates)

Emery Pt

Elliot Pt

Navy

Dries

Yards

Basin

Fisherman's
Wharf

Frances Bay

Dries

Darwin

4₉

Dries

5

Fort Pt

Stokes Hill Wharf

Fort Hill Wharf

0   1   2

Nautical Miles

Quarantine area

DARWIN ⊕ 12°28'S 130°51'E

Darwin

Darwin is the usual jumping off spot for yachts taking the southern Indian Ocean routes if they are not proceeding up through Indonesia to peninsular Malaysia and Thailand.

VHF Ch 16 for coast radio and port authorities. Ch 11 for Cullen Bay Marina.

Mooring

There are two main anchorages and a marina at Cullen Bay. Most yachts make for the anchorage at Fannie Bay which can be a little uncomfortable but not dangerous in the dry season.

Fannie Bay Anchor clear of the drying mudflats and beach off the Darwin Sailing Club or where convenient. The bottom is mostly mud and sand, good holding. Good shelter in the dry season (April to November) although there may be a ground swell making it uncomfortable but not untenable.

Frances Bay On the E of Darwin and more prone to a ground swell in the dry season than Fannie Bay. Anchor off the town on mud, good holding. Because it can suffer from swell it is less popular than Fannie Bay even though it is closer to town.

Cullen Bay Marina

Data Visitors berths. Max LOA 32m. Depths max 4m.

The marina is accessed via a 24 hour lock (Darwin has a 6m tidal range at springs). Call up the marina on Ch 11 for lock opening times and instructions for entering the marina. Berth where directed. Finger pontoons. Good all-round shelter.

Facilities

Darwin Sailing Club Has club facilities, a yard, and a grid for drying out. Water and fuel by jerrycan. Buses run along the waterfront to downtown Darwin.

Darwin Water and fuel at Fort Hill Wharf or Fisherman's Wharf. All repair facilities including good mechanical, electrical, electronic and engineering repairs. Sail loft. Chandlers. Large supermarkets.

Cullen Bay Marina Water and electricity at every berth. Fuel. Shower and toilet block. Yard and repair facilities. Shops and restaurants. Casino and golf course.

General

Darwin is the usual jumping off spot for the southern Indian Ocean and also for Indonesia and up to Southeast Asia. For this reason I include it here as the logical starting point for the section on the southern Indian Ocean. It is the last place before South Africa or the Mediterranean where you can source hard to find boat spares and specialist skills and also the best place to stock up with basic provisions.

For additional information on Australia see *Australian Cruising Guide* by Alan Lucas.

For information on Indonesia see *Cruising Guide to Southeast Asia Vol II* by Elaine Morgan and Stephen Davies

Ashmore Reef

East Island 12°16'S 123°4'E
West Island 12°15'S 122°56'E
Australian dependency

Located approximately 520 miles W of Darwin and 100 miles S of Roti Island off the SW end of Timor. Ashmore Reef is composed of three small sand *cays* named East, Middle and West. They rise out of the same coral reef and with hardly any vegetation except a few coconut palms (reportedly four amongst the whole group) and some scrubby bush will not be seen until close to. The reef is a maritime reserve and in the dry season has a resident ranger on board a research vessel (M.V. *Aurelia IV* in 1997). It is also the haunt of Indonesian fishing boats although it is of course illegal for them to fish in the area. There are no procedures for clearing in an out and as long as you refrain from fishing (including spearfishing) around the group then it appears OK for yachts to break their voyage here.

It is possible to anchor in several places around the group although the best protected anchorage is the one used by the research vessel on West Island. There are a lot of bombies in the approach to the anchorage in the lagoon and the best policy is to see if the rangers will come out to guide you through the pass into the lagoon. In the dry season shelter is good in the lagoon.

The coral around the reefs is magnificent and the diving first rate. Because there is no fishing around the reefs the fish are tame. There are however a lot of sea snakes.

Christmas Island

Flying Fish Cove 10°26'S 105°40'E
Australian dependency

Christmas Island lies approximately 1050M W of Ashmore Reef. It is comparatively high (around 300m/975ft) and easy to pick up from the distance. The island has two high points joined by a saddle. The only anchorage is at Flying Fish Cove under the NE end of the island. There are no dangers in the approaches and once around North East Point the gantries and settlement are obvious in Flying Fish Cove.

Flying Fish Cove

Aus *608*

Approach

Straightforward around North East Point into the bay.

By night The approaches and cove are not lit, but with radar a night approach is possible although not advised.

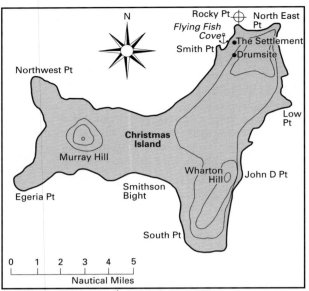

CHRISTMAS ISLAND ⊕ 10°25′S 105°41′E

VHF Ch 16 for Christmas Island Marine. You should call up to announce your arrival when 5–10 miles off.

Mooring

Tidal range 1·8m at springs.

Anchor in 6–20m where shown on the plan clear of the fringing reef. Care must also be taken to anchor clear of the chains holding the ship mooring buoys shown on the plan. The bottom is mostly coral or coral rubble and your anchor will likely snag something. It is a good idea to use a trip-line.

Shelter Reasonable shelter in the dry season (April to November) although the SE trades send some ground swell into the anchorage making it rolly. The barges charging around also produce a considerable wash being simply square water-pushers with big diesels.

Authorities Advise Christmas Island Marine on VHF Ch 16 when you have arrived. You must clear customs and immigration at the local police station ashore. No visas are needed.

Facilities

Water From local sources ashore.
Fuel Can be obtained from the barge jetty. Arrange for a tanker and then go stern-to the barge jetty with an anchor out to hold you off. When there is a big swell running this operation is best left for another day when there is less swell. Petrol by jerrycan from the settlement.
Repairs Some mechanical and hardware items available.
Provisions Most items can be found in the Settlement Trade Store including many items from Australia and also from Southeast Asia. Alcohol is duty-free.
Eating out Numerous restaurants including Chinese, Malaysian and pizza restaurants. At the yacht club fast food and drink is available on an honour basis

where you take what you want and enter it on the club ledger. Also showers and WC at the club. Remember to settle up your tab before leaving.
Other Bank. PO. Telephone and fax from the PO. Mail can be sent to Poste Restante, PO, Christmas Island, Australia 6798, Indian Ocean. Gas bottles can be filled by arrangement. Launderette. Mini-buses from the jetty to Drumsite and the lower settlement. Fortnightly flights to Singapore and Perth.

General

Christmas Island was named by Captain William Mynors of the *Royal Mary* who sighted it on the 25th December 1643. It was not actually claimed until 1888 when surveys revealed substantial phosphate deposits on the island. A company was formed and by the turn of the century phosphate was being exported. Chinese labour was imported and later augmented by Malays. These two groups now make up the major part of the population.

Today the island is administered by Australia and continues to export phosphate although the deposits are running out and the future of the island is in doubt. Ships must moor to the system of buoys in Flying Fish Cove to take on the phosphate as the ground swell makes it impossible to lie alongside for loading. The fine brown dust finds it way into everything and ashore the buildings and streets are coated with it and if the wind is in the wrong direction yachts get coated with it as well. The dust has remarkable adhesive qualities and even green water over the decks fails to shift it.

Although phosphate mining is the mainstay of the island, it mostly goes on in the south of the island and it is then taken on the single line railway to Flying Fish Cove and transferred to the ships. Most of the rest of the island is covered in rain forest and is also home to the remarkable red crab. These are large crabs, around the size of a dinner plate including the claws when fully grown, which live in burrows in the highlands. At the beginning of the wet season around November the crabs migrate down to the sea to mate. The whole of the island is covered in red crabs and the road-kill is enormous. After mating the females lay the eggs in rock pools around the coast and the crabs return to the highlands. It is a spectacular migration with the crabs just walking through and over everything in the way including houses, shops, gardens, cars, and roads as their annual biorhythm pulls them to the coast.

One of the schemes in place to replace phosphate as the main earner for the island is tourism and a casino and hotel has been built to attract gamblers here. Given the addiction to gambling in Southeast Asia this venture has proved remarkably successful with Asians flying in to the casino resort to spend large sums on the gaming tables and in 1997 the casino had a turnover of over $100 million. It's probably not a good way to renew the coffers but, if you fancy a flutter, you might get lucky.

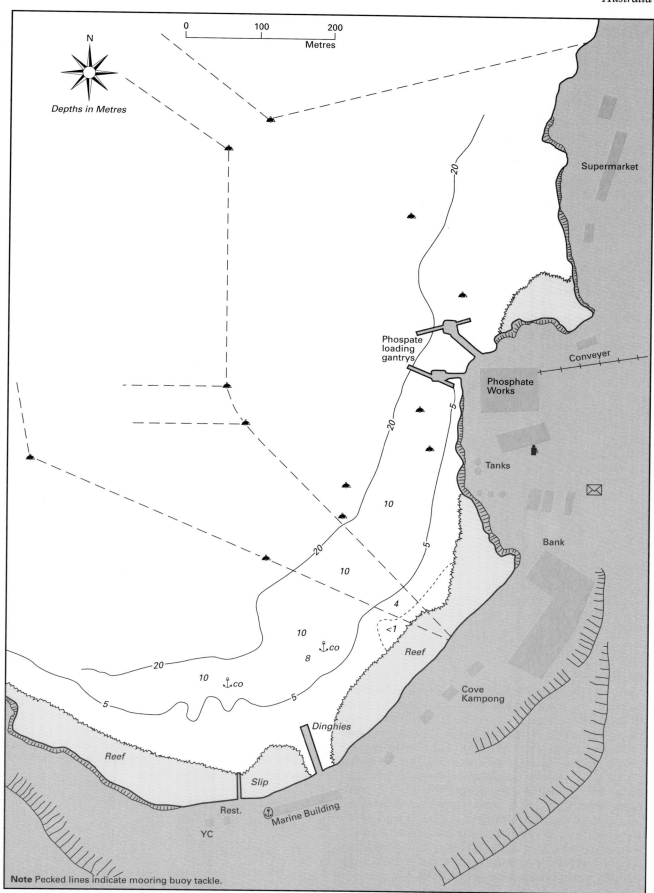

CHRISTMAS ISLAND/FLYING FISH COVE

Cocos Keeling

North Keeling 11°49'S 96°50'E
Direction Island 12°04'S 96°53'E
Australian dependency

Cocos Keeling lies approximately 530M W of Christmas Island and 600M SW of the SW extremity of Sumatra.

Cocos Keeling consists of two main island groups. North Keeling is an atoll with a continuous coral reef enclosing the lagoon and is covered in coconut palms. It is a nature reserve and all fauna and flora are protected. South Keeling consists of an atoll with a reef connecting the various main islands around the large lagoon. The main entrance to the lagoon is at the N end and most yachts make for the mini-lagoon lying under Direction Island at the northern entrance. Yachts can also go to West Island although the anchorage is exposed to the SE trades and there is little point in going here unless visiting the settlement for provisioning or communications. The islands are also covered in extensive coconut palms which will be seen from 10M off the coast. If an aircraft is landing the airport light is turned on and is reported to be visible from some 35M off the group.

Currents In general currents set NW past the islands at rates of ¾–1kt. Within the lagoon currents are tidal and generally set NW or SE. The tidal range is around 0·5m.

Weather

Prevailing winds in the Cocos Islands.

Month	Prevailing winds 0900	Prevailing winds 1500
Jan	E–SE/64%	E–SE/62%
Feb	E–SE/57%	E–SE/53%
Mar	E–SE/70%	E–SE/59%
Apr	E–SE/85%	E–SE/86%
May	E–SE/90%	E–SE/86%
Jun	E–SE/95%	E–SE/92%
Jul	E–SE/91%	E–SE/92%
Aug	E–SE/93%	E–SE/90%
Sep	E–SE/97%	E–SE/92%
Oct	E–SE/93%	E–SE/94%
Nov	E–SE/90%	E–SE/91%
Dec	E–SE/83%	E–SE/96%

History

The islands were reported by Captain William Keeling in 1609 and further explored in later decades. However they were not settled until 1826 when John Hare arrived on South Keeling. He was followed soon after by John Clunies-Ross and despite being business partners the two soon fell out. John Hare was restricted to Prison Island and soon left. Clunies-Ross imported labour from Malaya and built up a large copra plantation. The island was only declared a British dominion in 1857, although this didn't seem to phase Clunies-Ross and his family who kept on building up the plantation and in 1886 the descendants of Clunies-Ross were virtually awarded the islands by Queen Victoria.

In the First World War the cable station on

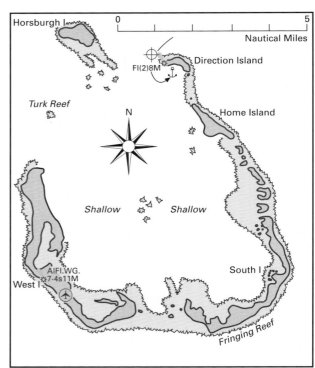

SOUTH KEELING ⊕ 12°05'S 96°52'E WGS 72

Direction Island was blown up by a party from the German cruiser *Emden*. The German ship was subsequently attacked by the Australian HMAS *Sydney* damaging the ship whereupon the German captain ran the *Emden* ashore on North Keeling. This is the historic wreck marked on chart 607.

Up to and after the Second World War administration for the island was given to various other British dependencies until it was made an Australian dependency in 1955. In 1978 the Australian government purchased the property from the Clunies-Ross' descendants except for a house and property on Home Island.

Home Island is the main settlement for the Malays left here and although administered from Australia, it is essentially self-governing at a local level.

Entry formalities

When approaching the 12M limit contact the marine officer on VHF Ch 20 to advise on your ETA. Note that the preferred channel is 20 and not 16. Vessels which arrive during the night must report at 0700 in the morning. All new arrivals must fly a yellow Q flag. Anchor off the quarantine area and await the arrival of the authorities. No person must leave the vessel or approach within 30m of another vessel until cleared in.

Direction Island

Aus 606, 607

Approach

From 8–10M off the coconut palms that grow extensively on the islands will be seen. There are no off-lying dangers until right up to the northern entrance to the lagoon between Horsburgh Island and Direction Island. At the lagoon entrance the depths come up quickly from 200–300m to 10m and less which can be a bit startling with the dramatic colour change from deep blue to turquoise. At the entrance the open lattice light tower on the W end of Direction Island will be seen. Yachts should proceed into the mini-lagoon under Direction Island, entering from the S after skirting the sand and coral bank running S from the light tower as shown on the plan. A small beacon marks the end of the shallow bank and should be left to port.

By night The W tip of Direction Island is lit Fl(2)8s8M. The light at the airport on West Island is Aero AlFl.WG.7·4s11M although it is reported the loom is visible some 35M off. The beacons marking the channel through the lagoon to West Island are lit including the leading lights, mostly Fl or Fl.R.

Although there is the light on Direction Island and the beacons marking the channel through the lagoon are lit, it would not be prudent to make a night approach, especially since most yachts will be heading into the lagoon at Direction Island where it is wise to eyeball the final approach into the anchorage.

VHF Ch 16 for the authorities on West Island. Ch 20 for customs and immigration. Ch 72 for ship to ship.

Dangers Care is needed in the final approaches to the anchorage under Direction Island and it is only prudent to have someone conning you in visually. Because the depths are relatively shallow and the water very clear it can be a little breath-taking getting in here. Depths over the sand and coral from the S are around 3·5m. Yachts drawing more than 3·5m should anchor outside the inner lagoon in Port Refuge. Often there will be other yachts in the anchorage and someone may come out to show you the channel in.

Note A yacht should not proceed to the basin at Home Island where a yacht symbol is shown on Aus 607.

Mooring

Proceed into the inner lagoon under Direction Island. Anchor off near the yellow quarantine buoy. Do not use the quarantine buoy to moor to. The bottom is mostly sand with scattered coral patches. There is also a wreck under the water with 2·5m

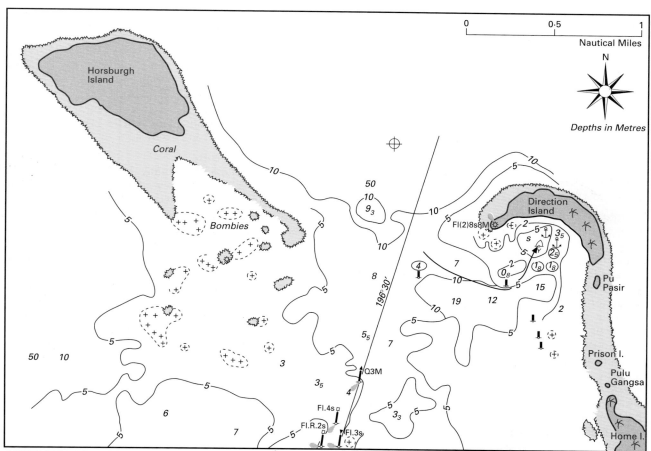

SOUTH KEELING: DIRECTION ISLAND ANCHORAGE ⊕ 12°05'S 96°52'E WGS 72

reported over it. Upon arrival do not go ashore or visit another yacht until the authorities from West Island arrive to clear you in. They can be contacted on VHF Ch 20. Once cleared in you can move closer to the beach wherever convenient, but clear of the swimming area and to the S of a line between the orange and red float buoys off the beach.

Shelter Good shelter from the SE trades.

Authorities The authorities from West Island visit the anchorage by launch on most days. Customs, immigration and quarantine officials will visit you in the anchorage and formalities are quickly completed. A visa is not necessary. South Keeling is an animal quarantine station for animals being introduced into Australia and therefore no animals are allowed ashore and any animal food or other waste must be burned off in a pit provided for that purpose on Direction Island.

Facilities

Water There is a tank on Direction Island to catch rainwater but it seldom has a lot in it. A tap on the jetty at Home Island has treated water. Toilets ashore.

Fuel At West Island settlement. It is expensive.

Repairs A slipway at Home Island although the reported max depth available is just over a metre. Limited mechanical repairs may be possible but do not depend on it. It is possible to arrange for spares to be flown in from Perth.

Provisions All provisions must be flown in and prices are accordingly high. It is much better to have done a big shop for basics at Christmas Island as prices at Cocos can be 1½ times higher than there or Australia. For large orders put your order in to the shop near the airport control tower well in advance so that items can be ordered from Perth. Cheques and credit cards cannot be used at the shop!

Eating out Barbecue facilities at Direction Island.

Other At West Island: PO. Telephone and fax facilities. Gas bottles can be filled. Resident doctor and a small hospital (call on VHF Ch 20). Ferry between Home Island and West Island. Fortnightly flights to Perth.

General

Direction Island is remembered fondly by visiting yachts. The anchorage is well protected and comfortable in the SE trades. There is an amiable camaraderie amongst the yachts here and beach parties and drinks on board are a regular feature of Direction Island life. There is a BBQ area ashore and the swimming off the yacht or the beach is excellent. In the lagoon the snorkelling is good and around the fringing reef on the weather side the fish life is prolific. Spear-fishing and cleaning fish is not allowed off the beach and swimming area (it attracts sharks) and the area off the SE corner known as the 'Rip' is a marine reserve and fishing of any kind is prohibited here.

Care should be taken to bury all rubbish in the pits provided on the island and to conform to the quarantine regulations concerning animals and animal waste. Rubbish of any sort should not be disposed of in the lagoon. There are others who will come after you and it is only right that you leave the place in the same (or better) condition that you found it.

West Island

Aus *607*

If you need to go to West Island for any reason then the buoyed channel through the lagoon can be followed to the jetty at the N end of West Island.

Approach

The channel is straightforward by day. Although the beacons are lit a night transit is not recommended.

Mooring

Anchor as close to the jetty as prudence dictates – usually in 2–3m. The bottom is weedy and reported not to be good holding. You will need to be securely anchored as the anchorage here gets the full weight of the SE trades blowing across the lagoon and a considerable chop is set up. It would be prudent to leave someone capable on board if at all possible or several cruisers can get together and make the trip on one yacht so that there is a spare body that can be left on board to keep an eye on things.

Facilities

It is around 4 miles into the settlement and it is a matter of walking it or trying to hitch a lift from any traffic between the jetty and the settlement. The facilities to be found are mentioned under Direction Island.

Chagos archipelago

Salomon Atoll off N pass 05°18'S 72°15'E
Peros Banhos Atoll off N pass 05°15'S 71°51'E
Diego Garcia off Main Pass 07°15'S 72°22'E

Current situation

The archipelago is formally British Indian Ocean Territory. This status was declared in 1965 when the Seychelles were given independence and the surrounding islands handed back to the new government with the exception of the Chagos archipelago. The group is administered by the British Navy and there is a Royal Naval Liaison Officer stationed on Diego Garcia. He in turn reports to the British High Commissioner on Mahe in the Seychelles. Diego Garcia is leased to the US Navy and US personnel are stationed on the island. DIEGO GARCIA IS OFF LIMITS TO YACHTS.

Technically a yacht must have prior permission to visit islands other than Diego Garcia, but in practice an accommodation has been reached whereby yachts may stop at the northern group (usually Salomon Atoll) to break the passage across the Indian Ocean. It must be understood that stopping here is entirely dependant on the goodwill of the authorities at Diego Garcia and yachts have no rights to stop here. In practice a yacht should not

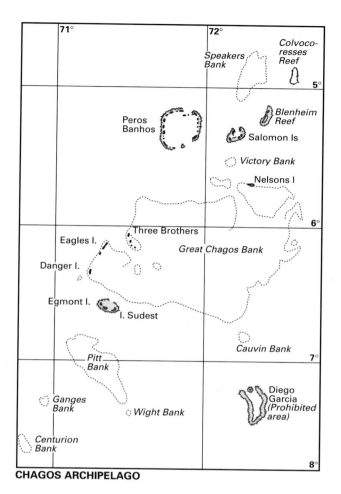

CHAGOS ARCHIPELAGO

be taken. You will then be escorted into the lagoon. A charge is made for entering and anchoring at Diego Garcia.

Data
Maritime claims Territorial 3M. Fisheries jurisdiction 12M.
Population Uninhabited except for British and US navy personnel on Diego Garcia.
Time zone UT+5

Geography and climate
The Chagos archipelago consists of six major atolls and a number of reefs and smaller isolated islands around the Chagos Bank. From N to S these are the Salomon Islands, Peros Banhos, Three Brothers, Eagle Islands, Egmont Islands and the largest island, Diego Garcia. The archipelago covers a large area which is some 177M long (between 04°44'S and 07°41'S) and 118M wide (between 70°47'E and 72°44'E). The islands are all atolls, mostly with coconut palms, and are surrounded by reefs. As with all true atolls the reefs are surrounded by deep water except in the Chagos archipelago where there are large areas of emerging reef with comparatively shallow water over them. Great Chagos Bank covers a large body of water between the northern and southern atolls with depths 10–80m and large areas which are imperfectly charted. The latest Landsat surveys suggest that the existence of some of the information shown on the charts is doubtful.

Coastal waters Within the lagoons depths are mostly considerable although there are numerous coral heads and patches of reef reducing the depths. Around the barrier reef on the drop-off depths are typically 200–300m. For the most part convenient depths to anchor in can be found in the Salomon atoll and also at Ile du Coin in Peros Banhos and in the atoll around the Egmont Islands.

The bottom is typically sand or coral. In places there are coral heads which easily snag anchor chain and it is useful to rig a trip-line. The reefs and marine life around the atolls are superb and there are few yachties who do not rave about diving and snorkelling in Chagos.

Climate The climate is equatorial and temperatures are pleasant with the SE trades blowing. During the wet season the ITCZ moves over or close to the Chagos group and rain and squalls are common.

Temperatures range from 25°–30°C throughout the year. Mean sea temperatures are 28°–29°C throughout the year.

Weather
Prevailing winds The winds are pretty much determined by the SE trades and the NW monsoon winds. However as the islands are close to the equator the SE trades are not as reliable here and can be patchy at times. However the warm water around the atolls tends to accelerate the wind over the island groups by 4–8kt so that there will generally be a little less wind away from the groups. During the NW monsoon there are often squalls and also days of calm or little wind.

stay more than one month (a more or less unspoken agreement) and should not contravene any regulations regarding the disposal of waste or destruction of the habitat. The islands are a designated conservation area and all flora and fauna are protected. Spear-fishing is technically illegal in the archipelago. In recent years there has been some blatant disregard by yachties for the environment with wholesale fishing, killing of turtles and makeshift camps ashore. Remember others come after you and your behaviour should ensure that others can enjoy the goodwill and environment you found here.

Documentation and visas
None is required although the patrol vessel of the British Navy visits on occasions, usually on a two week rota, and you may be required to submit a crew list and particulars. At times they also set up a barbecue on the beach with all yachts invited.

Diego Garcia can be entered in an emergency situation only. The Royal Navy will do their best to help in a serious emergency but the privilege should not be abused. This is not a place to go for a minor engine problem, a blown out sail or minor medical problems. Call the Royal Navy on VHF Ch 16 or 2182kHz and request permission to enter. A patrol vessel will meet you at the entrance to Main Pass and the yacht may be searched and particulars will

Gales The percentage frequency of gales in all seasons is low at <1–1%. However there are often squalls in which the wind can reach 30–40kt although they seldom last for long.

The area is not known for tropical storms although the records show that a cyclone hit the group in 1891 causing much damage. However the spin-off from a large cyclone tracking SW can cause severe winds (40–50kt) and very large seas in the group.

Tides

The tidal range around the islands is small at less than a metre, but because of the reefs and shoal water the tidal streams can be strong and have been recorded at up to 4kt in some atoll passes. In general the tidal set is less around the atolls and usually ½–1kt although the direction can vary. In most cases there is a set across or oblique to the pass direction requiring care when entering or leaving an atoll pass.

Currents

From January to April the Equatorial counter-current sets E through the group at an average rate of 1kt. From May to December the SW monsoon current sets E in the N of the group and the South Equatorial current sets W. Rates average ½–1½kt. It would be great if this generalisation applied wholesale, but it does not. Around the banks and reefs and atolls the current direction tends to be more variable and rates are also variable. When combined with the tidal streams the direction and rates vary. What this means is that a close eye should be kept on the cross-track error on the GPS and corrections made accordingly.

Across the banks there can be confused seas when a prevailing ground swell meets the currents around a bank. Across Great Chagos Bank confused seas up to 5m have been recorded when away from the bank the seas were more regular and the wave height less. On other occasions yachts have crossed the Great Chagos Bank without any apparent confused seas.

Navigation

The charts for the Chagos archipelago are acknowledged to be incomplete and many of the reported positions of reefs and banks are likely to be inaccurate. For the atolls themselves the surveys are more accurate and in general can be relied upon for detail although not for plotting GPS positions. That means that eyeball navigation is the preferred method of getting around near to and within the atolls.

Salomon Islands

Charts BA *3, 4*

Approach

The approach from the E is straightforward although a yacht should keep well clear of Blenheim Reef. There is everywhere deep water in the immediate approaches. The islands of the atoll are extensively covered in coconut palms which are visible when about 10M off. The pass into the atoll is on the NW end between Ile Anglaise and Ile de la Passe. The depths come up quickly from around 200m to 3–9m over the bar at the entrance. The deeper part of the channel is closer to Ile de la Passe with the reef extending W from the islet marked by a large coral boulder near its extremity. There are depths of around 6m through the deepest part of the pass. Once into the lagoon there are a number of coral heads with good room between them when proceeding towards the anchorage off Ile Fouquet.

Tidal streams The tidal stream is reported to set NNE–E across the entrance on a rising tide and NW–W on a falling tide. Rates are generally ½–1kt although at springs a rate of 2½kt across the bar has been recorded on a rising tide. Rates within the lagoon are negligible.

By night There are no lights and entrance should only be made by day and preferably before midday.

VHF During the SE trades there will likely be other yachts in here and contact can be made on Ch 16 or 69.

Dangers
1. The entrance over the bar is safe with the SE trades but should not be made when there are strong NW winds blowing (usually the NW monsoon is strongest in January and February).
2. Entrance through the pass and navigation within the lagoon should be of the eyeball variety.

Mooring

Yachts anchor in two places. The preferred anchorage is off Ile Fouquet. Anchor where convenient on sand and coral. The shelter here is good with the SE trades. Yachts also anchor off Ile Takamaka.

The alternative anchorage is off Ile Boddam although the approach to the anchorage needs some care as there are numerous bombies scattered around this SW end of the lagoon. Good shelter from the SE trades and also shelter from the NW monsoon in here.

A high-tide pass suitable for a dinghy exists between Boddam Island and Anglaise Island.

Authorities The patrol boat from Diego Garcia will visit from time to time. They will issue a clearance to any yachts present and charge US$55 for this service.

Facilities

None. However the atoll is popular during the SE trades and there can be substantial numbers of yachts anchored here. Yachts from South Africa

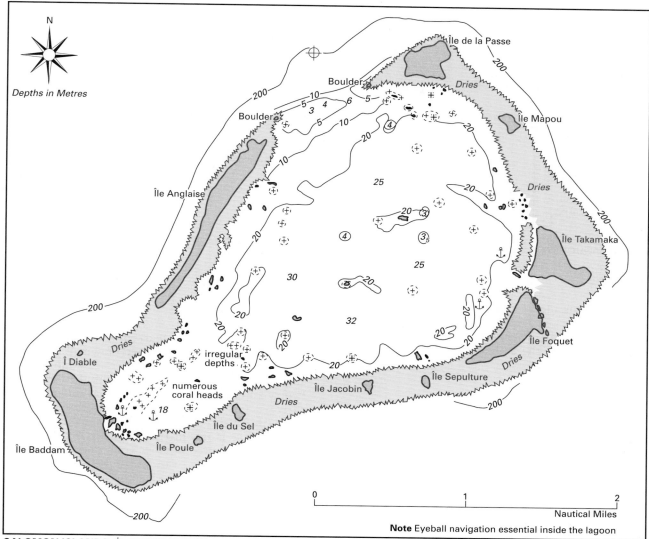

SALOMON ISLANDS ⊕ 05°18'S 72°15'E

regularly come up this way with Chagos as the turning point for the voyage. Yachts regularly connecting via the local marine net may be able to ask yachts in other places to bring spares or specialist equipment down to Chagos. Otherwise there is a good mutual support system between the various skills and resources distributed around visiting yachts.

General
Although the islands are technically uninhabited, in fact Salomon atoll has been inhabited by several unintentional castaways for some years. Pete and Tina (and Jess the cat) arrived here in their forty foot Hartley designed ferrocement yacht *Vespera* a number of years ago. While here the anchor dragged in a squall, the engine wouldn't start, and the yacht went onto the coral and was sunk in the lagoon. The other yachts here rallied around and decided the yacht could be repaired. It was eventually raised but then needed to be refitted and the engine rebuilt. This all takes time and the couple have become accepted as the involuntary castaways of Chagos.

Yachts travelling to the island have brought spares and supplies out to the couple who seem to have dropped into the castaway mode without too much of a problem. However it appears that with the yacht pretty much ready to go that the castaways may be going to leave what has been their home for a number of years.

Peros Banhos
Charts BA *3, 4*

Approach
This large atoll has passes on the N and S. From the N the usual pass is between Ile Parasol and Ile Longue. From the S the pass is between Ile Vache Marine and Coin du Mire. There are numerous coral heads in the anchorage so eyeball navigation from aloft is essential.

Tidal streams In the S pass the stream is reported to set SSE on a rising tide and NNW on a falling tide at around ½kt. In the N the stream is reported to set E on a rising tide and W on a falling tide at ½–¾kt.

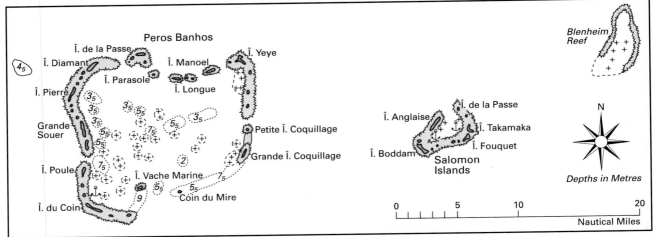

PEROS BANHOS TO BLENHEIM REEF

Mooring

Most yachts make for the anchorage off Ile du Coin which affords the best shelter from the SE trades. Anchor where convenient under the lee of the island where there are convenient depths. Shelter here is not as good as in the Salomon Islands.

Egmont Islands

Charts BA *3, 4*
Off the N pass 06°38'S 71°23'E

Approach

The islets around the atoll are covered in high coconut palms. The entrance to the lagoon is on the N side across a bar with reported depths of 2–4m. Inside the lagoon is peppered with coral heads and eyeball navigation from aloft is essential to thread your way through them.

Mooring

The anchorage under Ile Sudest is recommended as the best during the SE trades.

Seychelles

Current situation

After independence in 1976 the political history of the Seychelles has been marked by a series of coups and by the quasi-Marxist government of President Albert Rene. Rene reached power in a coup in 1977 and established single party rule with the Seychelles People's Progressive Front (SPPF) as the only legal party. A coup was attempted by mercenaries posing as South African rugby players under the direction of Mad Mike Hoare in 1982. Later in the same year the army attempted another coup and yet again in 1985 another coup was foiled. Rising discontent forced President Rene to legalise opposition parties in 1991. It has to be said that the possibility of another coup still exists although the country is at the moment stable. Despite all this the attempted coups have had little effect on yachts visiting here. One yacht that was here during the 1982 coup hardly knew anything was going on. In recent years things seem to have settled down somewhat and despite the apparent instability of the country in the past, there appear to be few problems for visiting yachts and the number of charter yachts based in the Seychelles has increased dramatically in the last few years.

Crime in the islands has been a problem in years past and it is recommended you stow all loose yacht gear below. Personal crime is relatively low and it is only boat bits left lying around that the locals are after.

Documentation and visas

Normal ship's papers and a valid passport for all crew members must be carried. Proof of cholera vaccination is required if arriving from Africa. You will need at least a dozen crew lists for the various departments.

Most foreign nationals do not need a visa and on arrival crew will be issued a visitors permit for two weeks. This can be extended up to 3 months although the process is a little tricky in that application must be made one week before the old permit expires.

Entry formalities

All yachts must enter and leave the Seychelles at Victoria on Mahe which is the only port of entry and exit. When 10–12M off call up port control on VHF Ch 16 or 2182kHz and advise them of your intended arrival. Yachts must fly a Q flag and on arrival anchor off where indicated by the port authority (usually E of Victoria lighthouse) until entry formalities have been carried out. Yachts must not proceed into the harbour unless advised to do so by the port authorities. Customs, immigration and health officials will come out to the yacht and complete the necessary paperwork. The quarantine officer will arrange for the yacht to be fumigated which is mandatory for all new arrivals. Once the paperwork and fumigation has been carried out a yacht will be directed to berth in the harbour, usually at Victoria Yacht Club. Within 24 hours (except weekends) the captain must report to the port office and complete an arrival form and hand over the ships papers which are kept until departure. All fees due must be paid here. In the past yacht fees were exceptionally high and in the early 1990s attempts were made to charge yachts $US100 per day. The charge for clearance and fumigation was around $US75 in 1997 and harbour taxes have been rationalised as follows.

Charges are *per day* and in $US at the 1997 rate.

Stays of < 5 days:		$18 for 0–20 tons GRT
		$31 for 20–100 tons GRT
Stays of 5-10 days:		$15 for 0–20 tons GRT
		$25 for 20–100 tons GRT
Stays of 10 > days:		$12·50 for 0–20 tons GRT
		$19 for 20–100 tons GRT.

These taxes apply for all anchorages around the Seychelles and must be paid before you can redeem the ship's papers from the port office at Victoria.

On some islands a visitors fee is also charged which is usually somewhere between $15–$25.

For all procedures it pays to keep a sheaf of crew lists handy.

On departure from the Seychelles application must be made to immigration two working days before the departure date. One day before departure port and customs clearance must be obtained.

If departing to visit other islands then port clearance must be obtained. Before departing port control must be advised on Ch 16 and a security clearance may be required. At the other islands clearance must be obtained from the local police or the island manager and the clearance form signed. This form must be returned to the port office within 24 hours of arriving back in Victoria.

If this all sounds like a bureaucratic nightmare – it is. But it is generally carried out in a friendly fashion although some patience is needed.

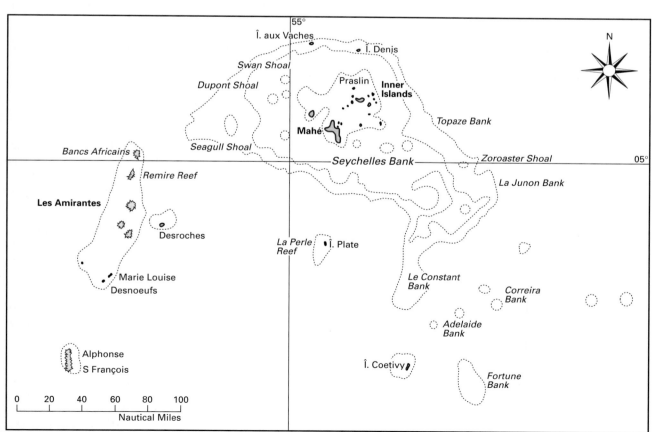

SEYCHELLES BANK & LES AMIRANTES

Data

Area 455km² (176M²)
Coastline 491km (265M)
Maritime claims Territorial 12M. Exclusive economic zone 200M.
Population 71,000
Capital Victoria
Time zone UT+4
Language English and French are the official languages. Creole.
Religion Roman Catholic 90%.
Public holidays
  Jan 1 New Year
  May 1 Labour Day
  Jun 5 Liberation Day
  Jun 18 National Day
  Jun 29 Independence Day
  Aug 15 Assumption Day
  Nov 1 All Saints Day
  Dec 8 Immaculate Conception
  Dec 25 Christmas
Government Democratic Republic (since 1991)
Crime Low levels of all crime.

Travel

Internal

There are ferries and internal flights between the major islands. Buses and taxis around Mahe. Water taxis. Hire cars.

International

To and from Mahe there are regular flights to many European destinations and to some African and Indian Ocean destinations.

Practicalities

Mail Reliable. Mail can be sent Poste Restante to Central Post Office, Independence Avenue, Victoria, Mahe, Seychelles.

Telecommunications IDD system. Country code 248. GSM phones are reported to work here if your supplier has an arrangement in the Seychelles.
Telephone and fax from Victoria at Cable & Wireless. Calls from hotels are very expensive.

Currency The unit is the Seychelles Rupee commonly abbreviated to 'R'. The currency is reasonably stable. No more than R100 can be exported.

Banks and exchange Banks in Victoria will exchange hard currency and travellers cheques. Cash advances on major credit cards are possible. Most of the hotels, up-market restaurants and many shops accept credit cards.

Medical care There is a hospital in Victoria but for major illness head for Europe or South Africa. The water is generally potable. On the coral atolls there are no natural water supplies and rainwater is the only source.

Electricity 240V 50Hz.

Useful books

East African Handbook Ed Michael Hodd. Footprint Handbooks. Includes a short section on the Seychelles.
Forgotten Eden A Thomas. Longman.

Underwater Seychelles Penny Verhoef.
There are a number of books on the fauna and flora and marine life produced locally.

Geography and climate

The coast The Seychelles are made up of two very different groups of islands. The northern islands called the Inner Islands are granite and generally high in aspect up to around 900m (2925ft). They are not volcanic but seem to have originated from an upthrust of the earth's crust some 650 million years ago. Over time fringing reefs have developed around the islands. The slopes of the high islands are generally covered in thick jungle and the Seychelles are home to a rich variety of flora and fauna, some of it unique including the well known *coco de mer*. The smaller islands in the north and the southern islands, called the Outer Islands, are typical coral atolls and as such low with a barrier reef and a lagoon. Most of the atolls have high coconut palms on them.

Coastal waters The Inner Islands sit on the Seychelles Bank which extends for a considerable distance around the group. This bank comes up quickly from considerable depths to a rim of shoal water around the edge of the bank which in places is only 10–20m deep. Once over the rim there are deeper depths inside although the rim is quite wide in places and there are also large areas of shoal water inside the outer rim. There are a few deep passages through the outer rim.

The Amirantes Group in the Outer Islands also sit on a bank whereas the other Outer Islands (Alphonse Group, Farquhar Group and the Aldabra Group) are more like other atoll groups with considerable depths a short distance off the barrier reef.

Those island groups sitting on a bank can have confused and large seas piling up on them. This is especially true of the E and S sides of the Seychelles Bank where the prevailing swell set up by the SE trades can give rise to disturbed seas. Once inside and up to the Inner Islands the seas are mostly calm and of little consequence. It also means that over the shallower parts of the bank amongst the Inner Islands that depths are convenient for anchoring in compared to some of the atoll groups such as the Maldives.

The Outer Islands are of a more typical atoll nature and depths come up quickly to the barrier reef and once inside the atoll depths can again be considerable for anchoring in.

The bottom is typically sand or coral. In many places there will be coral heads which easily snag anchor chain and it is prudent to rig a trip-line. The reefs have superb marine life over them and the diving is world class.

Climate The climate is equatorial with little variation in air and sea temperatures between the seasons. The dry season is June to November and the wet season December to May, but around the high islands there will also be rain showers in the

At Victoria	Av max °C	Av min °C	Relative humidity	Days 2·5mm rain
Jan	28	24	78%	15
Feb	29	25	76%	10
Mar	29	25	74%	11
Apr	30	25	74%	10
May	29	25	74%	9
Jun	28	25	75%	9
Jul	27	24	76%	8
Aug	27	24	76%	7
Sep	28	24	75%	8
Oct	28	24	75%	9
Nov	29	24	75%	12
Dec	28	24	78%	15

afternoon during the dry season.

Temperatures are generally 24°–31°C and sea temperatures 28°–29°C.

Weather

Prevailing winds near the coast Winds over the Inner Islands are mostly determined by the SE trades and the NW monsoon (the NE monsoon in the northern hemisphere curving around in the southern hemisphere).

During the SE trades from April to November the winds are generally from the SE and sometimes the E blowing at around 10–25kt. The winds are strongest in July to September when they will regularly blow at 15–25kt. At times E winds blow as a result of the diurnal heating and cooling of the land. Typical trade wind clouds form over the islands when the trades are blowing.

The NW monsoon runs from December to March during which NW–W winds prevail but are most consistent from January to the beginning of March. There is a noticeable diurnal effect with NW winds strongest at dawn and in the early morning and less strong in the afternoon. There are often associated squalls with NW winds and rain can be expected when distant islands take on a blue aspect.

In the change-over period between the SE trades and the NW monsoon there will often be variable winds although the general tendency to SE or NW prevails.

Month	Prevailing winds 1000	Prevailing winds 1600
Jan	NW–W/40%	NW–W/60%
Feb	NW–NE/55%	NW/NE/55%
Mar	NW–NE/55%	NW–W/55%
Apr	NE–E/40%	NW–E/35%
May	SE–E/65%	SE–E/60%
Jun	SE–E/70%	SE–E/45%
Jul	SE–E/80%	S–SE–E/80%
Aug	SE–E/75%	SE–E/75%
Sep	SE–E/75%	SE–E/70%
Oct	SE–E/60%	S–SE–E/75%
Nov	SE–E/35%	SE–E/25%
Dec	NW/30%	NW–W/50%

Note Figures are for Victoria. Other winds or calms make up the remaining frequency.

Gales The incidence of gales varies over the group. For the Inner Islands it is generally low with <1% during most of the year except for July to September when the incidence is 1–2%.

For the groups further S the incidence is 1–2% except around Farquhar Group where the incidence is 5% in the April to September period.

Squalls associated with thunderstorms pass through and wind speeds can exceed 40kt for short periods although generally less. One piece of local lore states that if the islands look bluish in the distance then rain and associated squalls may occur.

The Inner Islands lying near to the equator are not subject to cyclones although heavy swell from cyclones passing to the S of the group can make things unpleasant. The Outer Islands are in the track of cyclones although most swing S and miss the islands.

Tides

Around the Inner Islands the tidal range at springs hovers around 1m (0·9–1·1m). Around the Amirante Group the range at springs can be higher in places up to 1·4m. Despite the small range, tidal streams over the comparatively shallow waters of the Seychelles Bank can be strong and in places have been recorded at up to 4½kt. Mostly the rates are less at around 1–2kt, but care is needed especially where currents augment or deflect the tidal stream.

Currents

From December to April the Equatorial Counter-current sets E over the Seychelles Bank. The rate is highest in December and April at the beginning and end when it is reported to run at 1½–2kt. In the other months it runs at around 1kt. In May to June the South Equatorial Current moves northwards and sets E in the N, and W in the S. By July it extends over the whole Seychelles Bank and sets W until September. In October it moves S again until by December the Equatorial Counter-current setting E again dominates.

This all occurs around the Seychelles Bank, but over the bank itself the currents are deflected by the marine topography and by tidal streams. There is often an onshore set towards islands and reefs, the 'reef-sucking' current again.

Because the bank is shallow in places there can be overfalls and confused water where the current is squeezed by land or reefs and where it opposes the prevailing swell or a tidal stream. Currents around reef passes can be considerable and care is needed.

Navigation

Much of the Seychelles Bank and the Outer Islands are not well charted and care is needed plotting GPS positions. All navigation near to and within the atolls must be first and foremost of the eyeball variety backed up by prudent use of the GPS and any other aids to navigation.

Harbours and anchorages

All anchorages in the Seychelles can be visited with the exception of the following which are prohibited for security reasons or because they are protected reserves.

Yachts cannot anchor at Police Base on Mahe, Anse Barbaron, and the Cocos Islands. For islands 60 miles from Mahe permission is needed from the IDC in Victoria, for islands 240 miles from Mahe permission is needed from the IDL in Victoria, and for the Aldabra group permission is needed from the Seychelles Islands Foundation in Victoria.

Around many of the islands there are moorings and these must be used rather than anchoring so that damage to coral is avoided.

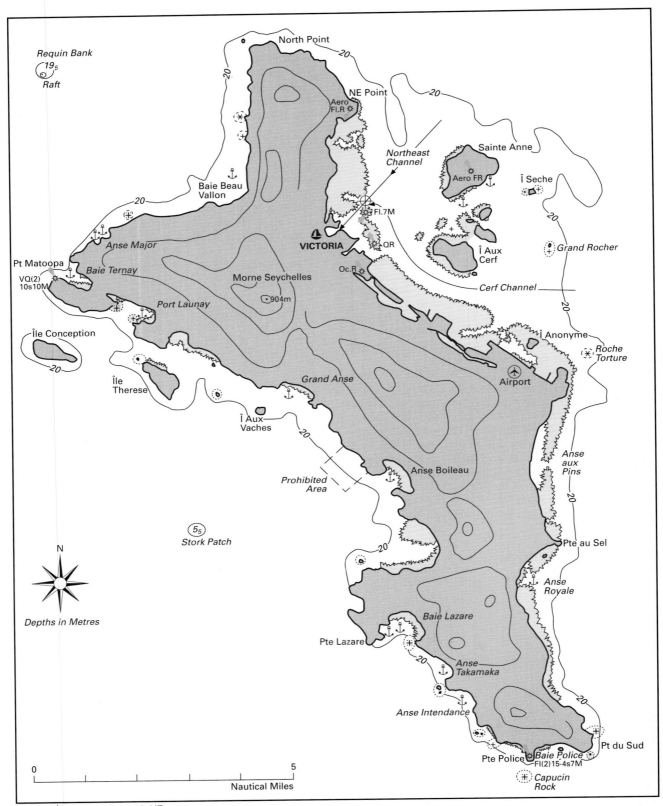

MAHE ⊕ 04°37·1'S 55°28·2'E

For additional details on anchorages around the Seychelles see *Les Iles Seychelles* (in French and English) by Alain Rondeau in the Pilote Cotier series.

Port Victoria

Charts BA *722*

Approach

For a first time entry into Port Victoria the NE Channel between Sainte Anne and the N end of Mahe should be used. The channel is deep and clear of dangers although care is needed in the final

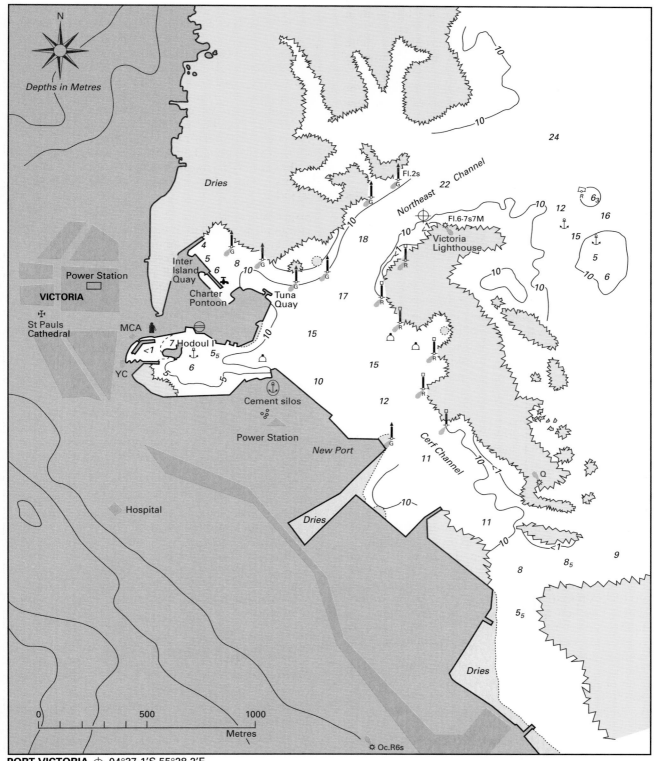

PORT VICTORIA ⊕ 04°37·1'S 55°28·2'E

approaches through the fringing reef. The Cerf channel can be used on subsequent occasions once familiar with the approach.

Conspicuous The high hills of Mahe and the high granite outlines of Ste-Anne and Ile au Cerf can be seen from some distance off. Victoria sits in a valley between the hills N and S of it. The buildings of Victoria are easily identified when making the approach through the NE Channel. The reef is only exposed at low tide so care is needed in the final approach although the white tower of Victoria light at the entrance to the reef is conspicuous. The beacons marking the pass through the reef show up well.

By night Although the approach is lit it is not recommended for a first time approach. On Ste-Anne there is an Aero F.R and on NE Point an Aero Fl.R. Victoria light (reef entrance) Fl.6·7s12m7M. Ldg Lts 210° *Front* Q *Rear* Oc.R.6s.

VHF Ch 16 for port authorities. Yachts should call up when 10–12M off.

Dangers Care is needed of the fringing reef in the final approach.

Note With care Cerf Channel is easily negotiated by day although it is wise to make the first approach through the NE channel.

Mooring

Visiting yachts normally anchor off in the old port on the E side of Ile Houdoul. It may be possible to get a berth on the yacht club pontoon which has 2–2·5m depths on the outer N side. Charter yachts use the pontoon at the Inter-island quay. The bottom in the old port is mud and good holding.

Shelter Good shelter in the old port although strong SE trades can produce a bit of slop when the reef is below water – bothersome rather than dangerous.

Authorities Harbourmaster, customs, health and immigration are all nearby. The port office is on the SE side of the old harbour/N end of the new harbour.

Facilities

Water Can be obtained ashore at the Marine Charter Association. To fill up tanks it may be possible to ask at the charter pontoon off the Inter-island quay where there is a tap on the pontoon.

Fuel There is a fuel dock on the Marine Charter pontoon, but depths are 1m or less at low tide. Enquire about depths before going onto here to pick up fuel. Alternatively there is a petrol station in town where you can fill jerrycans. For large amounts a tanker can be arranged and you will have to negotiate a berth on the Inter-island quay or in the commercial harbour.

Gas Gas bottles can be filled. Enquire at the yacht club or the Marine Charter Association.

Note It is wise to stock up on water, fuel and gas here as facilities are few and far between around the islands.

Repairs A yard at the SE end of the Cerf Channel and at the NW end of the airport can haul yachts up to 40 tons on a slipway. Enquire in advance about the passage through the reef to the yard. Mechanical, engineering, GRP and wood repairs can be carried out. In Victoria some electrical and electronic repairs are possible, limited sail repairs can be made at the yacht club, refrigeration repairs, and there are several chandlers around town.

Provisions Good shopping for all provisions in Victoria. Good *boulangeries*. There is a market everyday in town although it is best to get there early in the morning for the best produce and freshest fish.

Eating out Numerous restaurants ranging from Seychellois cuisine which is Creole style and features on seafood, chicken and pork to more 'international' cuisine which will be easily recognised and will cost more and not taste as good as local dishes. The yacht club has a restaurant and bar and is a popular meeting place.

Other PO. Banks. Laundry. Telephone and fax at Cable and Wireless. Buses and mini-buses to main towns around Mahe. Ferries to the other major islands.

General

Although around half of the inhabitants of Mahe live in Victoria, (and that amounts to near enough half the inhabitants of the Seychelles except for 10,000 or so), it is still a small place. Nonetheless good yacht facilities can be found here although at a price. It is not a cheap place to buy boating bits or any imported items for that matter. It is a convivial friendly place and the spell of Seychellois life can soon capture you and keep you here. The Seychelles were thought to be the original Garden of Eden when they were first discovered and although Seychellois life includes a few of the best of the Devil's ingredients, the islands and life here still have something of that mythic quality to them.

The French influence is much in evidence from the language to *baguettes* and *croissants* in the bakeries. The islands were also home to a number of French pirates in the early 18th century including Olivier Le Vasseur nicknamed the 'Buzzard'. He was finally caught and executed in Réunion although just before his death he threw a scrap of paper to the crowd which allegedly contained details of where his treasure was buried. A spot at Bel Ombre on Mahe is thought to be where the Buzzard's horde is buried and an Englishman, Reginald Cruise-Wilkins, bought the site and spent 40 years searching for the treasure – only to find a few coins.

Anchorages around Mahe

Sainte Anne Anchor off the SW tip on the W side. Suitable with NW monsoon.

Baie Beau Vallon Suitable with SE trades. Rolly. **Hotels and restaurants ashore.**

Anse Major Suitable with SE trades. Good holding on sand.

Baie Ternay Suitable with SE trades. National park. Mooring buoys. Anchoring prohibited. Gusts.

Port Launay Suitable with SE trades. National Park. Mooring buoys.

Grand Anse Calm weather. Rolly.

Anse Boileau Calm weather. Rolly.

Baie Lazaire Suitable with NW monsoon. Good holding on sand. Hotel.

Anse Takamaka Calm weather. Rolly.

Anse Intendance Calm weather. Rolly.

Baie Police Suitable with light NW monsoon. Poor holding.

Anse Royale NW monsoon. Passage through coral and anchorage in passage.

Praslin and La Digue

These islands lie just over 20 miles from Victoria and are the most popular destination for yachts. The *coco de mer* with its curious sensuous seed pod grows on Praslin, though the plant and its seed is now protected because of the numbers spirited away as curios.

Praslin

Baie Ste Anne Suitable in NW monsoon and light SE trades. Eyeball navigation necessary through the reef. Popular with tripper boats.

Grand Anse Suitable in NW monsoon. Difficult access and restricted depths through the coral.

Baie Chevalier Suitable in SE trades. Sandy bottom.

Anse Possession Suitable in light SE trades.

Anse Volbert Suitable in light NW monsoon. Hotels and restaurants ashore.

Ile Curieuse Bay on the SE suitable in NW monsoon. National park. Mooring buoys.

La Digue

La Passe Suitable in SE trades. Coral passage. Limited room to anchor under the mole. Restaurants.

Grand Anse Suitable in NW monsoon. Rolly.

Anse Cocos Suitable in NW monsoon. Rolly.

For detailed pilotage of these and other anchorages including the Outer Islands see *Les Iles Seychelles* by Alain Rondeau.

La Passe on La Digue island   *Seychelles Tourist Office*

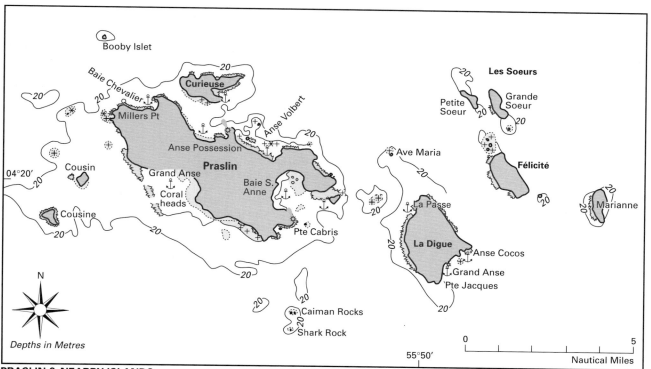

PRASLIN & NEARBY ISLANDS

219

Rodrigues

Rodrigues is a relatively high island (around 400m/1300ft) lying some 330M E of Mauritius. It is surrounded by coral reefs with the main harbour of Port Mathurin on the NW coast. It is not commonly visited by yachts, but those that do call here have been warmly received and speak well of the island. It is administered from Mauritius along with the Algalega Islands a long way to the N and Cargados Carajos Reef somewhat closer to Mauritius.

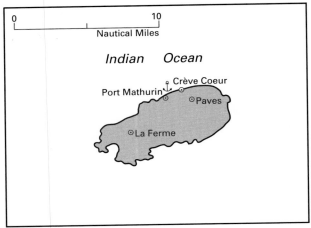

RODRIGUES I

Port Mathurin

19°41'S 63°25'E
Charts BA *715*

Port Mathurin is approached via either Western or Eastern Pass with Western Pass the recommended one. It should not be approached at night. Call port control on VHF Ch 16 or 2182kHz. The Western Pass is reported to be buoyed and to have a least depth of 9m.

Once up to the port you will be cleared in although clearance applies only to Rodrigues and not to Mauritius as well.

Mauritius

Current situation

Mauritius is possibly one of the most stable countries in the Indian Ocean. After independence was gained from Britain in 1968 its politics have been relatively clean and it has functioned as a multi-party democracy based on the Westminster model. There have been a few scandals, but no more than have affected European or American politicians. Its economy has also thrived through the hard work of the inhabitants and efficient government. The only recent blot on this paradise has been riots in 1999 after the arrest of a local reggae-style singer.

Documentation and visas

Normal ships papers and passports for all crew. No visa is required and anyone on a visiting yacht in transit will not require a visa as long as they depart with the yacht. For others a 3 month visa is granted on arrival.

Entry formalities

A yacht should go first to Port Louis to clear in. When 12M off call up port control on VHF Ch 16. The port office keeps a 24 hour listening watch. When up to the harbour call port control to advise on your arrival and request permission to enter harbour. You will be directed on where to berth and port control will also call customs and immigration to clear you in. There are strict quarantine laws and all animals on board will be confined to the boat and are not allowed ashore.

When clearing out yachts must normally return to Port Louis. You will need to purchase a clearing out form and stamps from the post office to go on the form. In some cases yachts have been allowed to clear out of Grand Baie.

Yachts are normally allowed to remain for three months although this appears to be flexible. After some period the yacht will be deemed liable to import tax.

Data

Area 1850km^2 (714M^2)
Coastline 177km (96M)
Maritime claims Territorial 12M. Exclusive economic
  zone 200M.
Population 1,120,000
Capital Port Louis
Time zone UT+4
Language English is the official language but French
  and Creole are widely spoken.
Religion Hindu 52%. Roman Catholic 26%. Muslim
  16·5%.
Public holidays
  Jan 1, 2 New Year
  Mar 12 Independence Day
  May 1 Labour Day
  Nov 1 All Saints Day
  Dec 25 Christmas

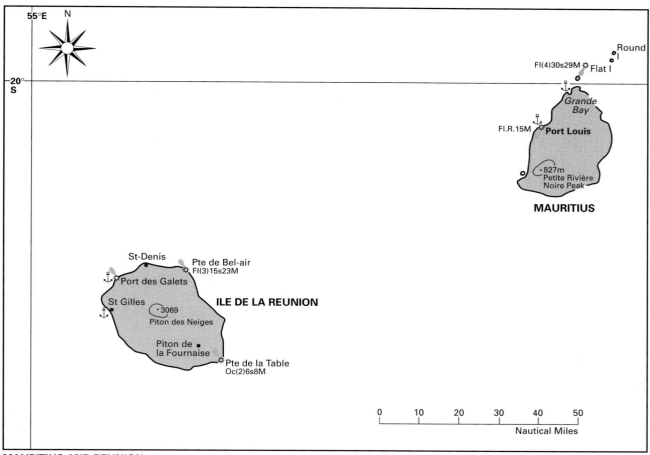

MAURITIUS AND REUNION

Moveable
    Id El Fitr (Ramadan)
    Jan/Feb Chinese New Year
    Jan/Feb Cavadee (Hindu Tamil festival includes body
    piercing)
    Mar/Apr Ougadi (Telegu New Year)
    Aug/Sep Gunesh Chaturthi (Tamil)
    Oct/Nov Diwali (Hindu Festival of Light)
Government Parliamentary Democracy
Crime Low levels of all crime.

Travel
Internal
There are bus services to most places although services finish early, usually 1700 for out of town services. Taxis are common although agree a price in advance. Taxi trains are share taxis operating along a more or less fixed route. Hire cars and motorcycles.

International
There are flights from most East African countries, from India, and from most European countries.

Practicalities
Mail Is generally reliable. Mail can be sent Poste Restante to Port Louis and there is also an *American Express* office here.

Telecommunications IDD system. Country code 230.

Telephone and fax calls from the OTS office in Port Louis. Calls from hotels can be very expensive, up to 3 times the going rate.

Currency The unit is the Mauritius Rupee (MUR) divided into 100 cents. The currency is stable.

Banks and exchange Banks will exchange hard currency and travellers cheques. Cash advances on major credit cards (*Visa* and *Mastercard*). Banks are open 0930–1430 Mon-Fri and 0930–1130 Sat. Many of the shops and restaurants take credit and charge cards.

Medical care Good medical care is available although for major problems head for Europe or South Africa. The water is potable. Not a malarial area.

Electricity 230V 50Hz

Useful books
East Africa Handbook Ed. Michael Hodd. Footprint
    Guides. Has a short section on Mauritius.
Guide to Mauritius R Ellis. Brandt.
*Mauritius, Réunion & Seychelles – a travel survival
    kit.* Lonely Planet.

Geography and climate
The coast Mauritius is a high precipitous island of volcanic formation. The highest peaks are in the vicinity of 800m (2600ft) and in most places it drops steeply to the coast. The lower slopes are cultivated

in sugar cane and sugar remains the principal export of the island.

Coastal waters The island is fringed by coral reefs although because the coast drops off quickly to considerable depths there are few real lagoons or reef protected anchorages. Most of the coral forms a shallow bank not far off the coast proper. There are few natural anchorages although the estuarine flats of some of the rivers provide natural shelter.

The bottom is mostly sand or mud with a few coral heads in places.

Climate The climate is tropical, although lying a fair way S, the winter and summer temperatures do differ. In winter (May to October) coastal temperatures are around 22–25°C by day and 16-20°C by night. In summer (November to April) coastal temperatures are around 27–30°C by day and 20–24°C by night. Rainfall is spread pretty much throughout the year although summer usually has the highest rainfall.

Weather
Prevailing winds near the coast Although Mauritius lies in the SE trades, the high island significantly affects wind strength and direction around its coast. The wind hitting the island will flow N or S around it from the SE corner and also gusts down through valleys. On the W coast of the island there are places where there will be little wind and others where the wind is deflected to greater strength. There is also a thermal component with the development of land and sea breezes which affects the constant SE trades. In general winds will be easterly, although depending on the location, they can blow from NE to SE. Wind speeds are generally 10–20kt, although in places there will be gusts and in others near calms.

Month	Prevailing at 0600	Prevailing at 1200
Jan	E–SE/60%	E–NE/65%
Feb	E–SE/60%	E–NE/65%
Mar	E–SE/70%	SE–E–NE/80%
Apri	E–SE/75%	E–SE/70%
May	E–SE/75%	E–SE/80%
Jun	E–SE/80%	E–SE/85%
Jul	E–SE/85%	E–SE/90%
Aug	E–SE/85%	E–SE/85%
Sep	E–SE/75%	E–SE/85%
Oct	E–SE/65%	E–SE/70%
Nov	E–SE/65%	E–NE/70%
Dec	E–SE/65%	E–NE/70%

Note Figures are for Pamplemousses which is inland from Port Louis. Other winds or calms make up the remaining frequency.

Gales There are significantly more gales this far S of the equator than there are closer to the equator. In general the gale frequency is around 5% through the year although this may rise to 8–10% in July to September. At times the SE trades may get up to 30kt or so in the seas around Mauritius, although this will be for a day or so only.

Thunderstorms with associated squalls and wind speeds of 30–40kt occur locally although these usually only last a matter of hours. They are most common from December to March.

Mauritius is within the area of the southern Indian Ocean affected by tropical storms and cyclones occur from November to April, although the most likely months are December to March. The frequency of cyclones is high with a probability of 11–20 in a 20 year period. Mauritius lies within the zone where cyclones in the southern Indian Ocean tend to start curving to the S from the original W–SW path. There are no hurricane holes known in the island and cruising yachts will normally try to leave the area before the cyclone season.

Tides
The tidal range around the island is generally fairly small at 0·3m at springs. Around the coast the tidal streams are not strong, but in some places where the water shallows in an entrance tidal streams can be stronger, although rarely more than 1½kt.

Currents
Mauritius lies within the South Equatorial Current setting W–SW at around 1kt. Around the coast the current is deflected, but usually in a straightforward fashion as there are few narrow channels and banks.

Navigation
Mauritius is reasonably well charted although care is needed with the use of GPS co-ordinates. Entry to Port St Louis and Grande Baie should be made using eyeball navigation to confirm position and dangers. Care is needed around the coast because the depths come up quickly to the coral fringing reef.

Port Louis
Charts BA *713*

Approach
Port Louis is situated on the W coast and the approach is straightforward with good depths in the immediate approaches. Close in Fort George, silos in the harbour and the buildings of Port Louis will be seen.

By night With care a night approach can be made. Use the leading lights on 127°30' *Front* Fl.R.2s10M *Rear* Fl.R.3s15M. Mer Rouge Al.Iso.WR.8s10M. Entrance buoys Q.G/Q.R.

VHF Ch 16 for port control 24/24.

Dangers There can be a considerable swell in the approaches although the entrance is safe except in exceptional weather.

Mooring
Proceed to the NE basin and berth where directed.
Shelter Good shelter.
Authorities Immigration, customs and health are all nearby. Do not go ashore until cleared in.

Facilities
Water In the NE basin.
Fuel In the NE basin or by jerry can from town.

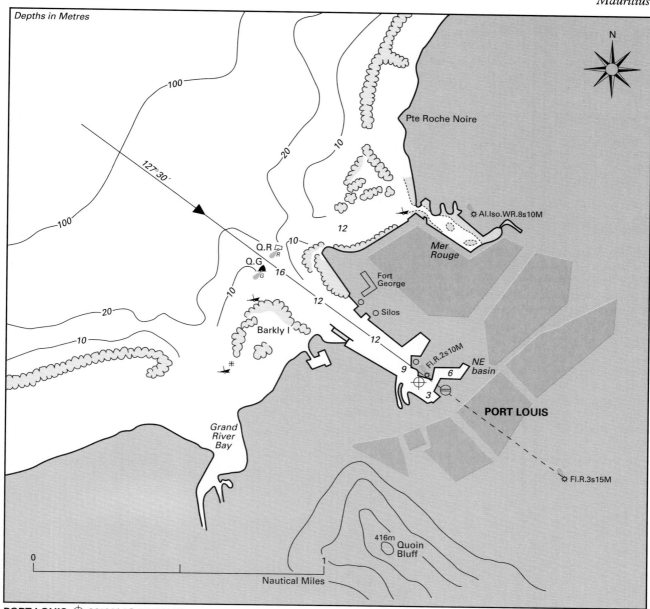

Depths in Metres

Pte Roche Noire

Al.Iso.WR.8s10M

Mer Rouge

Fort George

Silos

Barkly I

Fl.R.2s10M

NE basin

PORT LOUIS

Grand River Bay

Fl.R.3s15M

416m
Quoin Bluff

0   1   Nautical Miles

PORT LOUIS ⊕ 20°09´.3S 57°29´.5E

Gas Most gas bottles can be refilled.

Repairs Mechanical and engineering repairs. Hardware shops.

Provisions Good shopping for all provisions in Port Louis. Several large supermarkets.

Eating out Numerous restaurants nearby, many with good seafood cooked Creole style and Indian food. You can also get 'international' cuisine, some of it very good.

Other PO. Banks. Hospital. Buses and taxis.

General

Port Louis is the bustling capital of Mauritius with a population of around 150,000. The general affluence of Mauritius is reflected here in the range of shops offering luxury goods at not inconsiderable prices. Port Louis was established as the capital by the French in 1735 and its French and later English

antecedents can be seen everywhere from the architecture to the cuisine and general culture.

Mauritius has two claims to fame that most people know of, one concerning an extinction and the other a rarity.

The dodo was endemic to Mauritius and Réunion until visiting sailors and early settlers decided it was an easy source of food. The bird weighed around 20kg, couldn't fly, and looked and tasted much like pigeon. To make matters worse it laid only a single egg on a grass nest and consequently the eggs were easy prey to humans and introduced species like pigs and dogs. No dodos have been seen since the Dutch left in 1710.

The rarity is the Mauritian penny red stamp of which a thousand were mistakenly printed with 'post office' instead of 'post paid' in 1847. Around 15 penny-reds survive worth around US$200,000 each should you discover one lying about.

Grand Baie

This large bay on the NW of the island is where most yachts make for. It is a tourist area with numerous hotels and restaurants around the beach. There is reported to be a yacht club of sorts here.

Réunion

Current situation

Réunion is a stable dependency of France (Territoire Outre-Mer) with a Prefect appointed by the French government in overall control and a local council which decides on local matters. In all respects it is a safe place to be.

Documentation and visas

Normal ships papers and passports for all crew. No visa is required if you are from an EU country. Most other countries do not require visas except for Australians. A visa can be easily obtained in Mauritius, but in other nearby countries it can take some time. EU and most other nationals get 3 months on arrival. A yacht can be used for 6 months out of any 12 months here as in France itself. If a yacht is laid up ashore and the owner leaves Réunion this time does not count as part of the 6 month period allowed.

Entry formalities

A yacht must go to Port de la Pointe-des-Galets to clear in. When 12M off call up the *capitanerie* on VHF Ch 16, usually changing to Ch 12. You will be directed to a berth and must wait for immigration and customs to arrive. Animals on board will need a rabies certificate or they will not be allowed ashore.

Yachts can remain in Réunion for 6 months out of 12 months. If you need to stay longer it is best to go to Mauritius and then return to Réunion. Technically the 6 months out of 12 is cumulative, but in practice you get another 6 months.

Data

Area 2510km² (969M²)
Coastline 201km (109M)
Maritime claims Territorial 12M. Exclusive economic zone 200M.
Population 618,000
Capital Saint-Denis
Time zone UT+4
Language French. Creole and some English spoken.
Religion Roman Catholic 94%
Public holidays
  Jan 1 New Year
  May 1 Labour Day

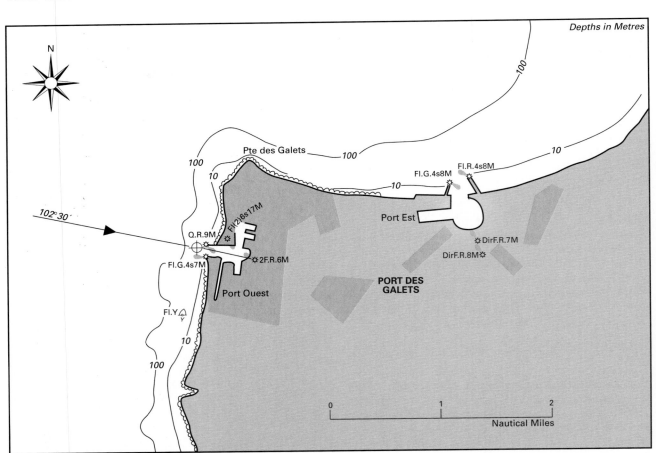

APPROACHES TO PORT-DES-GALETS ⊕ 20°55′·4S 55°17′·3E

May 8 Victory Day
May Ascension
Jun Bank Holiday
Jul 14 Bastille Day
Aug 15 Assumption
Nov 11 Armistice Day
Dec 25 Christmas
Government French *territoire outre-mer*
Crime Low levels of all crime.

Travel
Internal
Bus and *taxi collectifs* (share-taxis) serve all island destinations with an efficient service. Bus timetables are available in the main centres. Taxis can be found in the main centres. Hire cars and motorcycles.

International
Flights from some African countries and to France.

Practicalities
Mail Reliable and efficient. Mail can be sent to Poste Restante, Main Post Office, Rue du Maréchal, Saint-Denis, Isle du Réunion, Indian Ocean.

Telecommunications IDD system. Country code 262. Telephone and fax calls from the post office in St-Denis. Public phones use phonecards.

Currency Réunion uses the French Franc.

Banks and exchange Banks will exchange hard currency and travellers cheques. Cash advances on major credit cards (*Visa* and *Mastercard*) and some ATMs. Banks are open 1000–1900 Mon–Sat and 1300–1900 Sun. Many of the shops and restaurants take the major credit and charge cards.

Medical care Good medical care available although for major problems go to South Africa or France.
The water is potable and abundant.

Electricity 220V 50Hz.

Useful books
East Africa Handbook Ed. Michael Hodd. Footprint Guides.
Mauritius, Réunion & Seychelles – a travel survival kit. Lonely Planet.

Geography and climate
The coast Réunion is a high precipitous island of volcanic origin and still has an active volcano, Piton de la Fournaise, in the SE of the island. The first record of an eruption here was in 1640 and it lasted 10 years. The last eruption was in 1992. The highest point of the island is Piton des Nieges in the middle of the island at 3069m (10,069ft) and Fournaise in the SE at 2631m (8632ft). This makes the island easily visible from some distance off although cloud frequently obscures the higher ground. Like Mauritius much of the island is cultivated in sugar cane.

Coastal waters The island has some coral reef around it close to the coast as at Mauritius. There are no enclosed natural anchorages and the harbours and anchorages used around the island can be subject to heavy swell depending on wind and sea conditions. In fact Réunion is a venue for surfing

competitions which gives you an idea of what the seas around here can be like.

For details on climate, weather, tides and current see the section under *Mauritius*.

Port-des-Galets (Port de la Pointe des Galets)
Charts BA *1497*
20°55'S 55°17'E

Approach
The approach to Port des Galets is straightforward with good depths even quite close to the coast. Yachts should make for Port Ouest.

By night The approaches are well lit and with care a night approach can be made. Main light Port Ouest Fl(2)6s21M. Leading lights on 102°30' *Front* 2F.R.6M *Rear* F.R.6M. Entrance Q.R.9M/ Fl.G.4s7M. S basin F.R.

VHF Ch 16 for *capitanerie*/working Ch 12.

Dangers There is usually a strong swell setting onto the coast which will often be seen as surf.

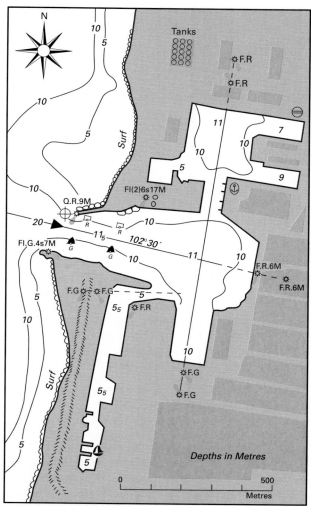

PORT-DES-GALETS: PORT OUEST ⊕ 20°55'.4S 55°17'.3E

Mooring

Where directed. Yachts proceed into the long S basin where there are 5–5·5m depths. To clear in you may be requested to go to one of the N basins.

Shelter All-round.

Authorities Harbourmaster, customs, health and immigration.

Facilities

Water In the yacht basin.

Fuel Can be arranged in the yacht basin.

Gas Most gas bottles can be refilled.

Repairs Mechanical and engineering repairs. Hardware shops in St-Denis.

Provisions Some provisions can be obtained but you are better off going into St-Denis to shop.

Eating out Several restaurants with Creole and other fare.

Other For most things like banking, telecommunications and the like you will have to go into St-Denis. There is a reliable bus and share-taxi service.

General

The area is a fairly grim port and industrial area with little to recommend it except the secure yacht berths. The coast is black basalt onto which a heavy surf pounds so it is difficult to go swimming.

St-Gilles

There is reported to be a harbour used by yachts here at the entrance to the river. Numerous restaurants and hotels here where the coast has some beaches.

Comoros

The Comoros are made up of the other three islands of the four-island Comoros archipelago which includes Mayotte. The Comoros achieved independence in 1975 from France. Since independence the names of the islands have been changed from Grand Comoro to Njazidja, Moheli to Mwali and Anjouan to Nzwani, but most people still refer to them by the old names. The islands are not particularly stable with a corrupt and precarious government and numerous coups have been mounted and bloody retribution exacted when one or other faction has won. The last coup attempt was in 1996 led by the French mercenary Bob Denard who has been on the Comoros scene before, although this attempt was less successful and the French arrived in force to restore order and return Denard to France for trial.

The poverty, restless political situation and fundamentalist rule from ruling parties (*shariya* law was recently introduced) makes the Comoros somewhat unstable in the region, but nonetheless it is visited by yachts as a convenient stepping-stone between east Africa and Madagascar. The islands are spectacular granite outcrops and the waters

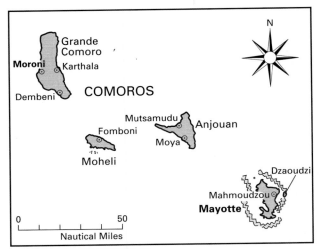

COMOROS AND MAYOTTE

around the islands are clear and rich in marine life. The diving is reported to be excellent.

For detailed pilotage on the islands refer to *East Africa Pilot* by Delwyn McPhun.

Moroni

Charts BA *563*

Approach

Moroni on the W coast of Grande Comoro is the port of entry for the islands. The approach is straightforward as depths are considerable all around the island with only a little coral around some parts of the coast.

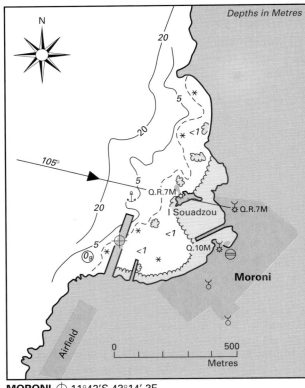

MORONI ⊕ 11°42′S 43°14′·3E

By night Leading lights on 105° *Front* Q.R.7M *Rear* Q.R.7M. Also a Q.10M near the inner basin. A night approach is not recommended.

Tides Tidal range 3·8m at springs.

Mooring

Anchor off in 5–15m where shown. For reasons of security it is best not to go on the mole although depths look adequate off the end.

Shelter An open anchorage suitable in the S monsoon although it is reported to be uncomfortable with a considerable ground swell.

Authorities Port captain, customs and immigration in town. You can buy a visa on arrival. There are numerous unofficial 'fees' so negotiate how you will.

Facilities

Water Near the quay in the inner basin.
Fuel By jerrycan from town.
Provisions Reasonable shopping for basics, bread, and fruit and vegetables.
Eating out Local restaurants in town.
Other PO. Banks. Taxis and hire cars. Internal flights to the other islands and international flights to Paris, South Africa, Dar es Salaam, Madagascar and Mauritius.

General

Although the town is a fascinating spot to stop over at, the reports of most cruising yachts talk more of the uncomfortable anchorage, venal officials and persistent requests for fees or *baksheesh*. This is no reflection on the inhabitants which away from Moroni are said to be friendly and welcoming or the island itself, which if you get to explore it, is said to be spectacular. Different yachts have had widely disparate experiences here so I suggest you try it for yourself, but with some street-wise suss.

For information and pilotage for Grande Comoro and the other islands see *East Africa Pilot* by Delwyn McPhunn.

Mayotte

Mayotte, although geographically and ethnically a part of the Comoros, voted not to join the other islands when they opted for independence and remains a *territoire outre-mer* of France. This means that it gets a good deal of aid from the parent country and consequently it is wealthier and generally more accessible for Europeans. Yachts must go to Dzaoudzi to clear in, but a glance at the chart shows there are numerous other possible anchorages inside the barrier reef which encircles most of the island.

For detailed pilotage refer to *East Africa Pilot* by Delwyn McPhun.

Dzaoudzi

Charts BA *2741, 2744*

Approach

The main pass is through Passe M'Zamboro which is about a mile wide between N and NE reefs. The pass and the channel to Dzaoudzi is buoyed and has leading marks to get you through. Depths are generally 10m plus.

By night Although the leading marks (with the exception of the first set) and the buoys are lit, a night approach is not recommended for the first time through here.

Tides Just over 3m range at springs. The comparatively shallow waters of the lagoon mean that tidal streams can reach 3kt at springs although usually less.

VHF Ch 16 for the *capitanerie*.

Dangers Care is needed not to stray from the access channel as the lagoon is peppered with coral heads.

Mooring

In the S monsoon (SE trades) anchor on the N side of Dzaoudzi. In the N monsoon anchor on the S side of Dzaoudzi.

Authorities Harbourmaster, customs and immigration at Dzaoudzi. Visiting yachts are usually allowed to stay for 3 months on entry.

Facilities

Water On the quay. Reported potable but check first.
Fuel By jerry can from town. For duty-free fuel there is a quay.
Gas Most gas bottles can be filled.
Repairs There are reported to be places to dry out alongside the quay. Mechanical and engineering repairs. Hardware shops.
Provisions Good shopping for provisions. Many items are imported and prices are accordingly high. Many hard-to-find items including good wines and spirits from France and all sorts of tinned delicacies. Baguettes and croissants in the bakeries.
Eating out Good restaurants in Pamandzi with French food available as well as Creole, Indian and Chinese!
Other PO. Banks. Laundry. Free ferry ('the barge') across to Mamoudzou.

General

Dzaoudzi is the small islet off the W side of Pamanzi and is largely occupied by the military. The bulk of the population lives in Pamanzi and Mamoudzou opposite on Grande Terre. The place is something of a haven, albeit an expensive one, with an ordered life guaranteed by the French military and shops sporting all sorts of goods out of Europe. The French franc is the currency here and between the freshly baked baguettes and imported French wines, it is a welcome respite in this part of the world.

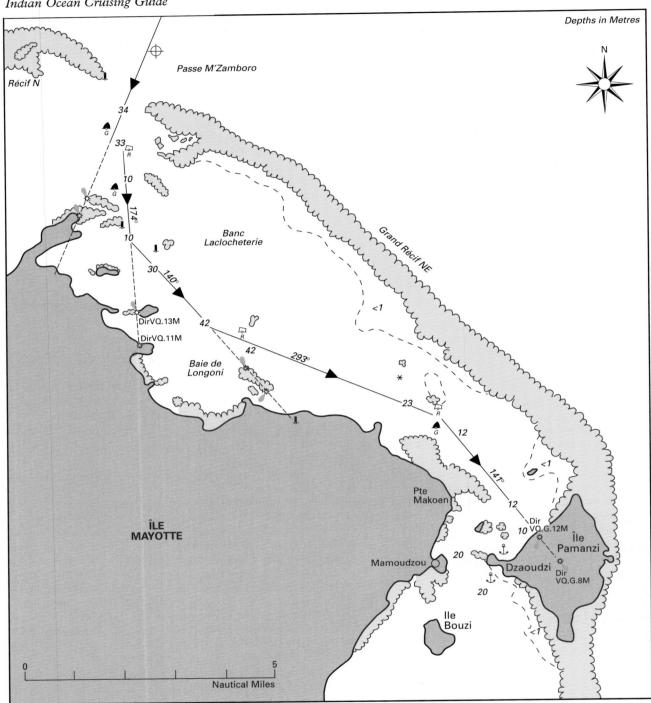

Depths in Metres

PASSE M'ZAMBORO TO DZAOUDZI ⊕ 12°35′S 45°08′E

Calendar of the Winds

The Mahorais of Mayotte measure the year by the winds.

Kashkazi N monsoon from November to March. This is the 'bad' season when the seas are rough, it rains a lot and cyclones may hit the island as they did in 1984 and 1987.

Matulahi Inter-monsoon period between April and May. Wind is generally benign and from the E.

Kusi S monsoon from June to August – the 'happy'

season. The sea is calm, there is little rain and there are lots of festivals, marriages and social occasions.

Myombeni Wind veers to the W in the inter-monsoon period from September to October. Rain showers start.

Madagascar

Current situation

Under Didier Ratsiraka who controlled the country from 1975 to 1991, effectively as a totalitarian regime, Madagascar was something of a no-go area for yachts and tourists in general. He established a quasi-socialist state that was actively supported by the USSR and North Korea. This period was notable for riots, violence, corruption and attempted coups. With the breakup of the eastern bloc in 1989 Ratsiraka accepted that the end was nigh and a referendum in 1992 ushered in elections. In the 1993 elections Ratsiraka was defeated and Madagascar got its first democratically elected president for 30 years. So far the transition to democracy has been smooth, but elements of the military which supported Ratsiraka remain and the country cannot be described as stable just yet. This is no reflection on the Malagasy people who are generally honest and friendly souls. The visitor to Madagascar will be safe although it is wise to remove all gear from the deck, take precautions in some areas (particularly the SW) and be prepared for some corruption by officials which seems to have survived from Ratsiraka's era. If there are any rumours involving the military it would be wise to investigate further and possibly leave. In some areas it is unwise to wander around at night.

Documentation and visas

Normal ship's papers and a valid passport for all crew members must be carried. Proof of cholera and yellow fever vaccinations are required if arriving from Africa. Last port clearance papers are required. Carry some passport photos and a lot of crew lists.

All visitors require a visa. It is best to have a visa before arrival although one can be obtained on arrival. Visas can be obtained in the Comoros, Mayotte, South Africa, Réunion and Mauritius. If you do not have a visa then you will likely have to pay more for one when you arrive and perhaps an 'administration' fee as well. Visas are issued for 3 months.

Entry formalities

A yacht should go first to a port of entry. These are at Diego Suarez (Antisiranana), Hell-ville (Adoany) on Nosy Bé, Maharjanga, and Toliara. When 12M off call up port control on VHF Ch 16 to advise of your arrival although do not expect to always get an answer.

The clearing in procedure appears to vary from port to port as do the charges for clearing and out. Hell-ville is probably the most popular port for visiting yachts to clear in at although the administration here is not always popular. At Hell-ville in addition to the normal visa you are required to buy a transit visa and pay 'administration' costs. The latter are subject to some haggling. Clear in with immigration and the harbourmaster. You will be required to purchase a cruising permit and also pay port dues.

For further information on the intricacies of entry and exit see *East Africa Pilot* by Delwyn McPhun.

Data

Area 587,040km$_2$ (226,657M^2). The fourth largest island in the world.

Coastline 4828km (2607M)

Maritime claims Territorial 12M. Exclusive economic zone 200M.

Population 11,942,000

Capital Antananarivo

Time zone UT+3

Language French and Malagasy official. Limited English spoken.

Religion Indigenous (including animist) beliefs 52%. Christian 41%. Muslim 7%.

Public holidays
Jan 1 New Year
Mar 29 Independence Day
Mar/Apr Easter
May 1 Labour Day
May/Jun Ascension
Jun 26 Independence Day
Aug 15 Assumption
Nov 1 All Saints Day
Dec 25 Christmas
Dec 30 Republic Day

Government Democratic Republic (since 1992 in practice)

Crime Moderate levels of crime. Attention should be paid to where and when you wander around some areas. Madagascar is one of the poorest countries in the world.

Travel

Internal

To get any distance it is best to travel by air. Air Madagascar owned partly by the government and partly by Air France serves around 50 destinations on the island. A train service runs from Atananarivo to Tamatave with branch lines. It is slow but comfortable. Buses serve most areas but they are overcrowded and the roads are appalling with less than 10% paved. For short distances there are taxis (*taxi-be*) and mini-buses (*taxi-brousse*). There are hire cars (expensive) in some places and also hire motorbikes and bicycles. There are ferry services to islands like Nosy Bé.

International

From Europe there is really only Aeroflot from Moscow and Air Madagascar from Paris. From Africa and the surrounding islands there are services including South Africa, Malawi, Kenya, Comoros, Seychelles, Réunion and Mauritius. Flights are in general quite expensive.

Practicalities

Mail Unreliable. It is best not to have mail sent here, especially packages which may go missing. Get it sent to South Africa or elsewhere along the way where you might stop.

Telecommunications Generally primitive and unreliable. There are a few public telephones and the PO, but you will often have difficulty getting a line out.

Currency The unit is the Malagasy Franc (MGF). All currency must be declared when entering. When leaving the amount of currency and the currency exchange slips must tally. MGF cannot be exported and you cannot change it back to hard currency. The currency is not the most stable and there have been arguments with the IMF on its valuation.

Banks and exchange Banks will change hard currency or travellers cheques into MGF. Commission rates vary so look around. Some banks (BankynyIndostria-Credit Lyonnais Madagascar (BNI)) will give cash advances on major credit cards. Banks are open 0800–1100 and 1400–1600 Mon-Fri. Few places accept credit cards. The US dollar is the preferred currency to carry although French francs or SA rand are usually accepted.

Medical care Poor. There are a few foreign clinics around, but in general the best policy is to get out of Madagascar. Water is generally potable but check first as in some places it is not. Madagascar is a malarial area and the appropriate prophylactics should be taken.

Electricity Usually 220V but 110V in rural areas.

Useful books
East Africa Handbook Ed. Michael Hodd. Footprint Guides. Covers Madagascar.
Dancing With The Dead: A Journey Through Zanzibar and Madagascar H Drysdale. Hamish Hamilton.

Geography and climate
The coast Madagascar is not of volcanic origin like some of the smaller islands nearby, but is thought to be a part of the African continent which drifted apart over time. The topography of the island is quite different from the E to W coasts. The E coast is relatively straight with little in the way of natural indentations. The W coast is more irregular with some small islands off the coast and deep sheltered bays and is the most popular coast to cruise around. The most favoured area is the NW coast around Nosy Bé where there are more than enough anchorages to choose from. The SW coast is generally sandy and arid.

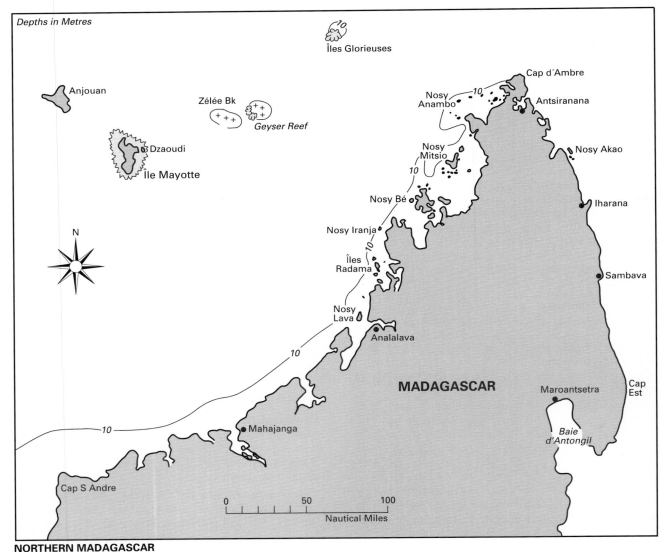

NORTHERN MADAGASCAR

From the coast the land rises up to a central plateau and then to the mountain ridge (maximum elevation 2880m/9360ft) lying closer to the E coast than to the W. The island has been extensively cleared for agriculture, but natural rainforest remains in pockets and is home to Madagascar's many unique species of flora and fauna.

Coastal waters Most of the coast is fringed by a shallow bank that extends out a considerable distance in places. There are extensive fringing coral reefs off much of the coast and around the islands and islets.

The bottom is mostly mud with some sand and coral in places. The diving off some of the offshore reefs is reported to be superb.

Climate The climate is tropical although over such a large island it varies significantly. A temperature of −8°C has been recorded in the mountains. Around the coast temperatures in the summer (Nov–Apr) are around 29°–31°C on the E coast and 24°–26°C on the W coast. Around the NW coast temperatures are generally higher at 31°–32°C in the summer and 28°–32°C in winter although they can fall to 15°–19°C at night.

Rainfall varies dramatically from coast to coast and N to S. On the E coast rainfall is very heavy for most of the year with 4000mm average at Maroansetra in the N. The W coast has a pronounced dry season from May to October. However the NW coast has a higher average rainfall than the W coast further S. The SW of the island gets very little rain and is arid.

Weather

Prevailing winds near the coast Although Madagascar lies within the area that the SE trades blow over, land and sea breezes play an important part in the equation. On both the W and E coasts land and sea breezes are well developed and either augment or detract from the SE trades between May to October. This means you need to take some care over where you anchor as an offshore breeze will later turn around to an onshore breeze. The SE trades are strong at the southern end of the island and decrease in strength and become variable in direction as they blow over the land. The exception is over the NW coast where the SE trades pick up again at the top of the island and are reliable and quite strong off the N end of Madagascar.

Between November and April NW winds blow over the northern half of the island, generally at less strength than the SE trades. At the N end of Madagascar the ITCZ affects it between January to February and there can be squalls and rain for periods.

Gales In general the frequency of gales is relatively low throughout the year at 1–2%. This does not take into account wind gusting down valleys and high winds associated with squalls which make the actual frequency seem higher. To the NE of Madagascar there is an area between the N end and N of the Farquhar group which sees a much higher frequency of gale force winds at around 5% between May and October. Winds often reach Force 7 which is not represented in the 5% frequency giving a much higher likelihood of strong winds accompanied by a lumpy sea which makes the sea area uncomfortable to sail through at this time.

Madagascar is within the sea area affected by tropical storms and cyclones which can occur from November to April, although December to March are the worst months. Typical cyclone tracks can move across Madagascar towards the SW and often curve back down through the Mozambique Channel. The frequency of cyclones is high with a probability of 6–10 every 20 years over the island and a higher probability on the E coast.

Tides

The tidal range around the island is high on the W coast and much lower on the E coast. The Mozambique Channel amplifies the tidal effect and can produce strong tidal streams over enclosed waters around the coastal bank. Around Mahajunga and Nosy Bé the tidal range at springs is 3·8m. Where the tidal stream meets a contrary current overfalls can be experienced.

Currents

The South Equatorial current divides when it hits Madagascar to flow N and S around the island on the E coast. Where the current curves around the N and S ends of the island the current can be strong and rates of 4kt have been recorded and close to the land rates of 8kt have been reported. With the SE trades blowing this can give rise to confused seas. In the Mozambique Channel the current sets SW on the African side and generally N–NE on the Madagascar side. Around the W coast of Madagascar the currents close inshore vary considerably and there will often be an onshore set and rates can be appreciable through narrow channels.

Navigation

Madagascar is not well charted and there are numerous reports of reefs and banks extending further than shown and some inconsistency over depths close inshore. GPS should be used cautiously and close to land or dangers to navigation eyeball navigation is essential. On average GPS positions are out by something like −0·2' latitude and +0·5'/−0·7' longitude.

Harbours and anchorages

Many of the anchorages useful for yachts are not well charted and for detailed pilotage reference should be made to *East Africa Pilot* by Delwyn McPhun published by Imray.

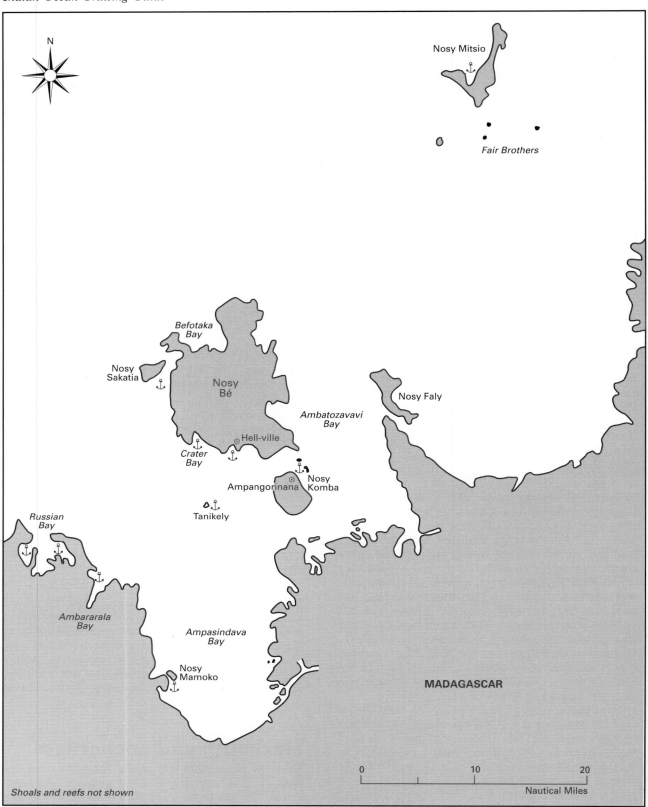

NOSY BE AND NEARBY ANCHORAGES

NW Coast

Most yachts make for Nosy Bé and surrounding anchorages when visiting Madagascar. The area is a ready-made cruising ground and conveniently placed between Chagos and the Seychelles archipelago and South Africa.

Nosy Bé

Charts BA *706*

Yachts clearing into Madagascar should head for Hell-ville/Adoney on the S end of Nosy-Bé. Some care is needed over the shoal water off the N end of Nosy-Bé and of the reefs and shoals in the channel between Nosy-Bé and Nosy Komba.

Hell-Ville (Adoney)

Charts BA *706*

Approach

Approach should be made from the S to avoid the reef and shoal water between Hell-ville and Crater Bay. A red buoy marks the E extremity of the reef but cannot be relied on. Once at the entrance to the bay the buildings of Hell-ville are clearly visible.

By night A first time night approach should not be made. Leading lights on 021° *Front* Fl.G *Rear* Fl.G. The buoy marking the end of the reef may be lit Fl.R.

Tides Around 3·5m range at springs.

VHF Ch 16 for port authorities. Other yachts in the anchorage may be on Ch 16 or 69.

Dangers

1. Care is needed of the reef between Crater Bay and Hell-ville.
2. If coming from the E care is needed of the reefs and shoal water in the passage between Nosy Bé and Nosy Komba. You should have someone up high conning you through.

Mooring

Anchor off in 10–15m. There are usually other yachts in here to advise on where to go. The bottom is mud and good holding.

Shelter Good shelter although the land breeze at night and in the early morning can make it a bit bumpy – uncomfortable rather than dangerous.

Authorities Port captain, customs and immigration. Clearing in fees seem to vary considerably so take advice from any yachts already here.

Facilities

Water Reported to be unpotable.
Fuel On the quay.
Gas Most gas bottles can be filled here.
Repairs Basic mechanical and engineering skills.
Provisions Most basics and excellent fruit and vegetables in town. Good spices including vanilla, cinnamon, and cloves.
Eating out Local restaurants serving stewy things or *bredes*. Some seafood available.
Other PO. Banks. Buses and taxi-brousses. Ferry to the mainland at Antsahampano.

General

Hell-ville was named after the French Admiral de Hell and not for its location. The old colonial town is in a state of disrepair, like much else in Madagascar, but it has a sleepy charm for all that. The main tourist area is around the beaches at Ambetoloaka on the SW coast of Nosy Bé.

Nosy Bé   *Delwyn McPhun*

Nearby anchorages

Crater Bay Lies just W of Hell-ville separated by the fringing reef. Good anchorage. Hotels and restaurants ashore.

Nosy Sakatia The island off the W coast. Yachts anchor in the channel. Good shelter.

Nosy Komba Anchor off the village on the NE. Anchorage looks to be exposed.

Tanikely Anchor off the E coast. Exposed.

Nosy Mamoko Anchorage under the island on the W side of Ampasindava Bay.

Ambararata Bay Anchor in cove on the W.

Russian Bay Large sheltered bay. Suitable hurricane hole.

Most of this information comes from disparate and often brief scribbled notes from other cruising yachts. For detailed pilotage refer to *East Africa Pilot* by Delwyn McPhun which contains information on these and numerous other anchorages he has visited in Madagascar.

South Africa

Since the remarkable transition to democracy under Nelson Mandela, South Africa has developed its nascent yachting industry to become an important force on the yachting scene. On the African continent it offers the best facilities going for yacht repair and care. After the somewhat primitive facilities to be found elsewhere in the region, this is the place to do all those important jobs you have been putting off for lack of expertise or spares and materials.

Those cruising westabout around the bottom of Africa will probably head for Durban or Richards Bay before proceeding around the coast towards Capetown. For detailed information on South Africa consult the current *South African Nautical Almanac* by Tom Morgan available in South Africa or from Imrays.

Documentation and visas

Normal boats papers and a valid passport for all crew members must be carried. Proof of vaccination against yellow fever is needed.

Yachts arriving in South Africa are regarded as being in transit and a transit pass is issued. This means you cannot travel out of the port or city/town you are in. If you want to travel inland you must sign off the boat and obtain a visitors visa. A 3 month

MADAGASCAR TO SOUTH AFRICA

visitors' visa is issued free to most foreign nationals including Americans and Canadians, Australasians, and EU members. You may be required to show proof of sufficient funds or an onward ticket before a visitors visa is granted, although this does not usually apply to the owner and family.

Entry formalities
When 12M off call up Durban Harbour Radio on VHF Ch 16 or 2182kHz and request permission to enter harbour. At busy harbours like Durban you may be asked to stand off if commercial traffic is entering or leaving harbour. Request permission to clear customs, health and immigration and follow the instructions given to you. If you are coasting between South African harbours you must still clear with customs on each occasion.

On entry you will be directed to a quay, in Durban the International Jetty, where clearance with customs, health and immigration will be arranged. In general the harbour authorities are helpful to visiting yachts.

Durban
Charts BA *2088, 577*

Approach
The approach is straightforward and free of dangers.
Conspicuous The tall buildings of Durban are easily identified from some distance off and closer in the harbour breakwaters and entrance will be seen. There are often workboats and tugs coming and going which makes the entrance easy to identify.
By night The approaches are well lit making a night approach straightforward.
Main light (Anglo-American Building) Fl.7s25M
Holiday Inn F.8M
The Bluff Aero F.R.5M
Entrance Fl(2)5s6M/Fl.G.3s6M
Leading lights on 215°30' *Front* Iso.R.2s12M *Rear* Oc.4s14M

Tides Tidal range around 2m at springs. Although not large this can give a 3½kt stream flowing out and 2½kt stream flowing in at springs.

VHF Ch 16 for *Durban Harbour Radio* usually changing to Ch 12.

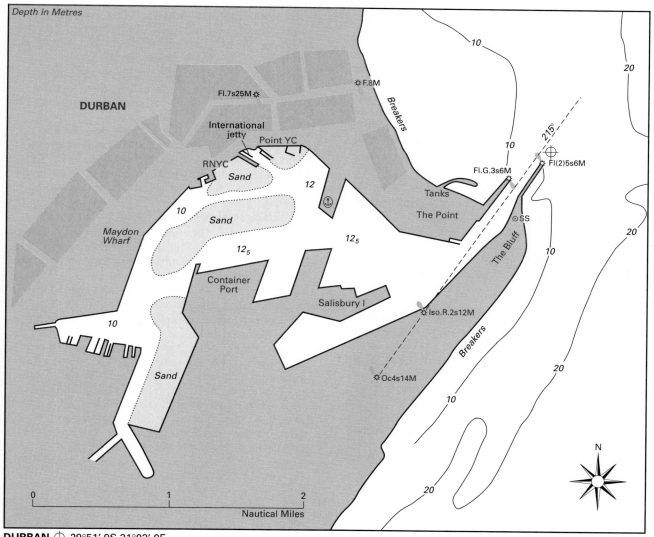

Dangers
1. Care is needed of commercial traffic entering and leaving the harbour. Commercial traffic has right of way and you may be asked to stand off for a while.
2. With strong SW winds there can be an appreciable swell in the approaches.

Mooring

Visiting yachts normally stay on the International Jetty where it is possible to stay for up to 3 months if there is room. The berths are administered by the Yacht Basin Development and Mooring Association (YBDMA) whose office is close by. The berths here are most convenient being right in the middle of town.

Shelter Good all-round shelter.

Authorities YBDMA. PO Box 2946, Durban 4000. ☎ (031) 301 5425 *Fax* (031) 307 2590.

If you need to stay longer or decide to move elsewhere there may be berths at the following clubs.

Point Yacht Club PO Box 2224, Durban 4000. ☎ (031) 301 4787 *Fax* (031) 305 1234.

Royal Natal Yacht Club PO Box 2946, Durban 4000. ☎ (031) 301 5325/6 *Fax* (031) 307 2590.

Bluff Yacht Club PO Box 21084, Fynnland, 4020. ☎ (031) 466 1386.

Point Yacht Club and the Royal Natal Yacht Club have pontoon berths while Bluff Yacht Club has mostly moorings. All of them have a clubhouse with a restaurant/bar and club get-togethers are very social affairs. They can also be used as a mailing address (mark letters 'hold until arrival'). They are all welcoming to visiting yachtsmen/women.

Facilities

Durban has extensive facilities of every kind and only a few are listed here. For more information refer to *South African Nautical Almanac*.

Services Water nearby at the YBDMA. Water and electricity at Point Yacht Club and Royal Natal Yacht Club. Shower and WC at all clubs.

Fuel On the quay.

Gas Most gas bottles can be refilled by Natal Gas Supplies.

Repairs There are three boatyards at Bayhead at the NW end of the harbour. Marina Yacht Lift has a 22-ton travel-hoist. Dorbyl and Elgin can crane or slip yachts. Yachts can also be hauled at Bluff Yacht Club. All yachts repairs are catered for in Durban including specialist GRP and wood repairs, sailmaking (North and Doyle have lofts), aluminium welding, and liferaft servicing. Most spares and yacht equipment are available or can be ordered. Chandlers and hardware shops.

Provisions Excellent shopping for all provisions in town.

Eating out Restaurants of all types and classifications from pizza to Chinese to posh French.

Other PO. Banks. ATMs. Telephone and fax services. Courier services. Laundry. Hire cars. Taxis

and buses. International flights and internal flights to Johannesburg where connections can be made for most international destinations.

General

Durban is a huge modern bustling city, a bit like a vision of the future in a sci-fi novel after some of the more simple places nearby. The noise and flurry of activity can take some getting used to although it makes a pleasant interlude for most with so much to do and see: eat in different restaurants, go to the movies, go shopping, accept invitations to *braais*, go on safari or just sight-seeing, maybe even do a bit of work on the boat.

Passage around the Cape

The passage around the Cape is one to be treated with respect. If you are in Durban then it is recommended you approach the Ocean Sailing Academy (near the International Jetty) where seminars are conducted on the passage around the cape. Often these will be taken by Chris Bonnet, a well known sailor in the area.

There are few places to stop on the passage to Capetown and the Atlantic. The following brief notes give you an idea of what to expect, but they must be fleshed out from local advice and the seminars at the Ocean Sailing Academy.

Durban to East London. Around 250 miles with no really safe anchorages or harbours en-route.

East London to Port Elizabeth. Around 125 miles.

Port Elizabeth to Knysna Lagoon. Around 175 miles. Difficult entrance and 2m max draught.

Knysna Lagoon to Mossel Bay. Around 45 miles.

Mossel Bay to False Bay. Around 200 miles. There are numerous marinas and anchorages around False Bay.

False Bay to Capetown. Around 50 miles.

After Mossel Bay there are some anchorages under headlands and a number of fishing harbours. Consult the current edition of *South African Nautical Almanac*.

For most people the worst bit of the trip is Durban to Port Elizabeth or Mossel Bay. The Agulhas Current runs strongly down the coast and when (not if) a SW buster comes through the wind against the current raises steep waves. Twenty metre waves have been regularly recorded. The advice most receive is to set off into the end of a SW buster when the barometer has just started rising. If you wait until the NE arrives after a SW blow then you will have lost time. Yachts usually stay around 10–12 miles off the coast where the Agulhas current can give them up to a 4kt boost in the right direction, though usually less. If a southerly blow should come through yachts head in towards the coast where there is less current and therefore less sea.

Ocean Sailing Academy, 38 Fenton Road, Durban 4001. ☎ (031) 301 5726/66/67 *Fax* (031) 307 1257.

Mozambique, Tanzania and Zanzibar

The east African coast from South Africa to Kenya is little cruised by yachts, but by all accounts it offers some superb sights ashore and excellent diving. The weather can be boisterous at times and tides and currents are considerable, but then to get to comparatively untrammelled cruising areas requires an element of risk and the desire to explore badly charted areas. Anyone cruising the coast will need a copy of *East Africa Pilot* by Delwyn McPhun which will take some of the pain away from getting to harbours and anchorages and provide a lot of interesting tid-bits on life and sights around the coast.

Mozambique

After the madness of the civil war here between the government (Frelimo) and the resistance (Renamo) sponsored by South Africa, things are reported to be on the mend. The country cannot be described as stable just yet, but neither is it in a state of flux any more since an accommodation was reached between Frelimo and Renamo in 1992. Since then things have improved greatly although there is still much poverty and isolated incidents from bandits. For the most part cruising yachts will know nothing of this as the coastal regions are rarely affected.

Tanzania and Zanzibar

Although Zanzibar is a part of Tanzania, it largely has self-rule and its own elections. A yacht cruising from the Tanzanian coast to Zanzibar will have to clear in with immigration although only a Tanzanian visa is needed for both Tanzania and Zanzibar. This area is redolent of spices and trading dhows and old myths and the cruising is described as superb. There are more than enough anchorages to visit within short distances and Tanzania as a whole has one of the most stable governments in Africa, although there have been some rumblings of discontent and a desire for independence in Zanzibar.

Further reading
East African Handbook Ed. Michael Hodd. Footprint Guides. Excellent guide.
East Africa Lonely Planet.

Kenya

Current situation
The re-election of Daniel arap Moi in 1997 continues the rule of the KANO party which has been continuously in power since independence and the first elections in 1963. Moi came to power in 1978 on the death of Kenyatta and at first seemed to usher in a period of greater freedom. That ended with the attempted coup by officers of the Air Force in 1982 and since then there has been increasing suppression of opposition parties, corruption that has crippled the whole infrastructure of the country, and a general repression of the population that has led to some instability. Allegations of human rights abuses and vote rigging have been made by a number of international organisations. The country, once the most prosperous in Africa, now has very real poverty and in places theft and muggings make it dangerous to go into certain areas after dark.

At the present time there is a risk of riots and violence between tribal groups which mean you should avoid certain areas and stick to well travelled routes. For the most part the coastal area north of Mombasa is one of the safest areas to be and yachtsmen have few problems here. For the future it would be wise to keep an eye on the situation in Kenya and consult others who have recently been there.

Documentation and visas
Normal boats papers and a valid passport for all crew members must be carried. Yellow fever and cholera certificates may be requested. The clearance papers from your last port of call will also be requested.

A visa will be issued at the port of entry and is valid for 3 months. This can be extended for another 3 months. When you leave and re-enter a new visa will be issued. The charge for a visa is around $50 per person, although this comparatively recent charge may be dropped if tour operators have their way.

Entry and exit formalities
A yacht must first go to a port of entry. From the S these are Shimoni, Mombasa, Kilifi, and Lamu. Along the coast you may be called up by the navy if they spot you and asked to identify yourself. At the port of entry you must report to customs and immigration within 24 hours. You will be issued with a transire which states what your next port is and that you are not carrying cargo or passengers. At each subsequent port you are required to present the transire and obtain clearance to the next port. At present there is no charge for clearing in and for a transire, but given the recent introduction of high visa charges, there may soon be a charge for the transire. A charge is made for light dues and port dues, but these are a matter of dollars rather than tens of dollars. When you leave the country the receipts for light and port dues must be presented before you will be given clearance.

Data
Area 580,370km^2 (224,082M^2)
Population 28,261,000
Capital Nairobi
Time zone UT+3
Language English and Swahili. Numerous other ethnic languages.
Ethnic divisions Kikuyu 21%, Luo 15%, Luhya 14%, Kalenjin 11%, Kamba 11%, Kisii 6%, Meru 6%, others 16%.

MADAGASCAR TO KENYA

Religion Roman Catholic 30%, Protestant 40%.

Public holidays
Jan 1 New Year
May 1 Labour Day
Jun 1 Madaraka Day (Independence)
Oct 10 Moi Day
Oct 20 Kenyatta Day
Dec 12 Independence Day
Dec 25, 26 Christmas
Moveable
Easter.

Government Democratic Republic. The KANU party has ruled since independence.

Crime The larger centres like Nairobi and Mombasa have a bad reputation for theft and muggings. Basically you should not carry any expensive items like a camera or camcorder, jewellery, and do not carry large amounts of cash with you. Confidence tricksters will regale you with hard luck stories and gangs often work a pick-pocket routine involving bumping into you or diverting your attention so that other members can relieve you of valuables. It is unwise to go into certain areas after dark and best to avoid some areas even in the daytime. Do not leave any loose items on deck and in Mombasa it would be wise to hire a recommended watchman. For most of the coast there will be few problems, but nonetheless be aware that theft does occur.

Travel

Internal
Good air and rail connections. Road connections are generally OK although the roads are falling to pieces.

Air Kenya Airways has regular flights between Nairobi and Mombasa and Kisumu. There may also be flights from Nairobi to Lamu.

Rail A good if sedate train connects Mombasa and Nairobi.

Coach and bus Regular buses connect Mombasa and Nairobi. It pays to take a more up-market bus. Local buses connect most places, especially along the coast.

Matatus and Peugeots Matatus are almost any vehicle which operates as a share-taxi. They operate along more or less one route and are fast and sometimes lethal. Peugeot estates are a little more up-market than a *matatu* and are a quick and relatively comfortable way of getting around on longer routes.

Car hire Relatively expensive and an alarming experience. Drivers in Kenya say that they don't stop because they might be robbed, so everyone ignores traffic lights, stop signs, any signs at all.

International
Kenya has good connections to Europe and particularly to the UK. It is one of the cheapest places to get to and from in East Africa with a number of airlines operating flights into and out of Nairobi and Mombasa.

Practicalities

Mail Is generally efficient and doesn't take too long to arrive. Parcels should be sent by registered post or they may go astray. They also have to be checked by customs so it can take a while before you are notified a parcel has arrived. It may be better to use a courier like DHL or Federal Express to get parcels out to Mombasa.

Mail can be sent to Poste Restante at any main post office, although if you can, get mail sent to a private address.

Telecommunications IDD system. Country code 254. The telecommunication system is generally good and you can usually get through without too much hassle. International calls can be made from public call boxes with a phonecard. Charges are typically around $4 a minute to Europe or the USA. Calls can be made from hotels but charges are typically double those from a call box or the PO. Faxes can be sent from the PO or a bureau in Mombasa.

Currency The unit is the Kenyan shilling (KSH) which is divided into 100 cents. With the political turmoil in recent years the KSH has not been stable and has progressively devalued against major currencies. $US are accepted in many places or are easily changed.

Banks and exchange In Mombasa there are banks which will change travellers cheques and cash. You can get cash advances on *American Express* and it may be possible to do so on *Visa* in Mombasa. Banking hours are 0800–1300 Mon–Fri and 0830–1100 Sat.

A black market exists but the rate is hardly worth it, being only marginally better than at the bank and it is also illegal. There are also scams where you go around the back of a building to change money and find yourself relieved of it without obtaining KSH in return.

Charge cards like *American Express* and *Diners* are widely accepted by hotels and upmarket restaurants and shops. Credit cards like *Visa* are accepted in some places and *Mastercard* is hardly accepted at all.

Medical care Is reasonable in large cities like Mombasa and Nairobi where good doctors can be found. In the country medical care is poor. Care is needed of malaria which is rife in this part of the world. More tourists get malaria in East Africa than in any other part of the world. Sexually transmitted diseases including HIV are also widespread throughout Kenya.

Care must be taken with the water in most places as Hepatitis A is common and can be caught from contaminated water. Suspect water should be boiled or bottled water used.

Electricity 220–240V AC.

For information on geography and climate, weather, tides, currents and navigation see *East Africa Pilot* by Delwyn McPhun.

Harbours and anchorages

Here I will describe just three of the harbours used by yachts, Mombasa, Kilifi and Lamu. For additional information on other harbours and anchorages around the coast of Kenya see *East Africa Pilot* by Delwyn McPhun.

Mombasa

Charts BA *616, 666*

Approach

The approach is reasonably straightforward with a buoyed deep water channel and leading marks. Yachts should head for Port Kilindini on the port side following the leading marks and the buoyed channel.

Conspicuous The high rise buildings of Mombasa are easily identified. To the N off Kenyatta Beach is a large cement factory with conspicuous chimneys. The main channel in has leading marks on 301–302° on a B&W striped tower. Once up to Ras Serani the second leading line into Port Kilindini is marked by two obelisks with a black vertical stripe. This channel is relatively straightforward with good depths.

By night A first time night approach is not recommended. Outer channel buoys Q.G/Q.R. Leading lights on 301°45' *Front* Q.8M *Rear* Fl.5s18M. Leading lights on 238° into Port Kilindini *Front* Q *Rear* Fl.

VHF Ch 16 for port authorities.

Dangers Care is needed of shipping and local boats charging in and out of the harbour. Do not expect any rules of the road to be obeyed.

Mooring

Tidal range 3·2m at springs.

Anchor off the Mombasa Yacht Club around the bend of Port Kilindini in 20–30m. The bottom is sticky mud and good holding.

Shelter Good shelter although traffic in the harbour creates a lot of wash making it uncomfortable at times.

Authorities Customs and immigration. Mombasa is a port of entry.

Note

1. Theft is a very real problem in Mombasa and it is best to employ a recommended watchman. The Mombasa Yacht Club can usually recommend a reliable watchman. In any case remove all items from the decks and make sure the yacht is locked up when you go ashore.

2. It has been reported that there are a lot of sharks in Mombasa harbour and it is not advisable to swim or dive, even briefly to free a fouled anchor.

Facilities

Water From the Mombasa Yacht Club. The water on the pier is non-potable.

Fuel A fuel quay near the yacht club. Alternatively fuel can be jerry-canned from town although this is a bit tedious.

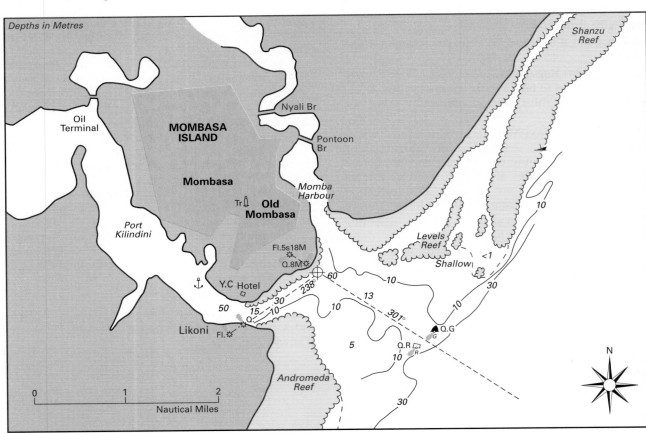

MOMBASA ⊕ 04°04'·3S 39°40'·7E

Gas Most gas bottles can be refilled.

Repairs Africa Marine next to the yacht club can haul yachts by crane. Most mechanical and engineering repairs can be arranged. Some wood and basic GRP repairs are possible. Good hardware shops in town and most basic mechanical components, bearings, filters and belts can be tracked down. Basic canvas-work and some sail repairs.

Provisions Good shopping for most provisions with supermarkets stocking imported European goods. Check sell-by dates carefully.

Eating out Good local restaurants with a variety of food and Indian and Chinese restaurants. Upmarket international cuisine at the hotels and some restaurants, most of them a bit out of town.

Other PO. Banks including Barclays. Hire cars. *Matatus* and taxis. Train and coach to Nairobi. Internal and international flights.

General

Mombasa is not often used by yachts because of the problem of theft. However those who visit here usually enjoy it for a taste of city life after more simpler places along the coast. It also has good connections to Nairobi and for flights out of Kenya, although Kilifi Creek is not far away and an altogether more secure place to leave a yacht.

Kilifi Creek

Charts BA *238*

Approach

The most direct entrance into Kilifi Creek is through North Pass approximately 1M S of the creek itself. There are least depths of around 9m following the leading marks. Leading marks show the passage through the reef and another set of leading marks show the passage into the creek. The first set of marks are two white beacons approximately 4m high on the low cliffs to the S of the creek and show the entrance in on 274°. Once through the reef the second set of marks are two white beacons (front 2m high and rear 5m high) on 328° which show the channel up to the creek proper. Once up to the creek there are good depths in mid-channel.

Before the bridge there are electricity cables across the river with 15m air height in mid channel. There is more clearance (up to 20m) closer to either shore where the cables curve up to the pylons. Beyond the pylons is the road bridge with 17m air height under the middle of the bridge although greater clearance (up to 20m) has been reported.

Conspicuous The buildings of Kilifi will be seen and a radio mast is conspicuous in the town. The creek proper cannot be seen until you open it from seaward when the bridge is conspicuous. The leading marks can be difficult to see until closer in, but Kilifi lighthouse will be seen.

By night A first time night entry is not recommended as the leading lights are not reliable. Kilifi lighthouse

LFl.30s9M. Leading lights on 274°: *Front F.R Rear* F.R. Leading lights on 328° *Front F.R Rear* F.R. Radio mast F.R.

Dangers
1. There can be a current in the creek of 1–1.5kt, usually flowing into the creek on the flood tide.
2. Care is needed of the reefs which are rarely above water and which combined with the poor visibility of the water make it difficult to spot them.
3. Care is needed of the fringing reef on either side of the entrance to the creek and in the creek proper.

Note It is also possible to use Takaungu Pass further S of North Pass, but the latter is the most direct entrance into Kilifi Creek.

Mooring

Tidal range 3.1m at springs.

Yachts will normally make for Swynford's Boatyard on the S side of the creek just past the road bridge. There are laid moorings and a charge is made for using them (US$1.50 per foot per month in 1997). Although there are a number of anchorages which can be used in the creek it is advisable to use the moorings at the boatyard both for the security of the boat and also for the facilities ashore.

Shelter Good all-round shelter and a boat can be safely left here.

Authorities Customs and immigration in Kilifi town on the N bank of the creek.

Facilities

Water Potable water at the boatyard. Showers and toilets at the boatyard.

Fuel Can be arranged by jerry can from the yard.

Gas Most bottles can be filled by arrangement with the boatyard.

Repairs Swynford's can haul yachts on a cradle up to 15m and 20 tons. Most mechanical and engineering repairs can be arranged. Other repairs can be arranged either in Kilifi or Mombasa. The boatyard also has a quay wall where a yacht can dry out alongside between tides for antifouling. You can also have mail sent to the boatyard.

Provisions Most provisions can be found in Kilifi town. Market.

Eating out Snack bar at the boatyard with a wonderful view. Restaurants and bars in Mnarani and Kilifi.

Other PO. Barclays Bank. Buses to Mombasa.

Swynford's Boatyard, Private Bag, Kilifi, Kenya. ☎ 0125 22479.

General

Most yachts headed for Kenya make a bee-line for Kilifi because it offers a relatively secure anchorage in pleasant surroundings. Some theft from yachts has been reported from Kilifi, but nothing on the scale of Mombasa. Sywnford's Boatyard employs night watchmen and the presence of other yachts keeps theft down. Kilifi is close enough to Mombasa

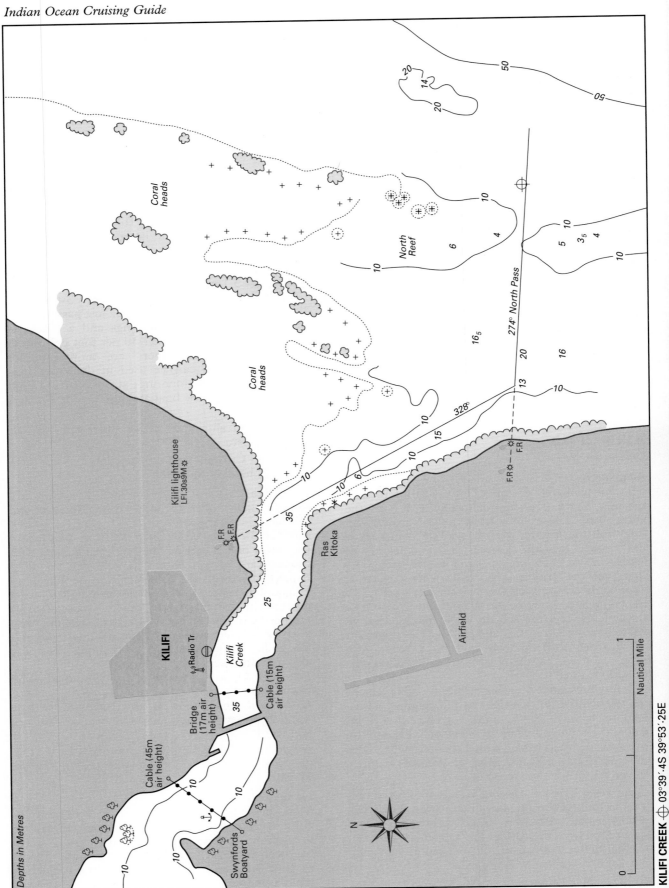

Depths in Metres

Coral heads

Coral heads

20
14
20
50
50
10
10
10
5
3₅
4
4
6
North Reef

274° North Pass
16₅
16
20
13
10

328°
15
10
10
10
6
10
35

F.R
F.R
F.R
F.R

Kilifi lighthouse
LFl.30s9M

Ras Kitoka

25

KILIFI

Radio Tr

Kilifi Creek

Cable (15m air height)

Bridge (17m air height)

35

Cable (45m air height)

10
10
10
10
10

Swynfords Boatyard

Airfield

N

Nautical Mile
1
0

KILIFI CREEK ⊕ 03°39'·4S 39°53'·25E

to make trips into the big city and is a good place to leave a yacht either for extended trips inland or when going back home. And the social scene around the snack-bar at the boatyard is an added bonus with some good parties and much swapping of stories and skills.

Lamu

Charts BA *668*

Approach

Lamu Bay with Lamu Island behind it can be recognised by the high white dunes of Lamu Island which reach 79m (257ft). The entrance channel into Lamu is on 015° with the lighthouse in line with a black conical beacon on the beach. The channel buoys shown on the chart are not all in place. The second leading line into Lamu is just before a sandbank marked by a red buoy and is on 033° marked by two red and white beacons. The white Peponi Hotel at Shela on the shore will now be seen. The channel on up to Lamu town is buoyed and generally follows the outside curve of the creek.

Conspicuous The high white sandhills of Lamu Island can be identified. Closer in the lighthouse on the W side of the entrance will be seen.

By night A first time night entrance is not recommended. Leading lights on 015°: *Front* Q.8M *Rear* Fl.5s8M. Leading lights on 033°: *Front* Q.2M *Rear* Fl.3s2M. There are other leading lights for the channel leading to Lamu and the channel buoys may be lit.

Dangers
1. Care is needed of Utend Rock in Lamu Bay.
2. There can be strong tidal streams in the entrance to the creek with as much as 3kt reported at springs.

Mooring

Tidal range 2·9m at springs.

If you are clearing into Kenya you will need to proceed up the channel to Lamu town and anchor off the town to clear in. Otherwise most yachts anchor off the Peponi Hotel at Shela just inside the entrance. The entrance to the inside channel and anchorage is marked by two beacons on two rocks.

Shelter Good shelter from the S monsoon. It can get a bit bumpy in here with the N monsoon and you may have to move to the E side of the channel. The strong tidal stream can also make things difficult although the bottom is reported to be good holding on mud and sand.

Authorities Customs and immigration at Lamu town.

Facilities

Water Can be arranged at the Peponi Hotel.
Fuel Can be arranged at the Peponi Hotel.
Gas Standard Kenyan bottles can be exchanged. Otherwise go to Mombasa.
Repairs Very basic mechanical and electrical repairs. For most skills and spares you will need to go to Kilifi or Mombasa.

Provisions Some provisions and a market in Shela. Better shopping in Lamu.
Eating out Good restaurant and bar at the Peponi Hotel. Other restaurants and cafés in Shela and Lamu.
Other PO. Bank. Bus to Malindi. Internal flights to Malindi and onto Mombasa.

General

Lamu is a fascinating place to visit, an old dhow trading port which still has sailing dhows although these are rapidly being converted to diesels in the interests of ferrying tourists to and from the reefs and beaches. Lamu town and the surrounding area is predominantly Muslim and you should adopt an appropriate dress code. In the surrounding area there has been some banditry in recent times and you should exercise care on excursions or on the bus trip to Malindi. In Lamu town it is probably wise not to wander around at night although off the Peponi Hotel theft is reported to be unlikely.

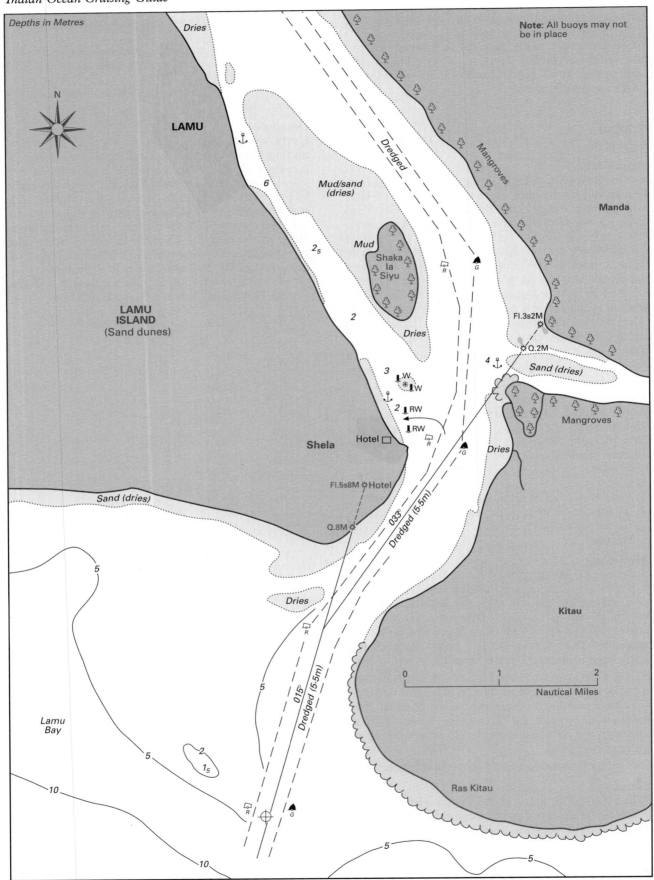

Depths in Metres

Note: All buoys may not be in place

N

Dries

LAMU

6

Mud/sand
(dries)

2₅

Mud

Shaka
la
Siyu

2

Dries

Mangroves

Manda

Fl.3s2M

☼Q.2M

Sand (dries)

4 ⚓

**LAMU
ISLAND**
(Sand dunes)

3

W.
✳W

2 ↓RW

←

↓RW

Shela   Hotel ☐

Fl.5s8M ☼Hotel

Q.8M ☼

Sand (dries)

Dries

G

Mangroves

Dries

G

5

Dries

R

033°

Dredged (5.5m)

Kitau

5

015°

Dredged (5.5m)

*Lamu
Bay*

5

2

1₅

0   1   2

Nautical Miles

Ras Kitau

10

5

R

G

5

10

5

Appendix

I. HYDROGRAPHIC PUBLICATIONS
BA publications
List of lights
NP 79 List of Lights Vol F Bay of Bengal and Pacific Ocean N of the equator.

NP 83 List of Lights Vol K Indian and Pacific Oceans S of the equator.

NP 77 List of Lights Vol D Eastern Atlantic, Western Indian Ocean and Arabian Sea.

NP 78 List of Lights Vol E Mediterranean, Black and Red Seas.

Radio Publications
281(1) Vol 1 Part I Communications: contains particulars of Coast Radio Stations in Europe, Africa and Asia (excluding the Philippine Islands and Indonesia)

281(2) Vol 1 Part 2 Communications: contains particulars of Coast Radio Stations in Philippine Islands, Indonesia, Australasia, the Americas, Greenland and Iceland

282 Vol 2 Radio Navigational Aids, Electronic Position Fixing Systems and Radio Time Signals

283(1) Vol 3 Part I Radio Weather Services and Navigational Warnings in Europe, Africa and Asia

283 (2) Vol 3 Part 2 Radio Weather Services and Navigational Warnings in Philippine Islands, Indonesia, Australasia, the Americas, Greenland and Iceland

284 Vol 4 Lists of Meteorological Observation Stations

285 Vol 5 Global Maritime Distress and Safety Systems

286(1) Vol 6 Part 1 Vessel Traffic Services, Port Operations and Pilot Stations – NW Europe

286(2) Vol 6 Part 2 Vessel Traffic Services, Port Operations and Pilot Stations – The Mediterranean, Africa, Asia

286 (3) Vol 6 Part 3 Vessel Traffic Services, Port operations and Pilot Stations – Australasia, The Americas, Greenland and Iceland

Sailing Directions

NP No.	Title
3	Africa Pilot, Vol III
13	Australia Pilot, Vol I
14	Australia Pilot, Vol II
17	Australia Pilot, Vol V
30	China Sea Pilot, Vol I
31	China Sea Pilot, Vol II
32	China Sea Pilot, Vol III
33	Phillipine Islands Pilot
34	Indonesia Pilot, Vol III
36	Indonesia Pilot, Vol I
38	India, West Coast of, Pilot
39	Indian Ocean, South, Pilot
44	Malacca Strait Pilot

Defense Mapping Agency Sailing Directions
SD171 East Africa and the South Indian Ocean (Enroute), 1995

SD172 Red Sea and the Persian Gulf (Enroute), 1993

SD173 India and the Bay of Bengal (Enroute), 1994

SD174 Strait of Malacca and Sumatera (Enroute), 1993

SD175 North and West Coasts of Australia (Enroute), 1994

Other
Ocean Passages of the World Data on power and sail routes including pilot charts.

The Mariner' Handbook Basic data on everything maritime.

II. YACHTSMAN'S GUIDES
Pilotage
World Cruising Routes Jimmy Cornell. Adlard Coles Nautical. Worldwide guide to cruising routes.

World Cruising Handbook Jimmy Cornell. Adlard Coles Nautical. Worldwide guide to data on cruising countries including basic data, formalities, communications, etc.

Cruising Guide to Southeast Asia Vol I. The South China Sea, Philippines, Gulf of Thailand to Singapore Stephen Davies and Elaine Morgan. Imray. Covers Hong Kong to Philippines.

Cruising Guide to Southeast Asia Vol II. Papua New Guinea, Indonesia, Malacca Strait, West Thailand Stephen Davies and Elaine Morgan. Imray. Covers Papua New Guinea, Indonesia, Malacca Strait.

Riau Islands Cruising Guide Mathew Hardy. Available locally.

Sail Thailand collated by Thai Marine & Leisure. Available locally or from Imray. Covers mostly W coast and some E coast.

Red Sea Pilot Elaine Morgan and Stephen Davies. Imray. Covers Yemen to the Suez Canal.

Imray Mediterranean Almanac Imray. Biennial publication includes light and radio data.

Mediterranean Cruising Handbook Rod Heikell. Imray. Data on Mediterranean countries.

Australian Cruising Guide Alan Lucas. Imray. General coverage of Australia.

East Africa Pilot Delwyn McPhun. Imray. Covers Kenya to South Africa including Madagascar and the Comoros.

South Africa Nautical Almanac Tom Morgan. Annual publication available locally or from Imray.

General
Cruising in Tropical Waters and Coral Alan Lucas. Adlard Coles Nautical.

The Maritime Radio & Satellite Communications Manual Ian Waugh. Waterline Books.

III. USEFUL BOOKS
In each of the introductions to a country there is a list of useful books relating to that country. Here I list just some general books on the Indian Ocean and topics like marine life and fauna and flora. This is not a bibliography, just some books I think are useful.

Narrative
Macpherson's Voyages ed by John Scott Hughes. Methuen 1946. OP. Droll and informative. Macpherson is little

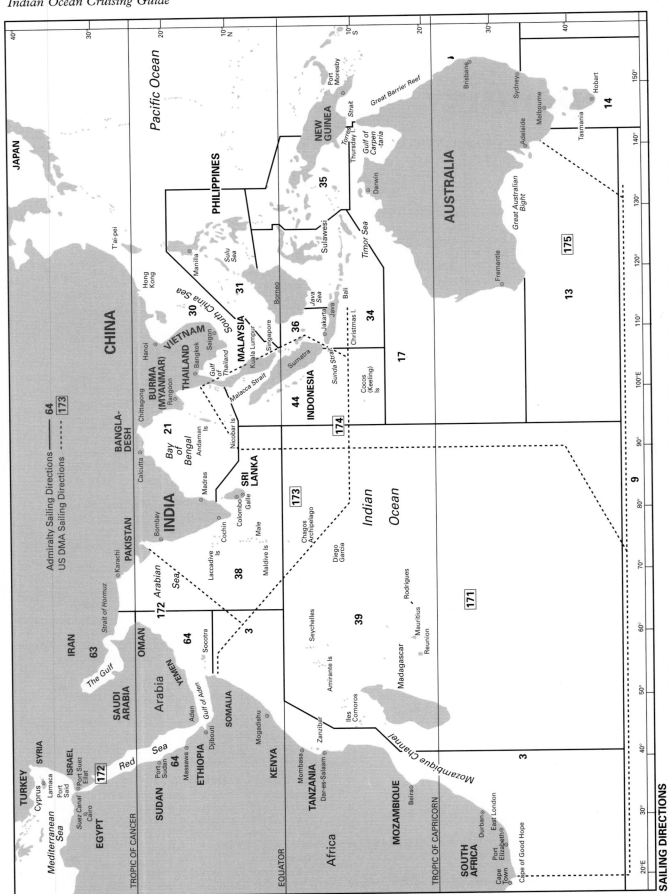

SAILING DIRECTIONS

remembered these days, but if you visit the National Maritime Museum at Greenwich you will come across the Macpherson collection, a wealth of nautical pictures and prints collected by Macpherson over many years and then bought by Sir James Caird for the museum. (Spell *Driac* backwards.) Macpherson started sailing late in life in his late fifties and the boat he sailed in was not dissimilar to *Tetra* at just 32 ft and of similar shape and displacement. Get hold of it if you can.

Sheila in the Wind Adrian Hayter. Hodder & Stoughton 1959. OP. Account of a passage eastabout after the war en route to his native N.Z. Useful information and a good read.

Somewhere East of Suez Tristan Jones. Bodley Head. Usual irascible style account of a passage eastabout in the trimaran *Outward Leg*.

To Venture Further Tristan Jones. Grafton Books. Journey across the Kra Peninsula in a Thai boat.

The Sinbad Voyage Tim Severin. Hutchinson. Retracing the steps of Sinbad in a replica ship from Oman to China. Recommended.

The Tigris Expedition Thor Heyerdahl. Unwin. Djibouti to Karachi and then on the Gulf in a reed raft.

South From the Red Sea Haroun Tazieff. Travel Book Club. OP. With Cousteau on the Calypso.

Breeze in the Sails Gulshan Rai. IBH Bombay. OP. Sailing down the Indian coast and from UK to shipwreck in the Red Sea.

From Southampton to Bombay Gulshan Rai. IBH Bombay. UK to India.

Sailing Around the World Gulshan Rai. IBH Bombay.

Hashish Henry de Montfreid. Penguin. Smuggling hashish in the Red Sea in the 1920's. Recommended.

Motoring With Mohammed Eric Hansen. Abacus. Sailing from Sri Lanka to shipwreck in the Red Sea and the return to retrieve his journals. Good on Yemen. Recommended.

General

Empires of the Monsoon Richard Hall. Harper Collins. Good and entertaining history. Recommended.

Further India Hugh Clifford. White Lotus. Reprint of classic 1904 work covering mostly Southeast Asia.

Arabia Through the Looking Glass Jonathon Raban. Fontana. Recommended.

The Last Sailors Neil Hollander & Harald Mertes. Angus & Robertson. OP. Covers some working sailing craft in the Indian Ocean.

The Indian Ocean Alan Villiers. 1952. OP. Collection of travelogue and history. Recommended.

Chasing the Monsoon Alexander Frater. Penguin. Recommended.

God's Dust Ian Buruma. Vintage.

World Conflicts Patrick Brogan. Bloomsbury.

Heroes John Pilger. Essays many of which concern contemporary Southeast Asia. Recommended.

Seven-Tenths James Hamilton-Patterson. Hutchinson.

Any of Joseph Conrad's relevant tales of the sea.

Marine Life

An Introduction to Marine Ecology R S K Barnes and R N Hughes. Blackwell Scientific. Excellent primer.

Underwater Guide to Coral Fishes Brent Addison and Jeremy Tindall. Southern Book Pub.

Indo Pacific Coral Reef Field Guide G R Allen and R Steene. Tropical Reef Research/Singapore.

Indian Ocean Tropical Fish Guide Helmut Debelius. Acquaprint.

South East Asia Fish Guide Helmut Debelius and Kuiter. Acquaprint.

Wonders of the Red Sea David Fridman and Tony Malmqvist. Isis. Available in Egypt.

The Greenpeace Book of Coral Reefs Sue Well and Nick Hanna. Blandford. More for the coffee table.

The Natural History of Whales & Dolphins Peter G H Evans. Christopher Helm.

Seashells of the World Gert Lindner. Australia & NZ Book Company.

Seabirds of the World Peter Harrison. Christopher Helm.

Collins Photo Guide Tropical Plants W Lotschert and G Beese. Harper Collins.

IV. CHARTS FOR THE INDIAN OCEAN
British Admiralty charts
Note Index references refer to sections in Admiralty World Catalogue NP131

Index A
The World – General charts of the oceans

Chart	Title	Scale
4060	Australasia and adjacent waters	10,000,000
4070	Indian Ocean – southern part	10,000,000
4071	Indian Ocean – northern part	10,000,000
4072	Indian Ocean – western part	10,000,000

Section 21
Indian Ocean Routeing charts

5126(1)	January	13,880,000
5126(2)	February	13,880,000
5126(3)	March	13,880,000
5126(4)	April	13,880,000
5126(5)	May	13,880,000
5126(6)	June	13,880,000
5126(7)	July	13,880,000
5126(8)	August	13,880,000
5126(9)	September	13,880,000
5126(10)	October	13,880,000
5126(11)	November	13,880,000
5126(12)	December	13,880,000

Index G1
West and South Coast of Africa, including adjacent islands and Cape Town approaches

577	Approaches to Durban	50,000
578	Cape Columbine to Cape Seal	1,000,000
636	Table Bay to False Bay	100,000
648	Maputo to Porto de Bartolemeu Dias	1,000,000
1232	Approaches to Saldanha Bay	100,000
1843	Approaches to East London	25,000
	East London Harbour	8,000
2080	Approaches to Richards Bay	50,000
	Richards Bay	18,000
2082	Cape Columbine to Danger Point	300,000
	Hout Bay	30,000
2083	Danger Point to Mossel Bay	300,000
2084	Mossel Bay to Cape St Francis	300,000
2085	Cape St Francis to East London	300,000
	Bird Island Passage	100,000
2086	East London to Port St Johns	300,000
2087	Port St Johns to Durban	300,000
2088	Durban to Cape Vidal	300,000
2089	Cape Vidal to Maputo	300,000
2095	Cape St Blaize to Port St Johns	1,000,000
2930	Jesser Point to Boa Paz	300,000
2939	Boa Paz to Baía de Inmambane	300,000
3769	Great Fish Point to East London	150,000
3770	East London to Mbashe Point	150,000
3793	Shixini Point to Port St Johns	150,000
3794	Port St Johns to Port Shepstone	150,000
3795	Port Shepstone to Cooper Light	150,000

Chart	Title	Scale
Index H		
Southern Indian Ocean, Zanzibar Approaches and		
Mozambique Channel, Northern Part		
3	Chagos archipelago	360,000
4	Plans in the Chagos archipelago	
	Entrance to Salomon islands lagoon	12,130
	Salomon islands	38,180
	Peros Banhos and Egmont islands	
	or Six islands	72,600
238	Ports in Kenya, Kilifi and Malindi	
	Entrance to Kilifi creek	12,500
	Kilifi Creek and approaches	25,000
	Malindi and approaches	37,500
563	Comores	300,000
	Anjouan: Port de Mutsamudu	5,000
	Grand Comore: Mouillage de Moroni	12,000
	Anjouan: Mouillage de Mutsamudu:	
	Muillage D'ouani	20,000
616	East coast, Kenya. Approaches to	
	Port Mombasa	50,000
642	Ports in Mozambique	
	Porto de Beira	25,000
	Porto de Bartolomeu Dias	50,000
	Porto de Sofala	50,000
	Porto de Chiloane	75,000
644	Baía de Maputo	75,000
646	Porto de Maputo	25,000
648	Maputo to Porto de Bartolemeu	
	Dias	1,000,000
649	Approaches to Porto de Nacala	100,000
	Porto de Nacala	36,000
650	Porto de Quelimane	50,000
653	Mokambo, Moçambique and	
	Conducia	100,000
	Moçambique harbour	30,000
661	Approaches to Kilwa Kisiwani harbour	75,000
	Kilwa Kisiwani harbour	35,000
663	Tanzania, Approaches to Tanga	37,500
	Tanga	15,000
665	Approaches to Zanzibar	50,000
666	Port Mombasa, including Port Kilindini	
	and Port Reitz	12,500
	Mbaraki creek	3,000
668	Lamu, Manda and Pate Bays	
	and approaches	75,000
	Lamu harbour and approaches	25,000
671	Outer approaches to Muqdisho and	
	Mark anchorage	300,000
	Muqdisho	15,000
	Mark anchorage	30,000
	Approaches to Muqdisho	60,000
674	Approaches to Dar es Salaam	50,000
677	Mananara to Ile aux Nattes	150,000
	Ambodifototra (Port Saint-Marie)	20,000
678	Ile aux Nattes to Tamatave	150,000
679	Anchorages on the east coast of	
	Madagascar	
	Rade d'Antalaha: Baie de Tintingue	25,000
	Sambava: Mananara: Antanambe	30,000
	Rade d'Angonsty	36,000
	Baie de Vohémar: Maroantsetra	40,000
	Baie de Loky: Baie de Mangerivy (Port	
	Leven): Baie d'Andravina	50,000
680	Anchorages on the east coast of	
	Madagascar	
	Manakara	15,000
	Mananjary	20,000

Chart	Title	Scale
	Itapere	24,000
	Fénérive, Foulpointe, Vatomandry	
	and Mahanoro	25,000
	Farfangana and Fort Dauphin	25,000
	Ste. Luce	36,000
681	Lindi Bay	25,000
	Lindi harbour	12,500
684	Mtwara and Mikindani harbours	36,300
	Mikindani harbour entrance	18,100
687	Kiswere harbour	24,200
688	Tamatave	32,850
689	Approaches to Mauritius and Ile	
	de la Réunion	550,000
690	Cabo Delgado to Mikindani Bay	72,800
	Channel and anchorage of Msimbati	24,000
691	Mtwara harbour	12,500
692	Rade de Tulear and Baie de	
	St Augustine	65,000
693	Dar es Salaam	7,500
701	Approaches to Baie de Bombetoke	150,000
	Baie de Bombetoke	50,000
704	Nosi Shaba (Beroja) to Moramba Bay,	
	including Narendri Bay	145,000
706	Iles Mitsio to Baie d'Ampasindava	100,000
711	Mauritius	125,000
713	Port Louis and Grande Rivière Noire Bay	
	Port Louis	12,500
	Grande Rivière Noire Bay	20,000
	Approaches to Port Louis	50,000
715	Rodriguez island	145,000
	Mathurin Bay	24,200
	Port South-east	48,400
718	Islands north of Madagascar	
	Farquhar group, entrance to	
	inner harbour	20,000
	Ile Picard	30,000
	Astove	50,000
	Assomption: Cosmoledo group	75,000
	Aldabra Island: Farquhar group	100,000
	Iles Glorieuses	150,000
721	Southern approaches to the	
	Seychelles group	750,000
722	Port Victoria and approaches	12,500
724	Anchorages in the Seychelles group	
	and outlying islands	
	Curieuse Bay, Baie Ste Anne to	
	La Digue, Grande Anse	25,000
	Bird Island	35,000
	Dennis Island	50,000
	D'Arros and St Joseph Is: African Is	75,000
	Coetivity Island	200,000
	Providence and St Pierre Is: Ile	
	Desroches	300,000
740	The Seychelles group	300,000
742	Mahé, Praslin and adjacent islands	125,000
758	Northern approaches to Madagascar	1,000,000
759	East coast of Madagascar –	
	Baie d'Antongil to Farafangana	1,000,000
760	Southern coasts of Madagascar –	
	Baie d'Ampasilava to Mananjary	1,000,000
865	Plans on the Tanganyika coast	
	Entrance to Pangani river	12,500
	Mto Sudi and Mchinga Bay	18,000
866	Plans in Tanganyika and Kenya	
	Moa or Gomani Bay and Wasin	
	channel	25,000
	Moa or Gomani Bay to Funzi Bay	50,000

Chart	Title	Scale	Chart	Title	Scale
708	Cape Comorin to Bombay	1,500,000	3460	Ports on the west coast of India	
709	Maldives to Sri Lanka	1,500,000		Veraval	20,000
828	Cochin to Vishakhapatnam	1,500,000		Porbandar	25,000
1011	Addoo atoll to North Huvadhoo atoll	300,000		Ratnagiri and Mirya Bays	40,000
1012	North Huvadhoo atoll to Malaku atoll	300,000		Approaches to Bhavnagar new port	75,000
1013	Mulaku atoll to South Maalhosmadulu atoll	300,000	3461	Ports and anchorages on the west coast of India	
1014	Maldives, South Maalhosmadulu to Ihavandhippolhu atoll	atoll 300,000		New Mangalore	20,000
1284	Port Muhammad Bin Qasim and			Quilon anchorage	30,000
	approaches	30,000		Calicut and Beypore anchorages	50,000
	Approaches to Phitti creek	50,000		Approaches to New Mangalore and Mangalore harbour	50,000
1470	Verával to Okha	300,000	3464	Ports and anchorages on the west coast of India	
1474	Savai bet to Veraval	300,000		Karwar harbour and approaches	25,000
1486	Gulf of Khambhat and approaches	300,000		Belekeri anchorage; Redi anchorage	35,000
1487	Approaches to Bombay	300,000	3466	Approaches to Kandla	40,000
1508	Vengurla to Murud-Janjira	300,000		Kandla creek	15,000
1509	Coondapoor to Vengurla	300,000	3518	Ports and anchorages on the northeast coast of Oman	
1564	Sacrifice Rock to Coondapoor	300,000		Port Sultan Qaboos and Muscat (Masqat)	12,5000
1565	Alleppey to Sacrifice Rock	300,000		Sur: Bandar Jişşah: Bandar Khayran	20,000
1566	Cape Comorin to Cochin	300,000		Khawr al Jaramah and Khawr al Hajar	25,000
1586	India and Sri Lanka − Pamban to Cape Comorin	300,000		Masqat to Mina'al Fahl	30,000
1587	Colombo to Cape Comorin		3519	Southern approaches to Maşirah	100,000
2067	Addoo atoll	25,000		Khalij Maşirah	50,000
2068	Anchorages in the Maldives		3522	Approaches to Masqat and Kina al Fahl	100,000
	Goidhoo atoll	30,000	3523	Outer approaches to Wudam	100,000
	Ihavandhippolhu atoll	50,000	3784	Ra's al Kalb to Ra's Marbat	750,000
2621	Inner approaches to Bombay	60,000		Nishtun	10,000
2624	Port of Bombay	20,000		Al Mukalla	37,500
2627	Jawahar Lal Nehru Port (Nhava-Sheva) and Trombay	20,000		Ash Shihr Termina	50,000
2736	Bombay to Dwarka	750,000	3785	Mina Raysut to Al Masirah	750,000
2738	Lakshadweep Sea − northern part	750,000		Marbat Bay: Madrakah anchorage	35,000
2851	Masirah to the strait of Hormuz	750,000	4701	Maputo to Muqdisho (Mogadiscio)	3,500,000
	Khalij-e Chah Bahar	150,000	4703	Gulf of Aden to the Maldives and the Seychelles group	3,500,000
2854	Northern approaches to Maşirah	100,000	4704	Red Sea	2,250,000
	Ra's Hilf anchorage	20,000	4705	Arabian Sea	3,500,000
2858	Gulf of Oman to Shaţţ al 'Arab	1,500,000	4706	Bay of Bengal	3,500,000
2888	Jask to Dubayy and Jazīreh-ye Qeshm	350,000	4707	Maldives to Sumatera	3,500,000
2895	Outer approaches to Mina Raysut and Salalah	100,000	**Index H3**		
2896	Approaches to Mina Raysut and Salalah	25,000	**Red Sea**		
	Mina Raysut	10,000	6	Gulf of Aden	750,000
2950	Plans on the coast of Somaliland		7	Aden harbour and approaches	25,000
	Elayu	7,500	8	Red Sea − Suez to El Akhawein	750,000
	Las Khoreh	12,500		Ash Sharma	100,000
	Bandar Gaan	14,500		Gulf of Aqaba	300,000
	Bosasso (Bandar Cassim)	20,000	15	Jizan and approaches	200,000
	Alula	20,000		Jizan	25,000
	Obbia	30,000	63	El Akhawein to Rabigh	750,000
	Dante (Hafun) − north and south anchorages	30,000	64	Approaches to Rabigh	50,000
	Eil Marina	40,000		Rabigh industrial port	20,000
	Bandar Beila anchorage	50,000	81	Sawakin to Ras Qassar	300,000
	Capo Elephante anchorage	50,000		Sawakin	12,500
	Candala, Oloch and Damo	50,000	82	Outer approaches to Port Sudan	150,000
	Itala	50,000		Sanganeb anchorage	25,000
	Illigh	60,000	138	Gezirat el Dibia to Masamarit islet	750,000
2952	Lamu Bay to Itala	1,000,000	141	Masamirit islet to Zubáir islands	750,000
2953	Itala to Ras Hafun	1,000,000	143	Jazirat at Ta'ir to Bab el Mandeb	400,000
2954	Gulf of Aden − eastern portion, including Socotra island	750,000	164	North and northeast approaches to Mits'iwa	300,000
3323	Malé atoll	150,000	168	Anchorages on the coast of Ethiopia	
	Malé anchorage and approaches	25,000		Dolphin cove	12,500
				Dissei anchorage: Port Smyth	15,000

Chart	Title	Scale
813	Colombo to Sangama Kanda Point	300,000
814	The Sandheads – Paradip to Raimangal river	300,000
816	Trincomalee harbour	10,000
819	Approaches to Galle harbour	25,000
	Galle harbour	10,000
821	Elephant Point to Chedúba Strait	342,000
823	Koronge Island to White Point, including the Gulf of Martaban	358,000
824	White Point to Mergui	281,900
825	Andaman islands	500,000
828	Cochin to Vishakhapatnam	1,500,000
830	Andaman Sea	1,500,000
831	Kyaukpyu harbour to Chedúba Strait	146,000
	Kyaukpyu harbour	36,318
832	Chedúba Strait to Ramree harbour	145,000
833	Rangoon river and approaches	60,000
	Port of Rangoon	25,000
834	Bassein river and approaches	72,600
840	Little Andaman to Great Nicobar	500,000
841	Plans in the Nicobar islands	
	Nancowry harbour and approaches	25,000
	St Georges Channel	50,000
842	Chowra to Great Nicobar	175,000
859	Raimangal river to Elephant Point	300,000
924	Tavoy river	72,600
1075	Approaches to Mergui harbour	75,000
1369	Mayu river to Kyaukpyu harbour	145,000
1398	Andaman islands – southern approaches to Port Blair including Duncan Passage	150,000
1419	Coco Passage and northern approaches to Port Blair	150,000
1583	Little Basses Reef to Pulmoddai Roads	300,000
	Batticaloa Roads	25,000
	Pulmoddai Roads	300,000
1584	Trincomalee to Point Calimere	300,000
1586	India and Sri Lanka – Pamban to Cape Comorin	300,000
1587	Colombo to Cape Comorin	300,000
1655	Approaches to Colombo	30,000
	Colombo harbour	7,500
1845	Moulmein river and approaches	
	Moulmein harbour	15,000
	Approaches to Moulmein river:	
	Moulmein river	60,000
1885	Sittwe	25,000
2058	Puri to the Sandheads	300,000
2060	Kalingapatnam to Puri	300,000
2061	Kakinada to Kalingapatnam	300,000
2062	False Divi Point to Kakinada	300,000
2063	Madras to False Divi Point	300,000
2069	Point Calimere to Madras	300,000
2197	Palk Strait and Palk Bay – eastern part	150,000
	Kankesanturai harbour	20,000
3052	Za Det Gyi Island to Mu Ko Similan	200,000
3265	Weligama to Little Basses Reef	150,000
	Hambantota	15,000
3481	Moulmein river to Ye river	145,000
3624	Pig Island to South Moskos islands	146,000
3700	Weligama to Colombo	150,000
	Weligama Bay	25,000
3771	Andrew Bay to Calventuras	145,000
3772	Calventuras to Bassein river	146,000
3941	Mu ko Similan to Ko Lanta Yai	200,000

Chart	Title	Scale
	Phuket	20,000
	Approaches to Phuket	50,000
3942	Ko Lanta Yai to Ko Tarutao	200,000

Index I1
Sumatera, Malacca Strait and Cocos or Keeling Islands to Christmas Island

Chart	Title	Scale
Aus 606	Approaches to Cocos (Keeling) islands	150,000
Aus 607	Cocos (Keeling) islands	25,000
Aus 608	Approaches to Christmas Island	100,000
	Flying Fish Cove	5,000
792	Sungai dinding and approaches	25,000
842	Chowra to Great Nicobar	175,000
843	Approaches to Bass harbour	50,000
1140	Tanjong Sepat to Port Dickson	50,000
	North western approach to Port Dickson	12,500
	Port Dickson	6,000
1312	Singapore Strait to Selat Karimata	800,000
1353	Tanjung Jamboaye to Permatang Sedapa (One Fathom Bank)	500,000
1358	Permatang Sedapa (One Fathom Bank) to Singapore Strait	500,000
1366	Approaches to Pinang harbour	60,000
1788	Ports in east Sumatera and adjacent islands	
	Jambi	20,000
	Tanjungpandan	25,000
	Kuala Niur	50,000
	Pangkalbalam	60,000
	Sungai Batanghari	300,000
1789	Pulau-Pulau Lingga	250,000
	Selat Lima	125,000
2056	Selat Sunda and approaches including Selat Panaitan	250,000
2149	Selat Sunda to Selat Gelasa and Selat Bangka	500,000
2152	Pelabuhan Kelang	15,000
2153	Southern approaches to Pelabuhan Kelang	25,000
	Selat Kelang Selatan	15,000
	Selat Lumat	25,000
2760	Sumatera – west coast – Pulau We to Pulau Enggano	1,500,000
2777	Indira Point to Teluk Aru and Ujung Kareueng	500,000
2778	Ujung Raja to Pulau Ilir	500,000
2779	Pulau Ilir to Pulau Nyamuk	500,000
2780	Pulau Nyamuk to Bengkulu	500,000
2781	Benkulu to Selat Sunda	500,000
2917	Plans in northwest Sumatera	
	Sabang	15,000
	Sibolga	20,000
	Teluk Tapanuli	100,000
	Selat Benggala and Alur Pelayaran Malaka	125,000
2918	Plans in Simeulu and Nias	
	Telok Delam, Rede Gunung Sitoli	25,000
	Lugu Sibigo	25,000
	Sinabang Baai and Telok Linggi	37,500
	Channel between Simeulu and Simeulu Tjut, Tandjung Tanah Nasi to Muzeuj River	75,000
	Rene Onolimbu	75,000
	Hinako Eiladen	100,000
2948	Plans on the west coast of Sumatera	
	Rede Meulaboh, Rede Tapa Tuan	50,000

Chart	Title	Scale
932	Tanjungpriok and inner approaches	
	Tanjungpriok	12,500
	Inner approaches to Tanjungpriok	20,000
933	Approaches to Tanjungpriok	55,000
941A	Eastern archipelago – sheet 1 western	
	portion	1,552,500
941B	Eastern archipelago – sheet 2 western	
	portion	1,552,500
945	Selat Madura and Selat Sapudi	
	including Madura	250,000
946	Ports in eastern Jawa, Bali and Lombok	
	Approaches to Ujung: Celukanbawang:	
	Tanjung Wangi	10,000
	Teluk Labuhantereng	30,000
	Pantai Timur: Padang: Probolinggo:	
	Panarukan	50,000
	Approaches to Teluk Labuhantereng	100,000
2056	Selat Sunda and approaches including	
	Selat Panaitan	250,000
2149	Selat Sunda to Selat Gelasa and Selat	
	Bangka	500,000
3706	Selat Lombok and Selat Alas	250,000
3726	Selat Bali to Pulau Kangean	250,000
	Selat Bali	75,000
3729	Tanjungpriok to Cirebon	250,000
3730	Cirebon to Semarang	250,000
3731	Pulau Panjang to Selat Surabaya	250,000

Index M
Australia

Chart	Title	Scale
Aus 413	Cape Fourcroy to Cape Leveque	1,000,000

American Defense Mapping Agency charts
Region 6 – Indian Ocean
Coastal charts

Chart	Title	Scale
61000	Algoa Bay to Cape Town	798,688
61003	Durban to Algoa Bay	830,131
61015	Giuba River to Zanzibar	971,600
61018	Hobyo to Kismaayo	973,000
61020	Mozambique Chanel – southern	
	reaches	1,000,000
61021	Ras Hafun to Obbia	964,515
61300	Madagascar – north coast	1,000,000
61400	Mozambique Channel – northern	
	reaches	1,000,000
61450	Mozambique Channel	1,000,000
61500	Madagascar – south coast	1,000,000
61550	Madagascar – east coast	1,000,000
62000	Gulf of Aden	1,000,000
62001	Red Sea	1,800,000
	Khalig el Suweis (Gulf of Suez)	500,000
62024	Al Masirah to Ra's Raysut including	
	Suqutra island	1,000,000
62028	Gulf of Oman and adjacent coasts –	
	Karachi to Al Masirah	1,000,000
63000	Karachi to Bombay, India & Pakistan	903,500
63005	Bombay to Cochin including the	
	Lakshadweep	1,000,000
63010	Cochin to Calimere Pt, with Sri Lanka	
	& the northern portion of	
	the Maldives	964,000
63015	Coast of India – Calimere Point to	
	Kalingapatam	945,197

South Africa

Chart	Title	Scale
61040	Yzervarkpunt to Cape of Good Hope	246,000
61050	Cape St Francis to Yzervarkpunt	246,530
61051	Approaches to Mosselbaai	40,000
	Mosselbaai	10,000
61060	East London to Cape St Francis	249,500
61061	Approaches to Port Elizabeth	40,000
	Port Elizabeth	10,000
61070	Mbashe Point to East London	251,860
61071	Approaches to East London harbor	12,000
	East London harbor	6,000
61080	Port Shepstone to Mbashe Point	256,035
61090	Durnford Point to Port Shepstone	260,460
61091	Approaches to Durban	25,000
61092	Durban	7,500
61100	Ponta do Ouro to Port Durnford	265,100

Mozambique Channel area

Chart	Title	Scale
61110	Limpopo to Ponta do Ouro	269,800
61120	Pont de Barra to Rio Limpopo	273,160
61130	Ilha Chiloane to Ponta de Barra	278,300
61140	Rio Zambeze to Ilha Chiloane	282,000
61141	Approaches to Beira	60,000
61142	Port of Beira	15,000
61150	Ilha Epidendron to Zambezi river	300,000
61160	Porto de Mocambique to Ilha	
	Epidendron	287,000
61170	Porto do Ibo to Porto de	
	Mocambique	300,000
	Porto Belmore	100,000
	Porto de Duarte Pedroso	40,000
	Porto de Nacala	75,000
61171	Porto de Mocambique including Baia	
	de Conducia and Porto de Mocambo	80,000
61172	Porto de Mocambique	25,000
61180	Mchinga Bay to Porto do Ibo	294,500
61181	Mikidnai Bay including Mikidani harbor	
	and Mtwara Bay	36,490
	Entrance to Mikidani harbor	18,780
61182	Plans in Mocambique	
	Porto do Ibo	46,100
	Porto Amelia	46,100
61190	Dar es Salaam to Mchinga Bay	300,000
61191	Dar es Salaam and adjoining anchorages	50,000
	Dar es Salaam harbor	10,000
61200	Dar es Salaam to Mombasa harbor	300,000
61203	Approaches to Zanzibar	75,000
61204	Zanzibar harbor	12,500
61210	Mombasa harbor to Manda island	300,000
61211	Approaches to Mombasa	50,000
61212	Mombasa harbor including Kilindini	
	harbor and Port Reitz	15,000
61220	Manda Island to Kismaayo	300,000
61301	Islands north of Madagascar	
	Aldabra islands	75,000
	Main Channel	25,000
	Assumption Island	75,000
	Iles Glorieuses	150,000
	Entrance to Inner Harbor	20,000
	Astove islands	50,000
	Approaches to West Island	25,000
	Farquhar group	100,000
	Cosmoledo group	75,000
61310	Comoros islands	300,000
61311	Plans in the Comoros and Mayotte	
	Niazidja – anchorage at Moroni	10,000
	Ile Pmanzi – Dzaoudzi	35,000
	Baie Fomboni	20,000
	Anchorages of Matsamuda and Ouani	20,000
61312	Mayotte (north side)	35,024
61410	Cap d'Ambre to Nosy Be	300,000
61420	Nosy Be to Baie de Bombetoka	300,000

Chart	Title	Scale
	Nosy Be anchorage	50,000
61430	Baie de Bombetoka to Cap Saint Andre	300,000
61440	Cap Saint Andre to Cap Kimby	300,000
61460	Cap Kimby to Nosy Lava	300,000
61470	Nosy lava to Cap Andriamanao	300,000
61510	Cap Andriamanao to Faradofay (Fort Dauphin)	300,000
61520	Faradofay to Riviere Faraony	300,000
61530	Faraony to Toamasina	300,000
61540	Toamasina to Cap Est	300,000
61560	Cap Est to Cap d'Ambre	300,000

Kenya and Somalia

Chart	Title	Scale
61220	Mand island to Kismaayo	300,000
61230	Kismaayo to Baraawe	300,000
61240	Cadale (Itala) to Baraawe	300,000
61242	Muqdisho	15,000
61250	Cadale to Ras Cusbad (Itala to Ras Assuad)	300,000
61260	Raas Cusbad to Raas Cabaad	300,000
61270	Raas Garmaal to Raas Cabaad	300,000
61280	Raas Garmaal to Raas Binna	300,000
62040	Suqutra island and adjacent islands	300,000
62050	Raas Aantaara to Raas Binna including Abd Al Kuri	300,000

Red Sea area

Chart	Title	Scale
56082	Difirswar by-pass to Bur Said by-pass (Suez canal northern part)	30,000
	Buheiret El-Timsah	15,000
56083	Bur Taufiq to Difirswar by-pass (Suez canal southern part)	30,000
62070	Raas jilbo to Raas Goragli	300,000
62080	Gulf of Aden − western part	300,000
62090	Gulf of Aden − western part	300,000
62091	Approaches to Berbera	75,000
	Berbera	15,000
62092	Approaches to Djibouti	100,000
	Continuation of Djibouti	100,000
62093	Djibouti and approaches	20,000
62095	Port of Djibouti	10,000
62097	Approaches to Bandar at Tawahi (Aden)	75,000
62098	Bandar at Tawahi (Aden harbor)	20,000
62100	Jazirat al Hanish as Saghir to Bab el Mandeb	150,000
62105	Perim Island and Small Strait	18,000
62110	Ed to Aseb including Az Zuqur and Jazair Hanish	150,000
	Aseb harbor	25,000
62111	Plans in the Red Sea	
	Aqiq	27,160
	Marsa Halaib anchorages	29,230
	Marsa Shaykh Ibrahim	16,240
	Sharm Dumaygh	7,170
	Edd Road	21,710
62115	Ra's Abu Masarib to Ra's Marjah	150,000
62120	North Mitsiwi Channel	150,000
62121	Approaches to Mitsiwa (Massawa) harbor	75,000
	Mitsiwa harbor	15,000
62130	South Mitsiwa Channel	150,000
62140	Approaches to Al Qadimah	150,000
62142	Approaches to Bur Sudan	25,000
	Bur Sudan	10,020
62143	Approaches to Bur Sudan and Sawakin	100,000
62144	Approaches to Sawakin	20,000

Chart	Title	Scale
62162	Bernice and approaches	50,000
	Bernice	20,000
62170	Approaches to Madinat Yanbu As'Sina'iyah	150,000
62171	Outer approaches to Madinat Yanbu As'Sina'iyah	75,000
	Yanbu Al Bahr	15,000
62172	Mina Al Malik Fahd (King Fahd) at Madinat Yanbu As'Sina'iyah	25,000
	Northern entrance channel	50,000
62177	Gaziret Zafaga and approaches	75,000
	Bur Safaga	15,000
62188	Approaches to El-Ghardaqa	75,000
	El-Ghardaqa	25,000
62191	Madiq Gubal to Ras Gharib	150,000
	Sharm El-Sheikh	25,000
	Ras Shukheir	50,000
62193	Bahr el-Quizum (Suez Bay)	15,000
62194	Approaches to Bahr el-Quizum (Suez Bay)	50,000
	Ain Sukhna	25,000
62195	Ra's Shukheir to Ra's el-Sudr	150,000
	Ra's Gharib	25,000
62220	Gulf of Aqaba	150,000
62222	Srait of Tiran	25,000
62225	Elat and El Aqabah (Gulf of Aqabah)	25,000
62230	Madiq Gubal to Geziret Zabartad	500,000
62241	Mina Jiddah	15,000
62242	Approaches to Jiddah	75,000
62250	Geziret Zeberged to Bur Sudan	500,000
62270	Bur Sudan to Sajid	500,000
62271	Jaza'ir Farasan and approaches to Jizan	200,000
62276	Port of Jizan	15,000
62285	Approaches to Madiq Kamaran	150,000
	Madiq Kamaran	35,000
62288	Plans of Al Luhayyah and Al Mukha	
	Al Luhayyah	25,000
	Mukha (Mocha)	25,000
62290	Sajid to Siyyan	500,000
62292	Al Ahmadi and approaches	75,000
	Al Ahmadi	25,000
62295	Ra's Isa to Ra's Mutaynah including Jazair Az Zubayr and Jazair Hanish	150,000
62302	Yemen (Aden) south coast	300,000
	Ghubbat Al Mukalla	25,000

Gulf of Aden to Persian Gulf

Chart	Title	Scale
62040	Suqutra island and adjacent islands	300,000
62046	Approaches to Suqutra	150,000
	Ghubbah Di-Hadiboh (Tamrida Bay)	50,000
62050	Raas Aantaara to Raas Binna including Abd Al Kuri	300,000
62070	Raas Jilbo to Raas Goragli	300,000
62302	Yemen (Aden) south coast	300,000
	Ghubbat Al Mukalla	25,000
62306	Ra's Fartak to Ash Shihr	300,000
62310	Ra's Fartak to Ra's Janjali	300,000
62312	Approaches to Ra'a al Madrakah	100,000
62313	Approaches to Mina Raysut	75,000
	Mina Raysut	25,000
62320	Ra's Sharbithat to Ra's Janjali	300,000
62330	Ra's Ad Duqm to Ra's Sharbithat	300,000
62340	Ra's Duqm to Ra's Al Hadd Khalij Al Masirah	300,000
62342	Northern approaches to Masirah	75,000
62344	Ra's Hilf anchorage	25,000
62350	Ra's Al Hadd to Masqat	300,000

Chart	Title	Scale	Chart	Title	Scale
62353	Ra's Al Hadd to Sur	37,500		Pondicherry	25,000
62360	Masqat to As Salamah wa Banatuha	300,000	63270	Palar river to Penner river	300,000
Eastern part of Arabian Sea			63271	Madras and approaches	50,000
62387	Gwatar Bay	70,000		Madras harbor	12,500
62388	Gwadar Bays	70,000	63280	Nizampatnam Bay	300,000
63040	Gwadar to Ra's Malan	300,000	63281	Machilipatnam anchorage	25,000
63050	Ras Kachari to mouths of the Indus	300,000	63290	Sacramento Shoal to Vamsadhara river	300,000
63053	Approaches to Karachi	75,000		Kakinada Bay	50,000
63054	Karachi harbor	15,000	63291	Approaches to Vishakhapatnam	50,000
63055	Port Muhammad Bin-Qasin and approaches	25,000		Vishakhapatnam harbor	12,500
63060	Ras Muari to Lushington Shoal	300,000	63310	Vamsadhara river to Devi river	300,000
63062	Gulf of Kachchh	150,000	63320	Devi river to Pursur river	300,000
63063	Approaches to Okha	30,000	63321	Hugli river approach	150,000
63065	Approaches to Kandla & Navlakhi	50,000		Entrance to Hugli river	75,000
63070	Lushington Shoal to Diu Head	300,000	63322	Haldia to Hugli Point	35,000
63080	Diu Head to Tarapur	300,000		Haldia	15,000
63090	Tarapur to Bankot	300,000	63323	Hiraganj Point to Calcutta	20,000
63091	Gulf of Khambhat	150,000	63324	Paradip and approaches	25,000
63092	Piram island to Bhavnagar	31,800		Paradip	10,000
63100	Bankot to Malvan	300,000	63330	Raimangal river to Elephant Point	300,000
63101	Agashi Bay to Kumbaru Point including approaches to Bombay harbor	140,000	63331	Pusur river	75,000
63102	Approaches to port of Bombay	40,000	63337	Approaches to Karnaphuli river	75,000
63103	Port of Bombay	20,000		Karnaphuli river	25,000
63110	Malvan to Bhatkal	300,000	63340	Naf river to Cheduba Island	300,000
63111	Approaches to Mormugao & Panaji harbors	100,000	63341	Cox's Bazar to Mayu river	143,160
	Mormugao & Panaji harbors	30,000	63350	Cheduba Island to Pagoda Point	300,000
	Port Mormugao	12,500	63351	Mayu river to Kyaukpyu harbor	144,086
63120	Bhatkal to Cannanore	300,000	63352	Kaladan river	70,000
63121	New Mangalore and approaches	100,000		Harbor of Sittwe	35,000
	Anchorage of New Mangalore	35,000	63353	Kyaukpyu harbor to Cheduba Strait	144,530
	Harbor of New Mangalore	10,000		Kyaukpyu harbor	36,320
63150	Cora Divh to Lhavandiffulu Atoll	500,000	63354	Cheduba Strait to Andrew Bay including Ramree harbor	145,100
63160	Lhavandiffulu Atoll to South Malosmadulu Atoll	200,000	63361	Andrew Bay to the Calventuras	145,930
63170	North Malosmadulu Atoll to Felidu Atoll	200,000	63370	Andaman islands – northern part	300,000
63172	Approaches to Male anchorage	20,000	63380	Andaman islands – central part	300,000
63180	Falidoj Atoll to Haddummati Atoll	200,000	63383	Port Blair and approaches	100,000
63190	Haddummati Atoll to Addu Atoll	300,000		Port Blair	15,000
63200	Cannanore to Alleppey	300,000	63390	Nicobar islands	300,000
63201	Cochin anchorage and harbor	25,000	63400	Andaman Sea – Burma to Sumatera	1,200,000
	Cochin harbor	12,500	63410	Goyangyi Kyun to Rangoon river including Preparis Island	300,000
63202	Addu Atoll – Indian Ocean	25,000	63411	Calventuras to Bassein river	146,966
	Gan anchorage	10,000	63412	Bassein (Ngawun) river and approaches	75,000
63205	Approaches to Cochin and Alleppey	75,000		Continuation of the river to Bassein	100,000
	Alleppey	25,000	63413	Rangoon river	50,000
63210	Alleppey to Cape Comorin	311,100		Rangoon	25,000
Bay of Bengal area			63417	Approaches to Rangoon river	100,000
63220	Gulf of Mannar – southern part	311,770	63420	Rangoon river to Launglon Bok Islands	300,000
63230	South coast of Sri Lanka	312,620	63422	Mali Kyun and vicinity	74,800
63231	Colombo to Ambalangoda	100,000	63424	Approaches to Moulmein	100,000
63232	Approaches to Galle	100,000		Moulmein river entrance	50,000
63233	Colombo harbor and approaches	15,000		Moulmein harbor	25,000
63234	Approaches to Galle harbor	25,000	63430	Launglon Bok islands to Nearchus Passage	300,000
	Galle harbor	10,000	63433	Approaches to Mergui harbor	75,000
Not for sale or reproduction outside the USA.				Mergui harbor	17,500
63240	Batticaloa Roads to Pt. Pedro	311,120	63440	Nearchus Passage to Ko Tachai	300,000
63241	Approaches to Trincomalee	50,000	71040	Ko Tachai to Ko Butang	300,000
63242	Trincomalee harbor	10,000	**Islands Eastward of Madagascar**		
63250	Palk Strait and Gulf of Mannar	310,350	61036	Seychelles with the Amirante and other outlying islands	638,000
53252	Tuticorin harbor	25,000	*Not for sale or reproduction outside the USA.*		
63260	Palar river to Muttupetai including Sri Lanka	300,000	61541	Mahe and Praslin and approaches	125,000
63268	Approaches to Pondicherry	75,000	61542	Victoria and approaches	12,500
			Not for sale or reproduction outside the USA.		

Chart	Title	Scale
61551	Plans in the Indian Ocean	
	Cargados and Carajos Shoals	91,240
	Agalega islands	123,380
	St James anchorage	18,760
	Ile Tromelin	30,080
61581	Ile de la Reunion	175,300
61582	Saint Denis to Saint Gilles-Les-Bains	40,000
	Anchorages of Saint Denis	10,000
	Port Des Galets	10,000
	Anchorage of Saint Pierre	12,500
61591	Mauritius	100,000
61592	Plans on the west coast of Mauritius	
	Approaches to Port Louis	50,000
	Port Louis	12,500
	Grande Riviere Noire Bay	20,000

Not for sale or reproduction outside the USA.

Chart	Title	Scale
61594	Grand Port (Mauritius)	25,000
	South entrance to Grand Port	12,500
61601	Rodrigues island	116,320
	Port South East	48,870
	Mathurin Bay	24,220
61610	Chagos Archipelago	360,000
61611	Diego Garcia	15,000
61612	Approaches to Diego Garcia	80,000

Region 7 – Australia, Indonesia and New Zealand
Coastal charts

Chart	Title	Scale
71005	Northwest Sumatera and the Strait of Malacca	1,000,000
71027	Pulau Bintan to Mui Ca Mau including north coast of Borneo and adjacent islands	1,091,700
71033	Western part of Java Sea and southern passages to China	1,613,850
71050	Great Channel (Indonesia – India)	300,000
72000	Java Sea	1,025,000
72021	Eastern part of Java Sea including Makassar Strait (Borneo east coast)	750,000

Sumatera and vicinity

Chart	Title	Scale
63400	Andaman Sea – Burma to Sumatera	1,200,000
71006	Tanjung Jambuair to Singkil	500,000
71009	Singkil to Padang including adjacent islands	500,000
71012	Padang to Bengkulu including Kepulauan Mentawai	499,326
71015	Bengkulu to Selat Sunda including Pulau Mega and Pulau Enggano	498,114
71040	Ko Tachai to Ko Butang	300,000
71042	Approaches to Ko Phuket	50,000
71043	Port of Phuket	10,000
71044	Kantang and Approaches	100,000
	Kantang harbor	25,000
71045	North coast of Sumatera (Strait of Malacca)	300,000
71050	Great Channel (Indonesia – India)	300,000
71058	Pinang harbor (Strait of Malacca)	17,500
71059	Northern approach to Pinang harbor	35,000
71061	Approaches to Pinang harbor	100,000
	South Channel entrance	35,000
71066	Lumut and approaches	75,000
	Lumut	25,000
71071	Approach to Belawan (Sumatera east coast)	25,000
	Port of Belawan	12,500
71091	North coast of Sumatera ond off-lying islands	106,835
71140	Ujung Katiagan to Tanjung Inderapura	269,500

Chart	Title	Scale
	Teluk Bayur	16,000
	Teluk Bayur and Teluk Bungus	53,000
71180	Selat Sunda and approaches	290,480
71210	Southern reaches to Bangka and Selat Gelasa	300,000
71220	Selat Bangka	
	Northern part	150,000
	Central part	150,000
	Southern part	150,000
71223	Air Musi – from the mouth to Pulau Karto	50,000
	Plaju roadstead and Sungaigerong	25,000
71230	Selat Durian to Selat Bangka	300,000
71239	Pelabhuan Sambu	12,500
71241	Selat Durian and approaches	100,000
71243	Selat Riau and vicinity	100,000
71244	Selat Bulan	25,000
	Sekupang	10,000
71247	Singapore harbour – eastern part	15,000
71251	Johore Strait and eastern entrance	25,000
71253	Harbor of Singapore – central part	15,000
71255	Harbor of Singapore – western part	15,000
71257	Singapore Strait – western part	60,000
71258	Main Strait and Phillip Channel	30,000
71259	Singapore Strait – eastern part	60,000
71261	Selat Bengkalis and Selat Rupat	75,000
	Pelabuhan Dumai	37,500
	Selat Rupat – southeast approach	30,000
71262	Plans of Port Dickson and Melaka	
	Port Dickson entrance	35,000
	Port Dickson	10,000
	Melaka anchorage	35,000
	Melaka	17,500
71265	Singapore area (Singapore–Malaysia–Indonesia)	200,000
71271	Approaches to Selat Kelang	75,000
71272	Northern approaches to Pelabuhan Kelang (north port)	15,000
	A.	30,000
	B.	15,000
71273	Southern approaches to Pelabuhan Kelang (south port)	
	A.	15,000
	B.	30,000
71275	Strait of Malacca – southern part	200,000
71281	Cocos (Keeling) islands	30,000
	North Keeling island	37,560
71285	Malacca Strait – central part	200,000
71295	Strait of Malacca – northwest part	300,000
71305	Strait of Malacca – northern part	300,000
71315	Ko Klang to Pulau Langkawi	200,000
71430	Southeast reaches to Singapore Strait	300,000
71440	Singapore Strait to Pulau Tioman including Kepulauan Anambas	300,000

Borneo and vicinity

Chart	Title	Scale
71036	Selat Karimata (South Java and China seas)	500,000
71410	Karimata Strait and southeast reaches	300,000
72040	Tandjung Putting to Tanjung Sambar (Borneo south coast)	201,090
72050	Tandjung Malatajur to Tandjung Putting (Borneo south coast)	200,980
72060	Tanjung Selatan to Tanjung Malatayur (Borneo south coast)	200,645
72070	Tanjung Selatan to Pulau Laut	201,020
72085	Makassar Strait – southern portion	500,000

Chart	Title	Scale
Jawa (Java) to Timor		
71018	Western portion of Jawa including Selat Sunda	497,000
71180	Selat Sunda and approaches	290,480
71182	Oedjoeng Genteng to Prinsen Eiland (Southwest coast of Java)	200,480
71185	Approaches to Jakarta	60,000
71186	Jakarta including Tanjungperiuk and Jakarta roadstead	20,000
71191	Christmas Island	51,430
	Flying Fish Cove	3,280
Region 9 – East Asia		
Coastal charts		
Chart	Title	Scale
71027	Pulau Bintan to Mui Ca Mau including north coast of Borneo and adjacent islands	1,091,700
93010	Gulf of Thailand	1,000,000
Vietnam, Cambodia, Thailand and Eastern Malay Peninsula		
93018	Kuala Terengganu to Ao Nakhon	496,000
93110	Pulau Tioman to Terengganu	75,000
93113	Approaches to Kuantan	75,000
93115	Approaches to Kertih	75,000
93117	Kertih and Kuantan	
	Kertih terminal	25,000
	Kuantan	15,000
93160	Kuala Terengganu to Laem Khao Phra	242,900
93180	Laem Khao Phra to Ko Kra	250,000
	Harbor of Songkhla	48,800
	Ao Pattani	149,900
93200	Ko Kra to Lang Suan Roads	241,300
93220	Lang Suan Roads to Prachuap Khiri Khan	240,000
93224	Prachuap Khiri Khan and vicinity	20,000
93240	Prachuap Khiri Khan to Ko Chuang	240,000
93241	Laem Krabang to Mae Nam Chao Phraya including Ko Si Chang	75,000
	Mouth of Mae Nam Chao Phraya including Bangkok Bar	35,000
93242	Bangkok Bar to Ban Bang Hua Sua	10,000
93243	Ban Bang Hua Sua to Sathu Pradit including Krung Thep (Bangkok) harbor	10,000
93244	Plans on the Gulf of Thailand	
	Approaches to Ban Ao Udon	20,000
	Approaches to Ban Patthaya	25,000
93245	Approaches to Ao Sattahip	75,000
93246	Sathu Pradit to Krung Thep (Bangkok)	10,000
93247	Chong Khram & Ao Sattahip	15,000
93260	Ko Chuang to Ko Kut	238,000

V. CONVERSION TABLES

1 inch = 2·54 centimetres (roughly 4in = 10cm)
1 centimetre = 0·394 inches
1 foot = 0·305 metres (roughly 3ft = 1m)
1 metre = 3·281 feet
1 pound = 0·454 kilograms (roughly 10lbs = 4·5kg)
1 kilogram = 2·205 pounds
1 mile = 1·609 kilometres (roughly 10 miles = 16km)
1 kilometre = 0·621 miles
1 nautical mile = 1·1515 miles
1 mile = 0·8684 nautical miles
1 acre = 0·405 hectares (roughly 10 acres = 4 hectares)
1 hectare = 2·471 acres
1 gallon = 4·546 litres (roughly 1 gallon = 4·5 litres)
1 litre = 0·220 gallons

Temperature scale

Centigrade to Fahrenheit $\quad \dfrac{C \times 9}{5} + 32 = F$

Fahrenheit to Centigrade $\quad (F - 32) \times 5 = C$

$0°C = 32°F$
$0°F = -17·8C$
So:

$70°F = 21·1°C$	$20°C = 68°F$
$80°F = 26·7°C$	$30°C = 86°F$
$90°F = 32·2°C$	$40°C = 104°F$

Index